John F MacDermaid
© 2007

ISABELLA COUNTY, MICHIGAN

FAMILIES AND HISTORY
2003

TURNER PUBLISHING COMPANY

Isbella County Court House, Mt. Pleasant, MI.

Turner®

PUBLISHING COMPANY

Publishers of America's History

www.turnerpublishing.com

Library of Congress Catalog Control No.: 2003113506
ISBN: 978-1-68162-190-6

Front and back endsheets: *Prints of Courthouse paintings by
John F. MacDermaid used in this publication by permission of
artist.*

*At left: Ann Arbor RR at the Chippewa River, Mt. Pleasant, MI,
circa 1900. Clarke Historical Library. This is the bridge James
Davis' horse tried to cross pulling a buggy when the animal became entrapped. The structure is located a block north of the Mt.
Pleasant Ann Arbor Depot. One can see an American Type 4-4-0
of mid 1880s vintage. It is pulling a passenger train north out of
Mt. Pleasant with an eventual destination of Frankfort on Lake
Michigan. To the front of the engine is "Fancher Flats" in the
background. In a few years this would become Island park. To the
rear of the train in the distance is Harris Brothers Mill on Broadway. The Ann Arbor discontinued passener trains in 1950 after
64 years of service. Today the new connector trail from Island
Park to Nelson Park would be along the bottom of this photo.*

*Jockey Alley, south of the courthouse square in Mt. Pleasant, circa 1920. Ege Photo. In ten years
scenes like this would be a memory preserved only in street signs. This view looks ESE from Main
Street at the present day intersection of Mosher Street. Mosher Street would be where the tree to the
left is located. Mosher Street ended at Fancher Street at the time and was extended to Main in the
1970s.*

TABLE OF CONTENTS

A.R. Muterspaugh Blacksmith Shop.

Acknowledgement

Isabella Genealogical History Book Committee. Front row: Marydeana Duckworth, Veronica Schutt, Lucille Cotter, Darlene Fedewa. Back row: Floyd Seiter, Linda Hopp, Jo Jennings, Don Cotter, Sheri Sponseller, Gary Anderson, Dan Grace.

There are many people to thank when one undertakes a project of this nature and if we miss thanking anyone we want them to except this acknowledgement as our heartfelt thanks.

First, we are very grateful to all the individuals who submitted their biographies and pictures for the history book. We also want to thank the businesses, churches, non-profits and other organizations for purchasing feature pages and submitting their histories to us.

We would also like to thank Mr. James R. Schafer, of *Mt. Pleasant Magazine,* for putting together an article on the history book at the very beginning of our project. Thank you!

A special thank you goes out to Mr. John F. MacDermaid for allowing us to use copies of his paintings of the Isabella Court House for our front and end pages of the history book. Another special thank you to Mr. Hudson Keenan for the articles he submitted and to Floyd Seiter for the pictures he provided for this publication.

A thank you goes out to the society's members for their help in submitting biographies and for contacting their friends and relatives to also submit information to the history book.

We would like to thank Virginia Forstat, of Turner Publishing, for her help in bringing this project to a successful ending. Her many hours working with us were of great help.

It is also important to thank our treasurer, Darlene Fedewa, for keeping track of the monies collected on this project. Her many hours of effort are greatly appreciated and we thank her for a job well done.

In closing, a big thank you to the History Book Committee made up of Gary Anderson, Sherry Sponseller, Dan Grace, Marydeana Duckworth, Arlene Leiter, Jo Jennings, Veronica Schutt and Darlene Fedewa. Their many hours spent compiling and organizing items for this book were greatly appreciated.

Isabella County History Book Committee

Publisher's Message

Turner
PUBLISHING COMPANY

Publishers of America's History

(270) 443-0121
(270) 443-0335 Fax
info@turnerpublishing.com

P.O. Box 3101
Paducah, KY 42002-3101
www.turnerpublishing.com

The people of Isabella County can be proud of the important role they and their ancestors have played in Michigan history. In this book, you will see how life evolved from the early days of the county to the present, meeting the people, families and communities that have played a major role in the development of Isabella County. This volume will allow today's generations to see where they come from and to see the events and heritage that shaped their lives. Future generations will benefit greatly from the wealth of information that has been recorded in this permanent hardbound book.

The Genealogical Society of Isabella County is to be commended for their outstanding efforts during the initiation and completion of the project. Special thanks goes to Dan Grace, president of the Genealogical Society of Isabella County for his perseverance and leadership. We sincerely appreciate the work of Gary Anderson, Sherry Sponseller, Darlene Fedewa, Marydeanne Duckworth, Veronica Schutt, Jo Jennings, Linda Hopp and other members of the book committee who devoted their time to the gathering, recording, and organizing of material for the book. We also recognize the valuable assistance of Printtech in spreading the word of the project.

We appreciate the many organizations and businesses that supplied histories and their support to the society in publication of this book. But perhaps most importantly, we than you, the residents of Isabella County, for your submission of biographies and photos, without which this book would not have been possible.

Turner Publishing is creating titles in many Michigan counties. It is with great pride that we now present to the people of Isabella County this volume, Isabella County, Michigan, Families and History, 2003.

Sincerely

Todd Bottorff

Todd Bottorff, President
Turner Publishing Company

Offices:

Nashville, Tennessee   Paducah, Kentucky

Isabella County Genealogical Society

Genealogical Society of Isabella

The Isabella County Genealogical Society began informal meetings in 1995 with a group of people who had similar interests in family history research. By 1998, a solid core of individuals was meeting regularly which allowed for a more formal organization. The charter membership was made up of 23 individuals.

The objective of the Society is to preserve and make available for genealogical research the records of our members, to encourage and assist the study of family history; to promote the exchange of knowledge and to encourage the deposit of genealogical records. The Society also cooperates with other societies and assists the area libraries in expanding and publicizing their genealogical holdings.

The Society has been actively developing a library of research books, created an annual obituary list from the local newspaper, established a society newsletter, offered classes to the public on family history and participates with the Michigan Genealogical Council. The group hopes to expand in the future and find a larger location where it will be possible for the public to have greater access to local records.

Current officers of the Society are Dan Grace, President; Sherry Sponseller, Vice-President; Marydeanna Duckworth, Secretary; Darlene Fedewa, Treasurer; and Linda Hopp, MGC representative.

Isabella County Time-Line

1850

1854 First tract of land entered by Aloney Rust (exact date disputed).
Feb Wm. B. Bowen settled in Coe Twp.
P.H. Estee, Daniel Brickley, John Stewart, Andrew F. Childs, James Campbell, George Reasoner, Charles F. Young and M.J. Hall entered claims of 1/4 section each. John Hursh claims 90 acres where part of CMU now stands.
1855 Treaty of 1855 to establish an Indian Reservation consisting of six townships.
1856 Chippewa Indians of Saginaw, Swan Creek and Black River began coming and selecting lands.
1857 Indian Mills built on the Chippewa River.
Isabella City exists already.
Salt River settlement began.
Methodist mission founded by Rev. George Bradley.
1858 Chippewa Township organized.
1859 Isabella County becomes independent from Midland County.

1860

1860 Census lists 1,443 people, 848 being Indian.
Current site of the county seat selected.
Court house accepted.
1861 Church of Christ at Salt River organized.
Isabella City platted by A.W. Fitch and F.C. Babbitt.
1862 James Birney is the second Isabella County judge, succeeding Wilbur F. Woodworth.
1863 Mt. Pleasant platted by David Ward, lumberman, replatted by George and Harvey Morton.
1864 Northern Pioneer newspaper, later to become the Enterprise, established by O.B. Church.
H.H. Dutton first stock of general merchandise.
First plat at Mt. Pleasant recorded.
1865 First log schoolhouse in Mt. Pleasant taught by Ellen L. Woodworth.
1866 Salt River Village platted.
1867 Winn post office established.
1868 Broomfield Township established and named after William Broomfield.
1869 The Lutheran Synod closes at the site of present day Embers Restaurant.

1870

1870 4,100 people living in Isabella County.
1871 Pastor Wugazzer is visiting each month from Big Rapids to hold services for the Broomfield Zion Lutheran Church congregation since its founding last year.
1872 Harris Brothers milling founded.
First Catholic Church.
1873 Last year of business in the village of Longwood for Major James Long, who platted the site south of the river from Indian Mills.
1874 Sacred Heart Church organized.
C. Kimball and R.E. McDonald are running a four-horse stagecoach from Mt. Pleasant to Clare.
IOOF established in Mt. Pleasant and elects first officers April 4.
1875 Much of the Mt. Pleasant business district destroyed by fire.
Mt. Pleasant incorporated as a village.
1876 Dushville (Winn) platted by William Wiley Dush.
1877 Isabella County Courthouse building is completed.
1878 Formal dedication of the Isabella County Courthouse.
1879 First RR Flint and Pere Marquette RR ran a small gauge from Coleman in December.

Mt. Pleasant's first library organized.
Sherman City schoolhouse built after previous frame building is blown down the previous year.

1880

1880 Census lists 12,159 people, 479 being Indian.
New Methodist Church built, remained until 1961.
J.E. Chatterton establishes retail grocery business.
First Presbyterian Church organized at Calkinsville (Rosebush).
1881 Exchange Savings Bank established by George A. Dusenbury & Co. Upton's opera house grand opening.
Dush's sawmill boiler explodes killing Andrew Gearhart at Winn.
1882 South side of Broadway destroyed by fire.
First mass at St. Joseph the Worker in Beal City.
Judge's brick house completed near Winn.
1883 Kane Brothers open grocery.
Calkinsville Presbyterian Church built.
1884 Portrait and biographical album of Isabella County published.
Forest fire destroys Methodist Indian campgrounds.
Post Office located at Horr.
1885 William's addition to Dushville platted consisting of 20 acres.
1886 Ann Arbor, Toledo and Northern RR comes from the South connecting Salt River, Mt. Pleasant, Rosebush and Clare.
Winn Masonic Cedar Valley Lodge #383 established.
St. Joseph the Worker church burns in Beal City
1887 Brinton platted by E.F. Coburn on land owned by Oscar T. Brinton.
Salt River village name changed to Shepherd.

St. Joseph The Worker
Beal City, Michigan

1882-1982

St. Henry's church has its first mass near Rosebush.
1888 Gorham Brothers veneer and basket factory.
 W.W. Dush, John Carr, and Albert Smalley killed in mill explosion east of Millbrook.
1889 Mt. Pleasant incorporated as a city.

1890

1890 Coomer Church built near Winn with the help of Rev. Barnes.
1891 Mt. Pleasant Improvement Co. begins establishment of Central Normal School.
 Indian Industrial School land is selected by the United States government.
1892 Indian Industrial School established by the federal government.
 Indian Industrial School cornerstone for main building is laid.
1893 John S. Weidman buys 8,000 acres where he erected saw, shingle and planing mills, founding the village of Weidman.
 Rosebush Center Methodist Church built.
1894 Weidman post office established.
1895 Central Michigan Normal School accepted by the state.
 Dushville officially renamed Winn by the Michigan State Legislature.
1896 A gymnasium is opened for membership in the Fireman's Hall by Thomas Dale, a well-known athlete in the city.
1897 Fire destroys Dittman's shoe store.
1898 Elton J. VanLeuven organized the private bank of Webber & Ruel.
 Fire in Weidman destroys the Damon building and the Dellsworth barber shop.
1899 Old Normal School building remodeled.

Department Heads at Isabella Sugar co., 1933. Seated: Henry C. Pety-Superintendent, James Gosler-Chief Engineer. Standing from left: Burt Granger-sugar end foreman; Arthur Grady-beet end foreman; Robert Stemler-filter press foreman; Maurice P. Pety-timekeeper; Joseph Falcon-sugar boiler; Lee Watling-chemist; Ray Ellis-chief electrician; Ted Turnbull-sugar warehouse foreman.

Mr. & Mrs. Barnes. Mr. Barnes helped build several of the churches.

1900

1900 James A. Cliff Lodge #424 of the Free and Accepted Masons chartered in Weidman.
1901 Fire in Weidman destroys residences and a block of businesses.
1902 500 cord of stone will be needed for the foundation of the sugar plant as smaller sheds are completed
1903 John S. Weidman purchased the private bank of Webber & Ruel in Mt. Pleasant July 1 the bank was incorporated as a state bank under the name of Isabella County State Bank.
 J.E. Chatteron & Son purchase Horning Elevator.
 Mt. Pleasant Light and Fuel Co. commences work on plant.
 Mt. Pleasant Sugar Company begins construction.
1904 Harry Kane elected state senator.
1905 Isabella County Creamery Company has 32 cream routes and 12 teams.
1906 First automobile in Mt. Pleasant.
1907 Waubenoo Chapter #360, Order of the Eastern Star organized in Weidman.
 Construction begins on Borden Condensery in Mt. Pleasant.
 New church of St. Joseph the Worker completed and consecrated at Beal City.
1908 Weidman Banking Co. founded.
 Winn Telephone Co. organized.
 Winn Bank established.
 Winn Masonic Temple dedicated.
1909 Central Michigan Normal builds its first gymnasium.
 Mt. Pleasant opera house presents *"Girls Will Be Girls."*

1910

1910 Chicory plant site chosen in Mt. Pleasant.
 A 50-foot bridge is constructed over the Harris Co. race.
 Residents are assessed for the paving of Broadway and Main St.
 Mt. Pleasant opens a new library with 650 books on the shelves.
1911 Isaac A. Fancher's Past and Present of Isabella County published.
1912 Citizens choose to keep Isabella County without saloons by a 1,068 to 226 vote.
1913 Boiler explosion at Thompson's Brick Yard three miles east of Mt. Pleasant kills three including Will Thompson, owner.
1914 Mt. Pleasant Lumber Co. begins operations.
1915 Weidman's first bakery started by Elizabeth Kaninsky.
1917 Mrs. Hannah Vowles is elected to the school board, becoming Mt. Pleasant's first woman to hold public office.
1918 Central Normal becomes a four year college.
 Transport Truck Co. organized.
1919 Isabella County War Chest created.

1920

1920 The Enterprise and the Times are bought and merged.
1921 Dedication of new Mt. Pleasant High School.
1922 Ice storm cripples area.
1923 Robert Aylsworth and Miles Drallette own a silver-black fox ranch in Weidman.
1924 Glen Oren's store moves from Bannister, MI to Shepherd.
1925 Administration building at Central Normal destroyed by fire.
1926 American Enameled Products install six car loads of machinery in the former Transport Truck Co. plant.
1927 Discovery of oil.
1928 Work begun on 130 foot tall Harris storage tanks.
1929 County's second oil well comes in at 125 barrels per day.

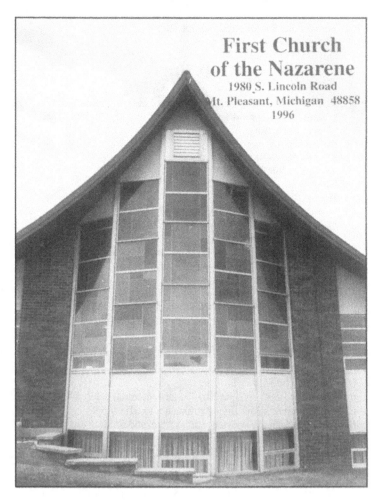

First Church of the Nazarene
1980 S. Lincoln Road
Mt. Pleasant, Michigan 48858
1996

1930

1930 Lew Maxwell blacksmith shop on west Michigan torn down to make way for George Harford garage.
1931 Struble No. I oil well fire kills nine and injures many more.
 Isabella County's first historical marker placed at Indian Mills.
1932 Crystal Ice Co. constructs an artificial ice plant on corner of Pickard and Kinney.
 Mt. Pleasant First Church of the Nazarene organized with 18 charter members under Pastor Howard Beadle.
1933 Central's Training School building burns destroying over 5,000 books.
1934 Closure of Indian Industrial School due to a policy change in Indian Affairs at Washington.
1935 Electricity comes to Winn.
1936 Fancher School built.
1937 Ferro Manufacturing Co. comes to Mt. Pleasant.
1938 J.F. Battle Motor Sales opens on the corner of Broadway and Arnold.
1939 State Highway Department garage built on south Mission.

1940

1940 Donation of funds to build hospital from the Commonwealth Fund of New York.
1941 Fire in Weidman destroys five businesses.
1942 Central Michigan College 50th anniversary.
1943 Central Michigan Community Hospital opens.
1944 German prisoners of war are housed near Sherman City.
 Rosebush Center Methodist Church burns.
 Rosebush elevator burns.
1945 New elevator built at Rosebush.
1946 Morey Brother's sawmill established near Winn.
1947 Last run for Mt. Pleasant Sugar Plant before being sold the next year and the equipment removed.
1948 Roosevelt Refinery fire.

1949   Island Park Swimming Pool opens.
        Pixie restaurant opens.

1950

1950   Fire downtown Mt. Pleasant destroys Economy Dime Store and
        damages Shephard Jewelry, Foland Optical, Dittman's, and
        Morris Dime Store.
1951   Pullen school opens.
1952   Maeder Sawmill established.
        St. Leo's church built at Winn.
1953   Blackstone Bar destroyed by fire.
1954   Bader Mill damaged by fire.
1955   New MPHS octagon construction begins.
1956   Old tires are burned under sheet iron to thaw the ground for the
        new High School.
        New library approved for Mt. Pleasant to replace overcrowded old
        building.
1957   Weidman Lion's Club chartered.
        Morbark Debarker Co. founded at Winn.
1958   Weidman Baptist Church established.
1959   Central Michigan College becomes Central Michigan University.

1960

1960   Borden Condensery closes.
1961   The Orchard Ave. Church of Christ centennial celebration.
1962   CMU converts first floor gymnasium to rifle range.
1963   Mt. Pleasant dedicates new water system and CMU dedicates Thorpe
        and Beddow Residence halls on the same day.
1964   Mt. Pleasant centennial celebration.
1965   Randell Manufacturing, Inc. founded near Weidman Community
        Memorial Stadium in Mt. Pleasant is completed.
        American Hotel on North Main St. to be torn down.
        Teen dance hall, The Whaler, closes after complaints from residents
        about noise.

        Weidman Dam approved to be constructed on Walker Creek creates
        Lake of the Hills development.
        Mt. Pleasant Junior High bond proposal approved.
        Holiday Inn opens 66 units to be followed by a restaurant, 42 units
        and meeting rooms.
1966   Abbott's Furniture Store founded in Weidman.
1967   21 apartment units built on the Isabella County Indian Reservation.
1968   Pixie South built.
1969   Weidman Church of the Nazarene founded.

1970

1970   Glady's McArthur Memorial Library opens in Weidman.
        Faith M. Johnston publishes *Through The Arch Of Experience.*
        Students occupy college gymnasium in war protest.
1971   Cashway Lumber grand opening of new location on East M-20.

Mt. Pleasant Centennial Parade on Mission St. 1964.

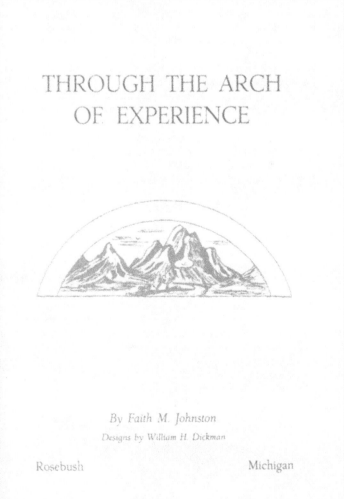

100th Anniversary

Wabou Lodge

No. 305

F. & A. M.

1872   1972

ZION LUTHERAN CHURCH

BROOMFIELD TOWNSHIP

1874

The Centennial Celebration of Mt. Pleasant Lodge No. 217 I.O.O.F.

1974

WINN AREA CENTENNIAL

1876   1976

WEIDMAN AREA CENTENNIAL

HISTORY BOOK

WEIDMAN, MICHIGAN
JULY 4, 1994

1972 Mt. Pleasant Public Schools Gordon Struble Memorial Forrest Shelter dedicated.
  100th anniversary of the Wabon Lodge F&AM.
1973 Schafer's Bait & Sporting Goods opens in Weidman.
1974 Keith Baumann builds new grocery store in Weidman across from Allen's Lumber.
  CMU Physical Training Building demolished.
1975 Western Auto opens in Weidman.
  Beal City Centennial celebration.
1976 Winn Centennial celebration.
1977 Herrick Park opens in the NE of Isabella County.
1978 20th anniversary of Shepherd Maple Syrup Festival.
1979 C&O makes its last run from Coleman to Mt. Pleasant.

1980

1980 Weidman VFW post chartered.
1981 Saginaw Chippewa Indian Tribe begins hosting Bingo games.
1982 Weidman Health Clinic completed.
1983 Shepherd Elementary institutes a "Family Style" lunch program.
1984 CMU begins work on a woodchip plant.
1985 Saginaw Chippewa Indian Tribe introduces card games into their bingo hall.
1986 Flood inundates area.
1987 Dedication of the Robert A. Wood Mill Pond Park project.
1988 Meijer, Inc. announces it will build in Mt. Pleasant.
1989 CMU Annex Chapel converted to art gallery.

1990

1990 Vietnam Veterans Memorial constructed at Island Park.

The First Hundred Years

A PORTRAIT OF
CENTRAL MICHIGAN UNIVERSITY
1892 - 1992

BRINTON!

I Used to go there
to Dances

Marilyn Geasler Fosburg

1991 Western Weekend parties turn to riot with crowd exceeding 2,000.
City of Mt. Pleasant okays recycling program in conjunction with county Material Recovery Facility.

1992 County Jail opens new 40 bed addition.
CMU football team defeats MSU 24-20.

1993 Recycling facility opens in Mt. Pleasant.
Rev. Jesse Jackson draws crowd of 6,000 at CMU's Rose Arena.

1994 Weidman area centennial celebration.
Brine spill of 840 gallons on farmland off Beal City Road near Leaton.

1995 City of Mt. Pleasant gives part of Franklin Street to Sacred Heart.

1996 Black Bear found in Scully subdivision off Lincoln Road.
Mt. Pleasant City Planners approve site for strip mall between Broadway and Michigan Street site of former Archie's car lot.

1997 Union Township to build wastewater plant. Cost estimated at nine million dollars.

1998 Claude Lemmer retires after 37 years as Shepherd band director.

1999 Honnegar Mill formerly Harris Milling demolished.
Delfield manufacturing plant sold to international British firm.

Eleven arrested at Tribal building sit-in.
Construction begins on Jack Locks Theatre complex on the corner of Pickard and Isabella.

2000

2000 Mt. Pleasant and Okaya, Japan celebrate their 35th anniversary of their sister city relationship.

2001 Robert C. Mills publishes *"Deer Camp: An American Tradition."*
Marilyn Geasler Fosburg publishes *"Brinton! I Used to go there to Dances."*

2002 Mill Pond dam demolished to make way for park improvements.
Gunman kills three in parking lot of Isabella County Courthouse.
Cinema 4 and Rally's demolished to construct Walgreens.

2003 Dittman's Shoe store concludes business history with auction and sale.
Isabella Bank and Trust Centennial.
Genealogical Society of Isabella County publish this family history album.

Beal City

Beal City was named after Mr. Nicholas Beal, who built the first general store on the northwest corner of Section 21, Nottawa Township in 1881. In 1882 Mr. Frank Vogel built a second store, which was to become the Tilmann Hardware in later years. After several owners, Ed Smith purchased the Beal Store in 1905 and ran it for 40 years. E.N. Smith also had a meat market in an annex next to his building and in 1934 he built a tavern beside his store. In 1945 the store was acquired by Mr. Walter Rau and became the Rau Grocery. Mr. Rau later moved his business across the street to the northeast corner where the building is located today.

In 1884 Peter Doll established a blacksmith shop. During the same year Joseph Doll and Peter Shafer started selling groceries and general merchandise from their new store. Doctors in Beal City have included Dr. Watley, Dr. Burch and Dr. Rondot.

The first church was built on land donated by Mr. John Pohl. This church burned, as did a second church that was built further north of town. The present church, Catholic School and Sisters Convent was completed in 1911.

Beal City Public Schools adjoin the Catholic school on the west and include both elementary and high school grades.

At one time there was a Gleaner Hall located on Main Street, which was built in 1913. This was used for dances and large gatherings. The hall was later removed when it wasn't needed because of the new Knights of Columbus Hall being built just east of town.

Blanchard, Michigan

The town of Blanchard is found in the township of Rolland in Isabella County. The two influences of this community were the large quantities of forests and the railroad industry. In 1876 Mr. Philip Blanchard from Maine came to the area with his family and purchased an existing saw-mill and much of the land in the area. His success with P.G. Blanchard & Sons prompted others to come to the area and the population grew.

In July 1878, the town of Blanchard was platted and by 1879, P.G. Blanchard owned 1,770 acres in the center of the township and another 80 acres south of the millpond. In 1880, P.G. Blanchard signed over all of his property to his sons and disappeared from the community and by 1891 there are no signs of the Blanchard family or business left in the area.

The area was very rich in lumber and by 1889, there were six lumber companies and three shingle mills in the small community. The only one left in the town today is descended from Mark Dewitt who came to the area and established a shingle mill in 1895. It was Mark Dewitt that developed the roadway that is still used today and provided a better access to the millpond.

As the forests were depleted, the residents recognized that they must turn to other ways of making a living or leave the area. Land was sold readily to those who were willing to clear the land and turn it over to farming. By the early part of the 20th century, farming was very profitable and over 16,000 acres covering Rolland and Broomfield townships was under cultivation.

The railroad coming to the area was a large factor in the succeeding of lumber and agriculture. Without the railroad, shipping of lumber or livestock would have been very difficult. Agriculture has maintained this community on through the years and developed a family-oriented area, which has held a stable population.

Mount Pleasant

In 1855 Mr. David Ward purchased land in Isabella County from the government that would, in time, become the city of Mount Pleasant. He had logged off the site along the east side of the Chippewa River and decided that the area would make a good location for a town.

Mr. Ward began surveying the land into lots with the assistance of I.E. Arnold and had soon completed the first plat of the village he named Mount Pleasant. It is believed that Mr. Ward may have named the village after his hometown of Mt. Pleasant, Ohio. He also donated five additional acres for county purposes.

On May 10, 1860 approval was obtained to move the County Seat to Mount Pleasant and construction was started on the new courthouse by W.H. Nelson at the cost of $140. The courthouse was completed and ac-

Early bird's eye view of Beal City, possibly taken from church bell tower.

Early picture of Broadway looking east, Mt. Pleasant.

Southwest corner of Main and Broadway Streets.

Broadway looking west from Normal Avenue in 1910.

cepted on July 12, 1860 and the first term of court was held in the new building that same year.

With the passage of the new land reform act (the Homestead Act of 1862) the county would see a large number of settlers moving into the area. The settlers could acquire land free simply by claiming it, making

Horse drawn fire truck, Mt. Pleasant.

Ann Arbor Train Depot on West Broadway, Mt. Pleasant.

Above and below: Train wreck north of Mt. Pleasant, Sept. 17, 1908.

Bennett Hotel stood at the corner of Broadway and Court Streets.

Bennett Hotel Dining Room

First motorized fire truck in Mt. Pleasant.

Canoeing on Main Street Feb. 23, 1922 after ice storm.

Central State Normal School, Mt. Pleasant.

Downtown Mt. Pleasant on Broadway Street looking east.

Dow Chemical Co. on East Pickard Street, Mt. Pleasant.

Roosevelt Oil Company and Refinery, Mt. Pleasant.

Albar oil well early 1950s.

improvements on it, and occupying it for a specified time. This was a great opportunity for individuals not in a position to purchase an improved farm.

In 1863 Mr. Ward sold his land to Harvey and George Morton. Since the original platting had never been recorded the Mortons again platted Mount Pleasant and this time recorded it in 1864. They built the first hotel in Mount Pleasant that same year. It was of frame construction and had 22 rooms.

From the earliest days of Mount Pleasant there was always a strong interest in education. In 1890, W.A. Jordan started the Mt. Pleasant Business College. A year later M.C. Skinner, who had been a teacher in the area for several years, became the new owner of the college and the name became Mount Pleasant Business College and Normal.

There was a great community interest in establishing a college for the community and after much hard work and several sessions of government, a law was passed in 1895 accepting Central as a state institution.

Near the end of 1928 oil was discovered at the Joslin No. 1 Oil Well in Isabella County. Mount Pleasant became a boom town. The two major hotels at the time, the Bennett and the Park, were usually filled to capacity with rooming houses and restaurants also being full. Oil drilling continued, new wells were discovered and a refinery was built in Mount Pleasant. Many of the oil companies and drilling contractors based their headquarters here. Mount Pleasant became the "Oil Capital of Michigan."

Mount Pleasant has continued to grow with the addition of the Soaring Eagle Casino east of town on the Chippewa Indian Reservation. An estimated 35,000 people visit the Casino and Mount Pleasant on a daily basis which provides a great stimulus for the businesses of the Central Michigan area.

From the Virgin Pines that were timbered off so many years ago, Mount Pleasant has grown to become "Someplace Special" to live in.

Rosebush (Half-Way/Calkinsville)

The village of Rosebush was originally called Calkinsville and also "Half-Way" because of its location between the Clare and Mt. Pleasant Stage Coach line. When the Ann Arbor Railroad came through around 1886 land was needed for a depot and a Mr. James L. Bush agreed to give the land to the railroad in exchange for the depot being named Rosebush after his wife, Elizabeth Rose. Later the depot name was applied to the village name.

In the early years there was a livery stable and hotel and as many as four grocery and general stores in Rosebush. Soon after the arrival of the railroad, Ned Johnson and later his son Wilbur ran a stockyard. The Rose-

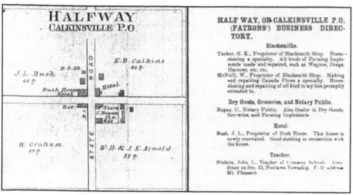

Plat of Half Way, Calkinsville, Rosebush.

Above and below: Kennedy Sawmill, Rosebush.

Shepherd, Michigan

The village of Shepherd began in 1857 at an intersection of two roads and named Salt River. The Salt River was very important to the community as a source of power for a saw mill and a flour mill. The first post office began in 1857 in the home of William Robbins and officially named the Salt River Post Office. By 1866, the village was platted out by Mr. Elijah Moore consisting of two blocks. Later two additions to the original plat was added and by 1884, the population consisted of 300 people.

The village now boasted of a blacksmith shop, cheese factory, hotel, attorneys, doctors, and several mercantile shops. Disaster struck the small village as fire destroyed businesses located close to the four corners and the Ann Arbor railroad came through but a 1/2 mile from the village causing the businesses to locate closer to it and left the four corners to rebuild as generally a residential area.

In 1885, I.N. Shepherd built a block of buildings close to the railroad and the village of Shepherd surrounded Salt River. Shepherd incorporated in 1887 and included a cider mill, clothespin factory, planing mill, canning factory, hotels and gristmills. The railroad brought a great deal of prosperity to the area. 1909 saw electric power brought to the village along with water and sewer services.

Through the years Shepherd's development has centered around a largely agricultural community with many service businesses for the people. It continues to grow as a family oriented community and boasts the annual Maple Syrup Festival each spring that is attended by thousands of tourists.

Aerial View of Shepherd, from water tower.

bush Bank was established in 1909 with Homer Campbell as cashier. Herb Gould, a mortician, was also in business until around 1915. The first barber was George McKnight and later, Claude Bullard, barbered from 1915-79. Some of the other businesses over the years were: Peck's Drug Store, Commort Brothers General Store, Arthur Johnson Store, F.C. Matteson Store, Alex Hyslop Store, Johnson-Hess Store, William Hunter Store and Hardware, Thomas Gray Elevator (later known as Johnson-Coyne Elevator and then the Rosebush Elevator), English Hotel, John Coyne Cobbler and Harness Shop, Terry and Bayliss Implement Store. Blacksmiths: Dennis Ragan, Abe Smith and Joe Clevenger and William Teeter ran a cream and milk station until around 1918.

There were four churches in the Rosebush area that included the Methodist, Presbyterian, Baptist and Standard churches. Medical doctors have included the names Ayres, Shaw, Johnson and McArthur.

The road that runs north and south through Rosebush was originally the old stage line, then later becoming US 27. It was graveled in 1918 and paved in 1930 and is now called Mission Road.

Ann Arbor Train Depot, Shepherd.

Weidman

The village of Weidman was platted by John S. Weidman in 1893 and contained 34 blocks divided into 450 lots. The village was partly in Sherman Township and partly in Nottawa Township and was located near the home he had built for his family that same year.

In 1894 the first post office was established with Horace Parsons as Postmaster. H.D. Scott and William Mills opened the first store in Weidman and sold groceries, dry goods and other merchandise.

Around 1905 the Holmes Milling Company was established. The company built an elevator and mill using the power from the Mill Pond, which had been created by John S. Weidman.

At one time there were two hotels in Weidman to accommodate overnight lodging for the stage line that ran between Mount Pleasant and Remus. Around 1908 one of the hotels became a furniture store and funeral home, a usual combination for this time period.

Mr. John Otterbine was a barber in Weidman from 1903-41. Eric Thompson operated a drug store and sold home-made ice cream from around 1907 until 1941. In the early 1900s there were two blacksmith shops owned by George Briggs and Asa Frantz that served the farmers of the area for a number of years.

The Weidman area had various schools over the years and in 1967 consolidated with the Barryton and Remus schools to become what is known as the Chippewa Hills School.

Winn (Dushville), Michigan

Winn, or Dushville, is located in Fremont Township of Isabella County. The village was founded in the early 1860s, primarily as a farming and lumbering community. The post office was founded in 1867 in a log house just about one mile from the location of Winn today. Franklin J. Williams was the first postmaster where mailed was delivered weekly.

In 1875 a young man come into the community by the name of William Wiley Dush. By 1876, William Dush had platted the village of Dushville and soon to follow was a steam-powered sawmill, a dry goods store and grocery, another sawmill and several other businesses. As Dushville grew and prospered, William Dush expanded his interests and became the postmaster after getting the name of the village changed to Dushville. By then, the populous numbered about 200 people and had a blacksmith shop, church, boarding house and a couple of general stores.

The town continued to grow through the years with the building of a hotel called the Commercial House. There was a dramatics club, a band, another church and a G.A.R. building. William Dush expanded his interests east toward Millbrook where he built another sawmill that took his life as well as that of two others. The name of the town continued to be confusing as it was called both Winn and Dushville. After William Dush passed away, a group of citizens petitioned to have the name re-established as Winn, which became effective in 1895. The post office did not change its name until 1898.

Broomfield Township

Broomfield Township is located in the middle of Michigan's mitten and begins about 10 miles west of Mt. Pleasant on M-20, at the top of a very significant big hill. The last big glacier ended at the "hill where the north begins" just north of Clare and this ridge runs through the lower 1/3 of our township, leaving 2/3's in the northern boreal forest. Native Americans came to our area about 15,000 years ago and mainly stayed around the Chippewa River to the north, Pony Creek in the southwest and around Hall's, Eldred and Woodruff lakes. Almost all Indian artifacts were located near water because the township was originally covered with an almost impenetrable pine forest canopy. Few deer, rabbits, turkey, bear, elk or other game were in the forest and could only live near forest edges near waterways.

Trappers and lumberman visited mainly by traveling the rivers and the first settlement was along the south bend of the Chippewa River, now part of the Lake Isabella Village. This was possibly an Indian Village to begin with and itinerant people would stay short periods, but it was never a permanent community in the usual sense.

Things remained pretty well in balance until the 1850s when the Michigan Government decided to build a road up the middle of Michigan from Ionia to the straits of Mackinaw. A general path was laid out and a businessman from the Detroit area named Edmund Hall was awarded the contract to build the state highway from near Deerfield and the west county line north, northeast to the top and middle of the township.

William Hutchinson walked up the proposed road sometime in the 1850s to look for a possible place to live. In 1861 he walked back up the road with his friend from Canada, William Broomfield, and both chose homesteads on the county line. Broomfield's property was at the county line and Deerfield Road and Hutchinson's was the next property to the south. An old letter from the Hutchinson Estate indicates that he and Broomfield walked up the state road to the settlement now called "Hall's Camp" in 1868 to have the first township meeting. They drew straws with Broomfield winning to become the first township supervisor.

The first registered marriage was Ithel Eldred, son of Judson Eldred. One of the first persons to live in Broomfield Township was Joe Lett, a black man, who resided in the township before the Civil War (early 1860s) and who later served in the Michigan Regiment during the Civil War.

Michigan had no money so they gave many sections of township forest to Hall in payment of his highway efforts. Logging probably progressed gradually, after the roads were improved and railways were established in the area. The towns of Chicago, Manistee and Holland all burned the same night in 1871 and the price of lumber sky rocketed and so did Hall's lumbering efforts. In 30 years lumbering crews cut essentially every pine tree, skipping many of the hardwoods. Frequent fires roared unstopped through the timber scraps and often sun-baked grasses. Hall left his name at Hall's Lake and what was once a verdant canopy of trees, as miles of charred grass and stumps. A total of about 10 lumber camps/mills were located in the township through 1900. Only Lett's Camp in Section 4 retains a name of current residents, the remaining appear to have taken their money and moved on.

Broomfield was pretty cagey, knew the ropes and got free land as a squatter. Other settlers bought the cut-off land at bargain prices and planted crops after pulling the huge pine stumps. At this time many schools also were established.

Before 1900 many farmers showed up and stayed in the township and included names such as Anderson, Green, Kimball, Diehl, Blackmer, Guy, Eldred, Norman, Thren, Strong, Todd, Richardson, Lett, Maxon, Esch, Sellers, etc. Folks came from all over the USA with the northwest corner of the township being settled by a large number of individuals from the south, escaping from civil war and racial horrors. Of the earliest pioneers in the 1879 plat book, only the Lett, Norman and Eldred names are still on property in the township in 2002.

Chippewa Township

Chippewa Township was one of the first townships organized in Isabella County. As early as 1850-51, there were several families residing in the township. Some of the early settlers were Norman and William Payne, William Foutch, George W. Howorth and the Reverend Charles Taylor. Mr. Taylor was the first minister in Isabella County of the Methodist faith.

In 1859 Mr. Norman C. Payne was elected the first township supervisor, a position he held through 1861. Some of the villages that were located in Chippewa Township at one time or another include Alembic, Denver, Wise, Delwin, Leaton and Tonkinsville.

Alembic had a post office from 1857-61, Wise from 1884-1906 and Delwin from 1880-1906.

Chippewa Township is bounded on the north by Denver Township, on the east by Midland County, on the south by Coe Township and the west by Union Township. It is numbered 14 north by 3 west.

Coe Township

Coe Township, located in the southeastern part of Isabella County, was the first township to be organized by the Legislature Act No. 151. The township was formed on February 13, 1855 and named for Albert G. Coe, who was the lieutenant governor of Michigan. In the spring of 1856 William B. Bowen was elected the first supervisor. Because Isabella County hadn't been organized, Mr. Bowen needed to go to the Midland County Seat to attend sessions of the board. The distance he traveled was about 18 miles through swamps, woods and marshes. The roads, if there were any, were very primitive.

Coe is bordered on the north by Chippewa Township, on the south by Gratiot County, on the east by Midland County, and on the west by Lincoln Township.

The population of Coe Township, in 2000, was approximately 3,000.

Farming is a major source of industry. The landscape of the township is primarily level land or gently rolling hills. There is adequate water from the Salt River, as well as sufficient drainage from the river's tributaries, all of which make the township ideal for agricultural use.

The land description is Township 13 North, Range 6 West.

Sources:

Isabella County Herald April 4, 2001 article: "My, how we've grown!" pages one and three.

Isabella County Michigan Atlas & Plat Book 1978, page 13.

Past and Present of Isabella County Michigan by Hon. Isaac A. Fancher, Chapter XXII Townships and Villages.

Portrait & Biographical Album of Isabella County, Michigan (Chicago: Chapman Brothers, 1884) page 543.

Saginaw News April 3, 1967 article: "Names of Townships Traced-History played big part."

Coldwater Township

Coldwater Township is located in the northwest corner of Isabella County with Clare County on the north and Mecosta County on the west. The first election was held on the first Monday of April, 1868 and J.J. Colley was elected the first township supervisor.

Coldwater Township had two villages, Sherman City and Brinton. Sherman City had a population of 150 in 1877 and was located on the Coldwater and Sherman Township line. Sherman City is about 25 miles northwest of Mt. Pleasant. In 1910 the population was 200 and there was a hotel, livery, saloons, grocery store, blacksmith shop and other places of business. Sherman City was named for General William T. Sherman. It had a post office from February 24, 1877 until October 15, 1913.

The village of Brinton, also known as "Letson," was settled in 1862. The first post office was established on April 17, 1888 and was used until November 30, 1906. Brinton is 7 miles south of Lake in Clare County or about 30 miles northwest of Mt. Pleasant. At one time Brinton had several general stores, a hotel, a farm implement store, harness maker and a blacksmith shop. By 1910 a hardware store, grocery store, drug store and a meat market had been added to the village.

As in many villages of the day, Brinton had a fire, which destroyed most of the buildings in the village. Today the area has some farming, mostly cash crops and a few dairy-farming operations.

Deerfield Township

Deerfield Township was organized in 1874. William Peterson was the first supervisor. Lumbering was an early activity to clear the land for farming. Logs were floated down both branches of the Chippewa River, and the Coldwater River, in the spring. The mill was located near the junction of those rivers. An early hamlet there was named Two Rivers. Deerfield is bounded on the north by Nottawa Township, on the east by Union Township, on the south by Fremont Township, and on the west by Broomfield Township

Denver Township

Denver Township, originally a part of Wise Township is located at the northeastern part of Isabella County, and was organized in 1876, making it one of the last townships to be formed. Denver was named from a suggestion of a resident who formerly had lived in Denver, Colorado. The first supervisor was Robert Pearson.

Denver is bordered on the north by Wise Township, the south by Chippewa Township, the east by Midland County, and on the west by Isabella Township.

The population of Denver in 2000 was approximately 1,150. The lay of the land is primarily low and flat, and farming is a source of industry.

The land description is Township 15 North, Range 3 West.

Fremont Township

Fremont Township was organized on October 16, 1863. The first election was held on the first Monday of April, 1869 at the home of Jerome Bachelder. The first township supervisor elected was William Tiffany.

Fremont Township's first post office was made of logs and was located one mile east of present day Winn. The first postmaster was Franklin J. Williams who was appointed in 1867.

Winn or "Dushville," as it was originally called, was the only village established in Fremont Township and was originally named after William Wiley Dush. Dushville had a few stores, blacksmith and repair shop and a boarding house.

On November 21, 1885 Samuel C. Williams laid out a plot of eight blocks, consisting of eight lots in each block in what was to become the village of Winn.

Fremont Township along with the rest of Isabella County was mostly a farming community after the lumbering boom left the area.

Gilmore Township

Gilmore Township, located in the northwestern part of Isabella County was organized in 1870 and named after Admiral J.C. Gilmore. Rufus F. Glass, one of the earliest settlers of the area, was elected the first supervisor of the township in 1870 and retained this position through 1873.

Gilmore Township is bordered on the west by Coldwater Township, Vernon Township on the east, Nottawa Township on the south and Clare County on the north. The township is not heavily populated as reflected by the 2000 Census, which showed only about 1,400 people living in the township.

The lay of the land shows heavily wooded areas, rolling hills, swampland and farmland. Hunting and fishing are popular pastimes in the township. The land description of the Township is 16 North, Range 5 West.

Isabella Township

Isabella Township was organized in 1857, two years before the organization of the county and originally embraced all the territory bounded by the county line, together with a part of Clare County, except townships 13 and 14 north, of range 3 west. Charles A. Jeffries was elected the first township supervisor and served from 1857-58. As the years went by Isabella Township was eventually reduced to the approximate size of the other townships in the county.

The boundaries of the township have Vernon Township on the north, Denver Township on the east, Union Township on the south and Nottawa Township on the west.

Calkinsville, a small village, is situated at the cross roads between Section 10, 11, 14 and 15. Calkinsville was named after Burton Calkins, a general store owner. In January 1899 a plot of land west of Calkinsville and the railroad tracks became what is now called Rosebush. James L. Bush named Rosebush for his wife, Elizabeth Rose Bush.

Jordan was a flag station on the Pere Marquette Railroad in 1884. Jordan was located between Mt. Pleasant and Coleman on the southeast Isabella and Denver Township line.

Other village sites in the township included Nippesing which was located southeast of Calkinsville-Rosebush and Whiteville which was located southwest of Calkinsville-Rosebush.

Whiteville was named for Omer L. White who was a store keeper and became postmaster in January 1884. The post office operated until February 1902.

The only village remaining in the township today is Rosebush.

Lincoln Township

Lincoln Township was organized on October 16, 1863 and is numbered 13 north and 4 west. It is bounded on the north by Union Township and on the east by Coe Township. It like other townships of Isabella County was heavily wooded when first settled. The clearing of the trees and draining of the land, has made the township a very productive agricultural site for many farms.

Some of the first settlers of the township were U. McKinstry, Edward Dugan, G.P. Ryder, E. Dunham, Samuel Woodworth, Nelson Ives and Warren Wardwell. The first birth in the township was a daughter to Mr. McKinstry. In the early days, there were two post offices in the township one at Crawford and the other was at Strickland.

Nottawa Township

Nottawa Township, organized in 1874 or 1875, was named in honor of an Indian chief of the Saginaw, Swan Creek, and Black River Indians who died in 1881 at the age of 100.

Coldwater Lake, fed by the Coldwater River, occupies all of Section

30. Coldwater River flows through the western part of the township and the Chippewa River flows through the eastern area. The township is bounded by Gilmore Township on the north, Isabella Township on the east, Deerfield Township on the south and Sherman Township on the west.

Rolland Township

Rolland Township is located in the southwest corner of Isabella County, and was organized from part of Fremont Township in 1866. How the township came to be named Rolland isn't clear. The first supervisor was William M. Peterson.

Rolland is bordered on the west by Mecosta County, the east by Fremont Township, the south by Montcalm County and on the north by Broomfield Township.

At the time the township was organized, lumbering was the main industry, however, as the land was timbered off, farming replaced it as the major source of industry.

Population of Rolland Township in 2000 was approximately 1,200. The landscape of the township is of beautiful trees (spectacular when the fall colors are at their peak), peaceful farmland, and rolling hills.

The land description is Township 13 North, Range 6 West.

Sherman Township

Sherman Township was organized October 12, 1868 and in 1869 the first election was held at the house of Cyrus Dunbar, who, with Milo T. Dean and Aaron Osborn, were Inspectors of Election. The first township supervisor elected was Wesley Ellis.

The township is bounded on the north by Coldwater Township, on the east by Nottawa Township, on the south by Broomfield Township and the west by Mecosta County. The Township is numbered 13 north and 6 west.

Sherman Township was sparsely settled and quite heavily wooded. The village of Sherman City was located partly in Sherman Township and partly in Coldwater Township. There was a post office at Sherman City along with a few buildings, but the town had no commercial importance except as a convenient trading point for the farmers in the area.

Union Township

Union Township was organized on March 19, 1861 with the first election held in a log schoolhouse. The Township is numbered 14 north and 4 west. There are two bodies of water within the township, the Chippewa River and Mission Creek which is a small stream and empties into the Chippewa.

The first settler in Union Township was John Hursh, who with his wife and six children located on a homestead in 1854. Others soon followed Mr. Hursh as the Homestead bill was passed by Congress which gave a settler 160 acres for a small amount of money, he had to build a residence and live for five years on the land. Following this, if improvements were added, a patent to the land was given.

Mt. Pleasant is the principal town in the township of Union and became a center of trade for lumber, farm products and businesses that flourished with the growth of the township. The first school was a log building built in 1855 and taught by Elizabeth Gulick. The township was first lumbered and then cleared into very good agricultural property.

Vernon Township

Vernon Township was organized on June 11, 1866. It lies in the northern part of Isabella County and is bounded on the north by Clare County, on the east by Wise Township, on the south by Isabella Township and on the west by Gilmore Township.

In July 1866 the first election was held at the home of George W. Stine. Mr. William Phinesey was the first township supervisor elected in Vernon with a total of seven votes cast. He served during the years 1866 and 1867.

J.L. Markley, a German, was one of the early settlers in Vernon Township and was founder of Vernon City. Vernon City is located on the north end of Vernon Township where the south end of the city of Clare begins in Clare County. Vernon City was settled long before Clare County was organized.

Burnham Crossings had a sawmill, boarding house and banking grounds for logs. Other mills were located in the area along with two brick kilns, a depot, and warehouse. The post office name was "Russell" in 1875. In 1896 fire destroyed the mill and the depot closed.

Farming is still in the area but it is mostly cash crops with some dairy farmers. A few oil and gas wells still exist.

Wise Township

Wise Township was organized on January 4, 1872 and aptly named after George W. Wise its founder. Wise Township is numbered 16 north and 3 west. The first election was held in the village of Loomis in April 1872. Lumber was the industry of the time with sawmills and a shingle factory. Soon to follow was a hotel called the "Hursh House" built about the same time as the Flint and Pere Marquette built the depot in Loomis. In 1872 a hemlock-extract factory was built at a cost of $15,000.

A school was built in 1871 with Miss Allen as the schoolteacher for the first term. Fletcher Tubbs had the first farm in the township and the first religious services were held in Wise & Loomis' sawmill. By 1884, Loomis was a thriving community of 350 people with two hotels, five stores, a church, blacksmith shop, drug store and two saloons.

Chippewa River, A.A. Railroad Depot and Harris Milling Co.'s mill.

Plat of Delwin, MI.

Top photo: The barn raising of David Seiter's barn. In the front is David Seiter on the rocking horse. Others include Edna, Mabel, and Margaret Nixon, Marie Bogan, Christian and Evelyn Seiter, Grandpa Seiter and Ethel Crawford.

Center photo: Barn raising of the Willey barn. David Seiter is in the far left corner, Richard Bogan sitting on the beam just above the ladder. Mr. Charles Hoover is holding the lamb on the high beam. Wonder how he managed to get it up there.

Bottom left: Barn raising day at the Andrew Irwin farm. This farm was sold in 1912 to Mr. and Mrs. Jacob Seiter. Mrs. Seiter and son, Robert, live there today. Perhaps you can pick out Jacob Seiter, left, on the top beam, and David Seiter in the center.

Bottom right: Construction of a bridge on a north and south road one mile east of the Vernon town hall. Far left is Albert Seiter, Earl Marshall, Clare Hoover, Charles Durnon, David Seiter, Andrew Irwing and Walter White. They help to date the picture.

Mt. Pleasant Bus Time-Table advertisement.

Early picture of Central Michigan Community Hospital.

Transport Model 22

TRANSPORT

MODEL 50
2 TONS CAPACITY

Chassis $2585
F.O.B. FACTORY

MODEL 50 SPECIFICATIONS

ENGINE, Continental C2. 4¼ bore and 5¼ stroke 4 cylinder cast enbloc. Oiling system plunger pump force and splash. Water circulated by large centrifugal pump. Crank case, aluminum, with all bearings fastened to upper half.

MAGNETO. Eisemann G-4 high tension. Manual control.

GOVERNOR. Duplex Model DMR centrifugal. Governor transmission control holds truck in high gear to speed of 16 miles per hour or 1180 r. p. m. engine speed. Governor engine control holds engine speed to 1460 r. p. m. which permits maximum power for low speed work when extraordinary power is required.

CARBURETOR. Stromberg M2 vertical. Float feed, gravity pressure. High and low speed adjustment. Choker attached to steering column. Hot air intake direct from stove on exhaust tube.

COOLING SYSTEM. Capacity over 7 gallons. Radiator armored design with spring cushion. Spirex core which is the most efficient type owing to the whirling motion of air as it passes through fins. Water is circulated by large centrifugal pump on engine. Radiator is cooled by 18 inch fan which runs on Hyatt bearing. Fan has extraordinary pulling power and is driven with flat leather belt.

CLUTCH. Fuller & Sons. Multiple dry disk 8 inches in diameter with 16 faces. Even and positive engagement at all times. Clutch pilot shaft bearing is of permanently lubricated type.

TRANSMISSION. Fuller & Sons GU. 4 speeds forward and 1 reverse. Ball bearing throughout. 1st speed and reverse gears 1" face, 2nd, 3rd, and 4th speed gears ¾" face. Final gear ratios: Reverse 53 to 1, 1st speed 39 to 1, 2nd speed 24.5 to 1, 3rd speed 13 to 1, 4th speed 8.15 to 1.

DRIVE SHAFT AND JOINTS. Arvac. Three 5" joints and two-piece tubular shaft. Intermediate joint carried on SKF Ball bearing.

FRAME. Pressed Steel. 208" long. 34" wide inswept to 31" between front wheels. 5¾" deep and 3½" wide at center. ¼" stock. Frame extremely well braced.

SPRINGS. Front 2½" wide, 40" long. 9 leaves. Rear 3" wide, 54" long. 12 leaves. Eye leaves of all springs Silico Manganese steel, balance high carbon steel.

REAR AXLE. Clark internal gear drive. Load carrying member, or dead axle, solid nickel chrome steel forging 3" in diameter. Power is transmitted to road wheels through jackshaft securely attached to dead axle by means of massive pinions meshing with internal gears bolted to road wheels in dust

proof housing inside of brake drums. Tread 58 inches.

BRAKES. Foot brake external contracting 3" wide. Emergency, internal expanding 2½" wide. Both brakes operate on 16½" brake drum.

FRONT AXLE. Columbia. Drop Forged I-beam 2" by 3" by ½" web, spindles are nickel steel. Tread 58 inches.

STEERING GEAR. Jacox Screw and nut type. Adjustable and accessible. Steering gear may be removed from frame without first taking out engine.

WHEELS. Hickory spokes and ash felloes. Front 36x4 with fourteen 2" square spokes. Rear 36x6 with fourteen 2½" square spokes.

TIRES. Goodyear standard equipment. 36x4 front and 36x6 rear.

WHEELBASE. 150 inches.

GASOLINE TANK. 20 gallons capacity.

EQUIPMENT. Tool kit with high grade tools, powerful jack, oil lamps located inside of dash also tail lamp, motometer, and odometer. Equipped for service.

Inasmuch as it is the policy of the Transport Truck Company to make such changes as may, in their opinion, better the truck's specifications and prices are subject to change without notice.

TRANSPORT TRUCK COMPANY, MT. PLEASANT, MICHIGAN

Transport Truck Co., Mt. Pleasant.

Sign from local Mt. Pleasant Oil Refinery.

Gould Rexall Drug Store located on North Mission, Mt. Pleasant.

Nickels, Mertz & Co. 5 and 10 to 50 Store.

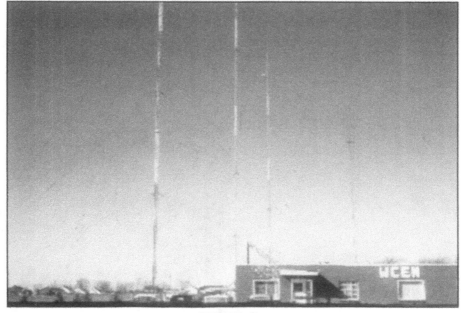

WCEN Radio

Bonnell Superior Furniture

In 1918 Edward J. Bonnell Sr. and Edgar Bixby purchased Foster Hardware and Furniture Co., located at the southwest corner of Main Street at Broadway. They renamed the business, which operated for 35 years, Mt. Pleasant Hardware & Furniture Co. Bonnell ran the furniture part of the business; Bixby the hardware, in this three-story brick building. Ed Bonnell Sr. was a charter member of Rotary Club and Mt. Pleasant Chamber of Commerce.

After serving in the Air Corps in World War II, Edward J. Bonnell Jr. worked for his dad in furniture sales until 1956 when he bought Superior Furniture, four miles north of Mt. Pleasant, from Bill Davidge, renaming it Bonnell Superior Furniture. In 1977 Ed sold the family business to his son, James Bonnell, who operated it the next 18 years, then sold it.

Ed Bonnell Jr. born in Saginaw, MI, has lived 84 of his 88 years in Mt. Pleasant, and has been an active member Kiwanis Club for 63 years. That was when Arlie Osborne, his high school coach, brought him and Lawrence Hood into Kiwanis. Ed was a scoutmaster and Kiwanis Club Boy Scout troupe representative. Ed played on the 1932 State Championship basketball team and attended Central Michigan University where he majored in business. Ed is a life member of the First United Methodist Church and was president of Methodist Men's Club when the new church was built in 1961. He is a present member of Isabella County Historical Society.

In 1947 Ed married Auburna "Burnie" Arnold of Traverse City, whom he met while she taught homemaking at Mt. Pleasant High. Ed and Burnie have four children: James, Helen, Bruce and Jean. When the children were enrolled at Pullen Elementary, Ed served as President of the PTA, while Burnie worked on school events and with Brownie and Cub Scouts. Ed and Burnie still live at 1608 East High Street, a home they bought from Stacey Myers, who built it.

Bourland TV & Appliance

James E. Bourland came to Mt. Pleasant from Aberdeen, MS, via Detroit in 1936. A friend he had worked with in Detroit encouraged him to come here to work for Johnson's Motors.

1951 Bourland T.V. & Appliance Grand Opening. James Bourland and Bessie Bourland, owners. Del Conkright, Mayor and Ray Brower, Appliance Rep.

Johnson's Motors was located on the corner of Michigan and College (University) St. The Firestone store next door on Michigan was owned by Floyd H. Johnson. Jim had a very small room for a radio repair shop. After a short time the store needed more room and it was moved to a back room in the building. Lowell Young was the manager of Firestone. Both the Firestone store and the radio shop needed more room. It was mutually agreed that Jim would move his operation.

He bought a store at 213 S. Main owned by N.D. Gover. The south half of the building was operated by Frank Sage as a music store. The north half was a jewelry store operated by Mr. Klunzinger. They both moved their businesses elsewhere.

Jim remodeled the store in 1951 and called it Bourland TV and Appliance. At the grand opening there were hundreds of people. The street from Michigan to Illinois was cut off to traffic due to the great numbers of people. The fire department came in to check and see if the floor was strong enough to hold everyone—it was. Mrs. Thering won the grand prize which was a hot water heater.

In the early 1950s he was instrumental in getting all the store owners north to Smith's Drug Store on the corner to remodel their store fronts. To the north was the Van Drie Bakery, the telephone office, ration board office, and Smith-Bonnell Drug Store on the corner. To the south was the Fire Department, American Cleaners, a shoe shop, dress shop, Lynch grocery, and Bill Segers Garage. Fire fighters at that time were Albert Whitaker, Al Pickens and Orem Flynn.

In 1960 a fire gutted Jim's store and it again was remodeled. In the late 1960s, Jim sold the building and semi-retired. He did repair service on radio's and TVs from his home and in the late 1980s, he retired.

At the ration board you would get ration stamps during World War II. With the stamps you could buy gasoline, tires, sugar, butter, shoes, and meat to name a few things. Jim Leonard was one of the board members.

Jim rode a bicycle to and from work to save gasoline and make his service calls. The government then issued him extra gas and tire stamps for transportation, as they wanted people's radios working.

Hafer Hardware, Inc.

Hafer Hardware was a full service hardware business that was started in 1947 by John J. Hafer and his stepfather, Gordon Jones. The original building had two separate businesses located in the same building. Gordon Jones occupied one half of the building and sold Maytag laundry equipment and General Electric appliances. Hafer Hardware occupied the other half of the building. In 1950 John J. Hafer took over the entire building and expanded his hardware business. This hardware store was a place where you could find almost anything and everything. It stocked house wares, plumbing, electrical, paint, sporting goods, lawn and garden supplies and more. It was the place to get those "hard to find" items. The store was always well stocked and really had more merchandise than there was room for. The store always employed friendly and knowledgeable sales clerks who could do everything from repairing

Hafer Hardware, Inc.

screen windows to mixing custom colored paint to threading pipe. The store was truly a "full service" hardware. John J. Hafer was always looking for new and different items to sell and in the early 1960s he started selling a new winter recreational vehicle called the snowmobile. Some of the early models were very crude in their design, but he later took on the Ski Doo line of snowmobiles and they soon became a huge hit. By the late 1960s he was selling upwards of 200 Ski Doo's each winter season. John J. Hafer retired in 1983 and sold the business to Mr. Glen Irwin who still operates the business today under the name of Hafer Hardware.

Hafer Oil Company

The Hafer Oil Company was located on the northwest corner of Mission Street (Business 27) and Pickard Rd. in Mt. Pleasant, Michigan and was owned and operated by Roy D. Hafer, his wife Flossie Hafer, and their children Roy, Milon and John. They purchased the property in 1926 and built a new home there. They built the gas station soon after and it opened for business in 1927. This was a "full service" station where attendants would pump the gas, check engine oil, and clean the windshield for their customers. The station offered Pure Oil gasoline and related products. The original gasoline pumps were known as "visible" style pumps. The gas station attendant would pump the desired amount of gasoline by hand into a large glass cylinder that sat on top of the pump housing. Then the gasoline would be gravity fed through a hose into the gas tank of the customer's vehicle. The maximum amount of gasoline that could be pumped into the cylinder at one time was 10 gallons, so if the customer required more that 10 gallons, this process would have to be repeated until the desired amount of gasoline had been delivered. The company also delivered gas, fuel oil, kerosene and other related products to local farmers, home owners, and oil drilling companies in the Central Michigan area. The Hafers also built another gas station east of Mt. Pleasant in Greendale Township. This building still exists and sits on the south side of M-20 just east of Oil City. The gasoline for that station had to be trucked from Mt. Pleasant several times per week and the trip there and back took most of a day to do. The Hafer Oil Company served gasoline from this location until the late 1950s. The building was then leased out and was used as a tire store, and later served as a Ski Doo snowmobile sales and service facility for Hafer Hardware. In 1981 the Hafer family sold the corner property and the gas station and the Hafer house were demolished. A Flap Jack restaurant was then built there, and later was re-named JW Filmore's restaurant.

McFarlane Dairy

Douglas McFarlane Sr. was born in Virginia to William C. and Clara (nee Schell) McFarlane in 1913. Shortly after his birth the family moved to Detroit, Michigan where Doug's mother died in 1921. Doug graduated from Cooley High School in 1931 and the following summer went to work for a road crew in northern Michigan.

In the fall of 1932 Doug came to Mt. Pleasant for a visit and his cousin convinced him to stay and enroll at Central. Doug was to meet Margaret (Peg) Brainerd and in the fall of 1934 they were married.

At this time Margaret's father, Hubert Brainerd, was running a small dairy business out of their home and delivering milk to a few households. Doug decided to join his father-in-law in developing the business. At the time Doug joined his father-in-law the business was only delivering about 24 quarts of milk per day so after Doug made the morning deliveries he would spend the rest of the day looking for new business. Over time the business would go from producing 24 quarts of milk per day to 600 gallons a day along with ice cream, cottage cheese and distributorship of Remus Butter for the area.

Prior to 1934 anyone could sell raw milk and as such there were about 17 dairies delivering milk in the Mt. Pleasant area. In 1934 the State

Bob Goffnett with his "Old Number 7" delivery truck.

This picture of the business was taken around 1930 and shows some of the company employees along with their fleet of delivery trucks. Pictured standing from left to right: John J. Hafer, Floyd Burgess, Roy D. Hafer, Otis Methner, and Gordon Armstrong. Seated in the far left truck is Milon Hafer and seated in the next truck to the right is Roy Hafer Jr. In the background to the right side of the picture the Kinney school building can be seen.

passed a law requiring milk to be pasteurized. Because of this Brainerd and McFarlane built their first building and installed pasteurizing equipment, completing this process in 1935.

In 1942, Doug became sole owner of the dairy. He continued operating under the name of Brainerd Dairy until 1948 when he changed the name to McFarlane Dairy. From 1935 on Doug began to obtain the other dairies in the county through mergers, purchases, etc., until all of the 17 dairies were brought together under the McFarlane Dairy name.

At the peak of Doug's business he employed six to seven people in the main plant, seven to nine drivers, two office workers and had four to six part time students. McFarlane Dairy delivered to the homes of most people in the city of Mt. Pleasant and Shepherd. He also delivered to the area schools and delivered commercially to the many stores throughout the Isabella County area. McFarlane Dairy also maintained a soda fountain area in the front of the main plant where individuals could purchase ice cream and such.

McFarlane Dairy drivers and workers

McFarlane Dairy drivers and plant workers

Doug McFarlane (far right) with his administrative and dairy store personnel

In the fall of 1968, McFarlane's sold out to the McDonald Dairy Company of Flint, Michigan and not long after, McDonald's discontinued home delivery and moved out the area.

Michigan Oil & Gas News

Since 1933, the Michigan Oil & Gas News magazine, published in Mt. Pleasant, has weekly informed both industry and public readership of drilling permit applications and issuance, drilling rig activities and drilling results, as well as legislative, regulatory, industry organizational and technological happenings relative to the Michigan petroleum exploration and production industry. The publication makes Michigan unique in the nation as the only oil and gas producing province with a weekly publication tracking petroleum industry activities exclusively in that province.

Two short-lived oil fields reporting publications came before the current Michigan Oil & Gas News publication, first published in June of 1933 from upstairs offices in the 100 block of South Main Street. The weight and rumble of the printing press, however, rendered publication offices on a second floor location unsafe. Founders John P. Murphy and James Dunnigan quickly moved to quarters in the 100 block of South Franklin Street, where the publication remained until the retirement of Murphy and Editor Norman X. Lyon in 1972.

To assure the continuance of the weekly communications flow provided by the publication, the Michigan Oil and Gas Association (MOGA) acquired the Michigan Oil & Gas News in 1972 and returned the publication to print at Mt. Pleasant under the management of Jack R. Westbrook, who retired in 2002 as Managing Editor. The publication, a wholly-owned subsidiary of MOGA, is currently under the management of Managing Editor Scott E. Bellinger and is now published from the 600 block of west Pickard, at the site of what were the Total Refinery offices.

In the past 20 years, the publication has:
• Published two books about Michigan's petroleum exploration and production history.
• Run educational series of articles on various aspects of the industry for the edification of other factions of the industry, as well as the public.
• Reported extensively and in a manner and format unequalled by any other publication, anywhere, the evolution and continued development of the Michigan Natural Resources Trust Fund.
• Run papers and guest articles by industry experts about innovations within the industry (geological series on deep formations) or impacting the industry (Miller Brothers Nordhouse Dunes Case).
• Published geological charts, drilling maps, and pipeline maps of Michigan for industry and public education.
• Extended knowledge of Michigan petroleum exploration and production history by having personnel make speeches to civic, educational and industry organizations about the petroleum exploration and production industry in general and Michigan in particular.

Mt. Pleasant — Oil Capital of Michigan

Larger cities absorb the presence of the oil and gas exploration and production industry as part of their economic diversity. Saginaw, where the discovery of the Saginaw Field in 1925 put Michigan into the ranks of commercially producing oil and gas states, was the site of some noted economic effect but made little to no change in the complexion of local life. So it was with Muskegon in 1927.

The 1928 discovery of the Mt. Pleasant Field between Mt. Pleasant and Midland, which basically proved that oil discoveries in Saginaw and Muskegon counties were not Basin-flank flukes and that petroleum production was possible in-Basin, led to establishment of the town of Oil City in Isabella County, the most obvious of local impact notice of the industry presence.

The Mt. Pleasant Field is credited with essentially shielding the town of Mt. Pleasant from the Great Depression. Overnight Mt. Pleasant became a boomtown with the arrival of a wave of humanity connected with every facet of finding and producing oil. The town flourished with new residents from all over the country, new housing, new businesses and best of all, new money. In 1929 the Mt. Pleasant Rotary Club hosted a wel-

Hearse in the 1935 Oil & Gas Parade.

1935 Oil & Gas Parade, Broadway Street, Mt. Pleasant.

come banquet with 40 oilmen as their guests. In 1935, at the opening of the first International Oil and Gas Exposition in Mt. Pleasant's Island Park, a parade was held which featured a hearse bearing an effigy of "old man depression" for whom a mock funeral was held.

The city became known as the "Oil Capital of Michigan" and the Mt. Pleasant High School athletic teams are still known as "The Oilers." It was at the Mt. Pleasant Field that in 1932 the first well was acidized, giving birth to the worldwide Dowell service company. It was at Mt. Pleasant that Franklin Oil Tool Company was born, later to expand worldwide in the 1970s as Franklin Supply Company.

So Mt. Pleasant became a hub of Michigan petroleum activity, first as an accident of geology and later as a convenience of geography (since the community lies close to the geographical center of the "mitten", thus located equal distance from anywhere in the Lower Peninsula). Primary oil and gas explorationists, petroleum supply and service companies, geologists (and later geophysicists), drilling contractors all headquartered in Mt. Pleasant to be accessible to the growing industry (now having seen oil and/or gas production from 64 of lower Michigan's 68 counties) no matter where the next oil or gas discovery was made.

Though later years have seen the intensity of field activity shift elsewhere in the state, Mt. Pleasant remains a viable center of petroleum industry activity with 98 business entities with Mt. Pleasant addresses listed as doing business with the industry in whole or in part in 2002 edition of the Michigan Petroleum Directory.

Mt. Pleasant Center

The history of the Mt. Pleasant Center, an agency of the Michigan Department of Community Health, begins in 1891 when the United States Congress directed that an Indian Industrial School be established in Isabella County, Michigan. The Act appropriated $25,000 for the purchase for not less than 200 acres of land and the erection of buildings. Land was acquired including several good farm buildings for $8,400. By January 1893, the Indian Industrial School opened. Peak enrollment at the school was 150 girls and 175 boys representing the Chippewa, Ottawa, and Pottaw tribes. Several buildings were built to accommodate the Indian Industrial School and they remain standing to this date. The original School Building (today known as the "Chapel") and the Cemetery were designated as historical landmarks in 1987 through the Department of State, Michigan Historical Commission.

In 1933, the Michigan Legislature passed a resolution directing then Governor Comstock to request the Secretary of Interior to relinquish the title of the Mt. Pleasant Industrial Indian School for the sum of $1.00. In 1934, by an act of Congress, the school, which included 320 acres of land, numerous buildings and a large amount of equipment was deeded to the state of Michigan. Following this action the Indian Industrial School was closed.

The Michigan Home and Training School was officially established in 1933 as a "colony" of the parent institution at Lapeer, Michigan. The school provided services to young men who were either mildly mentally retarded or of borderline intelligence. These young men provided labor to operate a large farm and dairy and engaged in contractual work of picking beets for the Michigan Sugar Company. The pay was $1.25 for a 12-hour day. Farm operations of this type were terminated in the mid-1950s by legislative action because the farms were not profitable.

From 1934 through 1945, the hospital unit at the Michigan Home and Training School served as the only general hospital in the Mt. Pleasant community and was located on the institution grounds.

The Department of Mental Health was established in 1945 and what was known as the State Hospital Commission was abolished by the legislature. The name of the Michigan Home and Training School was changed to the Mt. Pleasant State Home and Training School; with its first medical superintendent appointed in 1950. The school, however, was still a secondary operation of the institution in Lapeer. By 1956 the facility had a bed capacity of 1,460 and in the middle 1960s the census exceed 1,400 residents. Also in 1950, the Association for Retarded Children (ARC) established the yearly "Parent's Picnic" which was held on the last Sunday of July, as it is to this day. Although the ARC (now the Association for Retarded Citizens) no longer has a local chapter at the facility, the annual picnic has continued annually and is known today as the "Reunion Picnic."

In 1956 the Mt. Pleasant State Home and Training School became a freestanding institution and began an intense building program that lasted about 10 years. The buildings were designed to provide basic custodial care. At the conclusion of the building program, the Mt. Pleasant State Home and Training School had a capacity to service 1,460 persons diagnosed with mental retardation. As the buildings were completed, residents transferred into them from state facilities at Lapeer, Caro and Coldwater. During this time and into the late 1960s, there was, unfortunately, a tremendous growth of institutions across the United States, including Michigan. This resulted in Mt. Pleasant reaching a census of 1,460 persons. By 1962, the Mt. Pleasant State Home and Training School became a receiving institution and was assigned a catchment area that encompassed the 44 counties most northern in the Lower Peninsula excluding the thumb area.

Public Act 258, known as the Michigan Mental Health Code, was passed in 1974 by the Michigan legislature. This has paved the way for mental health services to Michigan citizens since that time. At that time, it was futuristic and extremely innovative. Among many other things, it clearly spelled out the rights of recipients of mental health services. The Act also stipulated that the objective of the Department of Mental Health was to shift the primary responsibility for the direct delivery of public mental health services from the state to the counties. The passage of the Mental Health Code also officially brought the end to institutional growth and, in fact, led the way for downsizing and allowed Michigan citizens with disabilities to live as other citizens do, within their home communities. The Mt. Pleasant State Home and Training School was renamed in 1975, becoming the Mt. Pleasant Center for Human Development.

As an incentive to provide greatly enhanced services, the Federal government in 1976 established the ICF/MR program for institutionalized persons (Title XIX). This allowed for 50% or more for the cost of care for people living in institutions to be reimbursed by the Federal government providing the State agreed to upgrade services as they related to programs, staffing levels, and physical plant requirements. By 1977, the Center for Human Development received its first certification as an intermediate care facility as prescribed by the Health Care Finance Administration. The Center was designated in 1978 as a full-fledged placement agency as well as continuing its role of a receiving agency. Partnerships were formed with community mental health organizations. Service delivery contracts were established to define the scope of community services. The Mt. Pleasant Center for Human Development developed and opened its first group home in 1978, which was located in Gratiot County.

In 1978, the name of the facility was changed to the Mt. Pleasant Regional Center for Developmental Disabilities. This name change stemmed from the passage of the Federal Act 91-517 of 1970 entitled the Developmental Disabilities Act. In the late 1970s, Citizens Advisory Councils were mandated. Their purpose was to advise the Directors of

Hospitals and Centers regarding administrative, policy, program, budgetary and recipient rights issues. The Mt. Pleasant Center has maintained Citizens Advisory Council to the present and they play an integral role in the development of its long range planning. In 1979 630 people resided at the Center and received services consistent with their needs.

As a result of the ICF/MR program and Federal reimbursement, the 1980s began with major renovations at the Mt. Pleasant Regional Center in the amount of $7 million. The Center began a conscience effort to assure individuals were being served in an atmosphere as natural as possible to the norm and in the least restrictive setting possible. The 1980's decade and beyond saw the closing and consolidation of many facilities operated by the Department of Mental Health as well as many private nursing homes serving people with developmental disabilities. The Mt. Pleasant Center played a major role in this endeavor as a resource agency as well as assisting with the expanded development of community alternatives for individuals. The community as well as the Center expanded community-based instruction and vocational training programs. By 1981, the Mt. Pleasant Center received 50% to 55% of their total budget from ICF/MR dollars. In 1983, the Center received a national two-year accreditation from the Accreditation Council for Services to the Mentally Retarded and Other Developmentally Disabled Persons (AC/NlRDD). The Mt. Pleasant Regional Center was the first state facility to receive a two-year award on the first survey, which signified the provision of quality programs.

The late 1980s saw a true implementation of Section 116e of the Michigan Mental Health Code (transfer of responsibilities to the community) and a dramatic change in the types of community alternatives being developed for people with disabilities. The role that the Mt. Pleasant Regional Center played in the public mental health system began to change. The point of entry for services was to become the Community Mental Health Service Provider organizations (CMHSP). The Mt. Pleasant Regional Center was to provide services to individuals on a temporary basis when services were unavailable in the community. In 1994, the then Michigan Department of Mental Health revised criteria for individuals to be admitted to a state developmental center.

The name of the Mt. Pleasant Regional Center for Developmental Disabilities was shortened to the Mt. Pleasant Center in 1995. The Michigan Department of Mental Health became the Michigan Department of Community Health in 1996. The Michigan Legislature amended The Mental Health Code in 1996 to further insure the provision of high quality services and protect the rights of people who received those services.

In October 1996, the Center renovated building 405 and the Habilitative Services department expanded to accommodate RESD School services, Adult Basic Education, Recreation Services, Speech Services, Occupational Therapy, Beautician and the Mid Michigan Industries on-grounds vocational program.

During 1996, the Mt. Pleasant Center began the transition of its treatment model to Person Center Services. From April through October of that year, the Center hired more than 150 persons to accommodate resident transfers from Caro and the loss of staff due to early retirement incentives. In September, residents from the Caro Mental Health Center transferred to Mt. Pleasant. Caro became a facility that provided services only to individuals with a mental illness. The Mt. Pleasant Center and Southgate Center were the only remaining Centers in the State serving persons diagnosed with a developmental disability. Southgate Center was closed in 2001 leaving Mt. Pleasant Center as the sole State of Michigan operated residential treatment for persons with developmental disabilities. The Center's census now, in 2002, is less than 170. The Center continues to enhance the supports and services available to resident's including: competency training, work therapy, and psychosocial rehabilitation.

The Center is an integral part of the State's continuum of services to persons with developmental disabilities. Over the past 100 plus years, the Mt. Pleasant Center has seen many changes in its mission. With the passage of the Mental Health Code in 1974, each change signaled a new commitment to provide higher quality services. As the millennium changed, the Mt. Pleasant Center prepared to celebrate its rich history at the 50th Anniversary of the Reunion Picnic, held July 30, 2000. Current and former residents, guardians, parents, present and retired staff and community members attended the picnic.

The Center remains committed to serving the citizens of Michigan!

The Real Horse Meets The Iron Horse Encounters near the Ann Arbor Depot in Mt. Pleasant

by Hudson Keenan

On occasion car train accidents happen today but 100 years ago the horse-driver and conveyance mishap of one sort or another was the situation one heard about. In those early days you had an additional variable to the mix not present today, the mind of the horse. The four encounters presented here all happened within a few hundred feet of the depot and fortunately, in these instances, no human lives were lost.

❧

A young man named Cuthbert made some good moves, saved his horse and his own life on a Saturday morning in early March 1900. He had just loaded lumber at the north side of West Broadway and was going west past the depot. The horses labored to pull the sleigh, loaded as it was, up the slight grade to the tracks. Sledding was good and with a little persuasion and a wrap of the reins Cuthbert urged his horses forward.

As he crossed the tracks a bolt broke on the runner of the sleigh. It jammed between the crossing tie and the rail with one end still firmly attached to the runner on the sleigh. The sleigh came to a quick halt. The team struggled wedging the bolt firmly in place. Cuthbert looked down and realized the problem but a glance to the north presented a greater problem by far. At the bridge north of the depot a cloud, of smoke could be seen as a south bound Ann Arbor Freight was approaching at a good rate of speed towards the crossing.

One reporter of the incident said Cuthbert had "rare presence of mind" as he jumped from the sleigh, got down behind the team and pulled the draw bolt as the train loomed closer. With the team released from the load they quickly moved away from the impending collision. The freight could not stop and demolished sleigh and its load scattering lumber in all directions. A crowd quickly assembled but fortunately no one was hurt and some of the lumber could be salvaged.

❧

Just about a block south at Rileys crossing another winter accident took place a few years later. (Rileys crossing today is on the trail west at end of Walnut St. going to the millpond). What happened to Claude Blizzard on January 9, 1905 is not all too clear as accounts don't seem to match entirely. All accounts do agree he lost his horse and buggy in a collision with a local switch engine on its way south to Gorham's Mill (Present site of Oak Tree Village)

The *Central Michigan Times* said Blizzard was in a blizzard and failed to see the engine moving from the north. The *Enterprise* newspaper, not using the play on words, said the engine was moving quickly and blew its whistle when almost at the crossing. In this account horse was said to have bolted on to the track in time to be struck by the engine's pilot and killed.

The young horse was reported as "looking like he had been cut up for the starving Russians" in the *Times*. The *Enterprise* said "some dealer might get glue, hide and old bones from the horse." One point there seems to be in agreement in all accounts. The almost new buggy was in pieces and its only value was scrap iron and kindling.

Claude had a box of live chickens in the buggy he was taking to market. They survived uninjured. Claude faired a little worse, he got some bruises and injured his left arm as he was thrown against a nearby fence. It was stated "he was much excited and nervous the rest of the day" and well he might have been. The journalism style used in reporting this mishap is worth noting. One would hope he would have gotten some sympathy from someone.

❧

In another instance James Davis from Deerfield Township west of Mt. Pleasant hitched his horse to his buggy on a fine day in early June 1914 and drove to town. He left his animal and rig at Dr. Hackett's barn in downtown Mt. Pleasant and went about his business.

What Davis didn't known, in the words of the *Enterprise* reporter, that his horse "likes railroading" but in a few minutes the statement would be justified. The horse with buggy attached broke loose and started north across Broadway moving along the Pere Marquette Railroad tracks east of the river. Next he passed what is now city hall north to Pickard Street.

Now the driverless rig veered west across the bridge continuing to the Ann Arbor Railroad before striking south on the tracks. All this time the buggy was bouncing along behind the trotting horse.

Everything came to a halt when the railroad bridge over the Chippewa River was encountered just north of the Ann Arbor depot. Not able to walk the ties he ran his legs through the openings and laid there with buggy still hitched. Fortunately the situation was discovered shortly before a train was due and several men extracted the animal. The horse was bruised and treated with arnica and courtplaster remedies. Apparently little worse for the experience horse and buggy were returned to a surprised James Davis.

🙞

Harry Cosford, native of England, was a shoe repairman for over 40 years at Dittmans Shoes in Mt. Pleasant. His home was along Bradley Road where he always displayed both the English and United States flags. He had been in the country but five years when he had an unlikely encounter on his way home from work at the Broadway crossing on a cold winter evening in January 1916. Cosford had passed the Harris Brothers Mill and was approaching the tracks when he heard an engine bell and looked up to see a rapidly approaching locomotive over the mill race bridge a few hundred feet south of the crossing. Glancing back to the right he saw a sleigh pulled by a team of horses carrying four men as they passed the mill heading for the tracks. The team had just come down the hill from uptown and they were on the run.

Harry Cosford was a man of slight stature but without hesitation he dashed into the street grabbed the harness and succeeded in turning the horses to the right towards the depot. The train roared through the crossing and all escaped a collision.

So unnerved by the encounter Cosford could not go on for awhile. When he did get home he could not eat supper. Reflecting back he said he thought the engine stopped and it was the engineer who told him he prevented a very serious accident. None of the men, in the sleigh said they saw the approaching locomotive.

Valley Chemical Company

The Valley Chemical Company was founded in Saginaw, Michigan in 1927. John J. Hamel, William F. Zingg and William J. Passolt were the founding stockholders.

The business plan was to pick up dead farm animals plus bones and fat scraps from meat markets and small packing plants. Animal hides would also be purchased. The material picked up was to be processed to get fat for the soap companies and the dry products for animal feed.

In 1931 the plant in Saginaw had a fire and was closed. In 1932 it was decided to move the manufacturing operation to Mt. Pleasant. In 1928 Valley Chemical Company had purchased the Mt. Pleasant Rendering Company from George Pregelman. The plant was located two miles north of M 20 and one mile east of U.S. 27 on Valley Road. A new building was erected and machinery was moved to that location, and it became the center of operation.

If you draw a line on the map of Michigan from Port Huron to Durand, St. Johns, Grand Rapids and Muskegon, Valley Chemical Company trucks covered all the area to Mackinaw City. Collection points were at Saginaw, Durand, Muskegon, Manton and Gaylord. Semi-trailers would be sent from Mt. Pleasant to bring the material to the plant.

The material brought to the plant would be coarse ground and then cooked in steam jacketed cookers. When done, the product would be pressed to get the fat out. The remaining product was dried for use in animal feed. After 1939 naptha was used to remove the fat and the mixture of naptha and fat was run through a still to recover the naptha.

In a normal month two and a quarter million pounds of material would be processed. Six hundred thousand pounds of fat would be recovered. Also, 700,000 pounds of dry material. The fat was sold to the soap manufacturers and the dry product ground fine for feed mixing plants both local and national.

Normal employment was 70 people. Thirty would be truck drivers and the rest would be in the plant. Each month 10 railroad tank cars of fat would be shipped out. Also

Valley Chemical Co., approx. 1955.

four cars of feed mix and two cars of hides. Seven cars of coal would be shipped in to fire the boilers.

By the middle 1940s, the business was wholly owned by the Hamel family. Paul D. Hamel, president, moved to Mt. Pleasant in 1935 and W. Glen Hamel, treasurer, moved to Mt. Pleasant in 1946. In 1961 the business was sold to a Detroit company and the plant was closed in 1962.

Wool Day On Main Street

Wool day on Main Street was an annual event where farmers and wool buyers met to do business. This sketch appeared in the *Isabella Courier Democrat* special edition of April 27, 1900. Like other material in this edition it was gathered from past issues. Compared with the earliest known photographs this illustration predates them by four or five years making the sketch circa 1895.

It appears the drawing was made from the upstairs of the present day Downtown Discount Store, a building over 125 years old on the N.E. corner of Main and Broadway. The unknown artist rendering is a view looking to the southwest.

To the left notice the brick structure with its elaborate cornice, Carr and Granger, two Mt. Pleasant merchants had this building built with a meeting hall on the second floor. When the building was two years old Susan B. Anthony delivered a lecture on Women's Suffrage here on March 19, 1879. The building was torn down in about 1908 to make room for the Exchange Bank.

The church steeple in the background is the old Methodist Church built in 1883. The present Methodist Church is on the same site.

The building with the balcony is the present day Brass Saloon.

The building with the words Taylor Drugs is now part of the Firstbank. The building where the Allen Boot and Shoes is located burned in 1905. Foster Furniture constructed a new and larger building later known as the Mt. Pleasant Hardware & Furniture and now the Firstbank.

Wool Day on Main St.

First Presbyterian Church of Mt. Pleasant

First Presbyterian Church of Mt. Pleasant, Main St.

It was a time when acres of stump-land surrounded the village and towering pines grew nearby. On a Sunday afternoon in September 1871 a group of professed Christians met with missionary clergymen and established the First Presbyterian Church of Mt. Pleasant. The first minister was Rev. Luke Nott whose missionary efforts aided in the church's establishment. Twenty-three men have served as lead ministers of this church. For years the congregation struggled to survive fire, flood, and financial panic which hindered church growth. The first church building, a frame structure on Court Street, was dedicated in 1875. Due to growth and added strength, a new brick and stone sanctuary was dedicated in 1907 on Main St. Again growth dictated expansion and in September 1958 the congregation entered their third home, a magnificent structure on Watson Road.

The Women's Aid Society, now called Presbyterian Women, has long been a strong support group within the church. It was started in 1867 to raise funds to establish a local church. In the intervening 135 years it has purchased church property, paid salaries, was steadfast during the church's separation period, assisted with weddings and funerals, held devotional studies, and supported many mission projects.

The church has been blessed with outstanding senior choirs and organists. They are complimented by hand bell and youth choirs. Some of the church's long-standing programs have included a Christmas Eve Candlelight Service, Easter Cross of Flowers, Vacation Church School, hosting the Isabella's Child Development Center's preschool program, and the popular Shrimp Boil. The church has maintained a ministry with students at the university. Presbytery has assisted by helping to fund an associate pastor to help direct this program. The church has assisted members of the congregation who entered the ministry (17 since World War II). It has also given sponsorship and assistance to foreign families settling in the community.

In the year 2002 the church was under the leadership of Rev. Stephen Shugert. The worship services, the music program, the Sunday School, and programs with youth and the university students remain strong. Today, from its tower, a Silver Spire holds high a golden cross now and forever the symbol of Christian fellowship. It is a fitting memorial to the many devoted men, women and children, from the tiny group of founders who had striven to further God's work on earth through the First Presbyterian Church of Mt. Pleasant.

First United Methodist Church, Mt. Pleasant, Michigan

The beginning of Methodism in Isabella County came in the person of the Indian Missionary, George Bradley in 1857. Services were held in private homes and out-of-doors. Later they were held in a log school house located on West Locust street, a one room frame building on Illinois Street then the old court house a mile and a half north of the village. Rev. Bradley was followed by Rev. Robert P. Sheldon. From Rev. Sheldon to Rev. J.K.Stark, fourteen itinerant ministers proclaimed the gospel. From 1882 to the present twenty-four ministers have served the church with one, Rev. Charles Mackenzie, serving for 29 years. A number of associate pastors have served the church over the years, many going on to full time pastorates.

INCORPORATION AND FIRST CHURCH BUILDING
In January 1863, the church was incorporated as The First Society of the Methodist Episcopal Church in Mt. Pleasant. Two years later work was begun on a building to be used exclusively for religious purposes. It was located on a donated lot on Chippewa Street near the court house. It was dedicated in August 1866 and served as the church until the second church was erected in 1882 at the southwest corner of Main and Wisconsin Streets.

THE SECOND CHURCH
The second church was described as "a splendid edifice," "a handsome brick structure of Gothic Architecture with an elegant sanctuary." The cornerstone of this new church was laid in July of 1882.

THE PRESENT CHURCH
Plans for a new church building were developed in the late 1950's and in 1960 the third church building was begun. Wisconsin Street between Main and Washington Streets were vacated, the old church razed and the new church and parking lot were constructed on the site. The first service in the new church, the present church building, was celebrated on June 17, 1961. During the 1960-61 construction, church services were held in the Ward Theatre.

EDUCATIONAL WING
In 1991 a building committee was formed to explore feasibility of a new three story educational wing and updating of the sanctuary. On Sunday June 30, 1993 a Festival Service of Consecration was held for the new addition and changes.

WOMEN'S, MEN'S AND YOUTH ORGANIZATION
From the beginning the women of the church have played a prominent part in the church. As early as 1864 the women were organized as "The Ladies Association of the Methodist Episcopal Church." The title was later changed to "The Ladies Society of Christian Service" and even later to the present name, "United Methodist Women". The Men's organization is the United Methodist Men and youth are organized as the Methodist Youth Fellowship.

INSTRUCTION
In 1886 the Mt. Pleasant Episcopal Church organized its own Sunday School. The location of a Normal College in 1892, later to become Central Michigan University, placed upon the church the responsibility of serving college students. They were served through Sunday school classes and in 1940 The Wesley Foundation was established on campus. Currently there are Sunday school classes for all ages.

WORSHIP
Worship services are designed to meet the different worship styles. One service focuses on more traditional worship while the other is a more contemporary style. Sunday School classes are available for all with a number of special interest topics for adults. Opportunities abound for Bible Study, Choir, Liturgical Dance and sports and social events. A television ministry and Stephens ministry are part of the outreach program.

Immanuel Lutheran Church

In 1976 the American Lutheran Church Michigan District, decided to extend a mission to the Mount Pleasant, Michigan area. This decision was prompted by a request by several members of the congregation and a subsequent careful analysis of the area's needs. Later that year, the Reverend William White was asked to consider the pastoral responsibilities of this new and yet unformed congregation. Upon coming to Mount Pleasant, Pastor White met with a few potential families, viewed an empty farm field as a potential church site, toured this small Midwestern town, and courageously accepted the challenge.

A meeting was arranged in November 1976 of interested families, and a Steering Committee was formed. The immediate tasks were many and included finding a temporary meeting site that would meet the needs of the young congregation, developing a worship format, and beginning an education program. All individuals willingly offered their time and talents to solve these problems. From these working sessions developed strong bonds of fellowship in Christ.

On January 30, 1977, the American Lutheran Church in Mount Pleasant began its worship life in the lower level of the recently constructed Masonic Temple on Lincoln Road. A newly developed liturgy of the American Lutheran Church became the basis of the worship service of the congregation. A Sunday school program for youth and adults was begun shortly thereafter.

On April 17, 1977 Immanuel Lutheran Church (ILC) was chosen as the mission's name.

On September 17, 1977, after nine months from conception we officially became a fully constituted body of Christ, calling and installing our Pastor, William White and receiving the membership. At the Congregational Meeting the Constitution was approved and the following individuals were elected to the First Church Council: Hans Fetting, Herb Fluharty, Ken Folkert, Norm Heikkinen, Yvonne Jackowski, Ron Johnstone, Dave Jorgenson, Fred Koenig and John Krumich.

On September 18, 1977, Bishop Robert Wietelmann of the Michigan District of the ALC installed Pastor William R. White.

On July 8, 1978, the first wedding was performed by Immanuel Lutheran Church. The groom was Don Armstrong and his bride was Esther McNeal.

1979 was a very busy year for the church and congregation. The church's first Confirmation took place on March 4, 1979. Sponsors presented a congregational gift (Lutheran Book of Worship) to each confirmand (the LBW gift became an annual custom.) Confirmands and sponsors included: Linda Allen, Sandra DeGraw, Michael DeGraw, Katherine Fetting, Daniel Flick, Scot Fluharty, Donna Johnstone, Matt Nelson, Susi Nelson, Stephanie Oana, and Leann Sandel. Then in May 1979, Immanuel Lutheran Church purchased the Zonta building and remodeled it for use as an education building. On June 18, 1979, the first funeral of an Immanuel member was Charles Dumon. Then, from September through November 1979, the Altar Guild was established, the Adult Choir started by John and Barb Krumich and the first participation in the ecumenical community Thanksgiving Service.

During 1980, Phase I groundbreaking took place for the multi-purpose building on Bradley Road, the Worship Committee developed a "Guide for Christian Burial," Immanuel initiated, organized and developed Christmas Outreach, and began the annual custom of presenting Bibles to Midweek Church School 4-year-olds and third graders. On October 26, 1980, the multi-purpose (Phase I) building was dedicated.

On September 14, 1983, because of increased attendance, Immanuel Lutheran Church began two Sunday morning worship services at 8:30 a.m. and 10:15 a.m. On December 7, 1986, the education wing (Phase II) was dedicated.

In 1987, the congregation of the American Lutheran Church voted to become part of the new Evangelical Lutheran Church in America (ELCA). Pastor White attended the ELCA constituting convention in Columbus, Ohio, as a delegate. Immanuel Lutheran Church celebrated its 10th anniversary on September 18, 1987. On November 26, 1987 the first Community Thanksgiving Dinner was prepared by Immanuel Lutheran Church.

In January 1988, Immanuel officially became a member of the Evangelical Lutheran Church in America (ELCA). In October 1988, the church's loan application through the Department of Housing and Urban Development was approved for Immanuel Village, 26 housing units for senior citizens and handicapped persons.

Groundbreaking for the new sanctuary (Phase III) took place on March 19, 1989, with the first worship in the new sanctuary taking place on December 17, 1989.

The new sanctuary and a new organ were dedicated on February 11, 1990. A groundbreaking for Immanuel Village took place on August 26th. On December 2nd of that year, the bell tower and bell (Phase IV) were dedicated.

On June 9, 1991, Immanuel Village was dedicated and the congregation bid farewell to Pastor White who accepted a call to his home state of Wisconsin on September 1. During 1992, the congregation was served by interim Pastors Michael Mersey and Andreas Teich. In November a call was sent to Pastor Terry Nordheim who accepted the pastoral duties at Immanuel Lutheran.

Pastor Terry Nordheim was installed as pastor of Immanuel Lutheran Church on January 24, 1993. In September 1993, a decision was made to call an associate pastor and add additional full-time office staff.

On June 19, 1994, installation of Associate Pastor Martha Hartman took place. Pastor Hartman served the congregation until August 13, 1995.

In September 1996, the 20th Anniversary Committee ha[s] [its first] meeting and set a goal of raising $20,000. The money would be [divi]ded equally between a fund for a Habitat for Humanity project in Papua, New Guinea, a local service project, and for a North Western Lower Michigan Synod mission.

On September 28, 1997, Immanuel Lutheran Church celebrated its 20th anniversary with the theme: Remember, Rejoice, Renew! Pastor William and Sally White returned for this special celebration.

On June 28, 1998, after a call was sent, Pastor Jonathan Todd Bruning was installed as associate pastor of Immanuel. Coming from Luther Seminary in St. Paul, Minnesota, Todd's ministry continued with Immanuel until June 7, 2002 after he accepted a call to be the mission pastor of a newly forming ELCA church in Ionia, Michigan (Living Faith Ministries).

On December 2, 2001, the first Sunday in Advent, Immanuel began the new church year and the kickoff of its 25th anniversary by dedicating new paraments, designed by member Deb Wentworth and sewn by many members of Immanuel. 2002 was highlighted by many events for Immanuel, such that it was the beginning of the 25th anniversary year (celebratory events occurred during the year) and a three-month sabbatical (January-March) for Pastor Terry Nordheim. Pastor Terry began his sabbatical with a one-month Habitat for Humanity (return) mission trip to Papua, New Guinea, traveling there with his wife Cathy; their two adult children, Dan and Laura; Immanuel members, Bill and Kathy Gallaher; Melody Ferguson; Barb and Chuck McCollom; former Immanuel members, Dr. Glenn, Melodie and son Neal Dregansky; friends, Tom Freeman and Pete Wiederoder; and the North/West Lower Synod of Michigan, Bishop Gary Hansen.

Another mission trip across the ocean to Tanzania, Africa was made in July 2002 for one month by Immanuel youth: Sarah Freeman, Nicole Moss and Matt Tilmann, along with member Rose Prasad, Pastor Todd, his wife Pastor Jamie and daughter Kaite Bruning, and three Saginaw/Bay City youth. Immanuel members graciously provided substantial monetary support for both 2002 mission trips. August 2002 also brought a new staff position to Immanuel with the hiring of Congregational Administrator Sue Hand.

The current 2003 Immanuel Church staff includes: Pastor Terry L Nordheim, Administrator Sue Hand, Office Manager Diane Tilmann, Custodian Marvin Bidstrup, Assistant Custodian John Emmons, Music Coordinator, Organist and Chancel Choir Director Mernie Bidstrup, Joyful Noise Director Cathy Nordheim, Totally His, Rejoice, and Creation Band Director Gail Caleca, Folk Choir Director Joe Caleca, Treasurer Cindy Schreer and Financial Secretary Kathy Hunt. Immanuel has been very blessed throughout its 26 years with many devoted servant hearts in its staff and membership.

Mt. Pleasant CommMunity Church

Mount Pleasant Community Church began as a non-denominational group in the summer of 1980, when the need for a church with an Evangelical outlook and a Biblical foundation was acutely felt. After four months of lay leadership, the new congregation called the first full-time pastor, Rev. Malcolm G. Brown. Meeting first in the Chapel of CMU, the congregation soon began to rent the larger facility of Mt. Pleasant High School.

In late 1981, the congregation voted to unite with the Evangelical Presbyterian Church (EPC), a denominational fellowship of Evangelical churches in the Reformed tradition. Looking to the instruction of the Scriptures and the guidance of the Holy Spirit, the EPC seeks to blend unity in Christ with freedom in the Spirit through the bonds of redeeming love.

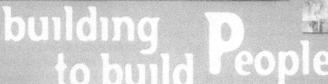

building to build People

1400 W. Broomfield Street, Mt. Pleasant, MI 48858   989-773-3641   www.mpcc.org

Mt. Pleasant Ward of the Church of Jesus Christ of Latter-Day Saints

The Church of Jesus Christ of Latter-Day Saints (commonly called the Mormons) held their first meetings in Mt. Pleasant Michigan in 1965-6 as a dependent Sunday School of the Midland Michigan Ward (A Ward is a local congregation of the Church.)

In the spring of 1966, a dependent branch was organized in Alma, Michigan, with meetings being held in the basement of the Bank of Alma. Jay H. Shurtliff, was the president of this new branch, with David M. Reid as 1st Counselor and Monte L. Higgins as 2nd Counselor. A year later the Alma Branch became independent. Under the leadership of President Shurtliff, members held many fasts to bring strength to the branch. As a result several families moved into the branch and new converts were added to the Branch membership.

In December 1968, the branch was relocated to Mt. Pleasant where meetings were held in Vowles Elementary School. In February 1969 the branch had grown large enough to be made into a Ward with Richard H. Headlee, called as its first Bishop. David M. Reid was called as 1st Counselor with Sherwood E. Bridges as 2nd Counselor. O. David Rogers also served as a counselor. At this period of its history the Ward consisted of members from Isabella, Clare, Mecosta and parts of Gratiot, Newaygo and Midland counties.

When Bishop Headlee moved his family to the Detroit area in 1970 Arlen D. Beck, was called as Bishop with Sherwood E. Bridges as 1st Counselor and O. David Rogers as 2nd Counselor. The congregation met in Vowles School until a permanent location could be obtained. Fund raising for a new building that had begun under Bishop Headlee continued. A building site was purchased and negotiations began to build a 1st Phase building at 1404 S. Crawford Road at the corner of Center Street. Robert Jellison and David Brant also served as counselors to Bishop Beck.

Frank Eldredge was called to serve as Bishop on June 24, 1973 after Bishop Beck moved to the Detroit area. David A. Brant was called as 1st Counselor and Roy Killinger as 2nd Counselor to Bishop Eldredge. Construction of the new building began in the fall of 1973. In August 1974 the Ward began to hold their first meetings in the Phase I building. At this time the membership was about 360 members.

Sherwood E. Bridges was called to be Bishop on January 30, 1977 with William C. Low as 1st Counselor and Jack A. Ware as 2nd Counselor. Richard Hardy also served as a counselor to Bishop Bridges. The second phase of the building was begun in April 1977 and completed in November 1979. The ward held an open house to celebrate the building completion with an organ recital on the new pipe organ. The pipe organ was purchased with donated funds and installed by Jack A. Ware. Melvin Dunn a Salt Lake Tabernacle Organist, was brought in to play an organ recital to celebrate the building opening with the public invited to attend. The building was fully paid for in March 1980 and was formally dedicated in September 1980. George Romney, regional representative of the church, and former Michigan Governor offered the dedicatory prayer and addressed the congregation. At this time membership stood at about 300 due to the creation of the Big Rapids and Clare County Branches of the Church. Each of these had their origins in the Mt. Pleasant Ward.

Thomas A. Martin, was ordained Bishop on Nov. 16, 1980 and served for two years. Monte L. Higgins, John Forester, David A. Brant and David M. Reid all served as counselors.

Jack A. Ware, was ordained Bishop of the Mt. Pleasant Ward on Sept. 26, 1982. During his administration the Ward continued to grow and construction began on Phase II of the building. Bishop Ware died in 1985 after a lengthy battle with cancer. He was instrumental in starting the Ward's successful Family History Center (then called a Branch Genealogical Library), and was the moving force behind the acquisition, design and construction of the church's pipe organ.

David M. Reid, one of Jack Ware's counselors was called and or-

Chapel at 1404 E. Crawford, Mt. Pleasant

dained Bishop on May 26, 1985. Monte L. Higgins, William C. Low, Daniel Morrison and Joseph Barden served as counselors to Bishop Reid. During Bishop Reid's tenure, Phase III of the building was completed. President Wayne M. Hancock of the Midland Michigan Stake of the Church dedicated the building.

Roger L. Hammer, was ordained Bishop of the Ward on February 14, 1988 and served until February 1991. William C. Low, Kevin Moore, David A. Kaiser and Robert L. Wheeler all served as counselors to Bishop Hammer.

Robert L. Wheeler was ordained Bishop on February 10, 1991 and served until his release in March 1996. Counselors serving under Bishop Wheeler included Robert T. Becker Jr., Charles R. Clarke and Roger L. Henrie. In March 1996 just prior to the release of Bishop Wheeler, the Alma Branch was created from the membership of the Ward, with Joseph L. Barden serving as its first Branch President.

Bishop Wheeler was succeeded by Robert T. Becker Jr., who was ordained on April 28, 1996 and served until December 1998. Counselors to Bishop Becker included David A. Kaiser, Roger L. Henrie, Richard L. Sheppard and Robert Marshall.

Bishop David A. Brant was called as Bishop on December 6, 1998 with William C. Low serving as 1st Counselor and Roger L. Hammer serving as 2nd Counselor. It was in Bishop Brant's term of office that the first LDS Temple was constructed in the state of Michigan in the Detroit area.

The Ward has had many activities, out reach efforts and special projects over the years, all accomplished with a volunteer, unpaid clergy and the strong devotion of its members. With the absence of a paid staff or clergy, every member of the church holds a position of responsibility in the Ward. The Ward has sponsored a successful Boy Scout troop since its organization, producing many Eagle Scouts. Its Family History Center has provided an invaluable free resource to the members of the community at large. Staffed by members of the church, and non-members alike, its dedicated volunteers have assisted thousands of patrons with searching out their ancestors. Without the hundreds of Sunday school teachers, youth advisors, primary leaders and teachers, relief society leaders, Scout leaders and many more, the work of spreading the gospel of Jesus Christ could not have been accomplished. This dedication of its members has ever been the trademark of the church. Of significance to the ward, has been the influx of members from other areas, particularly the inter-mountain west, to Central Michigan University, and the welcome addition of many new converts in the Mt. Pleasant area as the result of its emphasis on member missionary work. In addition many young men and women have been called by the Lord to leave the area and serve through out the world at their own expense as missionaries in spreading the gospel message. *Written by Robert L. Wheeler.*

St. John's Episcopal Church

St. John's Church is the oldest public building in Isabella County and one of the oldest churches in the Diocese of Western Michigan. This small intimate church seats 100 comfortably, creating a sense of warmth and belonging. From August 9, 1869 to 1882 a wandering congregation of Episcopalians gathered wherever to follow the church's liturgy and celebrate the faith, under the guidance of the Diocese of Michigan, with lay readers directing the services. Little by little the congregation felt prepared to have a permanent home. The church itself was the gift of one family, Mr. and Mrs. William Brown, who gave a gift of land at the corner of Washington and Maple. The land was cleared of its trees and the chestnut wood stored for the later building of the church pews, which are still in use. (A blight in the 1920s killed most of the remaining chestnut trees in Isabella County). The cornerstone of the church was laid on

October 19, 1882. An Edward Audlin laid the first stone, William Brown laid the second stone, and Charles Smith laid the third. The building was completed in December 1883, at a cost of $43,000. The church was designed in Elizabethan Gothic style, and the interior was supposedly copied from a church on the estate of the Duke of Devonshire. The building had four stained-glass windows and the inside was illuminated with two prism chandeliers. Bishop Gillespie consecrated the church on January 20, 1884. Mr. Brown hosted a 10-course dinner following the service at the Bennett Hotel.

The Rev. James McClone was appointed missionary to the church June 15, 1884. By the end of the year, he had added 67 members to the church through confirmations and transfer. Now needed was a rectory for their resident priest. The rectory was dedicated February 28, 1886, and the church was electrified in 1896. The same year the Ladies' Guild was established, only to become the most important force in the church. Mr. William Brown gave the rectory mortgage to the Guild; the women would own the rectory for the next half-century. It was the Guild, not the vestry, managing the church's finances.

By 1900 the church advanced from mission to parish status by the

diocese June 24, 1900. Two years passed without a rector and the church fell further in arrears. The church did not thrive again until the Rev. Charles F. Westman came from the Diocese of Dallas. In 1908 the building was enlarged to its present size. The apsidal sanctuary and the sacristy were added and the basement finished under the new additions. The Women's Guild was to pay off most of the debt.

Music has always been important in the life of St. John's. A vested choir first appeared in the church in 1910. Even when years would pass without a rector, there seems to have been a choir at most services. Once the impact of the discovery of oil in the 1920s was felt, prosperity slowly came to Mt. Pleasant and the town was spared the depths of the Depression. Throughout the 30s, St. John's had a series of rectors who came for short periods of time. In 1945 Father John Vincer became the rector. During his tenure the boys choir was one of the great prides of the parish. The choir had begun in 1939 under the leadership of Bernard Stone. Father Vincer encouraged the growth of the choir, which not only sang at the services at St. John's but performed all over the state. To this day men in Mt. Pleasant who came from different parishes remember "The Boys Choir." A memorial tracker pipe organ was a gift in memory of Paul Evett, built by Gabriel Kney of London, Ontario, in 1973. That instrument will be completed with the addition of a trompete stop in the Spring of 2003, with Mr. Kney completing a wonderful instrument that will provide generations of pleasure.

A major renovation took place in 1996, insuring room for growth and expansion. The Long-Range Planning Committee set aside space for a color-wheel garden and a newly seeded lawn facing Washington St. St. John's prides itself on doing little things lovingly and well to maintain the community and the fabric of the church. We strongly believe in the promotion of fellowship that frequently brings us together.

This is the history of a group of people striving to lead better lives by doing the work of the Lord. Generations struggled to keep the church going, some enjoying more success than others, each contributing to the life of the parish in their own right. Now it is the work of this generation. The task of the church is eternal.

Sacred Heart Church

Mt. Pleasant, MI

Good agricultural lands drew settlers to Isabella County mainly from New York, Ohio, southern Michigan and Ontario. Immigrating Irish Catholics from Ontario, Canada became the nucleus of the Catholic community in Mt. Pleasant. An estimated 25 Catholic families were present in 1875.

During those early days Father Richard Sweeney of St. Joseph's Parish, Saginaw made seven to eight trips a year to celebrate Mass and administer the sacraments in the Mt. Pleasant area. Catholic families continued to meet with a hope of having a church in the village. Isaac Fancher and wife Alletha were prominent early settlers. On August 7, 1872 the Fanchers, as a gift, deeded Bishop Casper Borgess of Detroit three acres of ground to be used as a site to build a church.

Seven years would pass before the frame church on Oak Street was a reality. In the first week of September 1879 Bishop Borgess and a young priest, Father James McCarthy, arrived by buggy from Clare. The Bishop consecrated the Church, naming it St. Charles and installed Father McCarthy as pastor.

An August 1880 report of the Diocese of Detroit listed St. Charles and missions with 200 families. The missions were at St. Louis, Irishtown, Beal City and Vernon all under Father McCarthy's care.

In June 1885 Father James Mc Carthy at the age of 31 was stricken and died within hours.

Father John Crowley, a newly ordained priest, was assigned as pastor of St. Charles by Bishop Richter of the recently formed Diocese of Grand Rapids to which Mt. Pleasant was aligned. Father Crowley had 19 years of teaching experience as a Christian Brother before ordination. When Father Crowley arrived plans were already being made to build a brick church. Subsequent developments would alter these plans.

The Ann Arbor Railroad extended its line to Mt. Pleasant in 1886. The three acre church site became prime factory real-estate. Within one year the Oak Street church site was sold for $3,000 dollars and the frame church moved to the southwest corner of Michigan and Lansing Streets. The entire block where the present Parish Hall, High School and gym are located was purchased for $1,600.

The new church was to be named Church of the Most Sacred Heart of Jesus. It was located on the Franklin and Illinois corner of the property. When the basement portion of the church was finished work was halted. Father Crowley quickly turned his attention to the now vacated St. Charles Church. Soon carpenters were framing up a second floor inside the structure, the outcome would be a five-room school opened in 1889. The completion of the Church was delayed while work on the school, convent and rectory proceeded.

Social life in the parish centered around the local Chapter Of Ancient Order Of Hibernians reflecting the Irish background of the early settlers. Twenty years later it would be the Knights of

Columbus which marked the ethnic diversity developing within the parish.

As the twentieth century approached the projects of the 1880's were taking root. Students were now graduating from Sacred Heart Academy and attention once again turned to completing the church. The twin steeples rose and the sanctuary covered the basement. Father Crowley would not see the completion of the first Sacred Heart Church. He had developed a heart and lung condition and died in June 1899.

Sacred Heart Church circa 1906

Two months later, in August, Father T.J. O'Connor was assigned pastor at Sacred Heart. In early 1900 the final decorations were finished and the last equipment installed. The church was completed after a dozen years of services in the basement. The parishioners rejoiced.

The twentieth century marked the end of the settlement period. The growing community was taking on a different look. Two government institutions were established in the city and Sacred Heart Parish served Catholics from these institutions.

Parish members became used to seeing Indian Children at Mass on Sunday. In addition to school duties the Dominican Sisters were instructing these children in religion. The children were students at the U.S. Indian Industrial School which was in operation for near 40 years in Mt. Pleasant.

For over a half century students from Central Michigan Normal, later named Central Michigan College, were regular communicants at Sacred Heart. Sunday morning groups of students could be seen walking up Franklin Street to Mass. The campus Mercier club, later named the Newman Club, had close ties to the parish.

During summers in Mt. Pleasant, especially in the 1920's, large groups of nuns, mostly Dominicans, were seen on the same street. They were traveling between the campus and convent working on certification and degrees. In some years the number of sisters in attendance was so great that a portion of Sacred Heart Academy was converted to a dormitory to handle the influx.

Father O'Connor, interested in education, pushed foreword the development and building of Sacred Heart School. When Father T.J O'Connor passed away in 1928 he was buried next to Father Crowley in Calvary Cemetery. The two pastors combined for over 40 years service to the parish.

In the decade of the 1930's Mt. Pleasant's population grew 40 percent as a result of oil discovery in central Michigan. Normal parish activities were continued. Father John A. Mulvey, the fourth pastor, was succeeded by Father Leo Farquharson in 1936 who would serve for the next 17 years. The physical condition of the parish remained much the same as the parish continued to slowly grow during the depression years. The influx of new parishioners added to the diversity in backgrounds of the group. Organizations such as the Holy Name Society, the Altar Society and the Knights of Columbus flourished. Sunday morning Mass included choral groups from the Academy. The Latin High Mass was sung by the men's choir.

From 1950 to the mid-1960s the growing educational needs of the parish depleted all available resources involving three major building projects. The convent, a gym and additions to the high school and the new elementary school building were completed. Msgr. Edward Alt was the pastor during most of this period. He stated the faith and charity of the parish was an inspiration second only to welcoming the many who joined the church during his time at Sacred Heart.

Meanwhile the condition of the church was becoming decrepit and much too small to accommodate the worshipers. It would fall to Monsignor Dumphy to head up the building of a new church. Vatican II necessitated new ideas being incorporated into the plans. A nearby new larger site was fortunately available as a result of the closing of the old Mt. Pleasant Junior High School. The first Mass was celebrated on Christmas Eve 1968 in the partially completed church. Dedication by Bishop Breitenbeck occurred in May 1970.

In late 1970 Father John Thome was appointed pastor. A few months later the Mt. Pleasant parish was transferred to the Saginaw Diocese. During this time many changes within the church were taking place as a result of Vatican II including the establishment of parish council.

The old church languished in disrepair until August 1978 when it was struck by lightning and partially destroyed by fire. Demolition of the church and adjacent old rectory followed. In 1979 on the east side of the cleared area the much needed Parish Hall was built during Father Cornelius Mc Eachin's pastorate.

Monsignor Frances Murray was pastor in the early 1980s. The next pastor, Father Richard Jozwiak, guided many renovations to

Present Sacred Heart Church

the interior of the church. In 1987 a group of parishioners lamented not hearing the church bells that were for years a signature of the old Sacred Heart church. They retrieved the old bell and with encouragement from Father Jozwiak purchased two new bells that were added in a tower erected in front of the church.

Father Thomas McNamara was pastor for eight years in the 1990s. He was especially interested in Sacred Heart Academy. He had been a teacher for 19 years before entering the priesthood. During his watch classroom renovations were made and a new gym now occupies the site of the old church.

Throughout its history Sacred Heart Church has been served by over 50 dedicated assistant pastors to as recently as 1999. They celebrated the sacraments and taught at the school before eventually being assigned to other parishes. Deacon Larry Fussman also has served Sacred Heart Parish for over 25 years. He has officiated at many marriages and funerals and been in charge of RCIA and other parish programs. In 2000 Sister Jane Eschweiler SDS joined the staff as Pastoral Associate.

Father Robert Byrne, pastor since 1999, has instigated changes in operational procedures to best utilize the talents of the parish staff. The rectory has been converted to offices and meeting rooms for staff and parishioners. As the main celebrant of the Eucharist and other sacraments Father Byrne also finds time to attend many parish and school and community events.

As the parish moves into the 21st century, our mission to Jesus can be summarized with "Our commitment will be fulfilled through the inspiration of the Holy Spirit and our generous stewardship."

St. Mary's University Parish

St. Mary's University Parish

On June 6, 1959, the then-bishop of Grand Rapids, Allen Babcock, set in motion plans for a "Catholic Chapel of St. Mary" on the campus of Central Michigan University. He came to Mt. Pleasant to break ground for the new center on September 18, 1959. Gathered for the occasion were many faculty and staff of the University, including President Judson W. Foust and President-emeritus Charles L. Anspach. Construction began immediately and was completed in time for the Fall semester, 1960.

The land on which the buildings sit was donated to the Diocese of Grand Rapids through the estate of Geneva Myrtle Stratton. Interestingly, the Stratton estate made similar donations of land to Lutherans, Methodists, and the Christian Reformed Church. That's how it came to be that Christ the King Lutheran Chapel is just north of St. Mary's across Library Drive, the Wesley Center across Washington, and Trinity Reformed just south on Washington. In the great building boom of the 1960s, the University, which had stopped north of us at Preston, hopped over us and built south, east, and west. Thus, by 1970, St. Mary's wound up near the center of the campus.

In the early 1970s, the name of the chapel was changed to "St. Mary University Parish" to make two things clear: 1) it was a full-fledged parish - and not merely a chapel or a "student parish" with all the programs and sacramental responsibilities of a parish; and 2) its primary responsibility was to the Catholic community at the University. In 1971, in a realignment of the Catholic dioceses in Michigan, Isabella County became part of the Diocese of Saginaw. Its bishop, Kenneth Untener, has been an enthusiastic sponsor of the parish.

Of late, St. Mary's has taken to advertising itself simply as "St. Mary Catholic Parish." The phrase "University Parish," while officially part our title, has been confusing for many on campus who believe that the parish is somehow sponsored or supported by the University. That is not the case. St. Mary's is a regular Catholic church responsible to the local Catholic bishop.

St. Mary's has grown steadily as both CMU and Mt. Pleasant have grown. When we first opened in September 1960, there were 10,000 students at CMU, 3,000 of them Catholic. In September 2003, there were very nearly 20,000 CMU students and 7,000 of them were Catholic. The remarkable population growth in the city has also led to an increasing number of "regular families," 286 of them at last count, calling St. Mary's home.

Weaving Faith Into Life

In April 1997, the parish undertook a major renovation of its buildings: roofs, lights, flooring, heating, furnishings. The place was getting a little rundown from its many years of service, but is once again a delightful shelter for our work and ministry.

Of particular delight to the parishioners has been the installation of faceted glass windows in the nave of the church. Designed by Michigan glass artist Mark Bleshenski, they depict in symbols the many life-professions represented among our parishioners, professions our students are working to enter. These stunning works of art are testimony to our belief that our work in the world is a portion of God's work in bringing about the Kingdom Jesus proclaimed. More information, including an on-line tour of these windows, is available on our website: www.stmarycmu.org.

Also of interest is the large circle in the center of the floor of the church depicting the cycle of the liturgical year in its seasonal colors. Fashioned from almost 10,000 pieces of ceramic tile, and installed by parishioners in 800 hours of donated time, the design helps the parish keep its eyes of faith focused on the cycle of our celebration of Jesus' ministry from his birth, through his death, to his resurrection.

In 1999, St. Mary's celebrated its 40th anniversary of service to the tens of thousands of Catholic students, faculty and staff who have attended the University through these years. That service has been spearheaded by many priests and lay professionals who have made up the parish's pastoral team over the years. Besides Fr. John McDuffee, the parish's first pastor, many will remember Frs. Roger Dunigan, Steven Vesbit, Jack Johnson, Robert Gohm, Robert Meissner, James Falsey, Richard Szafranski, Joseph Griffin, Jeffrey Donner, and these lay professionals: Sr. Annina Morgan, Joseph Frankenfield, Libby Tisdall, Mary Ann Ronan, Sr. Meg Majewski, Tina Moreau Jones, Karon Van Antwerp.

A pastoral team provides only one part of the energy that makes a community like St. Mary's thrive. Many parishioners have stepped forward to form our Education, Liturgy, Service and Justice, and Administration commissions.

The heart of a university parish, of course, is its students. St. Mary's has been greatly blessed by the leadership offered by many excellent young people from all over the country who have found St. Mary's an important part of their lives during their formative years at CMU. Each year, many of them gather to form a core group called Reach Out which plans and coordinates the parish's efforts to meet the needs of the thousands of Catholic students who call CMU home.

St. Joseph The Worker Church

In 1881 a delegation from Beal City made up of Peter Knipps, John S. Pung and Peter Schafer set out for Mt. Pleasant to meet with Fr. James J. McCarthy, pastor of the parish then known as St. Charles. They went there to discuss the possibility of starting a parish in Beal City. With Fr. McCarthy's encouragement they returned home determined to make their dream a reality. The parish they so greatly desired was founded in 1882. It was given the name St. Philomena. The name was changed in 1961 to St. Joseph the Worker.

The first church was built on five acres of land donated by John Pohl. The wood frame building (36' x 60') was erected by Henry Lorenz and John Minick. Fr. McCarthy presided at the first Mass celebrated in that church on November 8, 1882. The congregation at the time consisted of 28 families. Many of the family names are still familiar today: Zuker, Schafer, Yuncker, Elias, Miller, Reihl, Pung, Lorenz, Tilmann, Starr, Gross and Martin. There was a lone Irishman in their midst by the name of Michael McGuien. All the rest had names that bespoke of a solid German ancestry.

St. Joseph's has operated a parish school since 1883. The upstairs of the original church served as the classroom. When it burned in 1886, the foundations were reused to build a two-room schoolhouse in 1887. Until the second church was completed in 1890, Mass and various other parish celebrations took place in the school. This was also a wood framed building (60' x 112'), but it was finished in brick.

Three Marywood Dominicans arrived in the fall of 1901. The parish rented homes for them to live in until 1910 when the blocked fieldstone convent was finished. The first opportunity to go to school beyond the eighth grade was provided to those living in the Beal City area by Dominican sisters. A ninth grade was started under their direction in 1921. The first class to graduate from St. Philomena High School graduated in 1925. There were 10 students in the class. The class of 1948 was the last class to graduate from the high school.

From 1939 to 1941 a series of school consolidations created the Nottawa Township School District. The district received state aid and rented facilities from St. Philomena parish. The first superintendent was the pastor, Fr. Linus Schrems. He was followed by Fr. Julius Amman. The district operated under these arrangements until June 30, 1946, when it was denied state aid for the 1946-47 school year. It took several years to resolve the entanglement of the parochial and government schools. Finally in 1948 the parish ceased to operate a high school. Construction of the present elementary school started in the summer of 1948. The school in use at the time was moved back to the west. It caught fire and burned to the ground November 30, 1948. Six grades were in the new building by April 1949. There are currently 131 students enrolled in grades one through six. The principal is Mrs. Mary L. Hauck.

On the night of May 5, 1905 there was a severe electrical storm. The tower of the second church was struck by lightning and it started to burn. Due to the heavy rain the fire advanced slowly, so there was just enough time to remove almost everything of value, including the altar and pews.

In a span of less than 25 years the people of St. Philomena's faced the daunting task of building a third church. Fr. Alexander Zugelder came down from St. James, Beaver Island to lead the effort. Plans were soon underway to build a 52' x 128' church that would be as fireproof as stone and tin could make it. The walls are supported by blocked fieldstone, brick and mortar. Pressed tin was used to cover the ceiling and walls. The roof was done with metal shingles. The soffits and exterior trim are also metal. Bishop Henry J. Richter (Diocese of Grand Rapids) consecrated the church on July 18, 1907. A crew of 12 men under the direction of a stonemason from Petoskey, Herman Kepke, did most of the construction. Frank Doll and George Straus also played a crucial role in getting the masonry work

done. Peter Bierschbach was the lead carpenter. Mr. Kepke returned to Petoskey, when all was complete except the belfry. Frank Doll and Sam Bierschbach supervised the final construction stage. A picture postcard of the church postmarked, August 21, 1907 and addressed to a Mrs. Mary Klein of New Haven, Indiana by someone who signed her name, Katie, indicates it was built for $15,817.16. The note on the card stated that the labor was not included.

In November 1997 the charter members of the Pastoral Council, the Finance Council and the pastor, Fr. John Cotter, took a tour of all the parish buildings with the members of the Buildings and Grounds Commission. From this evolved the determination of both councils to develop a long-range master plan that would address building maintenance and much needed improvements before they became a full-blown crisis.

On December 1, 1998 a series of meetings took place throughout the day with artist and liturgical consultant Frank Kacmarcik, Obl. S.B. from St. John's Abbey, Collegeville, Minnesota and Traverse City architect, Kenneth C. Richmond, AIA. All available members of the Pastoral Council, Finance Council, Buildings & Grounds Commission and Worship Commission were involved. The most interesting idea inspired by the day's discussions was a proposal to connect the church and convent with a gathering area that included a new baptistery.

It took quite awhile to find out whether the idea was feasible. What would it cost? Could blocked fieldstone be employed in the new construction so that it would match the existing buildings? Was there strong parish support for a master plan on this scale? These and other questions were eventually resolved favorably so that the project could proceed. The groundbreaking ceremony took place on August 1, 2002. The dedication was July 18, 2003. The total cost of the project was $2 million. Construction of a 48' x 102' addition was the route chosen to make the two existing buildings into one.

St. Vincent de Paul Catholic Church

The history of St. Vincent de Paul Parish, Shepherd, Michigan, begins with the year 1908. It was at a time when Bishop Henry Richter was administering the sacrament of Confirmation in Alma, Michigan that a spirited people of approximately 35 families of German and Irish descent requested their own church.

Prior to that time, the early Shepherd area Roman Catholics attended Mass at Irishtown, Mt. Pleasant or Alma. After Episcopal permission was obtained, a vacated Baptist Church located on Wright Avenue in Shepherd was purchased and moved by logs, horses and much toil to their property on Maple Street. At one point, the church was mired in the spring mud for two weeks before it could be moved. Finally the building was placed on location by the church pioneers in the springtime of 1909. Father John A. Mulvey was the founding priest and served the new mission from St. Mary's in Alma, which was the Diocese of Grand Rapids.

With the purchase of an old farm house as a rectory, St. Vincent had its first resident pastor with Father John W. McNeil in 1919. Over the next several years, as numerous pastors served, other lots were purchased so that by 1954, a whole city block plus three lots of another block were owned by the parish.

With the appointment of Rev. T.J. Bolger, a social hall was constructed in 1949 which eventually became the parish school. The hall became the center of many parish activities, including religious classes and was the locale for the first Shepherd Maple Syrup Festival breakfast. It was also rented by the Shepherd Public School system for additional classrooms. Under the direction of Father Edward Roczen, a convent was built and the hall renovated into the parish school with the School Sisters of Notre Dame being the teaching staff. On September 4, 1962, the St. Vincent de Paul Parish School opened with an enrollment of 125 students. The school has played a very important role in the life of the parish. It is with sadness to note that the St. Vincent de Paul Catholic School will close at the end of the 2001-2002 school year.

Almost from the beginning, St. Vincent' has been frequently a parish with a mission church. In 1919, St. Patricks' of Irishtown was a Mission until 1938, during Fr. Joseph Henige's stay, when it passed over into the newly founded diocese of Saginaw. Since 1970 to the present, St. Leo's of Winn has been a mission to St. Vincent. Due to the lack of priests available, St. Patricks' of Irishtown also became a mission to St. Vincent in 1999.

During the pastorate of Father Edward Boucher at St. Vincent some important firsts and notable events occurred. During this time, the parish of St. Vincent was transferred into the Diocese of Saginaw; the new decrees of the Second Vatican Council were implemented, with the first

St. Vincent de Paul Catholic Church

Saturday evening Mass celebrated in November 1969. In February 1972, the debt for the school and convent was paid and a mortgage burning party was held.

In the winter of 1972-73 plans were considered for a new church. Under the pastorate of Father Noel Rudy, plans were finalized, construction commenced and the new edifice was dedicated September 26, 1976. The contractor was Lawrence Bardos. The cost of the church was $252,330 with the debt being paid by October 1986.

Under Fr. Ray Matuszewskis' direction (1984-1991) a new Parish Center was constructed and furnished at a cost of $280,000 and dedicated Aug. 25, 1991. Sad news was received in a letter from the School Sisters of Notre Dame informing the parish that the 1990-91 school year would be the last for their Sisters to service the school. Thereafter, Mrs. Diana Falsetta became the principal and lay teachers took their place. After the convent was vacated it was renovated into the present rectory for Fr. Ray Matuszewski. Fr. Christ Lauckner was pastor for a short time thereafter.

St. Vincent seems to be a befitting parish for a young priest to locate as their first parish as pastor; first Fr. Bill Rutuskowski, then Fr. Robert Howe. Upon the arrival of Fr. Bill Rutkowski in July 1992, the parish site saw a cheerful uplift. The old rectory was demolished, the St. Vincent's statue moved from the old rectory to the north side of the church; the cemetery greatly improved; also a grotto as a tribute to the unborn was placed where the old rectory once stood. In 1996 Fr. Bill Rutkowski was appointed pastor of St. Stanislaus Parish of Bay City.

Fr. Robert Howe now leads the flock, coming from Blessed Sacrament Parish of Midland in July 1996. Under his direction the interior of the church was redecorated.

The parish has enjoyed a growth from the original 35 pioneer families to the present 266 families.

Faith Evangelical Lutheran Church

Faith Evangelical Lutheran Church had its beginning in 1979 when several families gathered together and petitioned the Home Mission Board of the Wisconsin Evangelical Lutheran Synod to consider Mount Pleasant as a potential mission start up. Pastor Cary Grant, a recent seminary graduate, was then called to be their first resident pastor and Norbert Hall served as the congregation's first president. The congregation worshiped in various rented facilities until 1984 when its present property was purchased and a permanent building and parsonage was erected. The day before the facility was to be dedicated, fire broke out and nearly destroyed the newly erected plant. After making repairs, the church was dedicated in 1985.

When Pastor Grant left in 1989, Pastor Michael Biedenbender was called to serve this growing group of Christians. Raymond Grace was elected president of the congregation in 1990. That same year the congregation endeavored to expand their facility using primarily volunteer labor from the congregation and the community. They purchased more property to the east of their present location and began construction in the summer of 1990, dedicating that facility in October 1991.

The people of Faith have not only reached out to the community

with the Gospel, but also have done work with the college students at Central Michigan University. The congregation continued to grow and in the fall of

Faith Evangelical Lutheran Church

2002 endeavored to expand their facility yet again. Using all volunteers from the community and congregation, the people of Faith added a youth and college room and a preschool room to the current building.

Although a church is often measured by its structural presence in the community, the heart and essence of Faith Lutheran church is its people. Pastor Biedenbender remains as their full time pastor and Wayne Rhode presently serves as the president. The congregation has grown from 12 to 250 and has better than 50 children under the age of 5. They have a very active children's ministry and an active campus ministry.

Central Michigan University

Central Michigan University is a nationally distinguished university with a main campus in Mount Pleasant, Michigan, and a network of more than 60 extended learning centers that stretches across North America. CMU offers close to 170 programs at the bachelor's, master's, specialist's, and doctoral levels.

Although CMU is the nation's 43rd largest four-year public university, its main campus remains a friendly, reasonably sized learning environment where 19,000 undergraduate and graduate students can walk to classes together and experience learning through close interaction with full professors.

The university's park-like 480-acre campus blends classic early 20th century architecture with modern health, music, science, business, industrial and engineering technology, student activity, and library facilities. CMU currently has more than 150,000 living alumni, including many noted leaders and professionals.

A Brief History

Central Michigan opened its doors in 1892 as the Central Michigan Normal School and Business Institute. At that time, few of the state's teachers received any formal training in teaching. School founders, deeply conscious of the poorly prepared teacher applicants seeking positions in Mount Pleasant's schools, made teacher training their mission in founding the state's second normal school.

Thirty-one students attended classes in second-floor rooms over an office on the corner of Main and Michigan Streets in downtown Mt. Pleasant. Most students at the time were eighth grade graduates, attending the "Normal" for a few weeks or months prior to beginning their own careers as teachers.

Within the first two years, land was acquired following the sale of bonds and a $10,000 Normal School building was constructed where Warriner Hall now stands.

In 1895, the Michigan State Board of Education assumed control of the school, which had grown to 135 students, renaming it Central State Normal School. The school assembled its first football squad of 15 men in 1896, only to be defeated by Alma High School in the season's sole game. In the same year, Central became state-supported. Within a few years, Central's women were competing in inter-school basketball.

By 1918, the campus consisted of 25 acres with five buildings, one of which, Grawn Hall, is still in use, though substantially remodeled. Enrollment has more than tripled in 10 years to 450 students.

Central's educational offerings also had been growing more comprehensive. Students completing two years of schooling beyond high school began receiving their Life (teaching) Certificates in 1903. The school was accredited by the North Central Association for the first time in 1915. In 1918, the bachelor of arts degree was first awarded, and in 1927, the bachelor of science. Central's first graduate courses, supervised by the University of Michigan, were offered in 1938.

Fire destroyed the school's main building in 1925, and Warriner Hall was built to replace it. Prior to World War II, the school's name changed again – first to Central State Teacher's College, then to Central Michigan College of Education. Enrollment rose to more than 1,800 students.

In the post-war years of 1949-59, the first large student residence halls were built, and Central's first master's degree was accredited by the North Central Association.

On June 1, 1959, with 40 buildings standing on a 235 acre campus and an enrollment of 4,500 students, Central was renamed Central Michigan University, a designation that reflected growth in the complexity of the school's academic offerings as well as its physical growth in the post-war period.

Through the 60s, enrollment grew from 4,500 to more than 14,000 students. The enormous rate of growth caused significant change in the character of the university. Buildings constructed on the land south of Preston Road more than doubled the physical size of the campus.

The gift of Neithercut Woodland near Farwell and the establishment of CMU's Biological Station on Beaver Island gave the university valuable facilities for specialized studies.

With its enrollment climbing past 5,000 students and development of its first master's programs, Governor G. Mennen Williams on July 1, 1959, signed a bill changing Central Michigan College to Central Michigan University. That recognition sparked development of an array of new undergraduate and graduate programs and set the stage for a post-war construction and enrollment boom. Sixteen new residence halls were built between 1956 and 1970. Enrollment jumped to 15,580 students in 1989.

CMU's growing commitment to improve the quality of life of residents in every corner of Michigan was exemplified in two significant achievements during the 1970s: the establishment of the Institute for Personal and Career Development in December 1971 and the first 24-hour radio broadcast by WCMU in March 1973.

During the next three decades, CMU's fledgling distance learning program became one of the largest in North America, graduating more than 50,000 students, and WCMU becomes the flagship station of the largest university-licensed Public Broadcasting network in the nation. As the distance learning program evolved, its name changed twice more. It became the Division of Off-Campus Education in 1976 and the College of Extended Learning in 1990.

Central Michigan University athletes enjoyed many successes over the years – from a NCAA-II national football championship over Delaware in 1974 to four consecutive Mid-American Conference Academic Achievement Awards from 1998-2001.

One of CMU's crowning athletic/academic accomplishments celebrated the close association between quality in the classroom and healthy performance on the field: introduction in 1980 of the first sports medicine program in the nation.

Soon after Mike Rao became the university's 12th president in 2001, the combined on and off campus student enrollment reached a record 28,000, and the university achieved an important academic landmark – designation by the Carnegie Foundation as a Doctoral/Research-Intensive University.

Today, CMU offers more than 50 graduate programs, including nine doctoral programs, and CMU professors are respected for innovative applied research and creative activity that complements CMU's traditional strengths in undergraduate education, teacher preparation, and extended learning.

Sacred Heart Academy

Founded In 1889

Sacred Heart Parish embarked on a new venture in 1889. Father James Crowley, pastor, converted the original Sacred Heart Church into a two-story school. Five Dominican Sisters traveled from their New York Motherhouse to staff the new Sacred Heart Academy. The school boasted 150 students the first year.

Rose Donovan Campbell, Academy graduate, writes, "School days at the Academy began in the old wooden building which was the original church. In November 1908 students were moved into the new brick building on the corner of Franklin and Michigan Streets. It was an impressive curriculum for a small parochial school in a town of 5000."

In 1909, under the leadership of Father Thomas J. O'Connor the growing parish built a new school for $25,000. As enrollment continued to increase, an addition was built in 1923 for $14,000.

Gerald Cotter, class of 1922, at his 50th class reunion stated, "the great exploits of the football, baseball and basketball teams were reviewed, particularly the games played against St. Henry's in the cow pasture up on McConnell's farm and one played here at the sandlots. The combined score was reported to be 96-6."

Mildred O'Brien Young, class of 1922, writes, "No uniforms were worn because times were hard. Several students lived on farms and drove in by horse and buggy. The horses were kept in the livery barn where the parking lot of the grade school is now located."

Pastor John A. Mulvey arrived in 1926. His constant interest in the school kept the Academy open during the Great Depression. Succeeding him in 1936, Father Leo Farquharson guided the school to an enrollment of 380 students.

Earl Seybert and Edwardine Carey Curtiss, class of 1937 wrote, "There was no gym. Elementary rooms were on the first floor and in the basement. High school was on the second floor."

Dorothy Voisin Sheahan states her class of 1947 wrote the present school song, *Academy, We're for You.* In 1948 "Cor Jesu," the school yearbook, was first published and the name continues even today.

"The Academy football team had its first undefeated football team since 1933. Most games were played on Sunday afternoons," writes Jerry Powell, class of 1950.

In 1953, Monsignor Edward N. Alt undertook an extensive building program for the Academy. Additions included a gymnasium and seven classrooms. In 1964 a new elementary building was completed and over 800 students were enrolled in grades two through twelve. Kindergarten and first grade were added in 1975.

"Victory was sweet. Coach Utterback led the Academy team to the memorable 1967 Class C State Basketball championship," writes Joann Campbell McManus.

"Ten students from the class of 1988 were the first group of students ever to attend first through twelfth grade at the Academy. The golf team won the State Championship," writes Matthew Baumgarth, 1988 graduate.

Sacred Heart Academy celebrated the centennial year in 1989 and was designated as an historical site by the state of Michigan with a centennial plaque.

In 2000 the Academy commemorated the opening of a new gymnasium. Fourteen State Championship banners are displayed as symbols of an outstanding athletic program, respected statewide. The program continues to be successful. "We worked hard to win and went all the way to the Girls Class D State Quarter finals, a first for the Academy," states Christine Lilly, class of 2003.

The Dominican Sisters of Grand Rapids staffed the Academy as teachers and administrators from the very beginning. With the faithful and loving instruction provided by the sisters, Academy graduates obtained an outstanding education, shaping and molding successful futures. In the early 1960s, dedicated lay teachers and staff were added to the faculty and have maintained the important legacy of excellence in education. Academy students consistently achieve superior state and national test scores.

The Academy has been accredited with the North Central Association of Colleges and Schools since 1999. In the Diocese of Saginaw, the Academy is the only Catholic school embracing kindergarten through twelfth grades, supported by one parish.

Through a faith-based curriculum, the Academy is committed to developing the spiritual, intellectual, social, emotional and physical gifts of its students to their fullest potential. Well into its second century of service, Sacred Heart Academy continues to provide excellence in Catholic education and maintains a tradition of service to the Mt. Pleasant Community.

MPCA History

"I have no greater joy than to hear that my children walk in truth." 3 John 1:4

Our Christian Academy was founded in 1984 as a ministry of First Baptist Church in Mt. Pleasant and in May 1989, the first class of seniors received their diplomas. Many students have graduated from the Academy since then and graduates have been accepted at the following colleges and universities: Alma, Baptist Bible & Seminary, Bethel, Bob Jones, Calvin, Cedarville, Central Michigan University, Cornerstone, Liberty, Michigan State, Moody Bible Institute, Pensacola Christian, Taylor, Trinity International, University of Michigan and Wheaton.

MPCA draws students from five counties in central Michigan representing 28 churches of different denominations. Students are accepted based on a variety of factors and we seek those who value faith in Jesus Christ. An education at our school is more than just classes, papers, and exams. It includes getting involved in the community, developing life-long friendships with others, meeting new people, and deepening a personal relationship with Jesus Christ.

We offer a comprehensive program for 4-year-old kindergarten through 12th grade. In a traditional classroom setting, certified Christian instructors teach not only the core subjects of Bible, reading, language, history, mathematics, and science, but also home economics, broadcasting, art, choir and band. Keyboarding and computer applications are taught to students in our state-of-the-art computer lab. Additionally, a selection of enrichment and extracurricular activities are available such as spelling and geography bees, math olympics, and speech meets.

MPCA students have performed well on standardized tests. Each year students have participated in MEAP testing and Stanford Achievement Testing. On the average, ACT scores are 11% above state averages and 13% above national averages.

The sports program consists of soccer, basketball and track for males; basketball, volleyball, cheerleading, soccer, and track for females. MPCA was the 1996 Class D soccer champion. It is easy to get involved with our Eagles!

A Christian School is important because it is a safe place where students can solidify their values, determine their vocation, and choose their place in society.

Andersonville School

Campbell School, circa 1913-14

Deerfield Center School

Delong School, 1915

Demlow-Miller, 1916

Drew School, 1925

First Hummel School, 1910

Fritz School, 1910

Hauck School, 1913

Herring School, 1915. Top row l-r: Wallace Graham, Fred Funnell, Lloyd Schutt, Ernest Irwin, Henry Little, Erma Hoover, Vera Seiter, Jennie Wardwell, Zoe Little, Edwin House.
2nd row l-r: Arlie Graham, Onie Border, Vernon Page, Sadie Gardner, Ella Wardwell, Esther Irwin, Marie Seiter, Josephine Little, Archie Border.
3rd row l-r: Mabel Seiter, Beulah Border, Ruth Border, Erma Bowers, Esther Seiter, Beryl Little, Emma House, Mildred Schutt, Beatrice Walker, Ruth Funnell, Alma Irish.
Front row l-r: Albert Seiter, Arthur Irish, Velmar Border, Eldon Bowers, Otto Border, Vernon Funnell, Harvey Wardwell, Andrew Irwin II. The teacher was Mabel

McCormick School, 1889

McDonald School, 1914

Meridian School

MacFarren School

North Rosebush School

Pine School, 1881

Polish School District 3, Denver Township

Pony Creek School

Whiteville School

Winn School

Wise School District No. 5

History of Central Michigan Community Hospital and Preceding Hospitals

When the 20th Century dawned in Isabella County, there was no hospital. Surgery was carried out in the home. Curtains and pictures were removed, the kitchen table was scrubbed and draped with sheets, and both the table and doctors' gowns were sprayed with a phenol solution. Dr. C.D. Pullen did the home surgery then, assisted by Dr. Charles Baskerville, with Dr. L.J. Burch administering the anesthesia. The operating staff wore no rubber gloves in those days, although they scrubbed with a sterilizing soap, and chloroform was the anesthetic.

A few years later, Dr. Pullen opened the first hospital in the area, a small facility located in what is now the Mental Health Clinic on South University Street in Mt. Pleasant. In about 1912, another hospital was opened by Dr. Michael F. Brondstetter on Court Street, now the intersection of Court and Mosher Streets, appropriately named the Brondstetter Memorial Hospital. Following this, Dr. Pullen, growing elderly, gave up most of his surgery.

In 1932, Dr. L.F. Hyslop bought the Brondstetter Hospital from the widow of Dr. Brondstetter who had died the year before. Dr. Hyslop brought Dr. R.H.

Strange to Mt. Pleasant as his partner. They later opened a new hospital in a brick building which still stands on the corner of Mosher and Court Streets. When Dr. Hyslop left Mt. Pleasant. Dr. Stewart McArthur joined Dr. Strange and the facility was renamed the McArthur-Strange Hospital and Clinic.

The Community Hospital was opened in 1934 on the grounds of the former Indian School to be used by all doctors practicing in this area. Not long after the state of Michigan took over the Federal Indian School property for housing the Mt. Pleasant Home and Training School (now the Regional Center) and the hospital continued to operate on the grounds.

From 1937-43, Community Hospital had 25 beds, housed a total of 4,589 patients, recorded 973 births, and had a yearly budget of about $37,000. The first blood bank in Michigan, outside of Detroit, was started here in 1938.

The staff of the old Community Hospital began the efforts to construct a new hospital; because they knew they would need more space and also that their building would someday be turned over to the State Home. Two staff members, Dr. Davis and Dr. Hersee, called upon the local Methodist minister. Dr. Charles MacKenzie, to help them. Dr. MacKenzie had previously headed a very successful hospital drive in Coldwater prior to his move to Mt. Pleasant.

Dr. MacKenzie went to New York to contact the Commonwealth Fund, an organization established to help finance the building of hospitals in areas which needed them. After making several trips to New York on his own time and at his own expense, Dr. MacKenzie secured a grant of $225,000 from the Commonwealth Fund for the erection and equipping of a new hospital and nurses' home.

The residents of Isabella County were required to raise an additional $55,000 in order to qualify for the grant. Under the direction of the Mt. Pleasant Junior Chamber of Commerce and its president, attorney Ray Markel, $65,000 was eventually raised locally. Since construction took place during World War II, construction costs soared and the Commonwealth Fund increased their grant to $290,000.

Wartime restrictions and priorities delayed the opening of the new 50-bed Central Michigan Community Hospital until April 1943. On April 11, the first baby was born there: Nora Jean Carney, daughter of Mr. and Mrs. William Carney. Its first surgery was April 12, a tonsillectomy for Jo Ann MacGregor, daughter of Mr. and Mrs. Duncan MacGregor. The first superintendent, highly qualified Genevieve Jeffrey, was selected by the Commonwealth Fund. She was a graduate of Mayo Clinic, with post-graduate work at Cook County Hospital and a master's degree in hospital administration from Columbia University.

Since CMCH opened in 1943 with 50 beds, it has been expanded four times. It was increased to 74 beds in 1959 to 115 beds in 1963, and to 145 beds in 1978. The hospital expanded to 151 beds in 1982 with the opening of an adult and adolescent psychiatric unit.

A brand new emergency room was opened at CMCH in 1998 and the Medical Arts Building, attached to CMCH on the southwest end of the campus, was opened in 1999. As of January 2003, CMCH is licensed for 137 inpatient beds.

In January 1945, the Hospital Auxiliary was organized. This very active organization continues today to provide much-needed funding, equipment and volunteer services for CMCH.

The Medical Care Facility, attached to the hospital at its north end, was opened in October 1965.

Many services are shared by the two

institutions.

In 1996, the Davis Clinic, PC, operation was merged with CMCH and Central Michigan Healthcare System was formed. CMCH established physician practices and formed a network of services in preparation for the onset of a managed care environment. Because the only growth in managed care was in government-subsidized services, CMCH collapsed the system in 2002, continuing to offer a network of services under the hospital umbrella.

Central Michigan Community Hospital offers a full range of services to the residents of central Michigan, including a 24-hour emergency room with full-time physician coverage, surgery and same day surgery, laboratory, intensive care and coronary care, diagnostic imaging services, family-centered obstetrics, respiratory therapy, pharmacy, pediatrics, and clinical dietetic counseling. CMCH also owns and operates several physician clinics, including ReadyCare, the hospital's walk-in urgent care center, Central Clinic-Shepherd and Central Clinic-Harrison. CMCH's Wellness Central Building, located South of town near Central Michigan University, houses rehabilitation services, cardiopulmonary rehab, health promotion services, Wellness Central Fitness and the Central Occupational Medicine Program (COMP). Through cooperative agreements with several colleges, the hospital provides clinical experience to students in many medical instructional programs.

Central Michigan Community Hospital
Your Partner For Health

Chippewa Bowling

Chippewa Lanes Bowling

Chippewa Recreation was opened by Ed Smith in the late 1930s and was later sold to Ed Geroux. In 1956 Art C. Periard bought the bowling alley from Ed Geroux. The lanes were located upstairs in downtown Mt. Pleasant over what are now Logo's Galore and a vacant storefront to the south on Main Street. The lanes at that time not only had pin boys, they even had a foul judge.

Art Periard remembers how the foul judge would sit in a booth watching the foul line on all seven lanes. A foot pedal hooked to a bell provided the alarm, and the foul judge sounded it whenever a bowler crossed the line. One of those foul judges was John Frisch Jr. John states, "I got a quarter a game plus all the potato chips I could eat."

Pin boys had the harder job. At 8 cents per game, a pin boy working two lanes and covering two five-man leagues could earn $4.80 per night. It was dangerous work, "I stopped several fellas who were throwing too hard," Periard remembers. "Those pins would fly. Some of those guys had lots of speed and no skill." Periard remembers only one minor injury, but says today's bowlers could only imagine the give and take between bowler and pin setter. "Sometimes we'd have a yelling match between pin boy and bowler," he says. "That's the advantage of automatic pin setters. They can't call in sick, and they can't yell back at the bowlers."

Periard wasn't necessarily looking for a bowling alley. He'd owned a resort in De Tour, on the eastern point of the Upper Peninsula from 1946 to 1956. A desire to be closer to parents prompted the Periards, Art, wife Doris and two sons to seek something closer to relatives in Saginaw.

Two weeks after answering an ad in the Detroit Free Press, Periard had sold his resort and was the new owner of a tiny bowling alley in Mt. Pleasant. "I'd done a little open bowling, but I'd never been in a league," he recalls. "The first time I'd bowled they didn't even give me bowling shoes. I bowled in street shoes and my wife bowled in high-heels."

Conditions were much more challenging back in the 1950s. For one thing, oil was sprayed with a gun from foul line to the pins. This made the lane conditions much more variable than they are now. In addition, balls were made of solid rubber and the pins were heavier being three pounds ten ounces compared to today's three pound six ounce pins. Pins have changed in more ways than one. Today's pins are coated in plastic for longevity. In the 50s the pins were finished wood and were refinished every week. "We had a store room to refinish pins," Periard says. "Every Saturday, we'd replace the pins. Then the old ones were lacquered with a paint brush and left to dry for a week."

In 1958 the business was moved from the upstairs location on Main Street to the current location on Mission Street. By the time Art built his new bowling alley he had learned a thing or two about running a bowling alley.

For instance, there was the first time he waxed the wooden approaches to the alleys. First to use the freshly waxed alleys was a women's league. "The first two women went flat on their face," recalls Periard. "I'd waxed the floor, but I didn't buff it."

The old upstairs alley was built before the days of air conditioning and it could get kind of warm. So the front windows were usually open, with screens to keep the bugs out. There were six or seven windows facing Main Street and one night, Joe Cooper sat his ball in the window, and it fell through the screen and down on Main Street. He had to go three or four blocks to get his ball back.

In those days, bowling alleys didn't yet have beer and pop, snack bars or arcade games. Bowlers were allowed to bring their own snacks and refreshments and keep them in the nearby locker room. On occasion, a particularly thirsty customer might scoot down the stairs after bowling, pop into Cascarelli's Casa Nova for a refreshment, and hurry back before his next turn.

Between Art Periard Sr. and his son Art Jr., they have seen nearly 50 years of change in the bowling scene. For the Periards, the biggest change came when they built Chippewa Lanes on Mission Street, a move necessitated by the need for more parking and to keep up with the competition by installing automatic pin setters.

The new building on Mission Street housed 12 lanes, which was an upgrade from the seven at the upstairs location downtown. Chippewa Lanes now sports 24 lanes.

Art Periard Jr., who took over the business in the early 1980s, has seen other changes, too. It used to be you could just put a sign up and fill a bowling alley. Today you have to work to be a proprietor.

In 1999 the business was sold to Carl Malish. Art Sr. still lives in Mt. Pleasant although he no longer bowls. He's been a widower since 1998, when he lost Doris, his wife of 61 years.

Art Jr. still bowls at Chippwa Lanes on Monday and Wednesday nights. His wife, Mary, also bowls in two Wednesday leagues.

The old upstairs lanes, known as Chippewa Recreation are gone. They were remodeled into six apartments in the mid-1990s.

Coldwell Banker Mt. Pleasant Realty & Associates
A Full Service Real Estate Company

Coldwell Banker Mt. Pleasant Realty & Assoc.

Was founded in 1964 when Keith Feight bought out his then partner Jack Swift of Swift & Feight. Swift & Feight started in 1959.

Mt. Pleasant Realty was the new name change in 1964. Jack Neyer joined Keith Feight as a salesperson that year and in 1967 purchased half of the business and became an equal partner in Mt. Pleasant Realty. Over the years Mt. Pleasant Realty has grown into the largest Real Estate Company in the area doing over 50% of the Real Estate business in Isabella County. Doug Schuette was brought on board in 1979 and purchased 1/3 of the business in 1983. Keith has retired, but still retains his ownership. The company purchased a Coldwell Banker franchise in 1998, which has helped the company's growth. Today we are known as Coldwell Banker Mt. Pleasant Realty & Associates. We currently have 35 full time associates of which 31 handle residential sales and four associates handle commercial real estate in our commercial department. Dave Ebbinghaus is our office manager, Jack Neyer and Doug Schuette are general managers.

Our company looks to the future and feels our community will continue to grow and prosper because of our location in the State. Central Michigan University and Soaring Eagle Casino will help us greatly in the coming years. Areas we currently serve are all of Isabella County plus parts of Clare, Gratiot, Midland and Montcalm counties. Our commercial department handles real estate transactions throughout the entire state.

Our staff today consists of Broker/Owners Jack Neyer, Doug Schuette, Keith Feight; Office Manager Dave Ebbinghaus; Administrative Assistance Paula Brown, Debbie DeVisser and Sue Ryckman; Sales Associates Barb Allen, Wendy Allen, Joyce Arndt, Paula Arndt, Marnie Basney, Larry Bean, Rita Eisenberger, Annette Forbes, Pat Frasco, Beth Jennings, Maurice John, Jeri Jones, Dawn Krantz, Stan Lilley, Marge Mills, John H. Neyer, Connie Ososki, Judy Pape, Linda Partlo, Rhonda Reedy, Rosemary Reid, Bill Robison, Kathy Rouiheaux, Eileen Rush, Doris Sherwood, Gene Smith, Robin Stressman, Steve Stressman, Penny Swart, June Stalter, Jeremy Turnwald, Pam Westman, Vic Williamson.

Elliott Greenhouse, Inc.

The original buildings that house Elliott Greenhouse, Inc. at 800 West Broadway was built in the late 1800s. At that time a chicken farm was located there and the building had chicken coups and a processing area where the chickens were prepared for shipping to local markets.

Apparently around 1910 the business was converted into a greenhouse as the original greenhouses, now gone, had a building date of 1910 on them. Sometime between 1910 and 1945 Walter and Elizabeth Caple became owners of the business, which they called Mt. Pleasant Greenhouse. In 1944 Walter Caple passed away and Elizabeth did not wish to continue running the business so she contacted her niece, Maxine Elliott, to see if she and her husband Kenneth might be interested in purchasing the business. At that time, Maxine was working for her father in Saginaw as a bookkeeper at his coal yard business and Kenneth had just returned from World War II naval service and was contemplating what profession to work in.

In 1945 they took over the business and a few years later changed the name to Elliott Greenhouse, Inc. Both Kenneth and Maxine attended design and floral classes. In the old days the Elliott's grew their own plants and flowers and tended for them in the greenhouses located on the property. They also had an employee who worked nights to watch the boiler and make sure that correct temperatures were maintained in the greenhouses at all times. The flowerbeds in the greenhouses had to be changed every year with new soil to re-sterilize the soil. Plants were grown to a certain stage outside during the summer and then moved into the greenhouses where they would continue to grow and bloom during the winter.

In the late 1950s and early 60s, the Elliott's also grew hothouse tomatoes during the early summer months of June, July and early August and sold them to the various grocery stores in the area. The current parking lot and new store addition is located where a plot of carnations grew every year.

Paul Elliott joined his father and mother in the business around 1969 after graduating from Northwood Business School. In 1979 Kenneth Elliott passed away leaving Paul, his mother, Maxine and Paul's wife Linda to run the business. Maxine continued to work at the store until around 1992 when she retired. She passed away in 2002.

Elliott Greenhouse, circa 1950.

In 1982 Elliott's expanded their business opening Elliott Floral in the Stadium Mall in Mt. Pleasant. They were one of the first tenant's in the new shopping mall. Around 1990 they moved their location to the corner of Mission and Broomfield Roads, where they still operate today. In 1992 Elliott Floral added Kilwin's Confectionery along with additional products and gift lines and shipping of gift baskets for holidays and special occasions. Elliott's have also added Jelly Bellies and 21 colors of M & M's.

In 1981 the new building addition at Elliott Greenhouse, Inc. was completed, and in 1997 three new greenhouse structures were added to better serve customers and better display products. All but one of the original small greenhouses is gone and they don't grow their own plants anymore as they now buy from wholesale suppliers and large growers in California, Canada, South America along with local growers. In the last few years' product lines have also been expanded to include items for home and garden. Elliott's also maintain two wire services through FTD and Teleflora, which allow them to send flowers most anywhere. Elliott's remain full service florist's with the highest quality products and service and along with their expanded products and gifts lines continue to serve the people of Mt. Pleasant and Isabella County as they have for the last 58 years.

Fabiano Brothers, Inc.

Fabiano Brothers, Inc. has been a family owned business since its inception. Based upon a firm foundation of tradition and integrity, the company continues to thrive with the leadership of the fourth generation of the Fabiano family.

In 1899, George Fabiano immigrated to the United States from Santi Ippolito, Italy. His hard work and dedication allowed him to relocate the rest of his family to America in 1913. They settled in Eaton Rapids, Michigan, where they opened a fruit market and shortly thereafter another market in Lansing, Michigan.

The Fabiano family and business moved to Mount Pleasant, Michigan, in 1919 where George and his two sons, Frank A. and Joseph R., established the Fabiano Fruit Market as a retail and wholesale store. After prohibition was repealed, the company began distributing both beer and wine products to retailers.

In 1969, Fabiano Brothers incorporated. Frank A. Fabiano Sr. passed away in 1977. That same year, James C. Fabiano, Joseph's son, was appointed president and Joseph became chairman.

As consolidation became the trend in the beverage industry, Fabiano Brothers, Inc. acquired several more brands and purchased three other whole-salerships: Johnston Sales of Mount Pleasant in 1977; Krumrei Beverage of Grayling in 1985; and Central State Distributors of Mount Pleasant in 1986.

In 1991, a fourth whole-salership, Max R.H. Treu of Saginaw, was purchased. All of the associates were retained and service continues to be provided from the Saginaw facility.

Joseph R. Fabiano passed away in 1993. However, James C. Fabiano, president and chief executive officer of Fabiano Brothers, Inc. and his sons, James C. II and Joseph R. II, continue to carry on the family tradition.

In 1994, Fabiano Brothers, Inc. acquired certain assets of Cellars Beverage, Inc. of Bay City, including the majority of the company's beverage lines. Cellars was one of the largest wine and new age beverage distributors in the Tri-City area.

In 1997, Trans-Con was formed in partnership with two other Michigan wholesalers when the state of Michigan privatized the distribution of spirit beverages. Trans-Con distributes spirits from several suppliers to the entire state of Michigan.

In 1999, Fabiano Brothers, Inc. purchased the Petoskey Beverage Company and Primo Vin of Harbor Springs. These two entities combined to create our Petoskey division, which distributes beer and wine to several counties in northern Michigan. All of the associates were retained from each company and service continues to be provided from the Petoskey facility.

Currently, Fabiano Brothers, Inc. sells and delivers beer, wine, and sprits to retail licenses throughout 16 counties in Central, Eastern, and Northern Michigan. The corporate offices and main warehouses are located in Mount Pleasant. However, there are distribution centers located in both Saginaw and Petoskey. Today, Fabiano Brothers, Inc. employs several hundred associates at its three locations.

Fabiano Brothers, Inc. has been striving for excellence for over 80 years and looks forward to continued success and commitment for years to come.

Building of the Fabiano Brothers. Left inset: George Fabiano with sons, Frank and Joseph. Right inset: James C. Fabiano with sons, James C. II and Joseph R. II.

The Embers Restaurant

The Embers Restaurant

Clarence Tuma was born and reared in the city of Detroit. After graduation from high school he enlisted in the army and went off to World War II. At the end of the war when he was discharged from the service he came to Mt. Pleasant to attend Central Michigan College because he wanted to play football as well as get a college degree in teaching.

Clarence had always had a great interest in cooking so while he was attending Central he started working in the food commons. Upon graduation in 1950 Clarence had three choices for employment. The first was a teaching position in a small town in the thumb area of Michigan, the next offer was to play professional football for the Detroit Lions and the third position was to manage one of the three food commons on the Central Michigan College campus. He chose to stay at Central where two years later he took over all of the food service on campus.

In 1957 Clarence decided to leave the college to start building The Embers Restaurant with his partner, Norman LaBelle. The restaurant was built on the corner of old US 27 and Preston Street, which in 1957-58 was considered rural Mt. Pleasant. On March 15, 1958 The Embers opened its doors to the public and soon became well known for its elegant dining, superb cuisine and home of "The Original One - Pound Pork Chop." The partnership would operate together until 1967 when Clarence Tuma bought out the partnership rights of the restaurant from Norman LaBelle and became sole owner.

Over the years the Embers has won acclaim for being one of Michigan's finest dining establishments. The restaurant has also grown from its original size of approximately 7,000 square feet to more than 24,000 square feet. In 1961 the kitchen was expanded and an elegant cocktail lounge was added on. The Benford Room, one of the more beautiful banquet rooms available, was established in 1969 on the bottom floor of the restaurant. The office area also was enlarged at this time. In 1974, a beautiful new addition and a complete renovation was made to the Embers, increasing the public dining area and adding a new touch of elegance and atmosphere.

In 1978 Clarence Tuma and Keith Charters opened The Embers on the Bay in Traverse City, which they operated until 1994 when it was sold to Mountain Jack's Restaurants.

In 1988 Clarence sold his interest in the restaurant to his son, Jeff Tuma. Jeff continues the "Embers Tradition" with facilities for banquets, special parties, catering and elegant dining. The "Tease Grille" was later

Clarence Tuma with Famous "Original One — Pound Pok Chop"

added to the complex and allows for an additional 130 guests for the restaurant. With the Embers dining room seating up to 230 guests the Embers can accommodate up to 360 individuals. The Embers employs around 135 people of which 80 percent are Central Michigan University students.

The General Agency Company

Established in 1915, the General Agency Company is one of the areas oldest continuous businesses. Originally founded by Charles A. Carnahan, Chester Riley and Walter W. Russell, the agency has been family owned ever since. C.R. "Tip" Carnahan joined the agency in 1938 with his father Charles. Tip was selling Mack trucks in Toledo, Ohio at the time when his father prevailed upon him to move to Mt. Pleasant and join him in the insurance business, one of several jobs during the Depression Era, following his involvement in Europe during World War I.

Charles Carnahan passed away in 1951 with Tip then becoming the sole owner. Tip's son-in-law, Jack Weisenburger, following a brief professional baseball career, came on board in 1954 moving here from Muskegon, Michigan with his wife Sally Carnahan Weisenburger and their two sons at the time, Bob and Rick.

The General Agency was originally located on Broadway at the end of University (then College St.). They suffered a serious fire in 1952, as evidenced by the photo shown here. They remodeled and progressed over the years.

In 1965, Jack and Sally became the sole owners of the Agency, eventually moving their offices to its current location at 525 E. Broadway. (photo shown)

As business developed, along came growth and son Bob then joined Jack in the business in 1977. With Jack reaching retirement age, Bob became the sole owner in 1991. In 1987 Bob Weisenburger was joined by his brother Dave, becoming a fourth generation of family to operate the business as co-owners along with the valued and capable, Mick Natzel and John Olson who are partners as well.

The General Agency Company has served the needs of Mt. Pleasant and the Central Michigan area now for over 87 years. They have practiced and maintained the hometown attitude of attracting quality people to provide prompt, courteous, professional attention. Their home base has extended throughout the state of Michigan over the years with business accounts from the Detroit area to the western U.P. all the while maintaining that same strong "hometown" attitude and philosophy.

The General Agency Company, from its humble beginnings in 1915, insuring small farms and businesses as well as individual homes and the

Fire at The General Agency Co.

country's growing number of automobiles, began to expand its insuring by developing specialty coverage for the area's oil and gas industry. Discoveries of oil and gas in and around the Central Michigan area in the late 1930s helped fuel the General Agency's interest in providing these special coverage's that the agency has parlayed into many petroleum related ventures throughout the state and have gained wonderful growth and experience in handling involved commercial risks of all types.

The General Agency Company currently employs a staff of 37 well-trained and knowledgeable people, providing assistance and coverage to individuals and businesses. From homes, autos, to retirement plans, life insurance, and long term care to the specialty needs of involved commercial companies.

The agency is an independent agent representing many different companies to provide their clients with options in coverage's and prices. They have always been proud of the service and attention to detail they provide to their insured, and have every plan to continue the business for years to come.

Gray's Furniture Appliance TV

Gray's Furniture Appliance TV business was originated in 1945 by Allen Wood and was known as Household Appliance, Inc. The store was located on Main Street across from the Ward Theatre and operated there until 1956 when Mr. Wood moved his business to the "Harris Block Building" located on the corner of Franklin and Broadway at 222 E. Broadway Street. Mr. Wood and his son Bob ran the business until 1974. At that time they sold the business to current owners, Mike and Rosie Gray.

The building was built around 1903, has three stories plus a basement (approximately 19,000 square feet) and has housed various businesses over the years.

The top floor was originally used as a silent movie theatre and the old projection room is still overlooking the floor where people gathered to watch movies on their visits to Mt. Pleasant.

The second floor was used as a formal ballroom and the balcony where the bands used to play is still present and looks down on where the dancing was done with chairs lined around the sides. Mike Gray states: "I've had people tell me they've watched boxing matches up here so they did other things besides holding dances. And I've been told that during the prohibition there was a speakeasy up here, but I've never been able to prove it." An undertaker used the south side of the second floor. A sign still identifies the room as the "Undertaker's Room" which, as near as anyone can tell, was in use from the beginning until around the early 1940s.

The ground level floor has seen many uses and Gray's research has shown that the west side of the building has almost always contained a furniture store of some type. History books

Gray's Furniture and Applicance T.V. Store

also show that the gas and light franchise was opened in 1903 on the east side of the 1st floor. Earlier maps show that the site housed a livery in 1884, just 19 years before the current building was built.

The Gray's enjoy serving the Mt. Pleasant Community and are known to carry better quality furniture and accessories. They also enjoy searching for many unique furniture pieces, both old and new. Gray's is truly a unique shopping experience.

House of Cabinets

Harold Franke was a cabinetmaker that had worked for various general contractors during the 1940s. He married Clara Belle Taylor on March 11, 1945 in Wisconsin and moved to the Strickland area in the winter of 1951, this being the area Clare Belle had grown up in. They have lived in the same house ever since.

Harold went to work for the Mt. Pleasant Cabinet Company, which was owned by Mr. Beryl Woods, that same winter of 1951. The store was located on the corner of M-20 and South Bradley Road. Beryl Woods had a good reputation for quality cabinetwork, with many original ideas. Beryl having been a former wood shop teacher was a very interesting as well as pleasant man to work with. We built all of the cabinets at that time.

Mr. Woods saw the marine business as a possible profitable sideline and he kept getting more involved in that with the cabinet business being more my responsibility. In the late summer of 1959 I decided it might be better to have the two businesses separate.

That fall I built a shop at my home and the Strickland Cabinet Shop was born. In the early 60s James (Milne) Witbeck started working for me. I never had anyone that nice to work with. He's closer than a brother.

We kept finding it harder and harder to keep up with the demand so in the spring of 1972 we decided we needed a show room in Mt. Pleasant. At this time we formed a partnership. We needed a different name so we decided on the House of Cabinets. We rented some space in Howard Himes building on the corner of River Road and Mission Road. Originally we just rented one room but as the business grew we kept renting more space in his building.

At this time we found companies that would custom build cabinets and also added factory built cabinets. Installation was sub-contracted out with Harold and Milne overseeing the projects.

On July 5, 1979 we experienced the loss of our showroom and inventory due to fire caused by a gas explosion. We then moved into a temporary building and set up temporary displays and our office in the old Beard Building on N. Mission Street. In the fall of 1979 we purchased a residential home at 5800 E. Pickard and changed it into a showroom and sales office with a repair shop in the rear.

Milne Witbeck (previous owner), Joe McDonald (current owner) and Harold Franke (previous owner).

We operated at this location until October 1, 1988 when we sold our business to Joe and Jenny McDonald.

During the 1990s the McDonald's added some additional lines, which included Cork Laminate Flooring and Ceramic Tile and Stone selections. They also added a multi-purpose warehouse to the south of the sales area for storage and counter top fabrication. That new building now houses all of the cabinet and tile displays.

In 1996 Joe and his brothers, Scott and Fred, formed the Pinnacle Cabinet Company located on N. Fancher Street in Mt. Pleasant to handle their cabinet manufacturing.

The House of Cabinets provides a full service business from the original design work to the completed project through their project management. Their distinctive designs for kitchens and baths along with service to their customers have helped make the House of Cabinets one of the leading kitchen and bath companies in the Central Michigan area.

Joe and Jenny McDonald believe in what the original business was built on by Harold Franke and Milne Witbeck, "Take care of people and the business will take care of itself."

Helms Funeral Home

The present day Helms Funeral Home began in Mt. Pleasant in 1909 under the ownership of G. Jay Stinson. G. Jay Stinson began his training in Owosso where he worked for the Woodward Casket Company and later apprenticed with Jennings and Foster undertakers. G. Jay Stinson became licensed in 1908 after attending the Carl Barnes School of Embalming in Detroit.

He moved to Mt. Pleasant in 1909 and worked with Foster Furniture & Undertaking, which was located on the southwest corner of Main & Broadway, where Firstbank is currently located. Shortly, G. Jay began his own business in rented quarters above the Johnson Hardware store. He rented space over the Sno-White bakery, located where Stan's Restaurant is now on Broadway Street. In 1915, Mr. Stinson purchased the Courier Printing office where the undertaking business remained until 1941.

The January 19, 1941 edition of the *Isabella County Times News* highlighted the formal dedication of the new location of the Stinson Funeral Home attended by nearly 500 people. His sons Russel in 1930 and Donald in 1940 had joined G. Jay in the family business. The new site was located on the northwest corner of Wisconsin and University streets. The large, beautiful facility included a chapel, two slumber rooms, a private room for family use and an upstairs apartment where Donald and his wife would live.

Soon after the dedication, a young man named Harry Helms came to Mt. Pleasant to attend Central Michigan and become a teacher. He lived in a basement room of the Stinson Funeral Home and went on ambulance runs as well as performing any odd jobs that Jay required - all at "no pay." After only one year at Central, Harry was drafted and spent 1942 to 1945 in the United States Army. Harry returned to Mt. Pleasant after his stint in the Army and again worked for Jay Stinson but instead of returning to Central, Harry took Jay's suggestion and attended Wayne State University Mortuary Science Dept. Harry became licensed in 1948 and continued to work for the Stinson family.

Harry and Alice were married in 1950 and became residents of that upstairs apartment in the funeral home in 1958 where they lived and reared their family. Russell Stinson retired from the business in 1973 and Harry and Alice became owners of the business where he had worked for 32 years. The business name was then changed to the Stinson-Helms Funeral Home.

Sherman Rowley, a licensed funeral director, came to Mt. Pleasant from the Lansing area in 1979 and is currently the managing director. Harry passed away in 1980 and Alice took over running the business and continues to do so today. In 1989, the name was changed to the Helms Funeral Home. The business continues to serve the Central Michigan area with care and dignity as it has for many generations.

Heritage Automall
Chrysler, Jeep, Dodge, Dodge Truck, Oldsmobile

Above: Hertiage Automall Chrysler Showroom on Pickard Street.
Left: Heritage Collision sign on Broomfield Road.

Heritage Chrysler began its life in 1941, the same year that the Jeeps were born. E.W. Smith, then a farm implement dealer, was granted the Chrysler-Plymouth franchises and sold the cars from his location at 360 W. Wright Avenue in Shepherd, Michigan for 36 years.

In 1977 E.W. Smith agreed to sell his stock in the business, then called Smith Motors, Inc., to Jim Sisson. Jim started managing the store and in 1979 purchased E.W. Smith's remaining common stock and became the sole stockholder. The name of the business was changed to Heritage Chrysler-Plymouth, Inc.

In 1984 Jim bought property on Pickard Street in Mt. Pleasant and started construction of a new building. In 1985 Jim moved the business into the new buildings located at 4650 East Pickard Road (East M-20) in Mount Pleasant and was granted the Dodge-Dodge Truck franchises in the process. The business then became known as Heritage Chrysler.

By 1990 the service and body shop departments needed more room, so Jim and wife Lynn bought the building, which had formerly housed the Farrand Tractor business on East Broomfield near Isabella Road. The body shop was moved there and incorporated as Heritage Collision Repairs with Lynn owning and operating it. A few months later Jim bought the Jeep-Eagle franchises from the departing Oldsmobile/Jeep dealer, making him a full line Chrysler dealer.

In 1991 General Motors made Jim the Oldsmobile dealer in Mount Pleasant. Heritage Chrysler-Plymouth, Inc. (d/b/a Tradition Oldsmobile) was born and was located in the same building as Heritage Collision Repairs. Lynn has done a great job with the body shop, which is a Direct Repair Facility for many insurance companies.

All their businesses needed more room, so the Sissons purchased the former ICTC property next to Heritage Chrysler in 2001. At one time it had been the Lincoln-Mercury dealership prior to ICTC locating there. The Sissons renovated the building and it is

Heritage Automall Oldsmobile Showroom on Pickard Street.

Heritage Collision Building on Broomfield Road.

now a car dealership again. Tradition Oldsmobile was moved to this location in June 2002. Heritage Collison Repairs, Inc. expanded and now occupies the whole building at 4884 E. Broomfield Road, Mt. Pleasant. The car dealership name was changed to Heritage Automall, Inc. and the names Heritage Chrysler and Tradition Oldsmobile went into the history book.

The history of Isabella Bank and Trust started in 1903 when a man by the name of John S. Weidman (founder of then Weidman State Bank) purchased the private banking house of Webber and Reul located at 200 E. Broadway in Mount Pleasant. Shortly after his purchase, he incorporated the bank under the name of Isabella County State Bank.

As the years pressed on, so did the growth of Isabella County State Bank. In 1912 the bank was remodeled, featuring a new iron reinforced foundation supporting not only the building but the character of the bank for being known as "solid as a rock."

In 1964, in what was to be a cutting edge tradition for the bank offering new delivery systems to their customers, Isabella County State Bank opened their first "drive-in" branch office at the corner of University and Michigan streets in Mt. Pleasant.

Six years later in 1970, John S. Weidman's previous endeavor, Weidman State Bank, merged with Isabella County State Bank and continued business as a branch office of Isabella County State Bank.

As growth continued, the bank added a Trust Department to the list of services available and with that addition changed their name from Isabella County State Bank to Isabella Bank and Trust in 1973.

From 1982 to 1991 Isabella Bank and Trust acquired through purchase, merger or new construction, branch offices in Blanchard, Six Lakes, Shepherd, Beal City, Barryton, Remus, and Canadian Lakes.

In 2001 Isabella Bank and Trust built a new Operations Center on the south side of Mount Pleasant. The building houses bookkeeping, accounting, computer operations, and the mail room. During the same year, renovations took place at their Customer Service Center and Main Office in downtown Mt. Pleasant.

With 100 years under their belt, Isabella Bank and Trust has witnessed and survived a great deal of trying times in history. The main office continues to stand today at 200 E. Broadway as a testament to the longevity of the bank Isabella Bank and Trust has surely proven itself to be "solid as a rock."

During the last century, Isabella Bank and Trust has grown into the successful community bank they are today. Its employees commitment to excellence and outstanding customer service reflect their dedication to their customers and their communities.

Isabella Bank and Trust currently boasts 15 branch offices, a network of 26 ATM machines, more than 200 employees, over $500 million in assets, and a century of service to the Central Michigan area.

100 YEARS • 1903 - 2003

isabella bank and trust

A Century of Service - A Lifetime of Friendship

Member
FDIC

EQUAL HOUSING LENDER

Krapohl Ford Lincoln Mercury:

Still in the Family after 53 Years!

In 1950, Harold Krapohl left his job with the Firestone Tire Company and Bob Krapohl left the Ford dealership he managed near Grand Rapids. They met in the middle of the state in Mt. Pleasant where they took on the formidable challenge of resurrecting a Ford car dealership that had closed its doors under the previous owner. Together they built a dynamic dealership whose success has been marked by its repeated expansion over the past 53 years.

It all started on Court Street in downtown Mt. Pleasant, where two buildings were added to the original facility - until they were too crowded to supply customer needs. So, in 1970, the Krapohls moved their thriving business to its current location at 1415 E. Pickard Street.

In 1981, the Lincoln and Mercury car lines were added to the Krapohl vehicle line-up. At the same time, the company started to gobble up additional Pickard Street frontage, as well as considerable back acreage. More buildings were constructed too - a reconditioning facility, a large vehicle storage building, a huge state-of-the-industry body shop, and a fast lube operation giving Krapohl's one of the largest physical plants in the state.

In 1975, Bob and Harold Krapohl retired, leaving the dealership in the hands of Bob's son-in-law Brian Smith (now retired) and Harold's son Tom Krapohl. Today, the company is still in family hands. Bob's grandson, Mark Smith, and Harold's son, Tom, together own and operate the dealership, and Tom's son, Spencer, has also joined the family team.

How does a company stay on top for so long? At Krapohl's, success is attributed to its highly-skilled, loyal and long-time staff. Employee relations and customer relations have always been the primary focus of the company, something that has never changed in Krapohl's 53 remarkable years.

The business started in 1950 in two buildings, shown far left and far right, in downtown Mt. Pleasant. Later, it expanded to include the building in the center and also a building at the rear of the dealership.

In 1952, Bob and Harold Krapohl received a major sales award from Ford Motor Co. just two years after starting the dealership.

This is Krapohl Ford Lincoln Mercury as it is today - its size a testament to its amazing success over the past 53 years.

Lease Management, Inc.

Lease Management Office

Lease Management Warehouse on North Kinney St.

In the 1930s, the Gordon Oil Company moved their business to Mt. Pleasant, Michigan. I.W. Hartman became involved in the Gordon Oil Company and later brought his brother, Earl Hartman, into the company. The company later formed Gordon Drilling as a subsidiary of Gordon Oil Company along with Lease Operating Company.

Gordon Oil Company operated until the late 1950s when Earl Hartman dissolved the business. In 1959 Rollie Denison, who worked for Gordon Oil Company and Dean Eckersley, who worked for Gordon Drilling Company, decided to start their own business. On July 1, 1959 they formed a corporation and called their new business Lease Management, Inc. The new business pumped oil wells throughout the state of Michigan.

On April 15, 1962 Jack Harkins joined Lease Management and is currently co-owner with Rudy Kler who joined the company on April 1, 1968. Mr. Harkins is a native resident of Mt. Pleasant (his ancestors migrated here in the late 1800s) while Mr. Kler was born in Wisconsin, grew up in New Jersey and moved to Mt. Pleasant in 1966. Rudy worked for the local newspaper before joining Lease Management. Early field supervisors of Lease Management, Inc. were well known in the oil industry. They were, Fred Sawmiller, Cal Morgan, Earl Delong and Bud Hilliard.

On January 1, 1963 Lease Management acquired five service machines from Jack Long, which worked in the Albion/Scipo Oil Field in Jackson and Hillsdale counties of Michigan. As a result of this acquisition a subsidiary company called Lease Management Service Company was formed. Woody Haskin, who had previously worked for Gordon Oil Company, was the field superintendent for that company. Around 1972 this subsidiary was merged into Lease Management, Inc.

In 1973 Lease Management, Inc. became the first Michigan based oil service company to acquire a Single Derrick Service Machine. The operator for this machine was Ron Schied and wells up to 5,000 feet deep could be serviced with this machine. Lease Management would later acquire the first Double Derrick Service Machine in Michigan from the Ward/Wilson Drilling Company of North Dakota. This machine would service wells up to 12,000 feet. The office building was acquired in the late 1950s and is located on Industrial Avenue in Mount Pleasant.

In 1975 Lease Management bought a warehouse located on North Kinney Street in Mt. Pleasant. The warehouse is still being used at this writing.

On September 1, 1979 Dean Eckersley retired and Rollie Denison became sole owner of Lease Management. Rollie sold Lease Management on June 30, 1996 to Jack and Rudy but retained his ownership in the real estate and wells.

In the 1970s Lease Management operated over 300 wells, had up to 90 employees and 13 service rigs. Lease Management now operates 160 wells, has around 40 employees and has eight service rigs. Lease Management is very proud of all their employees and the work they perform. Lease Management's present supervisor, Rick Pieratt, has 19 years service and our office staff comprised of Carol Cherven, Kathy Courser, Mary Ellen Crain, JoAnn Hoggard, and Shirley Reed have combined years of service totaling 114 years. Two of the original employees, Freeman Hunt and Walt Hemminger, from 1959 are still working as part time pumpers for Lease Management.

Lease Management, Inc. was and continues to be a strong supporter of the Mt. Pleasant area.

Mt. Pleasant Agency, Inc.

The New Mt. Pleasant Agency Building.

Founded in 1959, Mt. Pleasant Agency, Inc. has been servicing the insurance needs for Mt. Pleasant and Mid-Michigan for over 44 years. The success of Mt. Pleasant Agency, Inc. can be traced back to October 1959 when Keith Feight and Jack Swift, both Equitable Life Insurance sales representatives, purchased the existing agency from Donald and Harold Stinson. The company was first located at 119 S. University (College St. in 1959) one block West of the company's current location. The business was then named "Swift and Feight" and conducted business in real estate and insurance sales. Keith and Jack both worked together for the Equitable Life Insurance Co. and saw the need to sell more than just life insurance to clients. They also wanted the benefits of being in the Independent Insurance Agency distribution system. This gave them the option of representing and selling for more than just one company. They provided excellent personal service and competitive prices with an emphasis on honesty, integrity, and building strong personal relationships with their clients and companies they represented. They sold auto, home, life, and business insurance.

In 1962, Keith Feight purchased Jack Swift's half of the company and renamed and formed three companies "Mt. Pleasant Agency, Inc." "Mt. Pleasant Realty. Inc." and "Mt. Pleasant Agency Life & Health." He also brought in two new partnerships, John "Jack" Neyer and Howard Pohl. Jack Neyer on the real estate side while Howard Pohl headed up the life and health insurance and Keith worked both businesses plus the property and casualty insurance business. The business relocated from University to 304 E. Broadway and from 1965 to 1987 the three companies conducted business at 304 E. Broadway.

In 1983 Keith's son, Kurt Feight, joined the company as an agent/producer. In October 1987 the company relocated to its current location at 119 South Franklin Street in Downtown Mt. Pleasant. The larger office and pleasant modern surroundings provide the perfect atmosphere for accelerated insurance growth and a professional image. In 1990 the agency purchased another local insur-

Left to right: Kurt Feight and Keith Feight in 1990.

ance agency known as Grinzinger Insurance Agency from Gerald Grinzinger. This merger and purchase doubled the size of the company. Also in 1990 Kurt Feight become 50% stockholder and the President of the company. In 2003 the Michigan Insurance Agents Association honored the agency as being a Total Quality Agency. This award is given to insurance agencies that have made a strong commitment to long range business planning, quality customer service and employee management. The agency employs seven full time positions and serves the insurance needs for over 3,000 individuals and businesses in the area.

Mt. Pleasant Country Club

BEGINNING. Mt. Pleasant Country Club was the first golf course constructed in the area. The *Mt. Pleasant Times* issue of May 26, 1921 stated "Golf enthusiasts met last Sunday afternoon at the Indian School and organized Mt. Pleasant's first golf course." The golf links was located east of Harris St. and north of Pickard St., across from the Indian School. The next year the club had to vacate the property. Approximately 70 acres were leased from the Dow Company on the present location on River Rd. The official opening of the new location was May 12, 1922. A small farmhouse with no indoor plumbing acted as the clubhouse. In 1927 a new clubhouse was built. In those early days the greens were hand mowed and there was hand weeding. Fairways were mowed with three mowers behind a team of horses. It is doubtful if MPCC would have ever "gotten off the ground" if it were not for two individuals, A.E. Gorham and E.O. Harris. It was largely their individual interest, initiative, physical effort and financial support that was responsible for the club's early success. Often while the men watered the greens, couples would sit, snack and visit under the apple tree near the 9th green. Perhaps the greatest tragedy in the club's history was of an indirect nature. In the infamous McClanahan Oil Well Fire of 1931 A.E. Gorham, to whom MPCC owed so much, died. A memorable date at the club was May 20, 1948 when Willard Dow presented the property deed to the club.

COMPETITION. As interest grew, MPCC became a charter member of the Central Michigan Golf Association in 1928. This alignment included clubs from Mt. Pleasant, Clare, Alma, Ithaca, St. Johns, Midland and Portland. This competition continued until 1974. Competition included weekly interclub matches, a team invitational, and the annual championship tournament. Many lasting friendships were established. In 1932 the women of MPCC had formed the Women's Association and they started competition in the CMGA in the 1930s. In 1955 they severed this relationship and joined the Saginaw Valley Golf Association.

In 1946 the club sponsored its first open bestball tournament for men. For 21 years this was considered one of the outstanding bestball tournaments in the state. Outstanding amateur golfers from across the state participated each year. This was replaced by the annual Member-Guest Tournament. Later the women adopted the latter format for their tournament, now the Women's Classic.

Golf leagues have been a fixture since the first league was started in 1958. In 2002 there were three men's leagues and two women's leagues playing. A Senior Golf Association has been very active with eligible golfers competing weekly and making monthly visits to regional courses.

CHAMPIONS. The most prolific champion at the club was Jean Murray.

Jean won the title 19 times, starting in 1966. Other women with a large number of multiple titles included Ruth Ward, 14 wins; Helen Renwick, 12 wins; and Chris Zeigler, 8 wins. For the men, Bill Theunissen led with 11 titles and was followed by Byron Gallagher and Mike Kostrzewa each with seven wins. Two MPCC "graduates," Dick Horgan and Doug LaBelle III, played on the professional golf tour.

The membership enjoyed the appearance and play of golf celebrities at the club. The incomparable Walter Hagen played in an exhibition match in 1938 and golf professional, Betty Hicks, appeared in 1949. Exhibition artist, Joe Kirkwood, entertained in 1948 and Paul Hahn displayed his trick shot artistry on two occasions. Leading tour stars Dan Pohl, Fred Couples, Fuzzy Zoeller, Bill Kratzert, and Cindy Figg played an exhibition here in 1984.

A tribute to the character of the course was demonstrated in 1938-39. The top professionals in the state appeared here in member-pro tournaments. Only one professional equaled par on any one day and no pro broke par.

NATURAL DISASTERS. Due to its location on the Chippewa River the club experienced course flooding on numerous occasions. After several minor floods, the first major flooding occurred in 1957, followed by several other wet springs. On September 11, 1986 the city of Mt. Pleasant and the MPCC experienced the worst flood in the area's history. This cost the club $53,000. Prior to 1950 the course was graced with some of the most beautiful American Elm trees in the area, tall and arching. In the 1950s and early 1960s these were all killed by the fatal Dutch Elm disease.

On June 21-22, 1985 a fire destroyed the clubhouse. The membership approved $750,000 to rebuild and the new clubhouse was dedicated July 9, 1986. Member, Jack Anson, headed this planning committee.

DINING. The club's fine dining facilities are open to the public. Members have the opportunity to participate in a variety of social and gourmet events throughout the year. The clubhouse is a popular site for wedding showers and receptions, plus other special occasions.

EXPANSION. MPCC remained a beautiful nine-hole course until 1967 when two new holes were constructed as alternates to two of the then present holes - "an 11 hole course." Earlier, in 1964, the club had approved the building of a swimming pool, watering of the tees and fairways, a new parking lot, and expanded clubhouse. In 1980 Jerry Matthews was hired as course architect to expand the plant to 18 holes. Bobb Wardrop, a member who had pushed for this expansion, represented the club and worked closely with Matthews over the next two years. The new 18-hole layout was dedicated on July 3, 1982.

In 1998 a Master Planning Committee, chaired by Terry Stacy, was appointed. After many meetings and professional consultations, the committee's renovation plan was approved by the membership in 2001. Jerry Matthews was again the architect. The approved $1,330,000 plan included a computerized irrigation system, major drainage improvements, new tees, deepening of the ponds, improved sand bunkers, additional cart paths, river erosion control, course-wide berming, increased parking, and the reconstruction of the 9th hole. The first two items were crucial to keep the club competitive with other area courses. The course was played under "abbreviated conditions" in 2002 while construction took place. This inconvenience proved worthwhile when the beautiful new layout was open for play in 2003.

National City Bank

This bank was first established as a private banking enterprise in 1881 by G.A. Dusenbury & Co., the members of the firm being George A. Dusenbury and his brother William C. Dusenbury. It was operated by them until 1889 when it was succeeded by Dusenbury, Nelson & Co. The business continued as a private banking institution, but adopted the name Exchange Bank. In May 1894, the Exchange Savings Bank was organized and incorporated as a state bank under the laws of the state. The original site of Dusenbury & Co. was a free standing building in downtown Mt. Pleasant. The bank moved to the west side of Main Street on the corner of Main and Broadway in 1888. The present site, on the southeast corner of Main and Broadway was acquired in 1909. The bank would see many changes over the next century as officers, directors and stockholders worked together to keep the bank on the cutting edge of the industry. Growth was the focus of the 50s, 60s, and 70s as the bank added branches on North Mission in 1956, South Mission in 1963, West High Street in 1972 and Beal City in 1977. The North Mission branch was the first bank facility to have a drive-up window. It was called the Auto Bank. During these decades the bank expanded services and in 1971 changed the name of the five office locations to American Security Bank. In 1983 the interior of the downtown office underwent extensive remodeling to capture some of the architecture and decoration of the original design. Automated Teller machines (ATMs) were added to all locations in the 1980s. A corporate bank name change affected all eight banks in the company at the time, naming them NewCentury Bank Corporation in 1984. In 1986 the highly respected bank First of America out of Kalamazoo, Michigan acquired the NewCentury banks bringing statewide access to its customers. Continued growth attracted Cleveland, Ohio Banking Corporation National City to purchase the First of America banks in 1998. Presently National City serves customers in three Mt. Pleasant locations, downtown, North Mission and South Mission. National City is the 11th largest bank holding company in the country.

The first and second homes of G.A. Dusenbury & Co., Bankers, and the Exchange Savings Bank. First, 1881 and second, 1888 to 1909

The new home of the Exchange Savings Bank of Mt. Pleasant, Michigan.

Past presidents of the Mt. Pleasant bank include:

1894-1900	Douglas H. Nelson
1900-1903	John Kinney
1903-1905	G.A. Dusenbury
1905-1926	A.E. Gorham
1926-1929	M.T. Kenney
1929-1935	W.E. Lewis
1935-1951	Edward O. Harris
1951-1971	Chester W. Riches
1971-1976	Joseph A. Hauck
1976-1979	Gaylord L. Courter
1980-1985	Leo Staudacher
1985-1987	Terry A. Stacy
1987-1990	Richard J. Ruis
1990-1996	Perry Christenbery
1996-1998	Mark B. Perry
2002-Present	Barbara R. Theunissen

Maeder Brothers Sawmill

In 1952 Gerald and Russell Maeder decided they wanted to start a sawmill business in the Weidman area. They drove to Deckerville to look at a used portable sawmill that was for sale. After looking over the sawmill they decided to purchase it and borrowed $7,000 from Isabella Bank & Trust to get the business going. At that time they also acquired 10 acres just east of Weidman on Weidman Road where they built their homes next to each other and also set up the business.

The first few years they cut logs during the winter months and did their sawing in the summer. They cut grade lumber, timbers and "cant's" (poor grade lumber used for pallets and such). During the early years they didn't have any buildings so all the cuttings were done outside with the portable sawmill they had bought.

Over the years the Maeder's have built six buildings, purchased about an additional 62 acres adjoining their original land and put up an office where once only a portable sawmill was located. Their equipment has changed from diesel driven saws to the high tech computer saws of today. They have also grown from two employees (Gerald and Russell) to 17 employees.

Over the years the annual board foot of lumber they process has increased from four million board feet to around nine million board feet per year. They produce log cabin homes and act as a wholesale outlet for tongue and groove lumber made at Spearfish, South Dakota. The Maeder's used to produce slab wood for fuel use but now produce wood chips along with bark chips for landscaping and sawdust for use by local farmers. As one can see, the Maeder Sawmill has cut many different kinds of timber over the years. Recently, they cut 10 X 12 by 12-foot long timbers for the Soo Locks and 12 X 12 by 16 and 18-foot long timbers for use in Springfield, Illinois. The Soo Locks job required eight semi-trucks loaded with 16,000 board feet in each one of them.

The Maeder's remember when the Large Six Lakes Gas Co. oil fire occurred. At that time they didn't have an office so they received a call at their house from the Gas Co. saying they needed all the timber the sawmill had to make Riffraff. Floris Maeder had barely reached the sawmill area to let Gerald and Russell know that semi-trucks were on the way when the first one appeared. By the end of the day there wasn't any timber left at the Maeder Brothers Sawmill. Red Adair was brought in to finally put the fire out.

Russell Maeder passed away October 14, 2001 and Gerald is starting to enjoy retirement. Russell and Gerald's children, Rick, John, Jane and Tom now run the day-to-day business of the sawmill. When asked what has made Maeder Brothers Sawmill so successful over the years they replied that "We always tried to give the customer what they wanted."

MLT, Inc.

MLT, Inc. is an independent trucking operation consisting of freight vans and food-grade tankers. Servicing the entire continental United States and parts of Canada, the business is owned and operated by Cornell LaLone.

In 1989, the US Government invented the "whole herd buyout" plan for the nation's dairy farmers. Those farmers wishing to discontinue shipping milk could put in a "bid" and the government could accept the bid and pay them to stop sending milk to market. This concept dramatically affected the milk hauling business operated, at that time, by Cornell LaLone, Brenda Johnston and Reg LaLone, all siblings. The reduction in the volume of milk being shipped to market initiated the need for other avenues of trucking. It was decided that a satellite business of Morval LaLone Inc. would be started under the name of MLT, Inc. The first freight loads consisted of roll stock paper. Soon the business was hauling other freight, mostly restaurant and kitchen equipment manufactured locally. The business grew quickly.

In the spring of 1997, Morval LaLone Inc. was divided into three separate entities. MLT, Inc. operated for two years out of a rented facility on Enterprise Drive in Mt. Pleasant. In July 1999, MLT moved to its new building located in the Industrial Park South near the intersection of Isabella and Broomfield roads. The business is situated on 10 acres of land with an office, maintenance shop and warehouse.

In the past five years, MLT has grown from 20 trucks to the 50 truck units that are in operation today. The van division hauls freight of all kinds and is still delivering new kitchens to restaurants, schools and institutions all over America. The use of unloading ramps, furniture pads and trailer logistics eliminates the need for crating.

The tanker portion of MLT is involved in the transporting of dairy products from one facility to another in the dairy industry. Raw milk for bottling, cream for ice cream production and sweet condense for candy making, plus butter and powdered milk products are all transported throughout the Midwest and the East Coast.

With son Curt and son-in-law Kraig Moeggenborg, Cornell and his wife Molly have worked hard to provide excellent service to their customers and maintain a quality fleet of trucks and drivers. The management of MLT takes particular pride in the cleanliness and beautiful appearance of their fleet.

S. Silverberg Finer Jewelers

In the early 1960s Arthur Silverberg and his partner, Jerry Nathanson, both businessmen that lived in Midland decided to open a new version of their discount store in Mt. Pleasant. There had never been a discount type operation in Mt. Pleasant and it was an immediate success. Carrying anything from penny candy to riding lawnmowers, there was plenty of variety to choose from. At this time, discounting had barely ever been heard of. The store was located in the old roller skating rink on South Mission in Mt. Pleasant just outside the old city limits. At that time Mission Road was a two lane street with little ability to handle the traffic of that opening day. The Sheriff's department was there directing traffic. Jerry's father-in-law had a friend in Michigan government that told him that they should put paper bags over the "no parking" signs on the road. There was no way that the parking lot could handle the onslaught of traffic that this event brought. Thus, the Dart store was born. There were "bull's eye" savings and the radio ads featured a talking horse boasting of the hot specials that could be had. Sometime in 1962, the partners had a falling apart, and Arthur ended up taking the Mt. Pleasant store while Jerry remained in the Midland store. The decision to remain in Mt. Pleasant was a good one. Business was brisk until the big operations started moving in. First, there was the Yankee store at Mission and Preston, and then the Kmart at its current location. Even the 44 cent watermelons for sale on the 4th of July weren't enough to ensure enough business for survival. There was a new movement in retail toward Catalog Showrooms. The conversion was made and it was a good one. Arthur even put carpet on the wooden floor in this step-up business. New fixtures, product mix, and even their own published catalog. It was an instant success, and business was prosperous for many years until the advent of the "super stores" such as Walmart and Meijers. In 1994, Arthur decided to retire from the retail business and sold his remaining assets and inventory to his son Steve after his retirement sale in December 1994. Steve divided the building into two separate units, leased out the north half of the building and opened S. Silverberg Finer Jewelers in the south half. Business is still good and enjoyable as of this publication. The best thing about Arthur's decision to retain the Mt. Pleasant store is the community. There is no better place to live and rear a family. While Mt. Pleasant has become a "big" little city, it is still one of the most friendly places to be. The Pleasant is not in the Mt., it is in the people.

Print Tech, The Printing Place, Inc

Print Tech was established in 1984 as the Printing Place by Loren and Denise Anderson, on South Mission St. in Mt. Pleasant. It was incorporated in January 1995 and in July 1998 moved to their present location on East Pickard. Print Tech is a full service commercial printer serving customers throughout Michigan. They offer design services, and

all aspects of the production of printed products as well as advertising specialties.

Print Tech has a rich heritage in the printing field in Michigan. This heritage had its beginning when the father of Loren, Earl Anderson, began his apprenticeship at the Merrill Monitor in Merrill, Michigan in 1916. Earl worked for a number of printers and newspapers in Michigan including the *Enterprise, The Times News,* and *The Central Michigan Tribune* as well as owning two newspapers and a shopping guide. Two other sons of Earl and Doris Anderson also owned print shops. These businesses have employed a number of family members over the years.

Print Tech is proud to be a part of the history of Isabella County and they host a collection of Isabella County historic items in the lobby of the print shop for public viewing.

Sidney Sowle & Son, Inc.

It was the early 1900s and in Mt. Pleasant, Michigan, Sidney Sowle and Andy Cuthbert were putting in another typical day. The founders and only employees of Cuthbert & Sowle Moving were picking up families' belongings with their wagon, or "dray" as it was called then, and team of horses. The goods were then loaded on railroad freight cars rented by the families. The days were grueling and physically taxing, but this was "moving" in 1907 and the beginning of Sidney Sowle & Son, Inc.

Upon Cuthbert's death in 1911, Sowle became the sole owner. His grandson, William "Bill" Sowle Jr., president of Sidney Sowle & Son, recalls stories of his grandfather stacking furniture on wagons with padding and packing china and crystal in barrels. "Furniture was more durable then; it took a lot to damage it," explains Bill.

On days when his grandfather was not moving customers, he hauled coal. The enterprising Sowle was also a Teamster and worked for lumber companies using his team to pull logs from the woods. The company's books were contained in his back pocket. "If his billfold was full, business was good. In his other pocket was a small carbon-type receipt book of those who owed him money." After buying his first truck in the mid-1920s, the senior Sowle finally limited his business to household goods.

Sowle-Mayflower Moving & Storage Services

In 1932 the agency joined Mayflower but found that during World War II it was difficult to obtain trucks and fuel and service was inconsistent. In 1942 the company became affiliated with another carrier.

Following the war, Bill's father joined the company and, in 1946, its name was changed to Sidney Sowle & Son. "My grandfather decided to take over the storage business, while my dad handled the moving busi-

Early Moving Van — Displaying how it used to be done in 1907, Sidney Sowle (right) takes a break to pose for a camera aboard his first moving "van." Founder of Mayflower Moving Co. the same year, the business still remains family-operated. The scene is at the corner of Broadway and Main Streets. The Home Furnishings Building or Campbell Building on the right is where the Mount Pleasant Town Center parking lot is currently located.

Agency founder, Sidney Sowle, behind the wheel of his moving van, circa 1919. The truck was built in Mt. Pleasant, Michigan, and had wooden wheels.

ness. They had two straight trucks. One was 1,600 cubit feet and the smaller one was 1,150 cubic feet. My father then installed a bookkeeping system to keep track of the growing business."

While still in high school, Bill got a "crash course" on the moving business when he was called upon to load the 1,600 cubic foot truck. "You learned very quickly about density when you had to load an entire house into that truck. Of course, we had tailgates back in those days, but a mover had to become very proficient in loading a lot of stuff into a small space."

In 1953 Bill's grandfather passed away and his father invited him to join the business. "He told me that while I'd probably never be rich, I'd make a good living because people were always going to move." After accepting the offer, Bill changed his college major from pre-engineering to accounting to become better prepared for the job. However, he did not join his father until 1957, after graduating from college and spending two years in the service stationed in Germany. Bill has remained loyal to the business ever since.

Together, the two worked to bring innovations to the company. "My father built the first commercial warehouse in Mt. Pleasant in the 1950s," explains Bill. "There were not a lot of warehouses at this time in small towns. Instead, goods were stored in old houses or barns." In 1964 the agency re-affiliated with Mayflower and was "one of the first small movers in the Mayflower Family to become computerized and adopt the CAINS system."

Sidney Sowle & Son, Inc. has a crew with years of experience under their tires. Five of the 12 employees each have 10 years of experience, while the remaining employees have 4-6 years. Their ages range from 23 years old to 70 years old. Arnnie Price and Jay Huber our two veterans, have a family heritage with Sidney Sowle & Son, Inc. Arnnie Price has worked here for a total of 32 years; he started as a helper and now is the warehouse manager. At the age of 51 he is still going strong. Arnnie's father, Ray Price, worked for Sidney Sowle & Son, Inc. for 38 years. Jay Huber has been an employee for 23 years. He began as a helper and cur-

rently is the general manger. His mother, Anna Marie Huber worked here for 11 years. "We are all sort of a family, only with a lot of uncles," says office manager Cynthia Welch. "We all do our parts to make sure that each customer has a worry free move."

Sidney Sowle & Son, Inc. has come a long way since 1907. A team and wagon has been replaced by fully equipped tractor-trailer units and versatile straight vans. These trucks are capable of transporting customer's goods across our nation safely and on schedule. Smooth "air ride" suspension has replaced steel springs to cushion the ride of a customers goods. Cartons are still used to pack personal belongings, but better equipment has evolved to move not only cartons but also furniture. At Sidney Sowle & Son, Inc., everyone is cross-trained in all moving aspects. Better training of our packers and movers to the most productive and safest techniques has held up our high quality of service. Being one of the safest and most efficient moving companies around is something on which we pride ourselves. Sidney Sowle & Son, Inc. won the Circle of Excellence Award every year since its origination in 1990. The Circle of Excellence is a award handed out by Mayflower Transit for those agents who give the best service to their customers, as told by the customers with surveys sent to them after the delivery has occurred.

Of the many moves the company has handled over the years, Bill recalls a particularly memorable relocation of a local developer. "My father had moved the man to the property when he originally required it. Later, he decided to dam up a stream and build his own castle overlooking one of the lakes he created." Needless to say, the agency was pleased to help this local "king" settle into his castle.

The Sowle family's hard work and achievements have played a prominent role in the history of Mt. Pleasant and helped the agency enjoy a high profile in the community. But as Bill is quick to point out, the foundation for the company's success has been its affiliation with Mayflower. "We are better known in the area as Sowle-Mayflower. While our corporate name is Sidney Sowle & Son, we still feel the Mayflower name is vital to our success."

Tuma's Country Gourmet

An 87-Year Family Tradition

In 1970, a time-honored family food tradition was continued when Clarence and Norman Tuma opened the Country Store in Mount Pleasant. Brother Jim joined the management in 1971. It was built on the foundation of quality and service much like the food market opened in 1916 at 661 Charlotte in Detroit by Amos Tuma, father of Jim, Norman and Clarence. The Detroit store provided the livelihood by which Amos and Edith Tuma reared their seven sons and two daughters.

Today's Country Store strives to maintain the friendly old-fashioned atmosphere offering personal attention to customer needs. At its inception, the Tumas felt there was a need in this area for such a store offering quality meats, choice foods and vintage wines. Their perception was correct and today customers come from a 100-mile radius to take advantage of this unique food-retailing center.

Carrying on the family tradition, Ted and Jerry Tuma use Grandfather Amos' 75-year-old recipe for the homemade pork sausage, always a popular feature of the meat counter. Though rich in old-fashioned tradition, Tuma's Country Store uses modern and innovative merchandising ideas and skill to the delight of their clientele. An overwhelming favorite is Thanksgiving and Christmas fresh stuffed turkeys with The Embers sage dressing. Baked and glazed smoked hams are Easter choices.

Special sales are a highlight of the year too. Of these are our whole pork loin, our famous ground round and whole beef strip sirloin sales. These choice beef cuts also are known as New York Strips.

In 1988 the store was purchased by Jeff and Vicki Tuma (Clarence's Oldest Son) and was transformed over to more of a "gourmet" store. Fresh

seafood, lunch and dinner to go, an in house baker, catering, and gift baskets were all added to the already full line of gourmet foods and custom butchering.

The name Tuma has become synonymous with quality and service. Our country store is where you get it!

Park Place Hotel on the NW corner of Main and Broadway Streets.

Art Reach of Mid-Michigan

Art Reach

Art Reach of Mid-Michigan was founded in 1981 by a group of art supporters who were interested in merging several local arts organizations and in creating broad-based financial support for the encouragement of the arts and arts programming in Mt. Pleasant. The Mt. Pleasant Community Arts Council, a group of university and arts community people, served as the organization that sponsored cultural programs and coordinated arts activities in Mt. Pleasant. The Fine Arts Guild represented individuals, many who were artists, worked to promote the arts through the acquisition of an arts center. The Town Arts Center Project group was formed when a local, historic church building went on the market. The group thought that it would make an appropriate "home for the arts." Late in 1980 and early 1981 these groups began working together and merged to become Art Reach of Mid-Michigan. The community wide drive to purchase the Christian Science Church took place. Through the generous support of individuals and businesses money was raised to not only purchase the building, but also accomplish the much-needed renovations to transform the building from a church to an arts center.

Since 1981 Art Reach of Mid-Michigan has not only offered the central Michigan area a "home for the arts" but arts programming as well. Art Reach has four eight-week terms of classes each year. Classes are scheduled for adults and children in the basics of drawing, painting, watercolor painting, creative writing, and drama. Popular arts and fine crafts classes such as basket making, jewelry, creative movement, quilting, cartooning, calligraphy, and papermaking are also offered.

Art Reach annually sponsors a series of chamber music performances, and in partnership with the public library, a series of jazz concerts. In partnership with the Central Music Teachers association, Art Reach offers concert opportunities to student musicians. A community arts Resource Room where teachers, students, and interested community members can use and/or checkout art books, videos, tapes, reproductions, and specialized collections is located in the art center. Other programs available through Art Reach for the Mt. Pleasant community and surrounding area are an annual downtown Art Walk, Day with the Artists in the schools, scholarships, visual art and music education out-reach programs to area schools and adult care facilities. A Gift Shop and Gallery are located in a downtown storefront. Services to artists and arts organizations and maintaining a community arts events calendar are an important part of Art Reach's mission.

The Art Reach Center

The Art Reach Center located on the northeast corner of University and Wisconsin Streets was purchased as an arts center in 1981. The structure was originally built in 1885 by the Richard Balmer family as their residence. The two-story home was used by the family until they moved to Lansing in 1907. The house was sold to a group who was starting a Christian Science Society. The building was changed, the porch and pillars were added, the stained glass windows installed, and an addition was added to the back to house the Christian Science Reading Room. The building is believed to be the first dedicated Christian Science Church in the state. The dedication having taken place on April 10, 1908. The office and classroom addition was built in 1955.

The building remained a church until 1981 when it was purchased for an arts center. With the exception of the 1955 addition the building essentially has remained the same since 1908. In 1984 Art Reach received a grant from the Michigan Council for the Arts to make the building handicapped accessible. This historic building has served the community for over 100 years and will continue to serve well into the future.

Dedicated to God, Home and Country

Isabella Chapter was founded in 1912 in Mount Pleasant and supports education, service, patriotism and historic preservation.

Isabella Chapter DAR
Charter Members

Cynthia Page Brooks, Mrs. Kendall
Gratia Dunning Brooks, Mrs. K.P.
Ruth Irwin Balmer, Mrs. G. W.
Minnie Louise Converse
Jennie Richmond Chamberlin, Mrs. George
Anna Coutant Crittenden, Mrs. J.L.
Blance Irish Gardiner, Mrs. S.E.
Emma Mable Holbrook

Bertina Bliss Keeler, Mrs. Fred
Lorena Barber Larzelere, Mrs. C.S.
Fannie Crawford Mathews, Mrs. Roy
Ida Pierce Sanford, Mrs. R.T.
Evangelia Hawley Morrison, Mrs. S.R.
Bessie Fancher Tambling, Mrs. Charles
Myrta Wilsey Burwash, Mrs. F.M.

Members 2002

Jessica Gayle Bair
M. Sue Sommerville Bair
Paulette Dean Meredith Benner
Barbara Joy Sarwin Bush, Mrs. Donald
Jane E. Mumford Butcher, Mrs. Gilbert
Janet E. Littell Caltrider, Mrs. Robert
Glenna J. Farr Clendening, Mrs. Byron
Elaine Smith Courser, Mrs. Stanley
Eileen Gilson Deunk, Mrs. Norman
Marydeana Davis Duckworth, Mrs. Gene
Saramichelle Duckworth Duris, Mrs. Christopher
Sue Lynn Amacher Eldridge, Mrs. Bruce
M. Gayle Somerville Gilchrist, Mrs. Gordon
Helen Louise Fellows Glady, Mrs. Edward

Jeanne E. Gilbert Grassley, Mrs. Earlen
Leslie Ann Johnson Hager, Mrs. Lowell
Caroline C. Millar Hartman, Mrs. Earl
Rebecca J. Simpson Gilchrist Marqulardt, Mrs. Fred
Annajeanelle Duckworth McInnis, Mrs. William
Jill Lucille Snider Morrison, Mrs. William
Lynn Anne Mulligan Pike, Mrs. Ray
Shirley Hazel Amacher Robinson, Mrs. Max
Mary Ellen Baker Ruark, Mrs. Jarl
Lucille Davidson Snider, Mrs. Dean
Maxine Ann Fellows Tanner, Mrs. M.
Barbara Jeanette Crapo Thayer, Mrs. George
Margaret Helmer Wood, Mrs. Roger
Jane Ann Amacher Zempel, Mrs. Randall

Independent Order of Odd Fellows
Mt. Pleasant Lodge No. 217
Mount Pleasant, Michigan

A Brief History of Odd Fellowship and of Mt. Pleasant Lodge.

The Independent Order of Odd Fellows was founded in the United States of America, 186 years ago, on April 26, 1817, in Baltimore, Maryland, at the Seven Stars Tavern by Thomas Wildey and four other brothers of the Manchester Unity of Odd Fellows.

The five brothers: Thomas Wildey, John Welsh, John Duncan, John Cheatham, and Richard Rushworth organized Washington Lodge No. 1, of Baltimore, Maryland, the Mother of the Independent Order of Odd Fellows.

Members of the Manchester Unity soon established other lodges in Maryland, Massachusetts, New York, and Pennsylvania. In the early 1820s Grand Lodges were organized in these four states. On January 15, 1825 the representatives of these Grand Lodges created the Grand Lodge of the United States. In the 1830s and 1840s Odd Fellowship spread westward and lodges were organized in the Mid-West, including Michigan, with the Grand Lodge of Michigan being instituted on November 5, 1844.

In the spring of 1874, five Odd Fellows: James L. Sweeney, Albert Holms, Martin K. Morse, Jared H. Doughty, and John R. Doughty, wrote to the Grand Lodge of Michigan requesting that an Odd Fellow Lodge be organized in the Village of Mt. Pleasant. The Grand Master of Michigan instructed the brothers of Magnetic Lodge No. 141, of St. Louis, Michigan to institute the new lodge that was to be known as Mt. Pleasant Lodge No. 217. The lodge was instituted on April 4, 1874 in a log cabin near the Court House Square. The officers of the lodge were elected, new members were initiated, and the First through the Fifth Degrees were conferred on the members of the lodge.

Two brothers of Mt. Pleasant Lodge have served as leaders of the Grand bodies of Michigan: Brother William R. Kennedy was the Grand Master of Michigan in 1907-08, and Brother Robert A. Philo was Grand Patriarch of the Grand Encampment of Michigan in 1965.

The present elected officers for the year 2003 are as follows: Noble Grand, John Osborn; Vice Grand, Jack Eaton; Recording Secretary, Kenneth L. Nichols; Financial Secretary, Gerald E. Servoss; Treasurer, Edward J. Doerr; and Lodge Deputy, Robert C. Grove.

Mt. Pleasant Lodge from 1874 to 1907 rented the upstairs of buildings on Broadway and on Main Street. On April 1, 1907 they purchased for $2,000 the original Presbyterian Church Building on Court Street, and they stayed there for 55 years. The Lodge in October 1963 purchased the present Temple located on the northwest corner of Broadway and Fancher Street, from The First Baptist Church.

Wabon Lodge 305 F&AM
Mt. Pleasant, January 11, 1871

Salt River Lodge 288 F&AM
Shepherd, January 13, 1871

James A. Cliff Lodge 424 F&AM
Weidman, January 23, 1901

Mt. Pleasant Chapter OES 55
Mt. Pleasant, October 4, 1889

Coe Chapter OES 98
Shepherd, October 11, 1893

Waubenoo Chapter OES 360
Weidman, October 10, 1907

Masonic Organizations

Of

Isabella County

Royal Arch Chapter 111
Mt. Pleasant, January 16, 1884

Job's Daughters Bethel 61
Mt. Pleasant, December 2, 1956

Mt. Pleasant Rotary Club

Rotary International was founded in Chicago in 1905. The founder was a lawyer, Paul Harris. It was 20 years later in 1925 that Mt. Pleasant became the home of the Mt. Pleasant Rotary Club. Joseph Schnitzler, a local attorney who was a triple amputee, had visited other Rotary Clubs and was convinced that such a club was ideal for Mt. Pleasant. To Schnitzler must give credit for the existence of the Mt. Pleasant Rotary Club. This club was the first service club organized in Mt. Pleasant and set the pattern for service clubs that followed. This would include a second club, Rotary Club II, which the parent club sponsored in 1973. Rotarian, Lyle Bennett, was primarily responsible for the establishment of this second Rotary Club in Mt. Pleasant (an early morning club).

There were 24 charter members in the club and Joseph Schnitzler was the first president. Weekly noon meetings were originally held in the Park Hotel. Meetings were held in the First Presbyterian Church from 1930 to 1995. Since then it has met at the Riverwood Golf Course. The first major project of the club was working with crippled children and this remained a strong emphasis for the next 40 years. In 1927 Schnitzler addressed the Rotary International Convention in Brussells, Belgium on this topic.

Four Mt. Pleasant Rotarians have served the area clubs as district governors. These four were John Hepler (1963-64), George Lauer (1967-68), Emil Pfister (1972-73), and Ken Schaeffer (1989-90). In the Rotary years 1978-79 and 1989-90 the District Governor instituted programs aimed at determining the "Number One club in the district." Both years Mt. Pleasant earned "Number One" rating. During Rotary International's 75th anniversary year in 1980, the local club's project "75 Benches-75 Trees-75th Year" was voted the district's best. The club later built an observation platform and distributed bird houses in the new Millpond Park. There have been many local Rotarians over the first 77 years who have lived the Rotary motto of "Service Above Self" and "He Profits Most Who Serves Best" – serving on community boards, planning groups, task forces, improvement projects, etc. The club presents two awards annually. The "Distinguished Citizenship Award" recognizes a member of the community who has demonstrated a period and quality of service that deserves special recognition. The individual performed the services(s) for no pay and little recognition. The second award is the "Vocational Excellence Award" to recognize individuals who have demonstrated excellence, honesty and dependability in their dealing with others through their vocation. Club members who have proven to be outstanding Rotarians may be awarded the Paul Harris Fellowship Award.

The Rotary Club has demonstrated leadership in education in the city. Rotarians serving as superintendent of the Mt. Pleasant Public Schools have included George Ganiard (1924-1939), Charles Park (1939-48), Russ LeCronier (1946-63), Robert Janson (1981-199_) and Gary Allen (199_). Presidents of Central Michigan College/University have included E.C. Warriner (1918-38), C.L. Anspach (1938-59), Judson Foust (1959-68) and Harold Abel (1975-85).

Throughout its long history the club has instigated and carried out many projects that have made Mt. Pleasant a better community in which to live. In 1925 the administration building at Central Michigan Normal burned down. When the state legislature in Lansing threatened to move the institution elsewhere, the Rotarians combined with the Chamber of Commerce to assist in keeping it in Mt. Pleasant. In 1940 all of the club's surplus funds went to supporting the Community Hospital Drive, resulting in a life membership for the club in the Central Michigan Community Hospital. In the 1940s and 1950s the club members presented the *Rotary Review* which were community entertainment highlights. Youth programs supported by the club have included sponsoring a Boy Scout troop, sending high school students to Leadership Camp at Lake Rotary and to Wolverine Boy's and Girl's State in Lansing, providing scholarships to college-bound students, contributing towards the Community Stadium, assisting in anti-drug and substance abuse programs, caring for children of migrant workers, medical care for the indigent, and promoting a Bicycle Safety Program. Other projects have included sponsoring crippled children clinics for the county, helping with "airplane spotting" in World War II, co-sponsors for a community fitness exercise trail, first community organization to support the present Millpond Park, and supporting Boy Scout Camp Rotary north of Clare. Rotarian, Dr. Andrew Bedo, chaired a committee to establish a Child Guidance Center in Mt. Pleasant. The club supported this project, as well as a building addition some 10 years later. In addition to its many hands-on projects, the club has provided financial assistance for hundreds of other community activities.

Rotary does not limit its assistance to local projects. One of the four avenues of service in Rotary is International Service. The extent and purpose of this area is one criterion that clearly separates Rotary from other service clubs. The club has sponsored students with graduate scholarships for study abroad – it has been the largest privately sponsored scholarship program in the world. The district periodically sponsors a Group Study Exchange team to a foreign country. Leaders of such teams have included local Rotarians John Hepler (South Africa-1971), Don Kilbourn (India-1979) and Howard Evans (Finland-1990). In turn the local club has hosted teams from South Africa, India, West Indies, Argentina, Scotland, Australia, Finland, Spain, France, Russia and Brazil. Youth Exchange is a recognized activity of the Rotary International. It is for high school students to study abroad for one academic year. The club has hosted 35 such students. At the same time Rotary has screened local students for inclusion in this program abroad.

The first induction of women into the Mt. Pleasant Rotary Club occurred in 1990. These "pioneers" were Eileen Jennings, Geraldine Wright and Shirley Helber. The club has been a strong advocate offering financial assistance to the Rotary Foundation. One visible service of this foundation has been the "PolioPlus" program which expects to eradicate poliomyelitis from the planet by the year 2005. Rotary International's "3-H Program" (Health, Hunger and Humanity) funds large scale humanitarian projects providing benefits of a long term, self-helping nature by improving health, alleviating hunger, enhancing human and social development. Mt. Pleasant Rotary strongly supported this foreign aid program. Presently the membership totals approximately 65 men and women who are collectively carrying out the Rotary motto "Service Above Self."

Veterans Memorial Library

In 1879 in the office of attorneys Fancher, Dodds, and Partridge, a group of citizens gathered to organize Mount Pleasant's first library. The Library, Literary and Musical Association was incorporated under the state law "the object for which the association is organized is to establish and maintain a library for the members thereof." At the home of Mr. and Mrs. William N. Brown on Wednesday, March 18, 1879, the organizers met to elect officers and directors. Mrs. I.A. Fancher was elected president and Mrs. D.S. Partridge was to be the librarian.

Books were contributed by each member of the board, with the largest donation coming from Mrs. Francis Babbit, who, following the death of her husband was moving back to Ohio. The Library was supported by funds raised from annual dues paid by members and from parlor entertainment during the winter months. Not open to the public, the over 1,000 volumes owned by the library were for the use of the association members only.

The "Library" was first housed in a small building next to Isaac Fancher's home on North Main Street. When Fancher moved to Detroit in 1882, the library was forced to find new quarters. This would be a frequent occurrence over the next several years.

In 1895, right before a history of the Library, Literary and Musical Associations was to be published, the building, which housed the library, was destroyed by fire. The association was faced with replacing most of its books and had only three cents in its treasury. Never being able to earn enough money to start over, the association faded away in 1896.

It was not until 1909 that the city council finally caved in and decided there should be a library in Mount Pleasant. However, only limited financial support would be given by the city. In March 1910 the library opened with an official library board, donated books and furniture. It was located in the Nelson block of Main Street. The Library had 650 books on it shelves. The library would be open on Saturdays from 2:00 - 5:00 p.m. and 7:00 - 8:00 p.m. The formal opening took place on Saturday, March 19, 1910. 150 books were loaned out that day.

Within five years the library became too small and was in need of a new building. In March 1915, Mr. and Mrs. L.N. Smith offered their brick house located at 412 East Broadway. Fifteen dollars per month and payment of the taxes and insurance were to be paid to the Smiths. Within five years the library was proud to have six thousand volumes on the shelves. However the Smith house was no longer large enough.

The vacant old Unitarian Church located on the corner of College (now known as University) and Wisconsin was offered to the library board in January 1920. With the interior needing to be remodeled, the library board called on the Mount Pleasant Women's Club for help. The Club voted without hesitation to raise $1000 to purchase floor covering, book cases, reading tables, chairs and other necessary items for the library. They ended up collecting $2,643.12. The "Mount Pleasant Public Library" formal opening happened on June 16, 1921 with Miss Mary N. Osgood, full time librarian and Mrs. Anna Crittenden, assistant librarian.

Needing desperately to expand, a proposed $40,000 general obligation bond issue was put forth and defeated on April 7, 1941. 1941 also saw the beginning of a branch library located in Rosebush. This branch would close in 1945. It wasn't until 1957 that a new library building was made a reality. On May 24, 1957 the new library was dedicated to Mt. Pleasant's Veterans of all wars and would be called Veterans Memorial Library.

Once again a need to expand, the library arose. On June 13, 1983, city voters went to the polls and approved a $1.2 million dollar bond issue for library expansion to be paid for in increased mileage rates. The library expansion would include a multipurpose room, a children's area and for the first time public restrooms. The 1957 building was gutted, and the walls were "bumped out" on three sides. The south side of the building was expanded to two stories and was in itself larger than the original building. In September 1985, a gala grand opening/dedication was held. Speeches were given by local and state dignitaries, Mount Pleasant High Schools band played and refreshments were served.

The Library of Michigan officially recognized the Chippewa River District Library System as a legally established district library on May 20, 1998. On December 21 of that year voters approved a mileage of 1.75 for 10 years. The district area encompasses the city of Mount Pleasant, the Mt. Pleasant Public School System and Union Township. The Faith Johnston Memorial Library in Rosebush is the only branch library within the district borders. However, through an agreement with the Isabella County Library Board, branches in other communities, which had been established over the last 30 years, continue to serve the outlying areas. The Coe Township Library in Shepherd, Weidman Public Library, Rolland Township Library in Blanchard and the Fremont Township Library in Winn, play important parts in the library's mission to serve all the people of Isabella County.

Veterans of Foreign Wars of the United States

Borley-Hanel Post No. 3033
Mount Pleasant, Michigan

Sergeant Omer Borley

The Charter of Post 3033

Corporal Simon E. Hanel

Sergeant Omer Borley, the son of Theophile and Marie Borley, was born in Belgium, and was inducted from Mt. Pleasant, Michigan. He served with Company D, 126th Infantry Regiment. On October 24, 1918, he was killed in France, and was buried there.

Corporal Simon E. Hanel, the son of Charles Sr. and Elizabeth Hanel was born on February 9, 1896 in Isabella County. He entered the service on November 19, 1917, in Company D, 39th Infantry Regiment, and trained at Camp Custer, Michigan, and Charlotte, South Carolina. Corporal Hanel went overseas in March of 1918, fought and was killed in the Battle of the Argonne Forest on September 26, 1918. His body is resting among his fellow comrades in Flanders Field.

Borley-Hanel Post No. 3033 was authorized and constituted on May 25, 1934, by 23 World War I veterans from the Mt. Pleasant area. In 2003, our 69th year, the post has approx. 250 members, they are veterans from World War II, the Korean War, the Vietnam War, and the Persian Gulf.

The elected post officers for the year 2002-2003 are as follows: Commander, Richard Fish, Vietnam War; Senior Vice Commander, Robert C. Grove, Korean War; Junior Vice Commander, Terry Russell, Vietnam War; Quartermaster, Ralph Fischer, Vietnam War; Post Advocate, Ivan Ayris, Korean War; and Surgeon, Frank Morrison, World War II.

The Post Home was constructed in the 1950s and is located at 4841 E. Pickard Rd.

Mt. Pleasant Area Historical Society

Mt. Pleasant Area Historical Society

The Mt. Pleasant Area Historical Society began with a group of concerned citizens in 1986 that were trying to save one of the city's landmarks, the Pere Marquette railroad station, from demolition. The group was meeting in the Veteran's Memorial Library and when attempts to save the building from the wrecking ball failed, they decided to find a permanent location. Through the help of Tony Kulick, then Director of Planning and Community Development, a grant was obtained and the group was able to purchase a large home on the north end of Mt. Pleasant at 523 North Fancher St.

This building has provided the group over the years with a meeting place for monthly meetings where speakers present programs to promote the history of Mt. Pleasant and Isabella County. It is at this location, where an annual neighborhood ice cream social is held each July complete with live music.

Through the years, the Mt. Pleasant Area Historical Society, has held fashion shows, conducted Christmas tours of older homes in Mt. Pleasant, recreated a wedding conducted in vintage clothing, had displays at the Isabella County Fair and promoted the local history through school programs. Meetings are open to anyone with an interest in history.

The National Retired Teachers Association

The National Retired Teachers Association began with interested retirees from Isabella County schools under the leadership of Mt. Pleasant teacher, Emma Sager, and grew slowly into a much broader based membership of all school retirees plus interested and affected Central Michigan College educational personnel. A local chapter was formed of the Michigan Association of Retired School personnel and called The Isabella Chapter of Retired School Employees. This chapter, formed in 1951, grew to represent some 440 members. They include teachers, administrators, clerical and all other non-certified personnel, as well. All county personnel, CMU included are those receiving benefits from the Michigan public schools retirement system. Leadership for the group has emanated from their many past presidents, some of them were Dr. Rolland Alterman, Emma Sager, John Cuming, Carlo Barberi, Jack Anson, Virginia Grubaugh, Ken Walker and others. Over 1,100 county school district retirees benefit from this association. Many participated in funding and building the Marsp Service Center located off Joy Road in Lansing, Michigan. Its state membership stands at nearly 40,000 members.

ISABELLA COUNTY FAMILY HISTORIES

Orr School — 1915

ADAMS-BUCHHOLZ. Buell Adams parents and Dean Adams grandparents were Henry Adams and Augusta Buchholz, both born in Germany but in different places and at different times. Henry was five years of age in 1845 when he came with older sister Ann and two other brothers, William and Nicholas, and a sister Barbara from the state of Hessen to the United States. Augusta Buchholz was born at sea on the sailing ship *Tarquine*, while her family was en route to the United States from the German state of Prussia in 1854.

Both families stayed in Ohio for a while and then came to Gratiot County where they settled and acquired property. Henry had learned the shoemaking trade prior to coming to Gratiot County, and he established a shoemaking business in Alma, MI. In 1874 he disposed of his village property by trading for 70 acres of wild land in sec. 35 in Isabella Twp., Isabella County.

Henry married Augusta Buchholz in 1876. They had four children: Minnie (Adams) Deihl, Charles Adams, Dora Adams and Buell Adams. Dean's father Buell, the youngest, was born on Valentines Day 1895. Henry acquired 120 acres south of Mt. Pleasant on what is now Wing Road, just east of Old Mission Road, and the family moved to that location in the late 1890s.

Roberta (Fall) Adams parents and Dean Adams maternal grandparents were Charles Fall and Rosa Cooley. They were born in Saginaw County, married in Saginaw County and came to Isabella County about 1880. Three children were born in Saginaw County: Dora, Stephen and Ethel. Twin girls, Roberta and Ramona, were born in Isabella County in 1895.

By 1917 Roberta had completed work at Central State Teachers College and obtained a Teaching Certificate. She was teaching at the Crowley School south of Mt. Pleasant where she met Buell Adams. Roberta had lodging with her brother, Stephen Fall's family, now Bluegrass Road at Mission Road. Buell had a car and frequently found the time to

Buell and Roberta Adams

give Roberta a ride too and from school. Buell was called for service in WWI in 1917. When he was discharged in 1919 they were married in March that year.

Both Buell and Roberta were residents of Isabella County all or their lives. Roberta died in 1982 and Buell in 1984. Dean was born near Rosebush Dec. 31, 1919. The family moved South of Mt. Pleasant on Old Mission Road where Dean attended Mt. Pleasant Schools. He graduated from MPHS in 1937, attended CMU and graduated in 1942 with a BS degree and a certificate to teach secondary school

Dean met Dorothy E. Pennington while they were students at CMU, and they married in September 1942.

ADAMS-PENNINGTON. Dorothy Elieen (Pennington) Adams (b. Aug. 28, 1922 in Mt. Pleasant, MI) is the daughter of Elwin and Ethel

(Holmes) Pennington. A brother Wendell S. Pennington has resided in Georgia since 1952, operating a cattle ranch. Wendell and his wife, Wilma V. (Clark) Pennington, have five children, two boys and three daughters.

The Elwin Pennington family moved to Flint in 1928 where both Elwin and Ethel taught in the Flint Public Schools. Dorothy and Wendell attended Flint Northern High School. Wendell graduated in 1937 and Dorothy graduated in 1940. At this time the family returned to their home on Drew Road near Weidman. Ethel and Elwin had established a children's camp in conjunction with farming activities.

Dorothy entered CMU in September 1940 where she met and later married Dean Adams. Dean Adams was born to Roberta (Fall) Adams and Buell Adams near the village of Rosebush on Dec. 31, 1919. His family moved to a farm in Union Twp. south of Mt. Pleasant in 1929. He attended Mt. Pleasant schools and CMU. Dean graduated from CMU in 1942, and Dean and Dorothy were married at her home on Sept. 19, 1942.

Dean and Dorothy E. Adams

Dean and Dorothy made their first home in Leland where Dean taught school until being called for duty in military service in WWII. Upon entering military service Dean was assigned to a series of USAAF bases in California, Arizona and Texas before graduating from USAAF advanced pilot training school at Luke Field AZ, Dec. 5, 1943. While serving as flight instructor based at Minter Field, Bakersfield, CA, their first child, Robert Dean Adams, was born July 25, 1944. The training group at Minter Field was moved to Lincoln, NE in May 1945 and the Dean Adams family went to Nebraska where Dean served as flight instructor until the end of WWII.

After WWII ended the family returned to Mt. Pleasant where Dean resumed teaching. On Jan. 11, 1947 a second son, Richard Buell Adams, was born. Then on April 28, 1948 Thomas Elwin Adams arrived.

In the fall of 1948 Dean was recalled to active duty with the USAF and was assigned duty flying four engine transport planes (C-54) on the Berlin Airlift (1948-49). He remained on active duty until September 1958, living in Texas, Bermuda and New Jersey. While in Bermuda a daughter was born Dec. 16, 1953. Dean continued to fly transport missions to Europe, North Africa and islands of the Atlantic until leaving the service in October 1958. During this time Dorothy spent her summer months (with their children), working at the Pennington Chippewa Ranch Camp, a co-ed camp for boys and girls near Weidman.

Upon separating from the USAF in 1948, Dean and Dorothy purchased a farm near Lake City, MI. There they operated the farm (240 acres) and Dean taught school in the Lake City and Houghton Lake Schools. Dorothy worked as an insurance underwriter. While living at Lake City Dean also worked with a USAF Reserve unit at Traverse City and completed requirements for USAR retirement in 1965.

In 1966, they decided to sell the farm and Dean took a teaching assignment at Okemos Public Schools near Lansing. The family moved to that area and lived in Haslett, MI. After three years at Okemos, Dean moved to Holt, MI as a school administrator where he remained until retirement from Michigan Public Schools. While in the Lansing area Dorothy became active in Real Estate Sales. They came back to Sherman Twp., Isabella County, where they lived at there home on Drew Road west of Weidman.

Robert Dean Adams is the father of Jennifer (b. Oct. 23, 1970) and Amy (b. May 20, 1972); Richard Buell Adams and wife Connie are parents of Kristel R. Adams (b. Oct. 22, 1976), Aric R. Adams (b. March 1, 1978) and Erin R. Adams (b. Oct. 9, 1981); Thomas Elwin Adams and wife Alice are parents of Jason Adams (b. Sept. 16, 1975) and Paul M. Adams (b. June 20, 1978).

ALBAR-AVARD. Aloyisous Henry Albar (b. Aug. 10, 1906) md. Mabel Avard on Aug. 4, 1933, and to this union was born a son, Lavigne Albar, and a daughter, Nancy Albar.

When Aloyisous was 16 years of age he went to work at Floyd Johnson's Garage located on the corner of Michigan and College Street (now known as University Street) as a mechanic. He worked on Model "T" cars and Fordson Tractors for five years.

Then he bought out a small auto electric shop, which was located on West Michigan Street where he repaired starters, generators and also did general auto repair work.

In 1928 his business was growing so he bought property located at 114 S. Washington Street. On this property there was an old Woolen Mill, which he converted into a garage. At this garage he started selling DeSoto and Plymouth cars for a man name Lawrence Barr. In 1934 he began selling Graham Paige autos and in 1938 he took on the Nash Dealership.

Albar Motor Sales

In 1941 he added his first addition to the shop, which was a showroom and an office. During the war years with no autos being built he sold Case Farm Machinery. In 1946 he sold out the farm machines and continued with the Nash Dealership. In 1947 he added onto the back part of the shop enlarging the service department where he operated the business until he sold the building to the Buyer's Guide and retired.

ALEXANDER. Pete and Lisa Alexander have lived at 8488 S. Loomis Road, Shepherd since their wedding day on March 4, 2000. They met while serving on the Shepherd Tri-Township Fire Department. Pete sells real estate, serves on the Shepherd Tri-Township Fire Department, works at the Mt. Pleasant Holiday Inn, and farms 280 acres.

Lisa helps with the farming and takes care of her family, which includes Logan (b. June 23, 1997) and Landon (b. June 29, 2001). The Alexanders have two dogs, Mattie and Otis.

Lisa and Pete Alexander with sons, Landon and Logan

They attend Potter House Church in Mt. Pleasant. Lisa is a Sunday school teacher and helps with the nursery. Other activities they do as a family include growing mums, raising chickens, and helping with the Shepherd Maple Syrup Festival. Pete is the president of the Festival Committee.

Logan attended St. Vincent de Paul preschool and is now enrolled in kindergarten at Shepherd Public Schools.

ALEXANDER-TOWERSEY. Raymond Carl Alexander (b. April 10, 1929 in Ferndale, MI) is the younger of Thomas and Carrie Alexander's four children. He has a twin sister Ruth and two older brothers, John and Tom.

Sarah Evelyn Towersey was born to Fred and Alice Towersey on Nov. 4, 1928 in Alma, MI. With her older sister June and younger twin brothers, Darrell and Delbert, she grew up on Orchard Street.

Ray and Evelyn Alexander

Ray and Evelyn met at Alma High School. Ray was president of FFA (Future Farmers of America) and Evelyn was president of FHA (Future Homemakers of America).

Following graduation, Evelyn went to Murphy Beauty School in Mt. Pleasant and became a licensed cosmetologist.

When Ray graduated from high school, he joined the Air Force and was stationed in Alaska for 28 months. On Dec. 1, 1951 Ray and Evelyn were married in the Alma Methodist Church.

Ray and Evelyn left for Ogden, UT as Ray was still in the Air Force. From Ogden, they went to Alexandria, VA. In 1952 Ray enrolled at Michigan State College. Connie was born in September 1952 and Wesley, three years later, in 1955. Those four years at MSU were spent living in the barracks on Chestnut Street.

Upon graduation, Ray accepted a job in Wisconsin with the electric company and they built a home in Racine. Peter was born in 1957 and Philip 18 months later. Ray was transferred to the head office in Milwaukee, so they sold their home and moved to Brookfield. Ray was transferred again. In fact, they had lived 11 different places in nine years. This time to Watertown, WI.

Being homesick for Michigan, the family moved to Shepherd in 1964. They bought an 80 acre farm at 8651 South Loomis Road from Harry and Retha McCormick. Evelyn got a job at the Masonic Home in Alma. Ray worked for Jamesway for a year, then landed a position with Consumers Power in Alma. In 1967, Benjamin was born at Gratiot Community Hospital.

Over the past 37 years in Shepherd, Ray and Evelyn (with the help of their kids) built and operated a trailer park, a gun shop, and a party store. They are members of the Shepherd United Methodist Church. Ray has been active with a number of organizations such as Rotary, 4-H, Boy Scouts, Shepherd Historical Society, the church's building committee, and the Michigan Sheep Breeders Association. In addition to being a full-time Mom, Evelyn found time to serve as the Chamber of Commerce president, Women's Club, WSCS of the Methodist Church, Cub Scout den mother, and the Maple Syrup Festival chairman of the dining room for three years. She loves to play bridge.

Ray and Evelyn went to Hawaii for their 25th wedding anniversary, and for their 50th, they only got as far as Mt. Pleasant! They have traveled across the country and Ray has visited every state in the nation.

Now retired, Ray and Evelyn enjoy spending their time at their farm in Shepherd and visiting their children. Connie is the pastor at the Edmore United Methodist Church; Wes lives in Virginia where he is the Southampton County Extension Director; Pete is a fire fighter, farmer, real estate agent and president of the Maple Syrup Festival; Phil lives in Gaylord and works for MSU Extension as a district agent for 21 counties of northern Michigan; and Ben is a lineman with Verizon in Lexington, KY.

ALLEN-EWING. Grant Kenneth "Kenny" Allen (b. Feb. 2, 1930 in Gilmore Twp., Isabella County, MI), the son of Elmer Victor and Flossie Florence (Winters) Allen. Grant attended High School at Farwell, MI and graduated in 1948. The year after graduation he enlisted in the Army. Grant was wounded in Korea in September 1950 and discharged June 6, 1952.

On Aug. 23, 1952 Grant married Velma Jean Ewing at Velma's parents home on Coleman Road in Gilmore Twp. Velma (b. June 24, 1933 in Corunna, MI) is the daughter of Earl Howard

and Laura Adrianna (Hubbard) Ewing. Velma moved to this area, with her parents, brothers and sister from Saginaw, MI in 1943. Velma attended school at Weidman, MI.

Velma and Grant Allen, 1987

Shortly after being married, Grant and Velma purchased their first home on Neier St. in Mt. Pleasant, MI. Velma worked at the state home for many years and retired from the same in 1984. Grant worked for Ferro Mfg. for 11 years, then for the state home for seven. Due to injuries received in Korea, Grant could no longer work, and now has a disability from the Veterans Administration.

In 1978 Grant and Velma sold their home in Mt. Pleasant and moved to their summer home on Littlefield Lake. They also enjoy spending part of their winter in Rockport, TX.

Grant and Velma have two children, Steven Kenneth (b. Nov. 7, 1956) and Darcy Jean (b. Sept. 23, 1958). They also have eight grandchildren.

Grant and Velma are also mentioned in the Isabella County biography book published in 1982.

ALLEN-FULMER. One of the early pioneers of Isabella County was the family of Joseph and Laura Allen who came to the county around 1869. Joseph was born in New Bedford, ME on July 10, 1842 the son of Frank and Deborah (Spooner) Allen. Some time in the next 20 years the family moved to Ohio where Joseph met Laura Fulmer. Laura (b. April 7, 1842) was the daughter of John and Laura Fulmer. On Aug. 24, 1866 Joseph (age 24) and Laura (age 24) were married in Wood County, OH.

At some period around 1869 they moved to Isabella County. On Dec. 22, 1877 they purchased a farm from Mary Ford in Fremont Twp. They lived on the farm with their children until March 12, 1912 when the farm was sold to their daughter Rose and son-in-law, Elias Wonsey. The Wonseys farmed the land until May 18, 1943 at which time they sold the farm to their son George and his wife, Muzetta.

Joseph Allen

Laura and Jessie Albert Allen

The Allen's had 10 children: George (b. 1867, d. 1920), Benjamin (b. 1869, d. 1922), Cynthia (b. 1871), Josiah (b. 1874), Lemule (b. 1874, d. 1957), Jessie Albert (b. 1877, d. 1956), Cornelia (b. 1879), Rose (b. 1881, d. 1957), Edward (b. 1885) and Josie (b. 1889, d. 1897). All of the sons and daughters were born in Isabella County with the exception of the first-born, George, who was born in Ohio.

After selling the farm in 1912 the Allens moved into Shepherd where they purchased a home at 338 East Cottage Ave. where Joseph died on June 3, 1913. Laura Allen remained in Shepherd until her death on Oct. 25, 1929. Both Joseph and Laura Allen are buried in the Taylor Cemetery east of Winn, just north of the farm that they owned for 35 years.

ALLEN-MYERS. Burton Phillip Allen was born Aug. 22, 1857 in Madison Twp., Lenawee County, MI, just south of Adrian. Burton was the son of Ambrose Peter, and Mary (LaFromboise) Allen. In 1858 or 59 Burton moved with his family to Genesee, Genesee County, MI, where they lived until October 1864 when his father Ambrose purchased land in Union Twp., Isabella County, MI. where Riverwood golf course sits today.

On April 28, 1880 Burton purchased from his father, Ambrose Allen, 40 acres of the family farm in Union Twp., Section 20. The 40 acres was the property lying just north of the Chippewa River. Then on Aug. 16, 1883 Burton purchased 40 acres in Section 36 of Deerfield Twp., Isabella County, MI.

On July 2, 1884 at Salt River, Burton married Useba Myers of Coe Twp., Isabella County, MI. Useba was the daughter of Joseph and Margaret (Sawell) Myers. Both of Useba's parents are buried in Coe Twp., Isabella County.

Useba Allen, ca. 1885   *Burton Phillip Allen, ca. 1885*

They had two children, Elmer Victor (b. June 19, 1885) and Alta Grace (b. Aug. 26, 1886). Both children were born in Deerfield Twp.

On June 22, 1887 Burton sold the land he had purchased from his father in Union Twp. and then on Nov. 9, 1889 he sold his land in Deerfield Twp.

On Oct. 14, 1889 Burton and Useba purchased 160 acres of sec. 6 of Gilmore Twp., Isabella County, MI. On this land Burton built a barn, and a small log cabin to which he moved his family. Later on Burton would build a much larger home for his family. Burton and Useba stayed on the farm until late in life when they moved to their daughter, Alta Bellinger's home in Grant Twp., Clare County, MI.

Alta cared for her parents until their deaths. Burton passed away May 5, 1947 and Useba

Nov. 28, 1951. They were both laid to rest in Cherry Grove Cemetery, Clare, MI.

ALLEN-OLSON. Steven Kenneth Allen was born Nov. 7, 1956 at Central Michigan Community Hospital. His parents were Grant Kenneth and Velma Jean (Ewing) Allen. He lived with his parents and sister Darcy (Allen) Straus at 716 Neier Rd. on the west side of Mt. Pleasant. When he was young he attended Ganiard Elementary School, then went to West Intermediate School, then onto Mt. Pleasant High school, from which he graduated in 1975.

He can't begin to describe all of the great times he had growing up in Mt. Pleasant. The neighbors he had on Neier Street can only be described as super. He thinks back on how the adults looked out for all of them, and how all the kids used to play together. It was a great beginning. As he went off to the intermediate school and high school, and left the neighborhood school behind, he started to develop a lot of friendships outside of the neighborhood, some of these friendships still exist today.

Thanks to his parents, he and his sister were able to spend summers on Littlefield Lake at the home his dad was building for their retirement.

These too were some very special times, a lot of swimming, skiing, bonfires on the weekends, and friends from all over the state.

During his freshman year at high school he started his first official job at the old McDonalds that used to be on Mission street. He worked there until his senior year. His first job after high school was at Arby's, not a great start, but a start; from there he went on to the Holiday Inn, then finally to Ferro Manufacturing. He spent two years working on the assembly line at Ferro. He remembers coming home from work one day and his dad asked him if he would like to go to college. It turned out that his father's disability from the Korean War would allow him to go to college under the GI Bill. Steve told him he wasn't sure. Then he got his senses about him and went off to Ferris.

He arrived at Ferris in September 1978 and turned 22 two months later. He enrolled in the School of Allied Health in the Occupational Safety and Health program. He spent four fantastic years at Ferris. He worked at Schubergs Bar on Michigan Avenue for three years until graduation in 1982. While at Ferris he joined the Pi Kappa Alpha fraternity; he never in his wildest dreams thought he would ever be in a fraternity, but it was an excellent time with some great friendships made.

After college he went to work at the Midland Nuclear plant, and spent two years in the Safety Dept. until the plant shut down. He has had a number of jobs around Michigan working in construction safety. He can't begin to tell you how many of the hospitals, factories, office buildings, roads, and bridges he has worked on in this state. He finally figured out that working in the construction industry had its ups and downs, so he went to work for the insurance industry as a risk control specialist (construction). He presently works for St. Paul Insurance out of his home just outside of Rockford, MI.

In 1985 he met his wife, Barbara Olson, daughter of Donald and Irene (Carbonneau) Olson, at a softball game while he was living in

Lansing, MI. They dated for a few years and were married on May 5, 1990 in Manistee, MI (Barbs hometown). They started their life together in an apartment in Grandville, MI. In 1991 they purchased their first home on Ramsdell Drive outside of Rockford, MI. This home is in the country about half way between Rockford and Greenville. They still live in the same house today.

On Feb. 19, 1993, they started their family with the birth of Alaina Leigh Allen. They thought they did a

Steve Allen in back, Alaina and Mara in center, front is Barbara, Kenna and Eva, 2001

pretty good job with Alaina, so they had Mara Anne on Oct. 25, 1994, Eve Meredith on Oct. 15, 1996, and Kenna Faye on Nov. 22, 1998. They were blessed with four perfectly beautiful girls. The girls attend Lincoln Heights School in the Greenville school system.

This brings us up to February 27, 2002. Barb and Steve are presently very involved with the day-to-day operations of rearing four daughters. Steve is also getting back into doing his family genealogy from which he gets a great deal of satisfaction. He has discovered that he is a direct descendent of John M. and Elizabeth (Brown) Hursh, the first family of Mt. Pleasant, and Ambrose P. and Mary (LaFromboise) Allen, another founding family of Mt. Pleasant. He has also learned that he has an ancestor, on the Ewing side of his family, who was with Admiral Perry in the Battle of Lake Erie.

This looks like a good place to close. He wishes he could go on with all of his experiences up until now, all 45 years of them, but there is limited space here.

ALLEN-SHERMAN-LAFROMBOISE. Ambrose Peter (Yankee) Allen was born Dec. 11, 1814 near Troy, Wayne County, NY. At this time it is believed his mother's name was Sophia and his stepfather was Elijah Hill of Macedon, NY. His father is unknown at this time.

Ambrose has the distinction of being one of the "Pioneer Settlers" of Michigan. Ambrose purchased land in Hillsdale County (Oct. 17, 1835) prior to Michigan becoming a state in 1837.

On Oct. 7, 1839 Ambrose sold the Hillsdale land while he was still living in Macedon, NY.

Sometime prior to 1843 Ambrose married Mary Sherman (believed to be in Macedon, NY). Ambrose and Mary purchased a farm on March 4, 1843 in sec. 28, Madison Twp., Lenawee County, MI. On May 16, 1844 Ambrose and Mary's daughter Maria Jane was born, tragically though, Mary would not survive childbirth and passed away two days after Maria was born. Maria J. would be sent to live with her grandparents, Sophia and Elijah Hill, in Macedon, NY.

On May 11, 1854 in Madison Twp. Lenawee County, Ambrose married Mary Raspberry LaFromboise. Mary LaFromboise was born May 13, 1823 in Montreal Canada. Mary was the daughter of Nicholas and Mary Josephete

(Fauteux) LaFromboise. Mary was also the sister of Felix LaFromboise, another resident and businessman of Mt. Pleasant.

Mary Allen, ca. 1885   *Ambrose Peter Allen*

Ambrose and Mary, his second wife, resided on the farm in Madison Twp. Lenawee County and started their family there.

Mary Ann Allen was born on Feb. 28, 1855. Mary Ann, after moving to Mt. Pleasant would marry J.D. Gulick from another founding family of Mt. Pleasant.

Burton Phillip was born Aug. 22, 1857 and Henry Edward Nov. 7, 1858. There were three other children who must have died prior to 1870, William, Joseph and Marian. Ambrose's daughter Maria J., from his first marriage, was also living with them in 1860.

Around 1860 the family moved to Genesee, Genesee County, MI area. Maria J. would marry Samuel Rhoades on Nov. 7, 1860 and stay on the family farm in Lenawee County.

Ambrose, Mary, Mary Ann, Burton and Henry would stay in Genesee County until Oct. 18, 1864 when he purchased 120 acres of Sec. 20 Union Twp. Isabella County, MI. This land is now Riverwood Golf Course. Ambrose purchased this land from John and Elizabeth Hursh, who have the distinction of being the first family of Mt. Pleasant. Steven Allen has learned that he is the ggg-grandson of John and Elizabeth Hursh on his Grandmother Flossie Winters side. So he is descended from two families that were pioneers of Mt. Pleasant. Ambrose and Mary would be his gg-grandparents.

Ambrose would spend the next 34 years of his life living on the section 20 farm. Through those years he purchased and sold a number of lots within the city limits of what is now Mt. Pleasant. Ambrose would end up selling 40 acres of the original farm to his daughter Mary and son-in-law J.D. Gulick, and also 40 acres to his son Burton. The remaining 80 acres was sold to his wife Mary on Dec. 26, 1882. After Ambrose died, Mary would sell this 80 to their son Henry and his wife Rebecca (Dibble).

Ambrose died on April 28, 1898 at the family farm, having reached the age of 83 years. Ambrose was laid to rest at Riverside Cemetery, Mt. Pleasant, MI. Ambrose was survived by his wife Mary; sons, Burton and Henry; and his first daughter Maria Jane who was now living in the Stanton area.

Mary would live until Dec. 20, 1903 also passing away at the family farm. Mary would be 80 years old at the time of her death. She was laid to rest at Riverside Cemetery next to Ambrose, and their daughter Mary Ann Gulick, who had passed away on Nov. 19, 1897. Ambrose and Mary are also mentioned in the Isabella County Biography Book published in 1982.

ALLEN-STRAUS. Darcy Jean Allen (b. Sept. 23, 1958 at Central Michigan Community Hospital), daughter of Grant Kenneth and Velma Jean (Ewing) Allen. Darcy attended school at Ganiard Elementary, West Intermediate, then graduated from Mt. Pleasant High School in 1976. She attended Central Michigan University for a short time after graduating from High School.

On June 16, 1978 she married Dennis Straus at St. Joseph's Church in Beal City, MI. Dennis (b. March 17, 1955) is the son of Gerald, and Katherine (Webber) Straus. Dennis lived just north of Beal City and graduated from Beal City High School in 1974.

After their marriage, Darcy and Dennis resided for a short time in Mt. Pleasant while their home north of Beal City was being built. Darcy and Dennis have four children, all were born at Central Michigan Community Hospital in Mt. Pleasant, MI.

1) Elizabeth Jean (b. Dec. 28, 1979) graduated from Ferris State University in the spring of 2002. She graduated with a bachelor's degree from their nursing program, and plans on working for Alma Hospital.

2) Jacob Gerald (b. July 10, 1981) is in his third year of electrical engineering at Ferris State University.

3) Sarah Katherine (b. July 21, 1984) graduated from Beal City High School in the spring of 2002. She plans on attending Western Michigan University.

4) Joshua Allen (b. Aug. 13, 1986) is in his sophomore year at Beal City High School.

Darcy returned to Mid-Michigan Community College and now is a registered nurse. Dennis has worked for Delfield Co. in Mt. Pleasant for a number of years. They presently reside at their home north of Beal City, MI.

ALLEN-UTLEY. Mary Eunice Allen (b. Aug. 22, 1887, Winn, MI, d. 1971) and Albert Jessie Allen (b. Oct. 1, 1877, Shepherd, MI, d. 1956) are both buried in Shepherd Cemetery.

Mary married Edward Utley in 1908, Isabella County, and he died in 1916. They had three boys, all born in Shepherd, MI: Lester (b. May 31, 1907, d. 1938); Ted (b. June 25, 1917, d. 1985); Vern (b. July 24, 1915.

Mary met Albert in Winn, MI. They married March 22, 1919 in Mt. Pleasant, MI and had four children, all born in Shepherd, MI:

Mary Eunice Garner-Utley-Allen and Albert Jessie Allen

Donna (b. Feb. 23, 1920); Retha (b. July 28, 1921, d. 1922); Tretha (b. Feb. 18, 1923); Kate (b. Dec. 26, 1925, d. 1986).

Albert was born and reared on the Allen homestead located west of Shepherd (now the Wonsey Farm). Rose (Allen) Wonsey was the sister of Albert. Our family moved to Lansing, MI in 1925. Albert worked at Rio Factory until 1929. He was laid off and forced to trade their home for a home in Shepherd, MI, where all of the children attended Shepherd High School.

Albert worked on a farm for $1 a day and was a caretaker of Shepherd Cemetery supporting their family of seven children.

Mary Allen was a midwife. When the children were growing up several families in Shepherd held square dances in their homes on Saturday nights for entertainment. The families always asked Mary to come play the organ. They would come with a trailer and pick up Mary's organ to use. There were three other people that played in the group, a violinist, guitarist, and drummer. All the children really enjoyed learning how to square dance at an early age.

ALLEN-WHITEHEAD-GALLANT. Tretha June Allen (b. Feb. 18, 1923, Shepherd, MI) attended Shepherd schools and married George Whitehead Sept. 24, 1939. They had six children and lived in and around the Shepherd area, the older children attending Shepherd High School.

Children are Robert (b. Aug. 1, 1940, Shepherd); Shirley (b. Oct. 6, 1941, Shepherd, d. 1962), buried in Shepherd Cemetery; Jerry (b. August 1942, Alma, MI, d. 1942), buried in Shepherd Cemetery; Duane (b. Oct. 13, 1944, Shepherd); Judy (b. July 15, 1946, Alma, MI); Lois (b. Oct. 4, 1947, Alma, MI).

Tretha and George divorced in 1949. In 1950 she met Harold Gallant, who worked at Ferro Stamping Co. in Mt. Pleasant. They married in 1950 and moved to Illinois in 1951, both worked at Bendix Aviation until 1955. They then decided to move to California where jobs were plentiful and education for the children was free. Both worked at North American Aviation until 1962.

Tragedy struck their household when oldest daughter Shirley passed away leaving three small children: Kathy age 4, Paula age 3 and Mark age 2. Assuming responsibility of raising her children, they returned to Mt. Pleasant, MI until 1967. The children attended school in Mt. Pleasant, MI. In 1968 they returned to California. Harold worked at Hughes Aircraft and Tretha at Interstate Electronics in Anaheim, CA until 1988 when they retired.

After successfully raising eight children they are now living in Las Vegas, NV, enjoying 17 grandchildren and 26 great-grandchildren, all of whom visit often. Harold and Tretha come to Shepherd every summer. Donna Bunker and Tretha are the only living children left in the Allen family.

ALLEN-WINTER. Elmer Victor Allen (b. June 19, 1885 in Deerfield Twp., Isabella County, MI) was the son of Burton Phillip and Useba (Myers) Allen. In 1889 Elmer moved with his father, mother and sister Alta to Gilmore Twp., Isabella County.

On June 28, 1919 Elmer was granted a land patent for 320 acres in section 29 of the Willamette Meridian, OR, after homesteading this land for three years. Elmer sold this land and returned to the family farm in Gilmore Twp., where he purchased 80 acres from his father and another 80 just north of the family farm. A few years later Elmer traded his 80 north of the family farm to his sister Alta, for the 80 she had that included the original farmhouse and outbuildings.

1957: Velma, Kenneth, Edith, Gerold, Al, Mom, Dad, Stevie, Betty, Maria, Louis, Larry, Aunt Alta and Barbara.

On Sept. 18, 1920 Elmer married Flossie Florence Winter in Farwell, MI. Flossie was born on May 7, 1896 in Surrey Twp., Clare County, MI (just south of Farwell), the daughter of Sterling Asa, and Josephene (Brown) Winter.

To this union four children were born: Edith Marjorie (Wicks) (b. 1925), Leona J. (Gott) (b. 1928), Grant Kenneth (b. 1930), and Mary Luella (Sherman) (b. 1939).

Elmer passed away at Central Michigan Community Hospital on Dec. 27, 1957, and was laid to rest at Gilmore Twp. Cemetery.

After Elmer's passing Flossie sold 120 acres of the old farm and moved next door to her daughter Leona and her family near Winn, MI. Flossie passed away at Alma Hospital on Nov. 5, 1977, and was laid to rest next to Elmer at Gilmore Twp. Cemetery.

ANDERSON-RANKIN. Gary Lee Anderson (b. March 12, 1958 in Flint, MI), the eldest son of Loren Earl Anderson (b. 1936) and Ruthann (Sanders) Barnes (b. 1940). His two brothers, Bruce Alan (b. 1959) and Mark Edward (b. 1964) were born in Mt. Pleasant, MI.

He came to Mt. Pleasant at a few months old when his father took a position with Lynn's Printing Service. An eye injury at the age of five left him mostly blind in the right eye and has accounted for lots of bumping into things over the years. While attending Mt. Pleasant Senior High he was co-drum major for the marching and pep bands. He is a graduate of CMU with a bachelor and master's degree in industrial management and technology. He has worked as senior computer repair technician and programmer analyst for CMU and teaches electronics for the Mt. Pleasant Area Technical Center, CMU, and the Saginaw Chippewa Tribal College.

In 1984 he was introduced to Kathleen Elizabeth Rankin (b. Aug. 19, 1961 in King City, CA). Her father, Delbert Eugene Rankin, and mother, Marilyn Francis (Westphal) had five additional children: Michael Norman, Belinda Garnet (Thrush), Pauline Margaret (Beutler), Edward Eugene and Mathew Eric. Kathy came to the Rosebush area in 1973 and later attended Michigan State University. Kathy has worked as a medical receptionist and is

Gary, Kathy and daughter Rachelle Anderson

getting into the antique business. On Aug. 30, 1986 they were married at the First Church of the Nazarene in Mt. Pleasant, MI which required a loan of $5.00 for gas to get there on time.

Rachelle Kristine Anderson (b. March 8, 1989 in Mt. Pleasant, MI) has excelled in school and made many friends as well as receiving an award for volunteer work.

ANDERSON-ROACH. Albert Gustov Anderson's maternal and paternal grandparents all came from Stockholm, Sweden. His father was Gustov Anderson and mother was Mary Andersen. They met on the ship as their families were on the way to Ellis Island. They settled near Rodney, MI and farmed for many years. They had five sons and three daughters. Albert G., as he was known, was one of the middle sons and was born in 1901. He became a barber and migrated to Pontiac, MI. He owned a 12 chair barber and beauty shop. Marguerite Roach worked for him and they were married in 1928.

Marguerite and Albert Anderson

Marguerite's grandparents came from Ireland and were ship builders. She was born in Newport News, VA in 1905. She had a sister Cecilia, a brother John Roach and a half brother Larry Booth. Their father John Roach was killed in France in WWI. Her mother Genevieve "Jenny" was an O'brien. She was a nurse and moved her family to Detroit and later the Bay City, MI area after her husband was killed. Marguerite had two sons, Frederick and Roland Pelton, by her first marriage.

In 1930 the Depression changed many lives and they lost their home and business in Pontiac and moved to Mt. Pleasant. They had three children: Patricia (b. 1930 at Pontiac), Dale (b. 1933) and Dave (b. 1935), both born in Mt. Pleasant. During the depression few people had cars so Albert walked to work in rain or snow. It was quite a walk as by then he had bought a home at 1212 W. Broadway.

Albert worked as a barber in the 1/2 basement of the Park Hotel on the NW corner of Main and Broadway. It had an outside stairway and when it rained, he sometimes had to stand in water cutting hair! He made $6-10 a week unless he traded haircuts for chickens or other items. Once a man traded a violin for cutting hair for his nine kids. Patsy learned to play it. Dr. Davis got haircuts in exchange for delivering Dale and Dave and also tending to family medical needs.

He studied geology nights at Central State Teacher's College, now CMU. He learned quite a bit about oil and gas and did leasing for Sun Oil Co. In 1939 Albert joined with Cliff Collins, along with several other men including a Mr.

Howard, owner of Polly's Market, investing in oil leases and wells. They made it big with a "gusher" in the oil city field. Oil was a booming business then.

Albert bought a large Victorian home on E. Broadway with 14 acres and a barn, across from Collin's Meat Market in 1941 and sold the little one on W. Broadway. The oil business helped many Mt. Pleasant people out of the depression. He bought a car and Patsy got her first new dress and coat that weren't hand-me-downs from her cousins. She also got a riding horse and Dale and Dave had a Shetland pony. Patsy had her own room and thought it was heaven even if snow sifted through the upstairs window and a glass of water would freeze on a shelf.

When WWII came along Albert had ordered a new car and a new bike for Patsy, but those kind of things were frozen for the duration and couldn't be delivered. Also there was meat and sugar rationing, gas and tires too. Older brother Ronnie at 18 was in the Marines and badly injured on Iwo Jima. He died at 47 from all the shrapnel he had. Dale at 17 was in the Navy in the Korean War. His ship was sunk and he barely survived.

He spent a year in the hospital in Japan from his injuries and was awarded many medals for serving his country. Today he lives in Mt. Pleasant but after strokes, he is in a wheelchair. Dave passed away at age 62 near Spokane, WA of cancer. Albert died at age 69 and Marguerite passed away at 45 of cancer. Patsy and Dale are the only ones living at this time. Patsy married Maurice John Jr. May 28, 1976.

ANDERSON-SAGE-CLARK. Marion Lewis Sage (b. 1873, d. 1958) was the son of Mark Lewis Sage (b. 1851, d. 1874) and Mary Jane (Liverton) Sage (b. 1853, d. 1908). He had two brothers, Alonzo Amos (b. 1872, d. 1951) and Harry Septer (b. 1875, d. 1944).

Mark Lewis was a traveling minister who was away much of the time. He died in 1874 of typhoid fever, leaving his family destitute. In 1875 Mary married Frank Anderson. They had a daughter named Elsie.

In December 1878 the Anderson family left Ionia County to move to a farm in Fremont Twp. They bought 80 acres of Sec. 24 Fremont Twp. from the Lou Hetherington family.

It took two days to move their belongs by sleigh and a team of horses. There were no roads anywhere only a few trails that criss-crossed across the township. The post office was at Strickland which was two and one half miles to the northeast of their home. Mail came about every 10 days.

The first winter was difficult with no feed for the cows and chickens and little food for themselves. In 1879 Frank cleared land to raise feed for his livestock. He used logs to enlarge the house and built a night corral for his cows. There were no fences, so they roamed the woods during the day. They were milked in the open with no restraints which often involved a bit of pursuit.

As youngsters, they attended the Davis School located to the northeast of their farm.

Lewis helped on the farm in the summer by farming and splitting logs into rails to build fences. In the winter he worked in the lumbering woods, cutting in the upper peninsula, to get money to buy his clothes, returning home in the spring to help on the farm.

Frank passed away in 1900. Lewis continued to work on the farm for his mother until her death in the spring of 1908. Lewis bought the farm from the heirs.

On June 24, 1908 he married Iva May Clark, daughter of Fortunatus and Josephine (Rick) Clark, one of Dushville (Winn) residents. They were the parents of two daughters: Verl Irene (b. 1910, d. 1989) md. Ora Walkington (b. 1908, d. 1989) and lived near Portland, MI. Lucille Vivian (b. 1911, d. 1987) md. James Roy Elkins (b. 1915, d. 1970) and lived near Mt. Pleasant. They each had six children.

He served Fremont Twp. as treasurer, justice of the peace, and sat on the election board for many years. He was a member of the Davis School board, also a member of the IOOF Lodge. She was a member of the same organization as a Rebekah.

They sold the farm in the spring of 1942 to Vern and Winifred Hetherington, a descendant of the original owners of the farm. They moved to Lake O'Dessa where she passed away Nov. 7, 1950 and he on Oct. 18, 1958.

ANDERSON-TAYLOR.

Thomas Earl Anderson was born Dec. 9, 1901 in Merrill, MI, the son of Loren Edward Anderson (b. 1868, d. 1942) and Charlotte Georgina (Woollard) (b. 1874, d. 1969). Earl had one sister, Laura M. (Yours, Griffin, Archimbald) (b. 1894, d. ?). Earl moved to Shepherd to work at the *Isabella Republican* newspaper. While in the county he met and married Doris Fern Taylor on April 20, 1927.

Doris was born a twin on March 13, 1908 in Weidman, MI. She and her twin brother Donald Claude (b. 1908, d. 1992) were the only children of Cyrus Claude Taylor (b. 1883, d. 1975) and Lilie Fern Sickels (b. 1886, d. 1949). After an early career as a mail carrier, Earl worked as printer having started with the Merrill Monitor in 1916 as a "printers devil." He was employed as a printer at Central Printers, *The Times News* and *The Central Michigan Tribune* in Mt. Pleasant. Doris was a secretary at Central Michigan College and was involved with the operation of the family printing business.

Doris Fern (Taylor) Anderson and Thomas Earl Anderson

Doris and Earl had five children: Charlotte June Knopp (b. 1929), Donald Vaughn (b. 1931, d. 1998), Loren Earl (b. 1936), Leland David (b. 1940), and John Wesley (b. 1947). After leaving Mt. Pleasant the Andersons owned newspapers in Tekonsha and Breckenridge, MI and a shopping guide in Highland, MI. Earl also worked for Slade Printing in Pontiac and the Edmore

Advertiser in Edmore where he also founded Anderson Printing. Earl, not finding a hand soap that was able to do the job, made a soap from an old recipe of basic ingredients which he mixed at home. It had the consistency and cleaning power much like current day gojo. He marketed this product for printers and mechanics in local stores including Alswedes Grocery. Earl passed away June 2, 1980 in Mt. Pleasant, MI. Doris passed away April 8, 1985 in Mt. Pleasant.

The family printing tradition continued with Loren entering the trade at the *Holly Herald* in 1949 and then moving to Mt. Pleasant joining Lynn's Printing Service, publisher of the Buyers Guide. He then became the first Graphic Arts teacher at the new Technical Center in Mt. Pleasant in 1968.

He operated Standard Printing on Broadway where all three sons assisted with the printing of wedding invitations and napkins. He and his wife Denise founded PrinTech in 1984. Son Mark worked for the *Morning Sun* then PrintTech as production manager and currently is employed by E & S Graphics in Ithaca. Their daughters Carrie, Kelly and Laura and Niece Tracy worked for PrintTech while attending school. Two grandchildren, Rachelle and Zack volunteer their services on a part-time basis at PrintTech.

John worked at Anderson Printing and upon Earl and Doris' retirement, he and his wife Joanne (Dykstra) purchased the business that they operated until its sale in 2001.

Don and his wife Joyce (Gable) purchased a Sir Speedy franchise in St. Charles, IL upon Don's retirement from American Oil and operated it until his death. Their son and daughter-in-law purchased the franchise and continue the family tradition.

June's husband, Wayne Knopp, left Haliburton to work as press operator at the Buyer's Guide in Mt. Pleasant. He then worked for PrintTech until his retirement. June worked for Del's Photo Shop/The Picture Place until retirement.

Lee worked for a number of years for Anderson Printing in Edmore. Lee is currently a machinist and he and his wife, Linda (Carrick), live at Coldwater Lake.

ANTHONY-METHNER.

Ann Delores (Methner) Anthony (b. Aug. 20, 1932 in Wise Twp., Isabella County) is the seventh child of William Methner (b. April 3, 1888 in Midland County) and Emma (Gilbert) Methner (b. Sept. 22, 1896 in Isabella County). She has two brothers, William Vernell (b. June 11, 1918) and Lavern Gilbert (b. Jan. 11, 1920) and six sisters: Velma Frances (b. Nov. 10, 1921), Ruth Doris (b. Oct. 1. 1924), Alta Mae (b. Jan. 11, 1928), Joan Lea (b. Feb. 3, 1930, Kathleen Nellie (b. Nov. 30, 1933) and Phyllis Pauline (b. May 15, 1935).

They lived on a 40-acre farm and Ann went to Orr School, which was a one-room country school through the eighth grade. She graduated from Coleman High School in 1951 and started working for Dow Corning Corporation in Midland immediately after graduation.

She married Clifford Anthony on July 24, 1952 whom she met in high school. He was born Aug. 19, 1931 in Midland, MI. They have three children: Julie Ann (b. June 18, 1957), Michael

John (b. Aug. 19, 1959) and Eric Robert (b. May 16, 1962).

Cliff graduated from Coleman High School in 1950, served two years in the Army and went to work for Dow Chemical Co. until retiring in 1986 as a journeyman in refrigeration and air conditioning. After retirement from Dow Chemical Co. Cliff and Ann moved to Florida, where they currently reside.

ASSMAN-HOUSE.

In the 1940s Esther (House) Assman, her husband Henry, their two sons, Norman and Warren, and a daughter Elizabeth, moved from New York to Mt. Pleasant. For Esther it was coming home as she was born and reared in the Rosebush area.

This was during WWII and dealing in scrap was a big business. Henry stated a scrap yard at the address of 3798 South Mission. There is a small mall and gas station there now. He bought everything from old wash tubs to old cars. Soon a customer needed glass for his car, then another. Thus started the Auto Glass business, and the scrap yard was cleaned up.

Soon people and businesses needed house glass replaced. A couple of businesses they did that are still in town was, Ric's, and Archey Brothers car sales, which is now Murray Distributing Co.

In the late 60s Norman wanted to go into the carpet business, so they added on to the building, and the Auto Glass, and Assmann's Inc. split. In the 70s all the property and buildings were sold and the businesses moved to different parts of town. Therein lies two more stories: Mt. Pleasant Auto Glass and Flag Shop and Assmann's Carpet and Paint.

BACON-RIFE-GILLETTE-DREW.

Birdie L. Bacon was born in Lenawee County, MI in 1870 to William J. and Helen Lucinda (Chase) Bacon. They moved to Virginia with their children Birdie, May and Bret sometime in the 1880s because Helen had a "lung condition." William had loved Virginia when he was there during the Civil War and felt that the mountains and the pure air would be of benefit to Helen. (He also had a

Joseph Rife and Birdie Bacon

"wandering foot.") She died there not long after they were settled.

Birdie married Joseph Rife and they lived in Charlottesville where their son Nello Franklin was born in 1881. When he was very small, Birdie and May got on the train and came back to Michigan, leaving William and brother Bret in Virginia.

Birdie then married Myron Gillette, who was a salesman for one of the distilleries in Detroit and had another son, Myron (Mike). She divorced Myron and she and Nello and Mike came to Two Rivers (Caldwell) in Isabella County where they lived for a time with her uncle, Henry Bacon, and his wife "Ran." Henry had a sawmill on the Coldwater River where it joins the Chippewa just south of River Road. Traces of the millrace can still be found.

Birdie worked as cooks helper in the lumber camps in the area and then went to "keep house" for Peter J. Drew, who had the farm which lies north of the cemetery. They married in 1909 and daughter Mary Helen was born March 3, 1910. Peter died in 1944. Birdie lived until 1953. They are both buried in the Two Rivers Cemetery.

BATTLE-MCGUIRE-MCCONNELL.
The Battles, McGuires and McConnells were early residents of northern Isabella County. They settled (and descendants still remain) near Rosebush, and were among the founders of St. Henry's Catholic Church.

It is believed that James Battle and Patrick McGuire were natives of County Mayo, Ireland. In the early 1830s they emigrated to Quebec and settled in Terrebonne County, north of Montreal. It is likely they and their sons farmed in the summer and logged during the long winters. James' son James and Patrick McGuire, Junior first came to Michigan as loggers in the mid-1860s They must have liked what they saw, as both families emigrated to Michigan between 1869 and 1872.

The younger James Battle, along with his widowed mother, Winifred Haley, brother Francis, and sisters Anna McKenna, Rose Levierier, and Winifred Scully, emigrated from Quebec first to Clinton, Iowa, probably in 1868. James didn't stay there long, as he was found in Isabella County in the 1870 census.

Most of his siblings remained in Iowa or emigrated further west; only his sister Anna, Anna's husband Christopher McKenna, and three of their children (Margaret, who married Dominic McGuire, Catherine, who married William Clark, and Frank, who married Mary Greff Flannery) came back to Michigan. James first settled on the Sl/2 of the NW1/4 of Sec. 36, Vernon Twp. They later bought the El/2 of the NEl/4 of Sec. 35, and part of Sec. 26.

James Battle (b. 1829, d. 1893) md. Julia McGuire (b. 1840, d. 1928) in Quebec in 1862; their three eldest children (Francis, Patrick and Catherine) were born in Canada, the remainder (Mary, Rose, James, Anna and Margaret) in Michigan. James lived the rest of his life in the Vernon Township farm, dying unexpectedly near Christmas 1893. Julia outlived her husband by 35 years, and was still walking long distances between her childrens' farms not long before her death at age 88.

Francis Battle (b. 1863, d. 1943) md. Elizabeth McConnell (b. 1870, d. 1940). He was a farmer and later worked for the Isabella County Road Commission, living for several years in Mount Pleasant. As a reward for his work on the highway, the road running past the old homestead was named after him, and Battle Road can still be found off Mission Road. Writer of this history is the grandson of Frank Battle's only son Francis. His father was born in the old homestead on Battle Road, but raised in Ontario before returning to Michigan during WWII.

Two of Frank Battle's sisters married brothers of his wife: Mary Agnes Battle (b. 1871, d. 1964) md. Dan McConnell (b. 1868, d. 1931) and Anna Battle (b. 1876, d. 1952) md. Joseph

McConnell (b. 1867, d. 1943). Patrick Battle (b. 1865, d. 1939) md. Mary Radey (b. 1876, d. 1954), Catherine Battle (b. 1867, d. 1923) md. Dan Walker (b. 1860, d. 1923), Rose Ellen Battle (b. 1880, d. 1937) md. Frank Scott (b. 1875, d. 1941), and Margaret Battle (b. 1883, d. 1946) md. James Morrison (b. 1880, d. 1931). James (b. 1873, d. 1898) never married. When all was said and done, Francis Battle had 40 first cousins! Many descendants remain in the area.

BAUGHMAN-BAILEY-MYERS-ZUKER.
The George Washington Myers family consisted of wife Margaret and six children: Sarah, Anne, Mary, Margaret, Lucinda and Daniel. They came to Michigan from Ohio in the fall of 1867. The family made the trip by wagon, settling in Chippewa Twp. where they cleared 40 acres and built a home. Later they moved to Mt. Pleasant and bought a house at 408 South Normal Avenue (now called University). They lived there until their deaths many years later.

Margaret Swickard Myers was born Feb. 21, 1823 in Jefferson County, OH and died in 1915 at the age on 92.

George Myers (b. 1816 in Cumberland, PA) at some point moved to Ohio. He served in Co. A 32nd Ohio Infantry during the Civil War, was wounded and captured at Harpers Ferry. He died at his home in Mt. Pleasant in February 1896 at the age of 81.

Lucinda Jane "Lou" Myers (b. 1861, d. 1944), the second eldest of the Myers children, married Charles H. Bailey, Feb. 14, 1879.

Charles H. Bailey (b. 1852, d. 1942) came from Jordan, NY, at age 16, arriving with his parents in southern Michigan shortly after the Civil War. He later made his way to Mt. Pleasant in 1871, when the population was only 300. Charles established a painting and decorating business in 1872, which remained in the family until the 1950s. He served as sheriff in the early 1900s, as well as held other town and county offices.

Herbert E.R. Bailey (b. 1879, d. 1964), the only child of Charles and Lou, was one of four graduates who received the first Life Certificates given at Central Michigan Normal School in 1902. Herb married Emily Mae Snider (b. 1879, d. 1956) in Mt. Pleasant on June 30, 1903. They had two children, Charles H. Bailey Jr. (b. 1908, d. 1993) and Lura Ann (b. 1907, d. 1977). Lura married a local man, Alva D. Rahl.

Charles H. Bailey Jr. met Agnes Marie Peters (b. 1905, d. 1992) while both were students at Central Michigan Normal School. Agnes graduated in December 1927, with a primary education degree. They were married on March 9, 1929 and had two daughters: Joan A. (b. June 9, 1930) and Sue Ann (b. June 9, 1934). Chuck, a retired boilermaker, and Agnes lived in Nokomis, FL after his retirement in 1972.

Sue Ann married a local man, Gale E. Pickens, in 1954. They have four children: Ivan, Kandie, Karla and Kathy. Gale is the son of Albert and the late Beatrice Pickens.

High School sweethearts, Joan A. and Ralph Jordan Baughman (who had moved to Mt. Pleasant in 1945) were married in the Mt. Pleasant Methodist Church July 29, 1951. Ralph is the son of the late Edith Merle Baughman Olsen and the stepson of the late Carl F. Olsen.

Even though they moved around the country while Ralph served in the U.S. Air Force (Korean Conflict), Joan managed to come back to Mt. Pleasant for the births of their three children: Cindy Lou (b. 1952), Cheri Lynn (b. 1955) and Mark Jordan (b. 1956).

Four generations, 1931: Standing l-r: Charles H. Bailey Jr., Lucinda Myers Bailey, Herbert E.R. Bailey. Sitting: Charles H. Bailey Sr. holding baby Joan Bailey (now Baughman).

In January 1962 Ralph became a partner with Sammy P. Pishos in Central Accounting and Tax Service, which brought the Baughman family back to Mt. Pleasant as residents again. With the family now back in the area, Joan resumed her studies at Central Michigan University, graduating in 1975. Ralph is a 1956 graduate of Michigan State University.

During the 22 years Ralph was in business in Mt. Pleasant he served with several civic and professional organizations, including Trustee and Board Chairman of Central Michigan Community Hospital.

Joan and Ralph have retired to their cottage on Blue Lake in Mecosta County during the summer, and New Port Richey, FL during the winter months.

Cheri Baughman Sjoberg lives in Mt. Pleasant and works at Central Michigan University.

Mark J. Baughman lives in Mt. Pleasant and works locally.

In 1972 Cindy Baughman married a local man, Phillip Joseph "Joe" Zuker. They have two sons: Brian Joseph (b. 1974) and Jeffery Jordan (b. 1977). Joe is the son of Norman and the late Donna Zuker. Cindy works for General Ins. Agency Co.

Brian lives and is working in the Mt. Pleasant area.

Jeffery Zuker lives in Mt. Pleasant and is married to Veronica "Vicky" Burgess. They are the parents of two little girls, Joslyne (b. 1998) and Jordan (b. 2001), who have become the eight generation to reside in the Mt. Pleasant area.

BAUGHMAN-DAVIDSON.
John Alvas Baughman (b. 1857, d. 1946) and Mary Ann Davidson (b. 1865, d. 1941) were married Jan. 14, 1883 in Putman County, Leipsic, OH. Around 1905 they moved to Michigan, settling in the Alamando area. The children attended the Alamando School. Later they moved to a farm in Wise Twp. near the village of Loomis. The younger children attended the Loomis School. Their children were Mary Margurett "Maggie," Clara, George, Fred, Theodore, Chester, Nancy Viola, Daisy, Otho and Edward Delos.

Mary Marguriett married Clark Allison. Their children are Ora, Cecille (Mrs. Wells

Johnson), Harley, Vernon, Willis, Violet (Mrs. Charles Price), and Leta (Mrs. Walter Sowers). Clara married Wheeler Brown. Their children are Stella, Charles, Wilbur, Robert, Mary (Mrs. Russell Hall), Dale and Don. George married Pearl Lamping. Their child was Helen (Mrs. Ervin Searight).

Theodore married Melissa Swan. They farmed in Wise Twp., later moving to Mt. Pleasant where he was employed in the oil fields and by Hafer Oil Co. Chester married Zelda Harris. Nancy Viola married Albert Vorce. She taught school in Wise and Maple Grove Schools. She had a son, David. Daisy married Edward Methner and resided on a farm in Wise Twp. Their children are Kathryn (Mrs. Lester Fike) and Isabella (Mrs. Peter Dominguez). Otho married Grace Childs in Detroit and worked at Ford Motor Co. before moving to Mt. Pleasant and working in the oil fields. Their children are Robert, Joyce and Adelia. Delos married Fern Methner and lived in Detroit and worked at Ford Motor Co. After Fern's death, he married Mildred Childs and they lived in Detroit before moving to Pratts Lake, North Bradley, and Coleman area, and working at Dow Chemical Co.

BAUGHMAN-METHNER. Alta Fern (b. Oct. 18, 1907, in Wise Twp., Isabella County, MI) was Frederick and Pauline Methner's fifth daughter and the "baby of the family" (a daughter was born in May 1909; however, she died three months later).

l-r: Alta Fern, Emma, Mrs. Methner, Caroline "Carrie" and Susie, probably in mid-1920s

Fern attended Orr School in Wise Twp. In her autobiography (written during her senior year at Coleman High School), she stated that because her parents thought she was too young to enter high school at age 13, she attended eighth grade at Orr School for a second year. She wrote the county examination at the end of each year (1921 and 1922) and received a diploma after each writing. In the fall of 1922 she entered Coleman High School and graduated in the spring of 1926. After completing high school, she attended a business college in Fort Wayne, IN, where she developed her secretarial skills.

Again from her autobiography, Fern tells about lightening striking the family's barn on Labor Day 1912 and it's burning to the ground. The animals and some tools were saved, but all the grain, hay and other provisions for winter were lost. Nineteen barns in the Coleman area were struck by lightening and burned that same day.

Fern also spoke about the grief and loss the family experienced when her father died in April 1925. She was a junior in high school at that time.

Like most of the Methner children, Fern loved music and became quite an accomplished violinist. She and her sister Emma, who accompanied her on the piano, would spend hours playing during the evenings. This was a great joy to their parents and the others in the family.

Fern was a happy, good-natured child and young woman. She thoroughly enjoyed her family, school years, and music and was looking forward to a joyous future.

After completion of her schooling in Fort Wayne, Fern returned to Coleman and soon married Delos Baughman. On November 22, 1933, Fern gave birth to their son; however, there were serious complications during the birthing process and Fern (age 26) and the baby died on that day. Her sister Emma believed that Fern's death, so soon after the loss of their father, was too great for their mother Pauline and that grief shortened her life (she died in July 1934).

BELL-LITTLE. William Henry Bell married Halcien Little on Sept 3, 1893. W.H. or Henry, as many called him, was born July 16, 1874 in Montgomery County, IN and Halcien was born Nov. 18, 1875.

Halcien and Rev. W.H. Bell

They began their married life as farmers in Indiana and Illinois. In 1912 Mr. Bell decided to enter the ministry; he read, studied and took bible instruction by mail. Reverend Bell's first official pulpit was in Lucerne, IN. The second church he served was near Evart, MI. The family lived at what was known as the "flowing well" farm and for some of the children, it was the first time they had seen inside plumbing. W.H and Halcien were absorbed and dedicated to the life of the Church of Christ and to the lives of the members, as well as all people in the communities in which they lived.

The Bells had six children: Russell (b. 1894), Maurine (b. 1897), Dorothy (b. 1905), Beatrice (b. 1907), Helen (b. 1911) and Betty LaRue (b. 1927).

Churches that the Bells served were in Lucerne, Covington and Crawfordsville, IN; Henning, IL; Evart and Lapeer, MI and Deerfield Center in Lapeer; as well as Alma Christian Church and Forest Hills in Gratiot County; Coe Church of Christ in Coe Twp., Isabella County and Orchard Avenue Church of Christ in Shepherd.

Reverend Bell was highly respected for his kindness, caring and his love of God. He was pleased at his popularity for weddings, church activities, and substitute preaching. After his formal retirement from the ministry, he began custodial duties at Shepherd Public School where he was loved by the children and staff members. In 1952 the high school yearbook was dedicated to Rev. Bell.

The Bells owned a home east of Shepherd and a cottage at Rock Lake near the Rock Lake Christian Assembly. Halcien died Oct. 1, 1953 and Rev. Bell died Oct 9, 1968.

BELLINGAR-MULL. William R. Bellingar of Lincoln Twp., Isabella County and Lydia Mull of Fremont Twp., Isabella County were married and reared six sons and one daughter. Scott married Etta Carr but died before his third child was born.

l-r: Sarah Mull, Scott Bellingar, Lydia Bellingar (child), Lena Bellingar, about 1900

Oren married his brother's widow and raised his children with his own. Anson never married, Elmer married Alta Johnson but had no children. Lucious married Clara Brown and had seven children. Luella married Grant Curtis and had twins. All the Bellingars were farmers in Isabella County.

In 1909 William Franklin and Ethel Clark were married and lived on several rented farms. They had five sons: Claremont (b. Jan 23 1910) md. Ruth Young and had four daughters; William Franklin Jr. (b. April 7, 1911) md. Marian Wheeler and had three children; Thomas (b. June 8, 1912) md. Angeline Parker, had two children and divorced; Ronald (b. Oct 20 1915) served in WWII, married Dorothy Kile and had three daughters; Kenneth (b. Sept. 5, 1918) md. Betty Keck and had four children.

In 1929 William and Ethel bought a farm on Wing Road from Ethel's mother, Laura Scott. Daughter Violet was born July 7, 1924. Another son Robert (b. Dec 4, 1927) served in Japan with the occupation army. He married Donna Earl and had nine children. Violet and Robert were the only ones of this family who remained in Isabella County.

On Deerfield Rd. stood the one room country school all the Bellingar children attended, as had Ethel before them and Violet's daughters after them. It is now a residence.

Violet married Cecil Potter shortly after his return from WWII, and together they took over the farm. They continued to live there until 1961 when they moved to Jordan Rd. near Beal City. Daughter Leila (b. Dec. 19, 1946) md. Maynard

Sansote, has two children and lives near Pestoskey, MI. A second daughter Rosanne (b. Feb. 9, 1948) md. and divorced Ed Smith. She has two sons and lives in Alaska.

There are still many Bellingars living and working in Isabella County.

BELLINGAR-MULL-DAVIS. Edward Bellingar was born Sept. 8, 1844 in Defiance County, OH. When he was a baby, his parents moved to Hillsdale County, MI. In 1861, at the age of 17, Edward and his father came to Lincoln Twp. They homesteaded a quarter-section of wild land. Edward eventually owned 250 acres in Sections 4 and 5. He had a stock and grain barn, which had cost $1,500, and a very large brick home that cost $2,000, to build. When he was a child, he received an injury to one knee, the only way he could walk was with the aid of crutches. This didn't hinder him from doing what was necessary to make his land produce well. He was very ambitious. He held school offices and was also treasurer of the township.

Edward was married in 1866 to Mary Mull, who had also come from Hillsdale County. They had five children. After Mary's death, Edward married Olivia Davis in 1887. They had three sons: Howard, Fremont and Robert. Edward died in 1913. The original house burned in the 1920s and a new house, which is still standing, was built soon after that.

After Olivia's death, Robert and his wife Goldie (Pepple) moved to the farm. They had six children: Clyde (died at age 5), Barbara, Robert D., Imogene, Edward and Terry.

Robert farmed and also worked in the oil fields, driving a truck all over Michigan and out of state, delivering pipe and supplies to well sites, until his death in 1965. Goldie continued living on the farm.

Edward served two years in the Army during the Korean War and was discharged in 1954. He built a house on family owned land, one-half mile away, and in 1966, his family, Joann (Heinlein) and children: Karen, Thomas and Richard, moved into the farm house. Goldie, his mother, moved into the house Edward had built. Ed worked as a heavy machinery operator, which he loved, taking great pride in his work.

He also loved working with wood. He did all the changes to the farm house and he and the children dug out the Michigan basement, taking the dirt out by conveyer, making it a full size, finished, basement, with a fireplace. Joann retired from Central Michigan University, where she was supervisor of academic records. Ed died in 1998, at the age of 66. Joann still lives on the Centennial Farm. Karen's home is also on the original farm.

BELLINGER-ELKINS. Marvin Gale Bellinger was born May 7, 1939 in Lincoln Twp. to Cecil Elton Bellinger (b. 1917-) and Lillian Lucille (Recker) Bellinger (b. 1921-). He is a life long resident of Isabella County.

He attended grade school in Shepherd, then Ganiard School in Mt. Pleasant. In 1957 his class was the last to graduate from the old high school located on Fancher Street. After high school he worked for Lobdell-Emery in Alma, then Campbell-Zingg. In 1963 Stanley Elmore offered him a job as floor mechanic. He went to floor covering school in Pennsylvania and worked for Elmore's 17 years laying carpet, formica, tile and linoleum.

While he was laying floor covering, he farmed at night and weekends. In 1980 he began farming full time. He bought a herd of cows and became a dairy farmer. His farm operation was successful for many years until he retired in 1999.

He is a very accomplished carpenter. He built his house and all his farm buildings with the help of family and friends. He enjoys making furniture for his family.

Sally Anne Elkins was born Jan. 11, 1942, in Fremont Twp. to James Roy Elkins (b. 1915, d. 1970) and Lucille Vivian (Sage) Elkins (b. 1911, d. 1987). She was born in a rent house on her grandfather's farm that was later sold to Marvin's parents. They moved several times and settled on a farm on Deerfield Rd.

She attended grade school at Fancher and went to Crowley country school that was located on the corner of Mission and Bluegrass (where a Marathon gas station is located today). She graduated from Mt. Pleasant High in 1960. She worked afternoons at Elmore's during her senior year and several years after.

After her youngest daughter started school, she worked several years at Elmore's and then Central Michigan University where she retired in June 2002 with 28-1/2 years of service. She is currently treasurer of Lincoln Township.

They were high school sweethearts and joined in marriage on June 17, 1961 at the First United Methodist Church in Mt. Pleasant.

l-r: Melissa, Sandra, Marvin, Sally and Phillip in back

They have three children: Phillip Scott (b. April 3, 1963 in Carson City) is employed by CME. Sandra Kaye (b. Oct. 14, 1964 in Carson City) md. Stephen Allan Goetz and lives in New Carlise, IN. She is employed by Crowe-Chizek in South Bend, IN. Melissa Lynn (b. July 17, 1967 in Mt. Pleasant, MI) is employed by Delta College. Both Sandra and Melissa graduated from Central Michigan University.

In the spring of 1960 they purchased land from his grandfather, Howard Bellinger, on which they built a home and reared a family. In 1980 they bought the remainder of the farm that his great-great-grandfather Adam Bellinger (b. 1812, d. 1873) patented from the government in 1869. The farm being operated and owned by the same family since June 1861. They still live on the farm. Part of the original farm is owned and operated by their son Phillip Scott Bellinger.

BELLINGER-RECKER. Cecil Elton Bellinger was born June 21, 1917 to Howard U.

Bellinger (b. 1888, d. 1967) and Lydia Ellen Sponseller (b. 1884, d. 1959). He had two sisters, Marie and Lucille, and three brothers: Ralph, Walter and Kenneth. They were raised on a farm in Lincoln Twp. Sec 4.

As a youngster he and his siblings attended the Hoag school located on the corner of Mission and Walton road. He graduated from Mt. Pleasant High School in 1935.

He stayed on the family farm, often working for a nearby neighbor. He worked for Chase Dairy (McFarlane Dairy), Austin Construction, Roosevelt Refinery (Lenoard Refinery), CMU and Michigan Ohio Pipeline. In 1976 he had a near fatal accident while digging up a pipeline. Dirt caved in on him covering him completely. He was rescued by his crew. He had severe injuries to his pelvic which made it necessary to retire in 1979 after 37 years with Lenoard Refinery.

Lillian Lucille Recker (b. June 7, 1921 in Lincoln Twp.) was the second daughter of Lawrence Andrew Recker (b. 1895, d. 1966) and Lydia Gazelle (Caszatt) Recker (b. 1898, d. 1962). She had three sisters: Dorothy, Phyliss (Jean) and Beverly, and one brother Larry.

She attended school at the Lincoln Center, located on Crawford Rd., through the eight grade. She retired from Central Michigan University in 1984 with 17 years of service.

Cecil and Lillian were married Feb. 22, 1938 with her sister Dorothy McDonald and his brother Ralph in attendance. In 1942 they moved a house to Crawford Road where they raised their family and live today.

They reared three children: Marvin (b. 1939) md. Sally Elkins and lives in Lincoln Twp. They have three children: Phillip, Sandra and Melissa. Elton Dean (b. 1941) md. Lynn Campbell and lives in Bellingham WA. They have one son, Byard. Bonnie (b. 1944) has five children: Mindy, Randy, Joseph, Michael and Sean. She lives with her third husband, Ron Green, in Pinebluff, NC.

BELLINGER-SPONSELLER-TAY-LOR. Howard U. Bellinger (b. 1888, d. 1967) was the oldest of three sons born to Edward Bellinger (b. 1844, d. 1913) and Olivia (Davis) Bellinger (b. 1869, d. 1942). His brothers were Fremont (b. 1891, d. 1955) and Robert (b. 1895, d. 1965). They were born and grew up on the farm that their grandfather Adam Bellinger (b. 1812, d. 1873) patented from the government in 1869, the farm being operated and owned by the same family since June 1861 when Adam with his wife Salana and sons: Phillip, Horace, Edward and George, moved there from Hillsdale County. The farm is now owned and operated by Marvin Bellinger, Howard's grandson.

Howard had one half-brother Frederick and half-sisters Lillian, Ednah and Iva, the children of Edward and his first wife Mary (Mull) (b. 1842, d. 1887).

As a youngster he attended the Gulick school where he became acquainted with his future wife Lydia Sponseller (b. 1884, d. 1959) the youngest of the children of George and Harriet (McMacken) Sponseller. They reared a family of six children.

1) The eldest, Marie, married first Roland Brookens, then married James Roche and they have a daughter Nancy.

2) Lucille (b. 1911, d. 1979) was severely handicapped with arthritis all of her adult life. She lived on the family farm on Crawford road section four of Lincoln Twp.

3) Ralph (b. 1913, d. 1994), the first son, married Neurita Nelson. They have a daughter Janice. She married George Ugolini and lives in Beacon, NY.

4) Walter (b. 1915, d. 1998) md. Esther Chivington and reared a family of three: James, Cheryl and Dennis. They lived most of their life in Portland, MI where they owned a hardware store.

5) Cecil married Lillian Recker, second child of Lawrence and Lydia (Caszatt) Recker. They have three children: Marvin, Elton (Dean), and Bonnie. Marvin married Sally Elkins and they have three children: Phillip, Sandra, and Melissa. They live on the homestead on Lincoln road of Lincoln Twp. Elton married Lynn Campbell and lives in Bellingham, WA. They have one son, Bayard. Elton graduated from the University of Michigan and California Institute of Technology. Bonnie married first Lyle Cotter, was divorced, married John Christman, was divorced. They have five children: Mindy, Randy, Joseph, Michael and Sean. She is now married to Ron Green and lives in Pinebluff, NC.

6) Kenneth (b. 1923, d. 1990) md. Louise Brown. They reared five children: Derry, Kenneth, Ricky, Rodney and Brenda.

Howard was a farmer all of his life and was Lincoln Twp. treasurer for many years. His second marriage was to Isabell Taylor.

BERRY-ARNOLD-RILEY.

Max and Carol Berry were married June 22, 1941. V. Max Berry was born March 14, 1920 in Kalkaska County, MI, and Carol Arnold was born Feb. 19, 1917 in Bemidji, MN.

Max grew up on a 320 acre farm in Kalkaska County, attended a country school until the eighth grade, and then graduated from Mancelona High School in 1939. Max's parents were born in Newago and Kalkaska counties. Carol's parents were born in Coldwater, MI and Bemidji, MN. The Arnolds moved to Michigan when Carol was 10 years old.

In the early years of their marriage, Max worked at a defense factory in Detroit. In 1946 they moved back to Kalkaska where they farmed for several years. They had two dairy farms. In 1950 Max began sales work for General Mills Larro Feed Co. Carol began teaching in Kalkaska and Antrim counties for six years after attending Antrim County Normal for one year, 1935-36.

Carol and Max Berry

In 1959 the Berrys moved to Shepherd where all five children graduated from Shepherd High School. Their children were Dan (b. May 20, 1943); Thomas (b. Sept. 24, 1945); Ralph (b. Jan. 20, 1947); Donald (b. April 21, 1950); and Marilyn (b. Sept. 24, 1951). Ralph purchased the Garber Funeral Home in 1970 which is known today as the Berry Funeral Home.

Max began work in Rosebush managing the Sohigro Fertilizer and Seed Plant; Carol continued teaching and finishing her degree at CMU in 1966 with a BS in education. Carol taught at Shepherd Elementary Schools from 1959 until the year she retired, 1980. Max and Carol were very active in school functions, were president and vice president of the SugarBush for the Maple Syrup Festival. Max is a third degree Mason, Salt River Lodge 288 and also a member of the Shepherd Rotary Club (a Rotarian since 1948). Currently Max is a board member of Community Mental Health of Central Michigan and a member of the Isabella County Board of Public Works.

Max retired in 1982. The Berrys then began a retirement of travel throughout the U.S. including Hawaii, their favorite retreat which they have visited many times. They traveled and visited most national parks, driving their motor homes or fifth wheel. In 1976 they purchased a summer cottage on Eight Point Lake.

Carol died June 15, 1994. Max married Suzanne Riley in May 1996; they too have traveled to Hawaii, England, Scotland, Wales, Ireland and France.

BIDLACK.

In the year 1690 Christopher Bidlack and three sons left England and settled in Massachusetts. They expanded into Connecticut and further west, but after losing their land in the Pennite Wars of the Wyoming Valley of Pennsylvania, 7-year-old Benjamin Bidlack's parents moved to Delaware County, OH. During the Civil War Benjamin's 12 sons and family were lured to Chippewa Twp., Isabella County after Fred Leatherman, husband of Alva's daughter Zelma, returned to Oakwood, OH from the Shepherd, MI area, bringing with him his suitcase which was filled with 20 locally grown potatoes!

The Bidlack's first year oat crop stood five feet high! But that winter, Geneva, Alva's wife, started a fire to get rid of some brush and stumps, and consequently set a 12 inch layer of muck on fire. The muck burned for three years and a bumper crop was never again realized on his sandy soil.

Alva Bidlack and team, Lester (this author's father) and Everett Bidlack with dog, and Geneva with chickens, Chippewa Twp. about 1913.

The farm Alva and Geneva purchased was part of a United States land grant to timber baron Aloney Rust in 1855. (Note: in 1948 there was still one pine stump over six feet tall that measured six feet across!). The land (E1/2 of NE1/4 Sec. 25) changed hands four times before Alexander Coomer's widow sold the property to Geneva Bidlack in 1912. There is no record of who built the house or planted the maple trees, however, in the Bidlack family picture of about 1913 the trees appear to be at least 20 years old

The picture is typical of poor Ohio family photographs of the time—i.e. it was customary to pose wearing your best clothes along with the family wealth (team, mowing machine, cow and a few chickens!).

Alva (b. 1860) lived until 1928 when the house was sold and moved away. Geneva (b. 1864) lived with daughter Zelma in Cheasning, MI. until 1931. Geneva had born 14 children but only five survived. Lester and Everett lived quiet lives in Detroit. Two other girls, Dora and Florence, both worked as Harvey Girls on the railroad and remember serving meals to Frank James - pardoned brother of Jesse James!

BIDLACK.

Amy Jo Bidlack was born March 17, 1964 in Midland, MI to Harvey and Norma Bidlack of Isabella County. She had a wonder-

Amy Jo Bidlack in 1989

ful childhood, even as an only child and was a great lover of animals which were abundant on the small farm where she grew up.

Amy's father, Harvey, worked at Dow Chemical in Midland and mother Norma was employed by Oren's Department Store of Mt. Pleasant, so consequently Amy spent many happy hours at her grandparents Lester and Gladys Bidlack's home on the corner of M-20 and Shepherd Rd. She well remembers sitting on the front porch watching traffic on two lane M-20 where one car may pass every minute or so, a far cry from the five lane highway that passes that corner now.

Shepherd Elementary School was the place Amy was educated until third grade when her parents transferred her to Holy Scripture Lutheran School in Midland, MI. During these years she was a member of 4-H and won an award for bread making as well as awards for her chickens and rabbits. She also showed her Shetland Sheepdog in obedience trials with success.

Eighth grade found Amy back in the Shepherd school system and reacquainted with friends from elementary school. in high school she was a member of National Honor Society and graduated in 1982 after receiving the Spanish and social studies awards for that year.

In the fall of 1982 Amy began her college career at Lake Superior State College in Sault Ste. Marie, MI studying nursing and did much of her clinical practice in Sault Ste. Marie, Ontario, Canada. She graduated in 1985 with an associate degree in nursing. She decided not to stay the full four years in the UP due to too much snow and cold weather and instead transferred to Michigan State University where her father had obtained his degree in the 1940s. In 1989 Amy graduated from MSU with a BS in nursing and was a member of Golden Key National Honor Society and a member of the national honor society of nursing, Sigma Theta Tau.

Amy started her nursing career performing private duty nursing and in 1987 went to work for Gratiot Community Hospital in Alma, MI with a focus on intensive care and emergency nursing and is still employed there until this day.

One thing that always fascinated Amy was her grandmother, Gladys Bidlack's stories of growing up as a child in Bermuda and she has fulfilled a lifetime dream of traveling to this tropical island and seeing the house where here grandmother was born and retraced her steps as a child growing up on the shore of the Atlantic Ocean.

Amy still lives on the farm in Sec. 25 of Chippewa Twp., Isabella County and avidly works to develop this land into a nature preserve by planting trees and culturing a new pond with plants and fish. She loves observing wildlife including deer, coyote, raccoon, opossum, squirrels and birds of all species. She also enjoys her pets which give her much love and affection.

BIDLACK-DALLAS. After a stint in the army in WWI, Lester Bidlack returned home to Chippewa Twp. to work on his parents' farm. During that time, Black Creek was excavated using a floating drudge. This method of digging required a lot of manual labor which was fortunate for Lester and his father Alva. They worked long enough to pay off the drain tax on that portion of Black Creek that passed through the Bidlack farm. The tax amounted to 150% of the value of the entire property. It took a while at those days wages!

The lure of an easier life drew Lester first to Lansing and then to Detroit where he found employment as a streetcar motorman.

For years one of Lester's sisters (Florence [Mrs. Wm. F. Johnson] of Mt. Pleasant and mother of Connie Wert of Shepherd) had reoccurring dreams about her little dark haired sister across the seas. The frequency of this dream was well known among the family members, yet all were surprised when Lester met and married 5'2", 102 lb., black haired Gladys Dallas from Bermuda.

Lester and Gladys Bidlack, 1962

To this union was born Harvey (b. Oct. 2, 1924), Barbara (Feb. 9, 1926) and Florence (Feb. 5, 1927). In 1928 Lester had to take his family to Bermuda to meet the in-laws. They stayed for nine months. In order to defray expenses, Lester accepted a job with the Bermuda government reclaiming land and building road

beds to connect the many small islets. He was the engineer on a narrow gauge railway and also was in charge of 50 Portuguese laborers. Lester didn't speak the language but he knew how to run the train and how to get laborers to do their utmost.

By 1936 Lester had become a full-time general insurance agent and enjoyed that occupation until he and Gladys retired to the Shepherd area in 1962 where he renewed acquaintance's with many old friends.

Lester expired in 1969 at the age of 75, but Gladys, who was five years younger, lived to the ripe old age of 92.

The Chippewa Baptist Church on M-20 at Loomis Rd. was their church home and it afforded them much comfort in their declining years.

BIDLACK-SCHWEIGERT. Harvey Bidlack was born to Lester and Gladys in Detroit in 1924. Harvey's father made sure that his son spent every summer in Isabella County. The summer that Harvey was 16 he worked on a casing crew that was contracted out to the Pure Oil Co. Almost got himself killed three times the first day on the job but stuck it out because of the fabulous pay of $2.00 per hour!

At 17 Harvey graduated from high school in Detroit and enrolled in Michigan State College majoring in agricultural economics. He was in the last ROTC Cavalry class to use horses. ROTC lead to the Enlisted Reserve Corps but three months later he transferred to the Marine Corps. (Note: Most of the Reserve Corps enlistees never saw army officer training, but rather ended up in the 101st Airborne as foot soldiers and were killed in the Battle of the Bulge). After a few months in the V-12 program at the University of Michigan, Harvey was sent to Marine Officer's Candidate School at Quantico VA, and finally served as a fleet marine at Pearl Harbor.

After WWII, Harvey graduated from Michigan State with a BS degree. That same year (1948) he and a friend went to Alaska to homestead. That didn't last long! Alaska made the puckerbrush of Isabella County look real good! After working for Pure Oil again for a short while, Harvey accepted a position with Remington Rand Corp. in Detroit working as a Univac installation technician. The work was hectic (sometimes 72 hours without sleep) and it didn't take long to discover the peace and quiet of the family farm.

Harvey's grandmother Geneva Bidlack had died in 1931 with no will. The land was left undivided and the five heirs were unable to agree on how to settle the estate. Harvey bought each one's share at $3.00/acre. At the age of 36 he married 36-year-old Norma Schweigert of Midland, MI. Norma had been born in the log cabin her father had built after homesteading the last piece of land in Midland County.

Norma and Harvey Bidlack, 1984

For the next three years Norma continued to work for Michigan Bell as the Midland office's service representative supervisor. Michigan Bell's company policy dictated that Norma had to retire four months before their daughter Amy was born. Two years later, Norma began her 12 year career in Oren's gift department in Mt. Pleasant.

Amy Bidlack earned a BSN degree from Michigan State College of Nursing. She is now the fourth generation of Bidlacks to live on this land in Isabella County.

Harvey retired from Dow in 1986. He was a senior research biologist and has been issued five U.S. patents—two were for solid rocket fuel composition and three for plant growth regulation. Some of his work has been published in both the U.S. and Russia.

Besides raising cattle at home during his tenure at Dow, he, as a Republican, was elected to four terms as Chippewa Twp. Supervisor. He served 23 years as Chippewa's tax assessor, was chairman of the Tri-Township Fire Department, which is made up of Chippewa, Lincoln, Coe townships and the village of Shepherd. He was responsible for the first modern fire station for the unit, and two major bridge replacements over the Chippewa River so that rapid, modern fire protection became available north of that landmark.

In 1969 the south 30 acres of the Bidlack property was deeded to the Lutheran Churches of the Reformation in order to establish a seminary and train pastors. After seven years the seminary transferred to Iowa and the land was returned to Harvey and Norma who have been very active Lutherans most of their lives.

BLACK FAMILY. In 1868 David Black and his wife Agnes came to Michigan from New York State. They settled on 40 acres in the southwest corner of Isabella County. They had four children: John, Jim, Janette and Wallace. David died in 1914 and Agnes in 1937. The three oldest children were deceased by then, leaving Wallace.

Early Black Farm

Current Black Farm

Wallace had two daughters, Marjorie and Dorthy, from his first wife who passed away. He married Mary Dangler in 1920 and they had six children: Wallace (died in 1921 about two months old), Carrie (b. 1923), Ernest (b. 1928), Olin (b. 1934), Mary Jean (b. 1938) and Nathan (b. 1942).

Mary died in 1963 and Wallace in 1965. Ernest, the oldest living son, and his wife bought the farm from his brothers and sisters. They had three boys: Gearold (b. 1947), James (b. 1948) and Kenneth (b. 1949). Ernest and his wife Joanne still live on the home place.

BLACK-HESS.
The David Wallace Black farm at 11837 S. Green Road, Lincoln Twp., Isabella County, MI that my brother and his wife Joann now own is the farm I was born on in 1923.

The following is some of the history of my grandfather as told to me, Carrie May (Black) Wieferich.

David Wallace Black (b. Sept. 25, 1838, Barr, Ayrshire, Scotland) md. Agnes Perscilla Hess. He came to the United States and settled in New York State where some of his children were born. Later he moved his family and their belongings to St. Johns, MI by train and on to the farm by horse and wagon.

Mary and Wallace David Black

My father, Wallace David Black and Mable (Rudler) Black were married and had two girls: Marjorie Emily Black md. Marshall F. Abbott and Dorothy Agnes Black md. William Bunker. Mable Black died in 1920, leaving Wallace Black with the two little girls.

In 1921 he married my mother, Mary Charlotte (Danglar) Black. They had six children with the first child dying at two months old. The children of Wallace and Mary Black were Wallace LeRoy Black (b. Nov. 13, 1921, died January 1922); Carrie May Black (b. Oct. 20, 1923); Earnest Lloyd Black (b. March 4, 1928); Alan Franklin Black (b. July 18, 1934); Mary Jean Black (b. July 26, 1938); and Nathan Edward Black (b. March 21, 1942).

Original homestead on Green Road

Mary Charlotte Black died in April 1963 and Wallace David Black died in June 1965. Mom and Dad pulled together on the farm as a team. Mom worked on the farm and so did all the children. Everyone worked together in the sugar beets, garden, strawberries, raspberries and chickens. Often bills were paid in dressed chicken, fresh strawberries or hanging wallpa-

per. I never heard my mom and dad argue. Daddy's favorite scripture was 1 Tim. 5:18 and mom's was Ephesians 4:26. "Be angry but do not sin, 27 and do not leave room for the devil."

BOGER-GEASLER.
Martin Boger (b. April 17, 1892) was the only child of Henry and Louisa Boger. He spent his entire life on the farm in Coldwater Twp. that was originally homesteaded by Solomon Shilling (his grandfather) in 1870. The farm is still in the family and is home to Maggie Boger and Harry and Virginia (Boger) Herman.

Martin went through the eighth grade in the Conley School which was located about a mile west of his home. He grew up loving the out-of-doors and spent much time hunting, fishing and trapping. As a young man he often spent part of the winter months living with his friends in a log cabin on the shore of Cranberry Lake, west of Lake Station. They spent their days fishing on the lake and fox and rabbit hunting. It was a life-style that today's young men could only dream about.

His life's occupation was farming and he was a very good farmer using advanced farming methods as they became available. His specialty was raising potatoes. More acreage was added to the farm and it was eventually 300 acres.

Martin was also extremely interested in conservation and environmental issues long before it became the popular thing to do. He planted trees, shrubs for bird feed and was a good steward of the soil.

He served in WWI during the years 1918-19. He spent his entire time at Fort Custer because he had the flu and was too weakened by it to be sent overseas.

Mr. and Mrs. Martin Boger

On Aug. 29, 1924 Martin married Maggie Geasler (b. Jan. 4, 1898), the daughter of Joseph and Myrtle Geasler. She was born in Isabella County but soon moved to the Upper Peninsula where her father worked in a lumber camp. Maggie was the oldest daughter in a family of 13 children, so she learned early the responsibility of caring for a home and looking after her brothers and sisters. When she was a teenager her family moved to Sherman City. Maggie has spent her life as a home-maker. She was an excellent cook. She was also a creative seamstress who has sewed and quilted as long as her vision allowed. But her greatest love is for flowers. Her beautiful flower bed along Coleman Road brought pleasure to many as they passed that way.

Martin and Maggie have three daughters: Virginia (b. March 2, 1925) was an elementary teacher in the Beal City and Chippewa Hills

School systems for 32 years. She is married to Harry Harman who was postmaster at Weidman for 31 years. They have one son, Thomas.

Pauline (b. July 17, 1926) md. William Estes who was supervisor of transportation for the Chippewa Hills Schools. Pauline was also employed in the same school system.

Ruth (b. March 26, 1929) was an elementary teacher. She married Ralph Turnbull who worked for the State Department of Education. They have two sons, Robert and Timothy.

Martin died on Oct. 21, 1976, but Maggie, at age 104, still lives in their home on Coleman Road.

BOGER-SHILLING.
Henry Boger (b. May 9, 1862 in Mercer County, PA) was one of the five children of Jeremiah and Maria Boger. He was raised in a German speaking home and knew no English until he was old enough to go to school. His years of education were received in a Lutheran School.

When he was 21 he came to Michigan to look for his sister Liza Wagerman. Liza had married and moved to Michigan but had not kept in touch with her family. After locating his sister he took a job working in a lumber camp. On May 9, 1886 he married Louisa Shilling.

Louisa (b. Nov. 20, 1856) was the oldest child of Solomon and Margaret Shilling. She had gone to school through the eighth grade, written the state teacher's exam and became qualified to teach school. She taught her first term of school in the Brown School District in a newly built log school. At the time Henry and Louisa met she was working for H.A. Letson in a store located on the northwest corner of Brinton and Coleman roads in Coldwater Twp.

After they married they bought 40 of the original 80 acres homesteaded by Solomon and Margaret Shilling. Later 40 more acres were added to the farm. Working together they cleared the land and built a log house. They farmed in the summer and worked in a nearby lumber camp during the winter months. Louisa was camp cook and Henry cared for the horses and equipment. Later he helped with much of the carpenter work on the original buildings in Weidman.

Henry and Louisa had one son Martin (b. April 17, 1892). As he grew up more acreage was added to the farm and he shared the farming responsibilities with his parents.

Henry died on June 23, 1941 and Louisa died March 26, 1943.

BONNELL-ARNOLD.
In 1918 Edward J. Bonnell Sr. and Edgar Bixby purchased Foster Hardware and Furniture Co., located at the southwest corner of Main Street at Broadway. They renamed the business, which operated for 35 years, Mt. Pleasant Hardware & Furniture Co. Bonnell ran the furniture part of the business and Bixby the hardware, in this three-story brick building. Ed Bonnell Sr. was a charter member of Rotary Club and Mt. Pleasant Chamber of Commerce!

After serving in the Air Corps in WWII, Edward J. Bonnell Jr. worked for his dad in furniture sales until 1956 when he bought Superior Furniture, four miles north of Mt. Pleasant, from Bill Davidge, renaming it Bonnell Superior Furniture. In 1977 Ed sold the family business to his son, James Bonnell, who operated it the next 18 years, and then sold it.

Ed Bonnell Jr. born in Saginaw, MI, has lived 84 of his 88 years in Mt. Pleasant, and has been an active member of Kiwanis Club for 63 years. That was when Arlie Osborne, his high school coach, brought him and Lawrence Hood into Kiwanis. Ed was a scoutmaster and Kiwanis Club Boy Scout troupe representative. Ed played on the 1932 State Championship basketball team and attended Central Michigan University where he majored in business. Ed is a life member of the First United Methodist Church and was president of Methodist Men's Club when the new church was built in 1961. He is a present member of Isabella County Historical Society.

In 1947 Ed married Auburna (Burnie) Arnold of Traverse City, whom he met while she taught homemaking at Mt. Pleasant High. Ed and Burnie have four children: James, Helen, Bruce and Jean. When the children were enrolled at Pullen Elementary, Ed served as president of the PTA, while Burnie worked on school events and with Brownie and Cub Scouts. Ed and Burnie still live at 1608 East High Street, a home they bought from Stacey Myers, who built it.

BOURLAND-REED. James E. Bourland was born Oct. 26, 1912 in Aberdeen, MS, to Gilbert and Liza (West) Bourland. Bessie Marie Reed was born Jan. 26, 1918, in Blissfield, MI to Harry and Emma (Wotring) Reed.

James family moved to Homestead, FL in 1924 due to his father's health. They survived the 1926 hurricane but lost all of their possessions. He worked in a music store selling records, repairing radios and later joined the fire department. Jim returned to Aberdeen then moved to Detroit in 1933 where he worked as a radio repairman. It was big business at that time installing car radios. He moved to Mt. Pleasant in 1936 where he worked at Johnson's Garage that was located at the corner of University and Michigan St. Later he opened an appliance and television business of his own.

After graduating from high school Bessie worked for several families as a caregiver in the Blissfield area. She then came to Mt. Pleasant to help her sister who was ill. Through the years she would come to Mt. Pleasant by train from Toledo with her grandmother and cousin. They would pack a lunch as it took the greater part of a day for the trip. Her father often cam to visit two of his sisters, Clara (Page) Wilt of Coleman, and Bessie Ann (Floyd) Johnson of Mt. Pleasant.

Bessie and Jim were married in Shepherd in 1936, the year of the big storm. Snow was piled as high as the telephone wires. It was also the year the viaduct on S. Mission was built. In 1944, they purchased the Chamberlain farm on Walton Rd., where they still live, and bought the building at 213 S. Main St. in 1945. At this site they opened Bourland Television and Appliance Center and had the first television set in Isabella County. In 1960, a fire gutted the interior of the business. Shortly after remodeling the store, Jim semi-retired and worked out of his home repairing radio and televisions.

Bessie received her practical nursing degree in 1962 and worked at the Mt. Pleasant Regional Center until her retirement in 1981. In earlier years she was the first woman school bus driver in Isabella County.

l-r: James II, Joyce, Sharron, Joann, Bessie and James I in 1957

Their four children: Sharron (b. May 3, 1937) resides in San Diego, CA; Joann (b. Oct. 26, 1939) md. Bruce Lyon and lives in Gladwin, MI; Jim (b. Feb. 13, 1942) and wife Beverly live in Rosebush, MI; Joyce (b. Feb. 13, 1942) md. William Theisen and lives in Indian River, MI. They all attended the Hoag School through the 6th grade, then to Mt. Pleasant High School and Central Michigan University.

James and Bessie have seven grandchildren and 14 great-grandchildren. James' siblings, Mary, William, Gilbert and Elizabeth, are all deceased. Bessie's siblings are Adah (Lee) Johnson of Mt. Pleasant, deceased; Charles Amos Reed (Vera, deceased) Mt. Pleasant; Woodrow W. Reed (Doris, deceased) Mt. Pleasant; and Archie Reed (Leola) of Adrian.

BRANT-CHERRY. Robert Anthony Brant (b. Jan. 12, 1969, Grayling, MI) attended school K through 12 at Shepherd, MI, during which time lived at 7338 S Lincoln Rd. on his parents farm. His responsibilities included caring for several quarter horses, homing pigeons and usually his own 4-H project, which was raising a steer each year to enter in the county fair. Also during that time, he was also involved in sports at school. Track and cross country were the sports he was able to excel at given his smaller size. That would not last long though, the following year after school he gained several pounds and grew several inches.

His first job was working on a construction crew for his dad. It was there that he realized how much he enjoyed working outside which would eventually lead him to a career in concrete construction.

In 1991 he met Lisa Cherry in Ogden, UT, and a couple of years later, they were married. Lisa brought with her three boys from a previous marriage, which they reared together from that point and lived and loved as much as a family could. Their names are Justin, Robert and Bryan.

Lisa and Robert Brant with Justin, Robert and Bryan

During that time in 1996, they moved to Michigan to take a job offered by his dad to handle the concrete construction in his condominium project.

They are still in Michigan seven years later. The boys are grown and moved out and Lisa and Robert are enjoying some time to themselves. Hunting and fishing is by far his favorite pastime as well as working on and maintaining their home.

BRANT-SCHAFER. Ryan Daniel Brant was born April 1, 1974 in Alma, MI, to loving father David Arnold Brant (b. Aug. 14, 1942, Alma MI) and nurturing mother Kathlene Kay Thurlow (b. Sept. 28, 1944, Saginaw MI). Ryan was one of six children: brothers Eugene David (b. May 15, 1967) and Robert Anthoney (b. Jan. 12 1969); sisters Deanna Jane (b. April 24, 1974), Sarah Lynn (b. May 15, 1975) and Christine Louise (b. March 24, 1980). He, along side his family, grew up in a country home seven miles west of Shepherd at 7338 S. Lincoln Rd. He attended the Shepherd school system and graduated from high school in 1992. He grew up hunting with his father, shooting guns (his father's passion) and tending to many farm animals. Ryan enjoyed sports and friends during high school, where he met his wife.

Ryan, Danelle and children, Blake and Bailey

On Oct. 26, 1976 Danelle Lee Schafer was born to Micheal Norman Schafer and Paula Diane Fowler. Micheal (b. Sept. 17, 1955 in Alma, MI) and Paula (b. Oct. 13, 1955, Alma, MI) married May 8, 1976 and resided at 257 Clark Street in Shepherd, where they had three children: Danelle Lee (b. 1976), Eric Micheal (b. 1978) and Erin Marie (b. 1980).

In 1984 the family moved to 3805 S. Chippewa Rd. Mt. Pleasant. Danelle attended Shepherd Public schools where she graduated in 1995. While attending school she met her devoted husband. In May 1996 Ryan and Danelle married with a pocket full of change and dreams larger than life, they began their journey. Within three years they were blessed with two amazing children, she was overwhelmed with the joys of motherhood. In 2000 she began her career with Consumers Energy. Danelle enjoys golfing, friends, family, and her very active children.

Ryan and Danelle joined together on a glorious, sunny afternoon May 25, 1996. They were soon joined Oct. 24, 1996 by a beautiful daughter, Bailey Joyce. At that time, they lived at 634 Oak St. in Mt. Pleasant. On May 24, 1999 they were blessed by the birth of Blake Micheal. In October of that same year, they moved to 10335 E. River Rd. Mt. Pleasant where they currently live.

In 2003, Ryan started his own trucking company, Blay Transport, named after Blake and Bailey. Ryan and Danelle look forward to nurturing and growing with there children. They have many aspirations and dreams, and hope life permits them to grow old together as they chase them.

BRANT-THURLOW. Dave Brant was born Aug. 14, 1942 to Pauline and Anthony "Bud" Brant in Alma, MI. Dave was reared on a farm near Coleman, MI and graduated from Coleman High School in 1960. He followed in his father and grandfather's footsteps in residential building. He worked with his father until he was drafted into the U.S. Army in 1964.

He married Kathy on Jan. 2, 1965. Kathy was born to Juanita and Harvey Thurlow Sept. 28, 1944 in Saginaw, MI. Dave was honorably discharged from the army in June 1966. He and Kathy bought a 40 acre farm on Lincoln Rd. Dave began attending Central Michigan University and working with his father. Kathy worked at the Student Book Exchange.

Dave graduated CMU in 1969 and began teaching building trades at Mt. Pleasant High School and remained there until 1988.

In 1970 Dave began a building business, "Residential & Commercial Contractors" in partnership with Woody Lehr. They also purchased an interior decorating store "Mission Paint & Wallpaper," in Mt. Pleasant. They expanded this business to Midland and Alma. The partners also began a rental business, "LeBra Enterprise." The businesses were run out of an office located at 1300 E. Pickard until the decorating stores were sold and the store and office space were rented out.

Rosewood East Condominiums is a project of Residential & Commercial Contractors with nearly 200 units sold as of January 2003. In 2003 a new office building was built and a new condominium project started - "Rosewood North."

Dave and Kathy are very active in their church, "The Church of Jesus Christ of Latter-day-Saints." They have both spent years working with youth. Dave has been active for many years in the Boy Scout" program. Kathy is currently serving as director of the Family History Center (a genealogical library) located at the church.

David and Kathlene Brant and children: (not in order) Eugene, Robert, Deanna, Ryan, Sarah and Christine

They are the parents of six children: Eugene David Brant, Robert Anthony Brant, Deanna Jane Marshall, Ryan Daniel Brant, Sarah Lynn Henrie and Christine Louise Brant. Dave and Kathy have 11 grandchildren. The

couple bought a 60 acre farm, also on Lincoln Rd., where they built a new home in 1973. This is where they reared their family. In 1999 they purchased 20 acres on W. Wing Rd. where they again built a new home and now reside there.

BUCHER-JOURDAIN. Elizabeth Bucher was born 1846 in Switzerland in the Tri Country area of France, Germany and Switzerland to Jacob and Mary Ann Bucher. She immigrated in 1853 with her parents and two brothers, Joseph and John, to Erie County, NY, and grew up near Getzville, NY.

Julius Jourdain was born in Bellfort, France in 1844 to Michel Francois Jerard Jourdain. He immigrated with his family to the USA in 1847 and settled on a farm near Getzville, Erie County, NY. In 1861 Civil War breaks out and Julius enlisted in the service and served with the New York 1st Light Artillery from Sept. 9, 1861 until June 23, 1865. He fought in many battles and ran for his life at 2nd Bull Run, stood his ground at Gettysburg and marched with Sherman to the sea.

After the war, Julius noticed the younger sister of a neighborhood soldier, Joseph Bucher. She is all grown up, had a pretty smile and would make a wonderful wife. The young soldier attacks and the battle settlement is at the justice of the peace, Stephen Huff, in Tonawanda, NY on July 14, 1868.

The couple lived just outside of Getzville and had four children. In 1877, Julius' sister, Eugenia Bronstetter, writes her brother from Michigan in Union Twp. in Isabella County. She says that "the soil is rich and the land is cheap" and he should come to Michigan.

In March 1878, the family moved to Deerfield Twp., Sec. 2 of Isabella County, MI. Then, in 1881, Julius and Elizabeth moved to Isabella Twp, Sec. 35. Five more children were born after arriving in Michigan. The children are as follows: Joseph (b. Nov. 12, 1868), Elizabeth Jourdain Farner (b. March 30, 1871), Anna Jourdain Thering (b. Oct. 16, 1872), Edward (b. Oct. 17, 1876), Louise Jourdain Thering (b. Aug. 9, 1878), Eugenia Jourdain Thering (b. Oct. 27, 1883), Eugene (b. March 31, 1886, Louis (b. June 21, 1888) and Benjamin (b. Sept. 27, 1871). Two children died as infants, Frank and Helen.

Julius was a successful farmer, parent, husband, Catholic and Civil War story braggart. In 1909 he retired and moved to Isabella City (Dog Town) and lived there until his death on Oct. 7, 1914. After Julius died, Elizabeth moved in with Louis and Imo Jourdain. Elizabeth passed away April 3, 1925.

BUFFORD-WING. James Harvey Bufford arrived in Mt. Pleasant from Maumee, OH with his parents, George and Elsie, a sister Grace and brother Dennis when just a boy. Their livelihood was farming. In 1899 James Harvey married Alice May Wing, daughter of Walter Wing and Amanda L. Deveraux. They lived on 20 acres that stretched from Rural Route 3 (Broomfield Rd.) to the Chippewa River.

James and "Allie" had six children: Bernice, Lloyd, Alta Irene, Irma, Dale and Ralph. Lloyd and other children in the area walked to the Maple Hill School. James died of a stroke in 1917. His wife reared the children on her own and cared for her ill mother in later years. If any-

one remembers the basket factory, that was her employment. She lived alone until her death in 1959.

James Harvey Bufford and Alice May Wing, 1889

In 1928 Lloyd Vincent, the oldest son, married Ernestine K. Albar, daughter of Henry Albar and Julia Theresa Starr. Their union produced five children: Frances Jean, William H., Alice, Juliann and Margaret. Lloyd was a bus driver for "Blue Goose Lines" and "Greyhound" doing most of his traveling between Bay City and Sault St. Marie. Ernestine passed away in 1969 and Lloyd in 1971. Their son William returned to Mt. Pleasant after four years in the U.S. Navy and worked for Jack Sharrar Shell Service and Spicer Oil.

William married Joyce Worley in 1955 and they have two daughters. He went to work for Skelgas and was transferred to the Jackson, MI office and still resides in that area.

BUGBEE-ENGWIS. For many years, George A. Bugbee (b. Nov. 16, 1872, in Homer Twp., Midland County) was a prominent lumber dealer in Mt. Pleasant. At the age of 18, he enlisted in Chicago for three years of army training.

On March 22, 1902, he married Elizabeth Engwis (b. Feb. 21, 1882) of Midland. Most of Elizabeth's family had been stricken during the influenza epidemic and only Elizabeth and two of her brothers survived.

Elizabeth Engwis Bugbee and George Bugbee (wedding 1902)

The couple moved to Bay City in 1906, where George was engaged in the lumber business. While in Bay City, George and Elizabeth had four children: Katherine, George Wilber "Bill," Gladys and Elizabeth. They later moved to Standish where George also was in the lumber business.

In 1940 this article appeared in the Mt. Pleasant paper: "Retirement this week of George Bugbee, president of Mt. Pleasant Lumber Co., marked the close of a successful business career which began in this community nearly 27 years ago.

"Enterprise, initiative, friendliness and a square deal might well be set as symbols by which this 67 year old resident rose from an insignificant business position to one of outstanding leadership in the community.

"Formerly employed by the Wolverine Lumber Co. of Bay City, Mr. Bugbee represented that firm in establishing the Standish Lumber and Coal Co., which he conducted for six years prior to his venture in Mt. Pleasant.

"With the late W.D. Hood as partner, Mr. Bugbee began building the lumber company which was incorporated at $10,000 but now is valued at $100,000. The partners, impressed by cordiality of the community, got off to a flying start.

"An electrical storm swept through Isabella County, burning down several barns. Joining in on a barn raising at the W.B. Robinson farm, west of Sheperd, Mr. Hood and Mr. Bugbee made numerous contacts which resulted in a series of barn reconstruction with supplies furnished by the new businessmen instead of outside cities.

"Offering something new in service at that time, they provided architectural drawings of homes and for many years offered the only architect service in the community." George continued with this well known business concern until his retirement in 1940, due to ill health."

During WWII Elizabeth Bugbee worked tirelessly with the Red Cross, much of the time spent rolling bandages for the military hospitals. She had two gold stars hanging in her window, for her sons, Russ and Herb.

George and Elizabeth had eight children. One child, Katherine "Kitty" was burned to death when she was 8 years old. The other children were: George "Bill" Wilber (md. Grace Ferguson); Gladys (md. Athel Zufelt); Elizabeth (md. William F. Sowle); Ruth (md. Dr. Jack Kelly); Russell (md. Esther Peacock); Doris (md. Ed Cote); and Dr. Herbert Bugbee (md. Mona Wooten).

George A. Bugbee was in the Army in WWI, but was discharged to go home and support his mother and aunt who were very poor and needed care. After his death, many people came forward to tell how George provided coal for heat during the winters for some poor widows in Mt. Pleasant. Although they were not "church goers," both George and Elizabeth were known for doing good works quietly in the background for both family members and residents of Mt. Pleasant.

George and Elizabeth are buried in Riverside Cemetery in Mt. Pleasant.

BUGH-COX. WCEN AM 1150 had already been on the air since the 1940s when Gary H. Bugh was hired as a staff announcer in April 1961. The owner was Paul Brandt who also owned the Economy Dime Store in downtown Mt. Pleasant. WCEN was a full service radio station offering news, sports, public affairs programs and a wide variety of music from country and pop to old standards and classical.

Eugene Umlor managed a large staff including "Word to the Wives" and local news commentator, Georgia Martin. Popular morning man Lou Williams woke up his fans at 5:00 a.m. with a mix of country and popular music. Neal Johnson was another favorite announcer for many years. Chuck Stevens handled local sports including live broadcasts of local teams. Danny Hole was the "Grooveyard" host playing rock and roll tunes weekday afternoons. "Polka Joe" Kisnosky, "Rapid Robert" Coxon, Rheba Dedie, Joe Caleca, Dick Taylor, Bob Banta, Janet Phelps, Dan Bethel, Wayne Kemp and morning

men, Jimmy James and Duane Allen, were household names throughout Central Michigan. Larry Wentworth and Mike Carey handled sales and Pete Fronczak and Dick Leonard shared engineering duties with part time help from Harold Zeoli.

In the early 60s veteran Michigan radio newsman, Jim Hughes, took over the news department with his opening "It was another relatively quiet night." Gary was host of "Coffee With Gary" from the early 1960s thru 1990. After Lou Williams moved on Gary took over the Wonderful Outdoors, a weekly half-hour outdoor and travel show. He sold radio ads from 1968-92. In 1978 Gary and his wife Patty Jo pioneered a half hour Christian show called "Come Together" heard on Sunday mornings.

94.5 FM was added in the 1960s featuring easy listening music. Two bright red Ford Sedans were always ready to respond to the latest breaking local news. "The Red and White Satellite," a small broadcast trailer, was hauled to remote broadcasts, country fairs and other events.

In the late 60s WCEN was purchased by a group of investors with Chuck Anthony as manager. 94.5 FM power was raised and many other improvements were made. In the mid-90s the stations were sold to Sommerville Broadcasting and managed by Dick Sommerville. A new 1,000-foot tower was built and 94.5 went to a hot country format.

Gary left WCEN in August 1992 to take a position as GM of a new contemporary Christian station WPRJ/Praise 101.7 in Coleman.

He and his college sweetheart, Patty Jo Cox, were married in 1962. In 1966 they built their colonial ranch style home, "The Beehive," on the high banks of the Chippewa River east of Mt. Pleasant on the Don and Rita Lackie farm. In 1963 Patty Jo graduated with a BS degree from CMU and began a 31-year career as a speech and language pathologist at Coleman Elementary School. In 1969 they adopted a boy, Shawn and his sister, Heather. Together they and their spouses have given them 12 lively grandchildren.

In January 1970, Patty Jo, received her master's degree in special education from CMU. Both Patty Jo and Gary have been active in civic and church organizations for many years.

As Gary writes this they are enjoying semi-retirement and are still very involved with WPRJ and volunteer activities. They love to travel and return to their most pleasant place of all, Mt. Pleasant. They are very thankful for that wonderful community which they have called home for some 42 years.

BYWATER-CARPENTER. Clyde Bywater was a special person, son, patriot, husband, father and friend. Clyde was born the 5th of 11 children on May 17, 1897 in Clare County near the town of Farwell to John and Jessie Truxston Bywater. Clyde, as a boy moved several places with his parents. He lived in Farwell 1897-1900, the south side of Houghton Lake 1900-05, on the second farm of 40 acres near Houghton Lake 1905-07, in the Rosebush-Farwell area 1907-10, Boon 1910-11, and in Van Meer East Munising Wexford County 1911-16. During these years, Clyde's schooling ends at the fourth grade.

He worked as a farmer, logger and field laborer to help support a large family. In 1916,

Clyde strikes out on his own through the west. He settles down for a job on a big farming operation in Idaho. WWI breaks out and Clyde answers the call of his country. The U.S. Army is his home now learning how to run, march, shoot a rifle, and say "yes sir" army style. However, just prior to going "Over There" the patriotic song meaning the German front, Clyde loses his right leg in a railroad accident. After six months of rehabilitation both physical and scholastic, Clyde came home on Dec. 8, 1918 to Lansing, MI.

He became involved with his brother Charley, buying, repairing and selling houses (a house jockey). While this job is very competitive, drilling and repairing of water wells is not. Clyde puts together an impact or driver well rig mounted on a model T frame 25-foot mast, rope activated, model T car motor powered. Its smooth running was a tribute to Clyde's mechanical ability. Business is good which gives him time to visit the family now spread out from Lansing, Ionia, Grand Rapids, Portland, Sherman City and Van Meer.

Clyde was also known for his low budget trips to Florida and California. While on one of his central Michigan trips in the fall of 1927, he gets a hot land prospect of a 40-acre farm at 8775 W. Walton Rd., Rolland Twp., Blanchard, MI. Sale price was $500 and they will stand some of the price of the land contract. On June 20, 1928, the deal is struck. Clyde provides $300 up front and they will hold the mortgage of $200. The mortgage was sold to Charles Tate on April 23, 1929. As of April 23, 1929, Clyde Bywater and his new wife have purchased a 40-acre farm from Lorenzo and Arizona Bovee of Blanchard, MI providing that Clyde can pay the 1928 taxes of $46.

Clyde finds spring and summer of 1937 very hard on the farm so he moves off to Lansing and his sister Mabel moves on. There is much better money in the well business. From 1937-42, they live at 2228 W. Dunlap Lansing, MI. He works as a well driller and a cabinet maker. From 1942-45 they live in Apalachicola, FL where he works as a beekeeper and a commercial fisherman. From 1945-50, they live at 2418 W. Dunlap, Lansing, MI while he works as a well driller and farmer. In 1950, Clyde moves his family to Rolland Twp., Isabella County, MI. He says that the Lansing area is not a good environment to raise children.

From 1950-71, Clyde's life reflects his life's values: devotion and care of his children, excellent care of farm animals and crops (if you take care of the land it will take care of you). Called by all a good neighbor, may it be repairing machinery, dynamiting tree stumps or large rocks, forgiving loans and just giving a helping hand (do unto others as you would have them do unto you). Clyde dies peaceful and a successful man on Dec. 28, 1971.

CAHOONE-PECK. The Cohoons/Cahoons/Calhouns of the United States are descended from William Cahoone who was captured by the British during the Battle of Dunbar in 1650. William was one of 600 survivors of 10,000 prisoners taken during the battle. He was born in Luss on Loch Lomond in Scotland about 1633. He was indentured to Beck, Bex, & Co. of London and shipped aboard the John and Sarah to Massachusetts where he worked in the Winthrop Bog Iron Mines (now West Quincy).

In 1661 he was indentured to Samuel Deering who with 16 of his friends bought Block Island off Rhode Island. These men and William Cahoone went to the Island where Cahoone again worked in the bog iron mine. A plaque, affixed to a large boulder there, has all eighteen names and reads as follows:

A Free Man At Last:

"Settlers' Rock" commemorates the venture of these first white settlers on Block Island: Thomas Terry, Samuel Deering, John Clark, Simon Ray, William Rosh, Thormut Rose, William Barker, David Kimball, William Cahoone, Duncan M. Williamson, John Rathbone, William Judd, Edward Vorse, Nicholas White, William Billings, Trustrum Dodge, John Ackurs and Thomas Faxun.

William became a free man May 4, 1664, married Deborah Peck, and settled in Swansea, MA. The couple had seven children: Samuel, Mary, Joseph, William, James, John, and Nathaniel. He was appointed sole brick maker. These bricks were black and smooth. There is one in the Swansea Museum.

On June 24, 1675, he and 10 men volunteered to get a doctor's help for friends who had been injured by the Indians. All were killed; the Indians were caught and hung. This began what is known in American history as King Philiip's War. There is a plaque with the men's name, two of which are Salibury.

After early Cape Cod residents abandoned cultivating cranberries, Alvin Cohoon in 1846 planted a bog in Harwick, MA. He was joined by his cousin, retired Capt. Cyrus Cohoon, who developed the now famous early black variety from which most of today's commercial cranberries are descended including those of Ocean Spray.

Many Cohoons of this area are descended from William's third son Joseph. to fourth generation Joseph and Nancy Parr Cohoon. They had eight sons and three daughters. Seven sons and two daughters came to Michigan. David settled in Wayne County. James went to Plymouth and is the ancestor of Judson Foust, former president of CMU. Henry lived in Trenton. Many of John's family live in Midland and West Branch. Samuel settled in Jackson but his son David was one of the early settlers of Mt. Pleasant. Twins, Abigail and Lucinda, lived in Wayne County. Sarah may have remained in New York.

Charles Cohoon settled in Alma, Gratiot County, and Lidick in Shepherd, Isabella County. Two of Lidick's family and one of David's is in the Shepherd Area Historical Biography, pages 38, 39, 85, 86, 71, 72.

A descendent of the fifth son James, Stephen Calhoun, lives in Fresno, CA and it is due to his research that much of the Cohoon history is known. A sixth son, called Capt. John, had family in the Beaverton area.

CALKINS-BOUCHEY.
Nelson (William) Calkins (b. Aug. 26, 1916) md. Ilene Bouchey (b. Sept. 29, 1918) on March 9, 1938. To this union was born one child, Lorna (b. Sept. 21, 1944), who married Lowell Wonsey (b. June 12, 1944) on Jan. 25, 1964. Nelson and Ilene farmed for a few years but Nelson's health caused him to leave the farm and go to work at Central Michigan University. Ilene worked at the State Home in Mt. Pleasant. Nelson and Irene wintered in Crystal River, FL for many years after their retirement. Nelson passed away April 3, 1996.

Lorna and Lowell had three children, Charmaine (b. Sept. 21, 1964); Adam (b. March 19, 1967) and Daniel (b. Sept. 20, 1974). Lowell died after a long fight with cancer. Lorna later married Ivan Gates. They still stay busy working on water wells, and camping with their friends.

CALKINS-FAIRCHILD.
Elias (b. 1818) and Lemira (b. 1822) married and by 1846 were living in Michigan, having migrated here from Ohio. By 1861 they had settled in the woods five miles south of Mt. Pleasant, which at that time was unbroken forest.

In 1872 Elias purchased land where present day Rosebush is located and a year later in 1873 platted an addition on the land and called in Calkinsville. The Calkins were the first whites to settle in this area. Calkinsville was later granted a post office.

Children of Elias and Lemira were John, Edwin, Burton, Levi, Ella, James, George and Fred.

Although Elias spent the last years of his life in Calkinsville, he spent his last days at his son J.W.'s in Clare and is buried in Cherry Grove Cemetery. Lemira passed away Sept. 15, 1902.

CALKINS-FROGETT.
William (b. July 4, 1883 in Calkinsville, Isabella County, MI) md. Jennie Irene Frogett (b. February 1885) and to this union were born William Nelson Calkins (b. Aug. 26, 1916); Dorothy Calkins (b. July 19, 1919); Ralph Calkins (b. Jan. 4, 1921); Lysle Calkins (b. March 4, 1923); Inez Calkins (b. Oct. 19, 1924); and Merle Elton Calkins (b. Sept. 24, 1926).

William and Irene Calkins with their children l-r: Merle, Inez, Nelson, Dorothy and Lysle.

William had a butcher shop and bakery in the village of Rosebush (formerly Calkinsville) that was west of the old Rosebush Bank building. They built a home in Rosebush, the third block west on the north side of Rosebush Road, which later became the Frank Lynch house.

William and Irene later sold the meat market and bakery and bought a 60 acre farm one mile north and one mile west of Rosebush on Denver Road. They lived on the farm the rest of their lives. They were both hard working Christian people who saw a lot of changes in their lifetimes. William passed away in 1968 and Irene died in 1974.

The Calkins family have handed down a favorite cookie recipe called Dad's Fruit Cookies. To make a full batch you need to use 10 lbs. of flour and the recipe yields 36 dozen cookies. The Calkins family later published a cookbook of their favorite recipes that have been handed down through the generations.

CALKINS-GARDNER.
Burton (b. 1850), son of Elias and Lemira (Fairchild) Calkins, married Augusta Ann Gardner (b. 1857).

Bert and Augusta Calkins

To this union was born Lua Mae (b. Feb. 28, 1875); Ida Belle (b. April 12, 1878); Frank Burton (b. Sept. 6, 1880); William Augusta (b. July 4, 1883); Arthur Burton (b. June 30, 1885); Myra Della (b. Dec. 14, 1887); Franklin Leroy (b. Sept. 16, 1891); and J. Lester (b. 1898).

Burton and Augusta eventually moved to the town of Clare where they became well-known. Burton was the carpenter who built the first store building in Clare. He passed away in 1923 and Augusta in 1938.

CALKINS-MOORE.
Lysle Wesley Calkins (b. March 4, 1923) md. Anna Louise Moore (b. April 12, 1925) on July 26, 1947. To this union were born Sally Irene on March 11, 1959; Penny Ann on May 28, 1961; and Raymond Lysle on Jan. 18, 1960. Lysle and Anna also reared Garry Potter (b. Jan. 22, 1946) and later adopted Gary.

Lysle and Anna farmed a large amount of land in Denver Twp. where they built their home in 1975. They have reared all their children in this home and still live in it today.

CALKINS-ROGERS.
Inez Calkins (b. Oct. 9, 1924) md. Harold Rogers (b. Sept. 1, 1920) on May 29, 1943. To this union were born four daughters: Helen Rogers born (b. Nov. 28, 1945) who married Mike Bragg (b. March 21, 1945) and had two daughters, Michelle Lyn (b. May 11, 1971) and Rebecca Megan (b. Nov. 12, 1973); Pat Rogers born (b. June 9, 1947) married David O'Farroll (b. April 22, 1947) and had two boys, Todd Patrick (b. Jan. 2, 1968) and Sean Michael (b. June 5, 1973); Mary Ann Rogers (b. Nov. 5, 1948) md. Bill Pritchard (b. Dec. 11, 1947) on Oct. 4, 1968 and had two girls, Polly (b. Oct. 14, 1972) and Amber (b. Nov. 13, 1974); Cindy Rogers (b. Dec. 5, 1953) md. Brad Niergarth (b. Nov. 16, 1953) on Jan. 11, 1975.

Inez and Harold were in the jewelry business for many years having stores in Evart and Big Rapids, MI. Inez currently resides in Cadillac and enjoys traveling around the world.

A brother to Inez named Ralph Harold Calkins (b. Jan. 4, 1921) passed away at the age of 13 from a childhood illness on June 19, 1934).

CALKINS-WILTSE. Dorothy Calkins (b. July 29, 1919) md. Robert Wiltse (b. April 4, 1911) and to this union were born five children: Carrol Wiltse (b. July 27, 1939); Gloria Wiltse (b. Nov. 6, 1942); David Wiltse (b. Oct. 24, 1944); Dale Wiltse (b. Feb. 2, 1946); and Nancy Wiltse (b. Nov. 9, 1949).

Carol married Dalene Bailey (b. April 23, 1941) on Oct. 15, 1983; Gloria married Walter Dunbar (b. Dec. 23, 1937); David married Sherry Banks (b. Dec. 4, 1947) on Feb. 15, 1969; Dale married Dianne Maarceau (b. May 3, 1947) on June 25, 1969; Nancy married Ron Pranzarone (b. Oct. 8, 1945) on May 15, 1971.

CALKINS-YAGER. Merle (b. Sept. 24, 1926 in Rosebush, Isabella County, MI) md. Marion Lucille Yager (b. May 12, 1926) on June 19, 1948. To this union were born Rhoda Lucille Calkins (b. May 8, 1953), Mark Elton Calkins (b. Nov. 19, 1954), Larry William Calkins (b. Nov. 16, 1956) and Merlin Nelson Calkins (b. July 20, 1959).

Merle and Marion Calkins

Merle went to North Rosebush country school through the 7th grade, then attended and graduated from Mt. Pleasant High School through the 12th grade. He worked on the family farm and also drove bus for a few years. He spent two years in the Marine Corp during the Korean War. After his military service he worked at Dow Chemical in Midland where he retired after 30 years of work on Jan. 31, 1981.

Merle loves to hunt and has some of his trophies mounted. He stays busy helping his children, working in his garden and yard and making things out of scrap metal and wood in his workshop.

Marion was raised in Coleman and her folks had a farm there. At the young age of 16, Marion quit high school and went to work at J.C. Penney's in Midland, MI. She worked in window displays and also made signs for the store. She stayed at home while her children were young but also did some upholstery work in her spare time. When the youngest child turned 13 or 14 she decided to work outside the home again and went to work in the drapery department at Oren's Department Store in Mt. Pleasant, MI. She worked there for about 4-1/2 years until the store was sold.

In 1977 Marion decided to start her own drapery shop, which she called Marian's Drapery & Unique Gifts. For about a year she worked out of her home, then opened a shop in Rosebush in the first building after the old bank on Rosebush Road. In 1984 she returned the business to her home using the converted garage into a shop where she operated until 1989 when she retired.

Some of Marion's hobbies include bird watching, oil flower paintings and making quilts. Both Merle and Marion treasure the times that they have when their children, grandchildren and family gets together.

Merle and Marion Calkins, their four children and spouses, and 10 grandchildren

Rhoda married Daryl Bigelow in 1979 and they have two children, Donald Barry Bigelow (b. 1981) and Rebecca Lynnette Bigelow (b. 1983). Mark married Dianne Holp in 1976 and they have two children, Nathan Mark Calkins (b. 1979) and Brent Mark Calkins. Larry first married Dawn Ferguson and they one son, William Gabriel Calkins (b. 1981). Larry secondly married Lenora Riggleman in 1981 and they have two children, Troy Tyler (b. 1986) and Matthew Lee Calkins (b. 1992). Merlin married Dianne Friesen in 1983. They have three children: Kendall Merle Calkins (b. 1983), Bethany Doris Calkins (b. 1988) and Jeffrey James Calkins (b. 1990).

CARPENTER-BYWATER. Lena Mae Carpenter was born the first of eight children to Colonel Edward and Helen Chambers Carpenter. At the age of 14, Lena loses her mother to pneumonia. This creates a break up and family unity deteriorates. Lena and Mary (next sister) are to pick up the mothering jobs. Their schooling and childhood takes a backseat to work. When a handsome, well-spoken well driller asks for her hand, Lena says "I will ask my father to consent" and he does. On Aug. 9, 1928, Lena becomes Mrs. Clyde Bywater.

Clyde and Lena have 12 children, three dying as infants. The nine living children are: Thelma (b. April 4, 1934), Fred (b. Aug. 7, 1936), Marilyn (b. Nov. 25, 1938), Juanita (b. Aug. 20, 1941), Floyd (b. Aug. 20, 1941), Rose (b. March 25, 1943), Madelyn (b. July 15, 1944), Carolyn (b. Feb. 1, 1947) and Janet (b. March 13, 1948).

In the summer of 1951, the marriage falls apart. Lena moves out having been married too young, the inability to settle down and not having sewn wild oats. Lena remarries and has one child, Ronald Broughten on June 22, 1952. Lena lived out the rest of her life in Macon, GA and died Nov. 15, 1970.

CHAPMAN-WILLIS. Peter Chapman (b. April 16, 1825, d. Dec. 7, 1888) and Lodema Willis (b. Jan. 17, 1830, d. Oct. 6, 1904) had nine children. Originally from Saratoga and Monroe counties, NY, they settled in Rolland Twp. Sec. 35 on 100 acres of farmland. They are buried in Pine River Cemetery, Rolland Twp., Isabella County.

Burton (2nd) (b. May 26, 1870, d. March 24, 1947) md. Lena Densmore (b. June 2, 1876, d. Feb. 3, 1916) on New Year's Eve, 1894, at her residence near Blanchard. Lena's parents were Frank and Edith (Jones) Densmore. They

took the train to Grand Rapids on a honeymoon and to visit relatives. They had seven sons: Lloyd, Merrill, Laurence, Everett, Clark, Milo and Grant. Bert, Lena, Laurence, Merrill and Grant are buried in Surrey Twp. Cemetery in Farwell, MI.

Bert (Burton II), Lloyd, Milo, Everett, Clark and Grant

Milo (b. Dec. 10, 1900, d. Aug. 8, 1984) left home at age 16, after his mother's death, and went to work on the farm for his cousin, Thorton Densmore. While there he met Retha Zufelt, daughter of Grant and Cena (Richardson) Zufelt, who was boarding there while teaching school. They were married at the Presbyterian Manse in Mt. Pleasant on May 4, 1929.

They moved to Lansing for a short period of time, then returned to live with Retha's parents. Milo farmed with Grant Zufelt. Five children were born there. They moved to a farm due west and had one more child. In 1944 they moved to a farm 1-1/2 miles north of Strickland Baptist Church on South Green Road, in Lincoln Twp. where he farmed until he retired in 1960 and moved to Rosebush, MI.

After moving to Rosebush, Milo and Retha remained active by maintaining a large garden, and cleaning a local church. Milo painted houses in the area and worked for Camiel VanAcker on his farm north of Rosebush. All six children of Milo and Retha attended the Davis (Fremont Twp.) and Green (Lincoln Twp.) elementary schools. They all graduated from Vestaburg High School.

Laurence, the oldest son (b. Jan. 13, 1931, d. July 3, 1997), served in the U.S. Army in Japan. He married Evelyn Olmstead of Charlotte and they had four children and nine grandchildren. Laurence retired from Kellogg Airfield in Battle Creek.

Shirley Richeson (b. Feb. 5, 1932, d. March 6, 1990) taught at Saginaw Business Institute and was a financial aid officer at Kirtland Community College and Saginaw Valley Institute. She had one son, Dan A. Richeson, who lives in Mt. Pleasant, and three grandchildren.

Clara retired from state of Michigan (Regional Center) and resides in Rosebush, MI.

Myrna lives in Lansing, is retired from state of Michigan (Community Health), married to Arlo Earegood since 1956. They had four children, six grandchildren, and one great-granddaughter.

Milo Jr. (Willis) resides in Mt. Pleasant. He married and divorced Patricia Kosa. They have three children and six grandchildren. He served four years in the U.S. Navy.

Roger (b. April 25, 1941, d. Jan. 28, 1991) married and divorced Paula Fisk of Vestaburg.

They had four daughters and nine grandchildren. Roger attended Ferris State University, and earned his bachelor's degree from Andrews University, Berrien Springs, MI in 1969. He was a social worker in Berrien County, taught school in Indiana, and was employed at a hospital in Walla Walla, WA at the time of his death, age 49. Laurence is buried in East Leroy Cemetery; Milo, Retha, Shirley and Roger are buried in Woodland Cemetery, Rosebush, MI.

CLARK-COMINS.

Charles Augustus Clark, son of George Thomas and Mary Ann (Stutter) Clark, both originally from Gloucestershire, England, was born May 23, 1902. His parents owned a farm at 656 E. Beal City Road, Isabella County. He had five brothers and six sisters, all born in Isabella County: George H. (b. March 17, 1884), Jesse Isaac (b. Jan. 15, 1886), Francis Mabel (b. Feb. 8, 1888), Frank W. (b. Sept. 9, 1889), Albert C. "Joe" (b. Jan. 14, 1891), Emma B. (b. March 5, 1892), Sarah Jane (b. Oct. 1, 1893), Laurie Iva (b. March 19, 1896), Gladys Mae (b. June 26, 1898), Thomas F. (b. June 29, 1900), Charles A. (b. May 23, 1902), Rosalie (b. June 23, 1904).

Charles married Mary Jane Comins (b. Sept. 21, 1904) on Sept. 1, 1926 in Mt. Pleasant, MI. Mary's parents, Clinton Levi and Edna Jane (Parks) Comins, were originally from Belleville, Ontario, Canada. Mary had a brother James Harvey (b. April 23, 1907) and a sister Bessie Irene (b. July 16, 1911). All three were born in Canada. Mary's mother Edna died in 1914 as the result of an accident.

Clint moved the family to Mt. Pleasant, MI where his parents, Harvey L. and Margaret Jane (Garrison) Comins, had come earlier for a visit and stayed for health reasons. Clint then married Lena Mae Phillips (originally from Ontario, Canada) in 1926 and had a daughter Jane Anne (b. June 8, 1927). Charles and Mary lived in Isabella County on several farms from 1926-39. At that time Charles' mother died, so they moved to the farm at 2540 N. Whiteville Road to care for his father. His father died in 1943.

Charles and Mary had seven children, all born in Isabella County: Charles Jr. (Jan. 15, 1927), Marian Edna (Nov. 15, 1928), Joseph Clinton (b. July 15, 1937), Virginia Lee "Sue" (b. Nov. 22, 1941), George Franklin (b&d. Aug. 29, 1944) and twins Carol Ann "Tillie" and Harold Richard "Mike" (b. April 23, 1947).

Clark Family, l-r: Charles Jr., Virginia Lee "Sue" Embrey, Mary Jane (Mother), Charles Augustus (Father), Marian Edna Harrison, Joseph Clinton "Joe" and twins, Carol Ann "Tillie" Embrey and Harold Richard "Mike." Taken 1962 at Jr.'s home near Shepherd, MI.

During the Depression Charles worked for the WPA, clearing forests and logging. A tree accidentally fell on his left leg and crushed it between his knee and ankle. It took considerable time to get him to medical help, and he came very close to losing his leg. He had gangrene at one point and thus it took a long time to recover. Due to the accident, this leg was shorter and left Charles with a limp after that. He had also lost a finger down to the knuckle on his left hand. However, he still maintained a good sense of humor, was a hard worker and loved to farm. He was a good father and dearly loved and enjoyed his grandchildren.

In 1947 Charles and Mary moved to a 120-acre farm at 2990 N. Meridian Road and farmed crops and raised dairy cows, pigs, chickens, ducks and geese. The farm was taken over in 1958 by their son Joseph Clinton and his wife Lois Jean (Nicholson) Clark. Charles and Mary moved to an 80-acre farm at 3386 N. Whiteville Road where they lived until Charles death on June 1, 1965. Mary stayed on the farm until 1971.

When Charles and Mary's children married, they all lived within 30 miles of home. For many years they would all come home for Sunday dinners, along with their 24 grandchildren.

After Charles death in 1965 Mary was asked to teach at St. Joseph School in Beal City. She had received her teaching certificate from Central Michigan Normal (CMU) in 1923. She taught for a few years before moving to Mt. Pleasant in 1971 to care for her Aunt Julia (Comins) McKnight. Her aunt died in 1972, but Mary continued to live at 203 E. Chippewa Street until she passed away on May 12, 1997 at the age of 92. Mary's family all called her "Gram" and loved her very much.

COHOON-GALLUP.

Benjamin Arthur Cohoon was born Aug. 10, 1837 in Onandaga County, NY, to Lidick and Martha (Pickard) Cohoon, natives of New York. He came to Jackson, MI with his parents at 10 years of age. Benjamin's father went to Shepherd in 1857 after his wife died to buy land and returned in 1859 to settle on Sec. 19. Benjamin remained with his father until

Benjamin A. Cohoon

he was 23. From January through August 1961 he went to work logging on the Muskegon River.

When President Lincoln asked for volunteers, Benjamin returned to Jackson where he enlisted in the 9th Corps of the Eighth Voluntary Infantry Sept. 9, 1861. He was discharged Dec. 28, 1863 for the purpose of re-enlistment in Rutledge, TN, serving until June 13, 1865.

During his first enlistment, he was captured at the Battle of Secessionville on James Island, SC and spent four months as prisoner in Libby and at Columbia, SC until his exchange. During his second enlistment, he was captured May 6, 1864 at the Battle of the Wilderness and was at Andersonville Prison and then, before Sherman's army overran Atlanta, he was moved to Florence Prison where he remained for five months. He

was released March 1, 1865 at Wilmington, NC, and discharged at Camp Chase, OH June 13, 1865.

At Andersonville, no utensils were given to measure the food until a small tin can was found. Prisoner Benjamin Cohoon cut a strip off the top of the can for a handle with a pair of vest pocket shears and used a penny and made three rivets to fasten the handle to the cup. This cup was used by Quartermaster Ransom Brooks of Lansing to measure each prisoner's ration of corn gruel for 24 hours. Benjamin's cap and one boot he wore at Andersonville are in the possession of his descendants. Descendants also have a letter Benjamin wrote to his father and brother May 7, 1863 from Carver Hospital in Washington, DC describing the Battle on the Rappahannock.

After the war, Benjamin returned to Jackson and married on June 17, 1867 to Eudoria Gallup, daughter of William and Lydia (Page) Gallup. Eudoria was born Dec. 29, 1842 in Jackson County. Eudoria and Benjamin settled on Sec. 19 Coe Twp. Isabella County, MI and were the parents of Lenora (b. May 27, 1867), Ransom M. (b. Oct. 16, 1871), Lillian E. (b. Sept. 2, 1874), Henrietta L. (b. April 9, 1878) and Cora E. (b. Oct. 15, 1880). Benjamin died two months after his 50th wedding anniversary. Eudoria died Dec. 28, 1919. Both were buried in the Shepherd Cemetery.

There are descendants of Lillian in the area (see the Shepherd Biography, pages 71, 72, 85 and 86). Cora married George McGarry on Sept. 21, 1910 in Mt Pleasant and lived in Shepherd all her life. They had three children: Robert Dale and Christine Louise, both deceased, and Edna Eudoria now living in Midland with her daughter Mary and son-in-law William Dennis. Robert Dale's son Robert Eugene McGarry currently lives in Shepherd.

COHOON-MCGARRY.

Cora (Cohoon) McGarry was born Oct. 15, 1880 at home on Pleasant Valley Road west of Salt River Corners, Coe Twp., Isabella County on land purchased by her grandfather, Lydick Cohoon, on March 10, 1857 from the U.S. Government. Cora's father Benjamin Cohoon (b. Aug. 10, 1837, Onandaga County, NY) and his family moved to Jackson County, MI in 1847 and Isabella County in 1859.

Cora (Cohoon) McGarry

In 1861 when President Lincoln requested Civil War volunteers, Cora's father, Benjamin, enlisted. He survived incarceration in four prisons and told Cora he lost his eyelashes and eye brows in Andersonville because "all they were fed for a 24 hour ration was a cup of corn gruel, ground cob and all."

When the war was over Benjamin courted and married Eudoria Gallup on June 17, 1867 in Jackson. Eudoria (b. Dec. 29, 1842) was the daughter of William and Lydia (Paige) Gallup who were natives of New York State and moved to Liberty Mills, Jackson County, MI before Eudoria was born. After the wedding on June

28, 1867 Benjamin brought Eudoria to the log cabin in Coe Twp. where Benjamin's father and brother lived. Upon seeing the the cabin, Eudoria told Benjamin she was returning to Jackson until he built her a proper house.

In January 1868 Benjamin and Eudoria moved into their new house on 80 acres next to his father's log cabin on land which Benjamin had purchased the year before. Benjamin and Eudoria farmed and raised sheep. They spun the wool into yarn and knitted socks which they sold to help pay off the mortgage. One of the farm buildings had a mill used to grind wheat into flour. Prior to that, Cora said her father walked to St. Johns and carried sacks of flour home on his back.

Cora (b. Oct. 15, 1880) was the youngest of five children born to Benjamin and Eudoria. Her brothers and sisters were Lenonora (b. May 27, 1869), Ransom (b. Oct. 16, 1871), Lillian (b. Sept. 2, 1874), and Henrietta (b. April 9, 1878.

Cora lived all her life in Coe Twp. and graduated from Shepherd High School in 1880. She passed a teacher's examination and obtained her first teaching job at Leaton School which was a one-room school with several grades. She rode her bicycle with wooden wheels to work each day. She continued to teach until her marriage in Mount Pleasant, MI on Sept. 2, 1910 to George McGarry who she met at a Civil War Reunion meeting in Harrison. George was born in Livingston County to Thomas and Emily (Thorne) McGarry Dec. 22, 1882.

Cora and George purchased a farm on South Leaton Road Coe Twp. where all their children were born: Robert (b. May 22, 1911), Edna (b. Oct. 24, 1912) and Christine (b. Oct. 2, 1914).

Cora became blind from glaucoma as did her brother, father and grandfather. She died Oct. 5, 1962 at age 82.

COLE-EWING-WIXSON-HUBBARD.

James Cole (b. Sept. 7, 1863 in Kingston, Prince Edward County, Canada) came to Mount Morris, MI in 1865 and married Eva Angeline Cram on May 3, 1901.

Their son Paul Manley Cole (b. Jan. 13, 1902) was delivered at Sand Lake by Mrs. Jennie Cline from Rockford, MI. Paul married Halena Francis

Eva A. (Cram) Cole and James Cole

Wixson on May 3 1921, and had three daughters: Norma Constance Cole Mossell (b. Oct. 1, 1924); Vilma Virgina Cole (b. May 22, 1927) spent her life in a wheelchair as the result of a birth injury now called Cerebral Palsy; and Audrey Delores "Pat" Cole Ewing (b. Dec. 27, 1931). Audrey was born at home and delivered by Dr. Rondo.

On Aug. 27, 1949, Audrey married Franklin William Ewing, son of Earl Howard and Laura Adrianna Hubbard Ewing who married April 25, 1924. Earl and Laura moved into Ed and Zean Olger's home, which was across from Earl and Peet Douglas and one mile east of Paul Cole's home. Earl and Laura had eight children: Earl

(Betty) Ewing and Velma J. (Grant Kenneth) Allen, both living at Littlefield Lake; Paul (Joanne) living in Lansing area; Russell (Daisy) of Bay City; Walter (Lilly) from Shepard; Frank (Pat); Duane (Marie); and Doris (Lee) Hillaker in Tuscola County.

Paul M. Cole, Halena Wixson Cole; Vilma, Connie and Audrey Cole

The Ewing home burned shortly after they moved to Isabella County and they built a cement house that stands today (2003). After their death in 1955, Doctor Chamberlain from Mount Pleasant purchased the property.

Eva told that after her father died she was left a cow, and that she walked from Cedar Springs down old state Road, now know as West Coleman Road, to her home in Gilmore Twp. After James died in 1933 She married Frank Sherman, and they lived in a log cabin just west of Littlefield Lake on what is known as Stevenson Lake Road. The log cabin burned in 1967. Sid Struble, a barber, and his family from Mount Pleasant bought the property.

Eva often would walk west past Hank and Jim Purdy's home, turning south at George Skinner's corner, past Fred Wardwell's farm, chatting as she walked along, casting a glance at Mike Kripa's home, which often had a barking dog. Leon Hart had a berry farm next and as she approached the fruit farm, Martin Bolger's corner, she would turn east and would go past her friend Willard Spencer, then pass her old farm that George Hamilton's family now owns. She would then be a welcomed sight at the foot of the hill, her son Paul's home.

Eva told many stories of her life, one was about an Indian family who lost a tiny baby and were not allowed to bury the baby in the graveyard, so she offered a spot on her farm. She also told of a dying friend who said how she longed for some fresh fish, so Eva took her bamboo pole and walked to the lake. Not having a good day, she caught a dandy batch of undersize fish, then caught a ride home with two game wardens.

Audrey can remember her Grandma Eva and Frank Sherman taking her with them to Ray Geislers Store at Brinton in a one-horse wagon. She once danced at Brinton.

Audrey's grandfather, John Henry Wixon, was born Feb. 1, 1873. His parents were William and Mary Ann Bawkey who married Jan. 1, 1868. They came from Seneca and Wood County, OH. He married her grandmother, Louisa Wiggins (b. March 27, 1881 in Bay City). Her parents James and Fanny (Colosky) Wiggins came from Canada. James and Fanny married Aug. 28, 1876.

John Henry and Louisa married Jan. 30, 1897, and to this union a large family was born:

Edward (Clara), James (Beaula), Clarence (Ethel), Chet, Dave, and Bill Wixson, Helen (Fred) Wardwell, Dorothy (George) Courte[r] Lucille (Julius) Albee, Hilda (Dave[)] Winegardner Sampson, and Halena Franci[s] Wixson (Paul) Cole.

Wixson Family: (not in order) John Henry, Louisa, Helen, Louisa (Wiggins), Edward, Halena, Dorothy, Lucille, Bill, Dave, Chet, Hilda, Frank Ewing

Paul Cole worked for the WPA building bridges in the area. His boss was Jim Bent from Mount Pleasant, and he later became a close family friend. Dad then went to work for Vanderveen Construction Co., near Grand Rapids. He worked the stone crusher as they traveled building highways. Frank said that Paul told him that he poured the fastest mile of highway of anyone at that time. The money was good, but kept him away from home weekdays.

Paul then started his own cement finishing business, hiring many of the men in the area. Paul was one of the top finishers in Michigan. Halena kept a neat, clean and happy home while Paul worked. She took Audrey with her to return her father's team and wagon to Jersulem Hills and they made it in good time. She never drove a car.

Paul attended the Case School a mile east of the farm. Audrey's sister Connie graduated from the eighth grade there, Vilma enjoyed the school pot lucks, and all of them received their vaccination there as well. Audrey transferred to Weidman, Sherman Twp. Rural Agricultural School, in fifth grade.

Some of the families who also attended the Case School were, Gatehouse, Purdy, Hampilton, Fields, Kent, Seymore, Olger, Lumbert, Spencer, Hart and Shanner. A few of the teachers were Mrs. Monk, Mr. Sloan, Mrs. Geisler, Miss Fordyce, Miss Cook, and Mrs. Willy. Audrey remembers one occasion when Earl and Peet Douglas brought a black bear to school on the hood of their car, kind of like "Show and Tell." Audrey graduated from Weidman with a fine group of classmates "The Forty Niners," they meet each year at a local restaurant and, what else, talk and eat.

The Free Methodist Church shared the same property as the school. Audrey's Sunday school teacher was Mrs. Kitty (Lon) Brown; other teachers were Mrs. (Mate) Maybee and Frank and Mary Walters. Floyd and Bessie Seiters and their son Leon, held services. They used a bus to bring those families who needed a ride on Sunday. Audrey remembers them using a Flannel board to tell bible stories and made it almost as good as the movies. They would bring their motion picture camera and filmed the Hampiltons,

Ewings, Coles, Seymores, Kents, Browns, Courters, Wixson, Allen, Albee, Mossells and other families she doesn't know. She has a copy of their film, which was copied 30 years ago. Across from the church in the late 30s lived the young family of Theron Jarman. Her parents bought their property and her sister Connie and her husband Joe Mossell lived in the log cabin in 1947.

Frank and Audrey lived in it in 1950 and again in 1954. Audrey expects many of the

Pat and Frank Ewing

families mentioned have loved ones buried in Gilmore Cemetery, though Frank and Audrey are in no hurry to join them, that will be their final resting place. God willing the Beginning and not the End. Amen

CONROY-GORMAN.
Oct. 23, 1913 was a beautiful autumn day. That morning, at Sacred Heart Church in Mount Pleasant, Mary Alberta, daughter of Daniel and Frances (Evans) Gorman of Deerfield Twp. became the bride of George Edward, son of John and Bridget (Corcoran) Conroy of Chippewa Twp. They were attended by Anna Gorman, sister of the bride, and the groom's brother, Frederick.

Both, the Conroy and Gorman families, came to the New World from Ireland in the 1840s, the Conroy's to New York and then to Canada before migrating to Michigan in 1879. The Gorman's came directly to Canada and came to Michigan in the same year, 1879.

George and Bertha (she never used her baptismal name) went to live in Detroit, where he was a motorman for the City Transit System.

In 1918, they returned to Isabella County having purchased the Gorman farm in Deerfield. It was there that the writer first saw the light of day on Nov. 27, 1919.

The first six years of Robert Conroy's life was spent on this farm where he has many very vivid memories: Clyde Lyons pulling into their driveway with his big steam engine and thrashing machine complete with a water wagon. Also, his first day at the Townline School and his teacher, Miss Anna Marie Murphy and all those kids.

In 1924, his parent's wedding attendants, Anna and Fred, decided to "tie the knot" and took up residence at the Conroy farm in Chippewa Twp.

In 1926, his parents and Fred and Anna Conroy decided to become partners at the Conroy farm in Chippewa Twp.

There, Robert was enrolled at the Landon School where he continued through the eighth grade. In 1933 he entered good old MPHS, graduating in 1937. After graduating, he enrolled in the Industrial Training Institute in Chicago, a school specializing in air conditioning and refrigeration, graduating in 1939.

In 1940 he decided to seek his fortune in the "Big City," so went to Detroit, got a job in his chosen field, and continued to take classes at the University of Detroit and Wayne State, however he remained undegreed.

It was in Detroit, that he met the love of his life, Marjorie Surridge, and they were wed in 1942. She still retains that title after almost 60 years. In that period, they have been blessed with six children: Colleen, Kathleen, Michael, Patrick, Kevin and Brian, along with 15 grandchildren and at last count, four great-grandchildren. It is only fair to say, at this point, that all of this would not have been possible without the co-operation of three beautiful daughters-in-law and two terrific sons-in-law. We have been blessed!

As Robert approaches his 83rd birthday, he can look back over all those years and enjoy all those memories which he and Marge have accumulated, and can thank many people who have had a real impact on their lives, including many, many from good old Isabella County.

COOMER-OSGOOD.
Noah Virgil Coomer, son of Benjamin G. and Mary Isabella (Cooley) Coomer was born in Farmington, Oakland County, MI, Jan. 19, 1848 and died in 1926. As a young man he saved enough to buy a village lot in Morenci and built a home on it. He married Ella A. Osgood, the only daughter of Josiah Osgood and Mary (Foster) Osgood, on June 9, 1873.

Picture taken Jan. 18, 1904. Noah Virgil Coomer was 56 and Ella Ann Coomer was 50 years old.

They lived there a few years. Sold it and bought a new 120 acre farm in Deerfield, Isabella County and moved onto it. This place is about nine miles southwest of Mt. Pleasant and far enough from cleared country to give them a good deal of experience of pioneer life. They had a school house, a church (Coomer) and a cemetery on part of the farm. The school was burned by an arsonist some time later.

Noah held several offices in the town and in the church. He had served at least three terms as Justice of the Peace, and was census enumerator in 1884. At this time he received the appointment from Postmaster General Wanamaker to be the Postmaster General of the Coomer Post Office.

They had four daughters: Mary Florence (b. Feb. 11, 1875), Martha Viola (b. March 30, 1877), Lilly Mable (b. Aug. 2, 1879, d. Dec. 26, 1964), Laura Eva (b. Aug. 1, 1882, d. March 1, 1965).

Ella was a school teacher, and her great-granddaughter, Margaret Lucille Cotter, has her Teacher's Special Certificate for District No. 10, Deerfield Twp., Isabella County, MI, dated Oct. 26, 1883. Her pay was $20.00 per month.

Many may think, Noah and Ella are buried in the Coomer Cemetery, but not so. Margaret, her grandmother, Mable (Coomer) Stacy their third daughter, and Margaret's Mother, Beulah M. (Stacy) Ferris, have decorated and cared for

their graves in Riverside Cemetery in Mt. Pleasant since their deaths.

Great-Grandmother, Ella Coomer, died on May 22, 1921 at age 67 in West Seattle, WA and was shipped back to Mt. Pleasant, where funeral services were held in the M.E. Church on May 31, 1921.

This information was taken from a hard bound book of the "History of the Coomer Family," author, Benjamin G. Coomer and comments written by N.V. Coomer. Noah kept a daily diary for many years and this is in the possession of Margaret Lucille Cotter, his great-granddaughter.

COTTER-GOFFNETT.
Mable Coomer, daughter of Noah V. Coomer and Ella A. (Osgood) Coomer, married Harley Mason Stacy, son of John and Mary (Nintz) Stacy, April 12, 1901. They had three children: Beulah M. (b. April 12, 1902, d. July 16, 1972); Howard L. (b. Oct. 4, 1903, d. Jan. 28, 1971) and Hazel Marie (b&d. same day in 1909).

Beulah married Lawson Henry Ferris, Jan. 28, 1922. He was the son of Charles Ferris and Lucy (Button) Ferris from the Vestaburg and Sumner area. He was born June 18, 1890 and died Jan. 25, 1935. He served in the Army in France, during WWI.

Beulah worked many years at the Glenn Oren's store in Mt. Pleasant after she became a widow and was left with six children. Howard was an accountant for Burroughs in Detroit.

Margaret Lucille (Ferris) (Goffnett) Cotter (b. Dec. 17, 1922) is the oldest of the children in the Ferris family. She married Stanley Goffnett July 13, 1941. Stanley was the son of Lawrence and Ethel (VanHorn) Goffnett, born May 20, 1921. He farmed their 160 acre farm and had a milk route for a number of years. They sold their farm after their oldest son was killed. Richard (b. May 31, 1943) was struck by a passing motorist sliding on ice Feb. 1, 1949. He was with a group of children on their way to the country school they attended. They moved and had a small grocery store, gas station and had a fuel delivery on old U.S. 27. Stanley passed away Sept. 19, 1957 following a drowning accident.

After Stanley's death, Lucille went to work for Cole's Campus Store where she was in charge of the book department. This was before Central Michigan University had a book department and she ordered books for the university classes. After the fire at the Campus Store on Good Friday, she went to work for Central Michigan University, working for the Registrar's office and Computer Services. She retired at the end of December 1986 after working at Central Michigan University for 23-1/2 years.

Donald and Lucille Cotter

On Aug. 15, 1962 Donald J. Cotter and Lucille were married. He had three children by his first marriage: daughter Roni Dell and two sons, Donald J. Jr. and Linden J. Cotter. Between the two of them, they have seven children, 14 grandchildren, and 18 great-grandchildren.

Donald worked at Dow Chemical Co., as a rigger for 31 years and retired in February 1987. They have traveled extensively to all the states, including Hawaii and Alaska in 1997, to England and Ireland and in the year 2000, to Australia and New Zealand. They have been to several provinces of Canada and to Mexico and have been on several cruises.

They are members of the First Church of Christ of Mt. Pleasant and the Genealogy Society of Isabella County. They both enjoy gardening and fishing. Lucille belongs to the Lincoln Center Extension Club and is a Gold Key Volunteer for the Commission on Aging. They also volunteer to help at the Red Cross Blood Drives and Don makes 911 signs for the Red Cross.

COURSER-CHAMBERLAIN-WRIGHT.
Ephraim Carter Courser, son of Jesse and Hannah (Elkins) Courser, was born Dec. 5, 1831, Abercorn, Quebec, Canada and died April 2, 1915 Rolland Twp., Isabella County, MI; buried Pine River Cemetery near Blanchard, MI. One party says he went to California hunting for gold in 1852.

He married first Alvina Chamberlain about 1857/8 in Canada. She was born 1839, died Dec. 26, 1859 in childbirth and buried Brock Memorial Cemetery, Glen Sutton, Canada. One child, Thurlow Courser (b. Dec. 26, 1859, d. March 31, 1935) came to Michigan with his father, married Eliza Jane Richardson and had children.

On May 8, 1860, Ephraim married second Martha Wright (b. Feb. 11, 1843, Richford, VT, d. June 16, 1905, Rolland Twp.), daughter of Abijah Wright and Orrisa ? of Orleans County, VT. Martha is buried beside her husband. They moved to Rolland Twp. near Pine River, Isabella County, MI in 1875/6. Some of his children could remember coming when they were very young. He was a farmer in Rolland Twp. and an old settler of the area. He spent the rest of his life in Rolland Twp. Their children:

Back, l-r: Elvina, Jessie, Thurlow, Simeon; middle: Hattie, Ephraim Sr., Martha, Ephraim Jr.; front: Lucinda, Cora (on floor in front), William and Hannah. Picture made between 1890-92 and not really sure who is in picture.

Elvina Courser (b. June 16, 1861, Ohio, d. Feb. 16, 1927, Ann Arbor, MI) md. Joseph Forquer.

Jesse Courser (b. Oct. 24, 1862, Michigan, d. Oct. 31, 1937, Deerfield Twp.) md. Isabella Gearhart.

Martha Jane Courser (b. Aug. 29, 1864 Vermont) md. George Pumfrey; died in childbirth (Isabella County Death Records) May 29, 1882, Rolland Twp.

Ephraim Carter Courser Jr. (b. March 13, 1866 New York, d. Dec. 28, 1933, Deerfield Twp.) md. Emma Gearhart; second Anna McLaren; and third Dolly Rareden.

Hattie Orrisa Courser (b. Sept. 23, 1867, Richmond, VT, d. March 4, 1934) md. George Woodward.

Lucinda Courser (b. May 29, 1869, Richmond, VT, d. Jan. 30, 1931, Edmore) md. William Crawford. He was killed in an accident and she married second Peter Hanson.

Rosannah Courser (b. Oct. 18, 1870 in Jay, Orleans County, VT, d. June 17, 1945 in Washington State) md. Lewis Koltz and moved west.

Simeon Sumner Courser (b. Sept. 18, 1872, Richmond, VT, d. April 18, 1934, Alma, MI) md. Martha J. McIntyre.

DeForrest Courser (b. April 26, 1874, Richford, VT; d. July 31, 1885, Rolland Twp.) died of diphtheria and his father had to take his body out a back window because of the contagiousness of the disease and so he wouldn't spread the disease.

William Courser (b. Jan. 7, 1877, Rolland Twp., Isabella County, MI, d. Feb. 5, 1959, Mt. Pleasant) md. Barbara Uebele; divorced; married second Anna Bunting; married third Austa Viola Howay.

Hannah Etta Courser (b. 1879, Rolland Twp., Isabella County, MI, d. Nov. 6, 1944, Mt. Pleasant) md. Charles A. Moody.

Cora Courser (b. June 18, 1882, Rolland Twp., Isabella County, MI, d. Sept. 15, 1968, St. Johns) md. Dan Burkholder; married second Burr Box; infant died in infancy, Rolland Twp.

COURSER-MCINTYRE-PARKINSON.
Simeon "Sim" Sumner Courser, son of Ephraim Carter and Martha (Wright) Courser, was born Sept. 8, 1872 in Richmond, VT, died April 18, 1934 in Alma, Gratiot County, MI and is buried in Pine River Cemetery, Rolland Twp., Isabella County, MI. According to his obituary, he came to Michigan when he was 4 years old, walking much of the way.

Martha J. McIntyre Courser, Allen Courser (child), Simeon Sumner Courser, about 1898/9

On May 19, 1895 he married Martha J. McIntyre, daughter of John and Margaret (Inman) McIntyre, born Oct 29, 1872, Goderich, Huron County, Ontario, Canada (who were immigrants from Ireland to Canada and from there to Peck, Sanilac County, MI in October 1886 - November 1892, and from there in November 1892 to Isabella County, MI). Their marriage license appeared in the "Isabella County Enterprise" May 24, 1895.

Simeon was a farmer in Fremont Twp., Isabella County, MI. Martha died in childbirth July 24, 1901 (Isabella County Death Certificate) and was buried with infant in Pine River Cemetery, Rolland Twp., Isabella County, MI. She left one son living, Allen Samuel Courser (b. Dec. 24, 1895).

Simeon married second Cora Parkinson in 1905 and divorced about 1930. Their marriage announcement can be found in the *"Central Michigan Times"* Sept. 29, 1905, page 4, column 4. They didn't get along very well and when they separated she took a lot of things that were his first wife's. He hid his money so she couldn't take it. He hid it in stone piles out in the field and in the cellar and wherever he thought would be a good hiding place. They found it in quart jars and tin cans, etc. She wouldn't let his young son Allen live there or come in the house. So he was "farmed out" to anyone that would care for him. Cora had a daughter Lillian Parkinson by a former marriage and Simeon and Cora had one child, Carrie Marie Courser (b. Aug. 25, 1914, d. Oct. 9, 1914). She is buried in Pine River Cemetery. (Isabella County Death Records).

COURSER-NICHOLSON.
Allen Samuel Courser, son of Simeon Sumner and Martha J. (McIntyre) Courser, was born Dec. 24, 1895 in Fremont Twp., Isabella County, MI. He married Lula Mae Nicholson, daughter of Herbert J. and Millie Cora (Johnson) Nicholson of Deerfield Twp., Isabella County, MI on March 15, 1917 in the Methodist Episcopal Parsonage in Mt. Pleasant. (Mt. Pleasant Times, March 1917.)

Allen and Lula Courser about 1917.

Allen was a farmer in Fremont Twp. and he pulled horses at the County Fairs. He had some of the nicest Belgium horses in the country. His red pole cattle were given the best of care. He worked at Central Michigan University in later years as custodian where he met Tom Tresh, the young man who became a baseball star with the New York Yankees.

After his mother's death he was farmed out to anyone who would take care of him. He had to work to pay for his room and board and did not get to go to school very often because he had to do the chores. He lived with people in Deerfield Twp. and Fremont Twp. He did not see his father very often, not even at Christmas time. He was not allowed in his father's house after his second marriage. When Allen did go to see him (after Allen had married) they had to go to the barn because the 2nd wife wouldn't let them come to the house. They would park down the road, apparently she didn't want them driving in the yard (information from the family).

Allen inherited his father's farm and lived there until Nov. 30, 1962 when he died of cancer in the same room he was born in. Lula died May 15, 1982 of cancer in a St. Louis Nursing

Home; both are buried in Union Cemetery, Fremont Twp. Lula's religion was Adventist. Their children were:

Stanley Allen Courser (b. Oct. 21, 1918).

Ernestine Ruth Courser (b. Feb. 6, 1921) md. Keith Foote, had children: Terry Lynn, Patricia Jan, Marsha Earlene, Corwin Keith and Darwin Arthur Foote.

Mildred Pauline Courser (b. Jan. 6, 1923) md. Paul Fisk, had Paula Jean, Lanny Herbert, and Susan Ann Fisk.

Emogene Arlene Courser (b. Dec. 6, 1924) md. Buhl Loomis and had Ronnie Buhl, Tommy Allen, Beverly Arlene, Kenneth Raymond and NaJean Joy Loomis.

L.J. Courser (b. May 29, 1927) md. Ida Carrick, had Allen Jay Courser; married second Marlene Farhat, had Scott Lee Courser.

Martha Millie Courser (b. April 7, 1929) md. Ronald McQueen, had Lonny Lee, Charlene Mae, Ann Elizabeth, Lynn Paul and Phyllis Jean McQueen.

Earline Mae Courser (b&d. March 14, 1932), premature birth (Isabella County Death Records), buried in Union Cemetery.

COURSER-SMITH.
Stanley Allen Courser, son of Allen Samuel and Lula Mae (Nicholson) Courser, was born Oct. 21, 1918, Deerfield Twp., Isabella County, MI and died Feb. 17, 1991, Zephyrhills, Pasco County, FL and buried Pine River Cemetery, Rolland Twp.

He began school in Two Rivers (about 1924), where he said "he had to walk five miles to school. His Aunt Bell Courser would watch out for him because he was just a little fellow." They moved to Fremont Twp. and he attended Delo School, then Demlow School in Fremont Twp. when they moved to the Courser Farm.

He enlisted in the Army with a friend, Thurman J. Barrett, on Sept. 10, 1940, was stationed at MacDill Field, Tampa, FL, then to Jackson, MS where he met his future wife. He was sent overseas when war was declared and spent 44 months in the South Pacific. When he came home from overseas, he was sent to an army base near Chicago, IL where he was discharged. Elaine took the train to Chicago where Stan met her. Then they came by train to Lansing where his mother, dad, sister Martha, and brother L.J. met them.

Stanley Allen and Elaine Courser and their children l-r: Stanley Carl, Sandra Ann, Kathie Jean and Candice Elaine on Elaine's lap.

On July 2, 1945 Rev. Charles MacKensie, Methodist minister in Mt. Pleasant, married Stanley Allen Courser and Elaine Coraleen "Connie" Smith, daughter of the late Rev. C.D. and Nettie (Beacham) Smith of Jackson, MS.

Stanley had his own garage in Winn for several years and then went to Mt Pleasant to work for Kraphol Ford. From there he went to the Coca Cola Bottling Co. of Mt. Pleasant and worked there over 25 years. He retired from there after heart surgery in 1981. Stan loved fishing and hunting and after retirement he bought old tools and furniture, refinished them and sold them at flea markets. Elaine worked for the Mt. Pleasant Regional Center over 16 years and is a member of the DAR, a Genealogist and a painter since retirement. She is of the Baptist Faith. Children are:

Sandra "Sandy" Ann Courser (b. June 9, 1946) md. Terry Gimmey, son of Donald and Bernice Gimmey, on Oct. 16, 1965. Children: Amy Jo (md. Doug Simon), Connie (md. Wade Peele), Terry A.J. Gimmey (md. "K.C." Koenig). Grandchildren: Threse Ann and Nicholas Gerard Simon; Anthony Jacob and Taylor Ann Peele; Robert Grant and Kailey Tilson Gimmey.

Kathie Jean Courser (b. Oct. 20, 1948) md. Phillip Mayercak on March 16, 1968, divorced; married second Greg Lozo on July 15, 1992, divorced; two children Kathie Jo Mayercak and Joshua Kingsley.

Stanley Carl Courser (b. Feb. 27, 1950) md. second Ginger Shantau on Aug. 1, 1972, divorced; two children: Julianne (md. Joe VanWyck) and Adam Courser. Grandchildren are Eric Michael and Alexander Allen Denslow.

Candice "Candy" Elaine Courser (b. Nov. 5, 1957) md. Mark Albert Uebele, son of Gerald and Maxine Uebele, on June 25, 1977, divorced; two sons, Warren and Derrick Uebele.

COURTNEY-HARRY.
Orah Courtney of Ohio came to Isabella County looking to the oil fields for his employment. While in this area he met and married Anna Isabell Benzinger on Oct. 18, 1931. They made central Michigan their home and became parents of three children: Kenneth Alvin (b. May 5, 1932), Dorothy Fern (b. June 22, 1933) and Karen Elaine (b. Dec. 31, 1942, d. Sept. 23, 1943).

Kenneth, the oldest, attended Mt. Pleasant Public Schools graduating in 1950. He worked for Roosevelt Oil Co. one summer. Being small in statue he found the work not for him. He went to work for Fortino's Food Market and while working there a friend, Mr. Joe English, asked him to be his sub. on a rural mail route. In 1956 he wrote and passed the federal test to become a postal worker at the Mt. Pleasant Post Office where he remained employed for 38 years, retiring in 1994. Many friendships were made over the years.

Ken and Phyllis Courtney

Kenneth married Phyllis Marie Harry (b. Dec. 17, 1932) on June 21, 1952 and to this union were born four children:

1) Troy Allan (b. April 6, 1953, d. Sept. 17, 2000) md. Diane MacDonald, had four children: Joshua Adam, Danielle, Kasey and Abagail.

2) Vicki Sue (b. Aug. 18, 1955) md. James Burton Henry and had three children: Shannon, Tracey and James II.

3) Clay Michael (b. June 21, 1958) md. Kelly Ann Struble; two children, Michael James and Heather Sue. He married second, Alma June Conley and they have two sons, Kenneth David and Edward Hoye. Mrs. Courtney had one daughter Stella Jo.

4) Dana Andrew was born April 19, 1960.

Phyllis M. Courtney was the daughter of Marion Francis Harry (b. Nov. 26, 1892), son of Peter Harry (b. Oct. 17, 1861, d. Nov. 8, 1927) and Eva Mae Francis (b. June 29, 1872, d. Aug. 4, 1939). Peter and Eva had two sons, Frank Leo and Marion Francis. Peter and his sons worked for the cloths pin factory in Shepherd. As a young man Frank went to work for J.L. Upton Hardware Store in Shepherd, later buying it and worked there the rest of his life.

Marion Francis was of a different nature; he liked the out-of-doors. He and his wife worked in the lumber camps during WWI. He, hauling timber, and she, cooking for the lumberjacks. Marion liked farming best but worked many jobs always coming back to the Shepherd area. They worked on the Great Lakes Boats, learned plumbing from Frank Worthington and The Shouey Brothers Plumbers of Shepherd. Many furnaces and water systems he installed in homes and schools around Shepherd. Marion worked for Harris Milling Co., Bador Milling and Sweeney Seed Co. Later years saw him at Bixby's Hardware and the Ace Hardware in Mt. Pleasant.

On July 2, 1913 Marion married Rose LaStella Rector of Mt. Pleasant, the daughter of James Rector and Sarah Alyce Craven. Mr. and Mrs. Harry were the parents of three daughters: Violetta Fay (b. July 24, 1914) md. Vernon Fairchild; Donalda May (b. Sept. 15, 1921) md. Edward Carigan; and Phyllis Marie (b. Dec. 17, 1932) md. Kenneth Courtney.

COYNE FAMILY.
The Coynes came from the British Isles by way Canada to Rosebush. Daniel (1861) and Hannah (Walton) were married in Clare. Daniel Coyne came from Brampton, Peel County, Ontario, Canada, through Port Huron, MI on April 11, 1880 to reside in Rosebush, MI. They had two children: Lorne and Velma.

Velma received her teaching degree from Central Michigan Normal and attended many other universities. She was a teacher and counselor in Saginaw and Ann Arbor. Velma traveled the world summers and worked with the International Students at the University of Michigan.

Lorne graduated from Ferris institute and served in the U.S. Army during WWI. Lorne and Elsie (Fenner) were married in 1921. Daniel G. was born in 1925. Lorne was in the elevator and farming business previous to 1930. It was then that he was hired by Standard Oil Company, Ind. to be the commissioned agent. This agency stocked and sold petroleum products to farmers, businesses and homes. The products were gasoline, distillates and numerous specialty items.

Dan was active in scouting, receiving the Eagle Scout Award. Dan served in the U.S. Navy during WWII, also he joined the Reserves and served a total of 26 years. Dan received his degree from CMU in 1951. He married Melva (Krogman) in 1950. Their children are David D. (b. 1951), Dana L. (b. 1952) and Mark K. (b. 1956).

In 1954, Lorne retired and Dan became the agent with Melva handling the office. S.O.C. changed the name to Amoco Oil Co. Through the years, many employees and part-time employees assisted in having the Coyne family survive in the petroleum business.

A petroleum refinery was built around the bulk plant-causing many independent competitors. The idea projected by Lorne was to sell the best products available and give the best service and this has always been the Coyne theme.

David joined the U.S. Coast Guard in 1970. Later he joined the Reserves and served a total of 28 years. David worked in the business and attended CMU, majoring in industrial supervision. Dana received her degree from CMU and is an art teacher in the Detroit Public School System. She also has a degree in counseling. Mark graduated from Ferris State University and attended CMU, majoring in industrial supervision.

In 1976 Amoco changed to jobberships. Dan retired and David and Mark took the job over serving the customer base built up over 46 years. Coyne Oil Corporation was founded at this time.

Coyne Oil Corporation

David married Linda (Russell) in 1981. Their children are Daniel D. (b. 1986), Michael D. (b. 1989) and Kelsey L. (b. 1992). Linda is a very important part of the office staff along with her role as wife and mother.

As the business grew, it became necessary to move the office from the home to a larger location - first to 600 W. Pickard and then in 1990 to a new office and large warehouse at 914 W. Pickard. The company added propane deliveries and commercial fueling (franchise with Pacific Pride). In 1995, COC became dual branded: Amoco and Citgo. The lubricant line is Petro-Canada. A convenience store (Pickard Street Citgo) was built.

COC continues to grow with a loyal staff of transport and tank wagon drivers, warehousemen, office staff and store workers. Family interest through the years includes skiing, motorcycles, tennis, golf and antique vehicles.

All Coynes work in the business in some capacity.

CRAFT-REYNOLDS-LAWRENCE.
During the early settlement of new areas, people frequently moved in kinship groups. The families of Samuel Craft, Charles Reynolds and George H. Lawrence, which settled in Deerfield Twp., were one such group. Samuel Craft's sister Laura was married to Charles Reynolds. George H. Lawrence's sister Jenett married Samuel Craft. These families established successful farms which were maintained through the end of the century; but in 1878 these early settlers' path to their new farms was described in Charles Reynolds' obituary as "a narrow track through the forest."

All three families were active in the development of their community in Caldwell, MI. They participated in the Deerfield Farmers' Club, the Methodist Episcopal Church, and school functions. The men held various local offices or performed services for their township. Samuel Craft's activities were described in the Isabella County Portrait and Biographical History published in 1884, with his portrait and family biography included.

Charles Reynolds and Laura Craft were joined in marriage on Nov. 7, 1844 in Branch County, MI. They established their own farm, and became the parents of Oscar, Robert, Asa, and Ruth. During the 1860s and 1870s the three sons married and began families of their own. Charles, Laura, Ruth, and the three sons with their wives and children, bought land and began farming in Deerfield Twp. in 1878. Ruth married Thomas Forquer April 29, 1879, and would eventually have seven children.

In 1850, George H. Lawrence arrived in Branch County, MI from New York state at the age of 11 in the company of his parents and two sisters, Jenett and Mary Jane. George married his first wife Salli in 1863 and daughter Lillian was born in 1864. After the Civil War, George moved his family to Greenville, MI and worked as a stonemason. During the 1870s, Salli and three children died. He married his second wife Emma in Greenville in 1876. George moved to Deerfield Twp., Isabella County in 1878 with two daughters from his first marriage, Lillian and Minnie, wife Emma, and new baby daughter Ethel. While farming, George also worked as a mason.

The diphtheria epidemics of the 1880s brought sadness that was difficult to bear. Death could be sudden, without warning. Oscar Reynolds lost all three of his children, and nearly his wife Mary, during the first week of August 1883. George H. Lawrence and Emma had lost their small daughter Ethel to diphtheria as well on July 31, 1880.

Samuel and Jenett Craft raised their three children safely to adulthood on the farm in Caldwell. Burt Craft worked in lumber camps, on the farm, and on the railroad before his marriage to Mary Oliver on Jan. 12, 1884. Florence Craft taught school before her marriage to Thomas Dougherty on Sept. 21, 1892. R.S. Craft worked on the farm and married Phoebe Fleming on Sept. 1, 1897. He was also employed as a cigar maker before returning to farming in 1907.

DENNIS-METHNER.
Kathleen Nellie (Methner) Dennis (b. Nov. 30, 1933 in Isabella County, Mt. Pleasant, MI), daughter of Emma Vera Gilbert (b. Sept. 22, 1896) and William Methner (b. April 3, 1888). They were married Dec. 25, 1916 and nine children were born between 1918-35.

Her parents farmed and her dad also did carpenter work, building nearly all his brothers

and neighbors barns. Mom was always busy with children, planting gardens, canning everything, sewing and mending during the winter months.

Kathleen and her siblings grew up in the Orr Community in Isabella County. The first memories she had was living in a tiny house and sharing a bed with three sisters. During those years her dad went to town on Saturdays and always brought back chocolate covered candy for them.

Farming involved jobs for everyone. They had to pump water and do lots of hoeing. They played ball and watched the Methner Brother Ball Team play on Sundays and afterwards got an ice cream cone. They looked forward to free shows on Wednesday night in Coleman. That was one day none of them grumbled. Some days dad would hoe with them and because he loved listening to the Detroit Tigers almost immediately after lunch, they would suggest that maybe the game was starting early and they could stop, but it didn't work—it was always 2:00 p.m.

They attended the Orr one-room, country school. All seven sisters graduated from Coleman High School. Kathleen was lucky and rode the bus, but her older sisters had to walk or get a ride with cousins/neighbors.

After graduation Kathleen worked at Dow Chemical as a filing clerk. She became engaged to Don Dennis, a neighborhood boy. His parents, Clark and Marian Dennis, were farmers in Isabella County too. Don graduated in 1951, worked in the oil fields, then went into the Army during the Korean conflict.

After getting out of the service, Don and Kathleen married April 2, 1955. Don began working at Dow then. We gradually bought 40-acre farms while they were rearing five children, four girls and one boy:

Don, Kathleen (Methner) Dennis family in 1999

Kelly (b. Feb. 20, 1958) md. Tom Zamorski from New Jersey and lives in Colorado; Kathy (b. Dec. 21, 1959) md. Jerry Ratliff from California where they now live; Donald (b. July 24, 1962) is single and lived in Chicago, Detroit and now in Colorado; Karla (b. May 15, 1965) md. John Ferguson from Chicago and they live in

California; Kara (b. Oct. 22, 1968) md. Patrick Hughes of New Jersey and lives in Colorado.

They have four grandchildren. Don and Kathleen both retired in 1986, he as foreman in the plant and she as an executive secretary for the chairman of Dow's board of directors. He continues to farm and she enjoys being active in church, the neighborhood and community.

DENSLOW-THOMPSON. Issac Denslow was a sixth generation son of Denslows in the United States. He was born in 1876 near Sherman City in Isabella County. He married Laura E. Thompson of Horr.

"Ike and Laurie" spent their early years together near Horr coming to Broomfield Twp. in 1903, settling on a farm, three and a half miles east of Remus, later labeled by a painting on the barn as "Wild West Farm." They brought with them two small sons, Dewitt and Wilber, having lost their first-born when just over a year old from burns. A set of twins, Milford and Mildred, were born to them in 1907 and later another son and daughter, Billy D. and Zella Mae. Billy D. was lost in a road-building accident at the age of 20 and Zella Mae died when only 7 from scarlet fever.

The family built the big brick house in 1913, a familiar landmark today. It is noted Sam Sly of Grand Rapids did the brick work for a total of $55.

Ike was a farmer, raising sheep, horses and potatoes. He will also be remembered as Isabella County Supt. of Roads and as a Broomfield Twp. Road Commissioner for several years. The first mile of gravel road in Broomfield Twp. was built under his supervision. The family lived in Mt. Pleasant during some of those years. It was said "I" is for Ike, the boy with a smile. When he laughs, you can hear him a mile.

They celebrated their Golden Wedding Anniversary in 1944 with an Ox Roast for family and friends. The family grew up and spread out as all families do. Dewitt married Lena Thren, daughter of a family neighbor, and after a few years in the area settled in Stanwood as a mail carrier.

Wilber and Milford chose farming as a way of life and settled in the local area— Wilbur, east and north of Remus and Milford, north of Remus. Many a Remus High School student will recall the backaches acquired while picking up potatoes on their farms.

Wilbur married Beatrice Walker of Blanchard. She was a first grade teacher in Remus School. They had a family of four: Robert, Jola, Harriet and Reginald. Beatrice passed away in 1943 and Wilber later married Lila Bennett and they had a daughter, Ruthie.

Milford married, Magial Cullimore, of Winn and reared a family of five on what was once known as the Sunrise Potato Farm. Milford's children were Donald, Keith, Milton, Rex and Dorma Lee. Donald, a teacher at Montabella School, was lost in a car accident in 1967. Magial, a joy to all who knew her, passed away in 1973. Milford worked many years in the ASC office in Big Rapids.

Mildred married Robert Diehm, a son of the Adam Diehms. Their early years were spent in Remus, but they later moved to Stephenson in the U.P. where Robert was a well-respected

mortician. They had a family of five, losing a son in infancy. Their children were Darwin, Nick, Sally and Susan.

DIEHL. Generation I of the Diehl family to live in Broomfield Twp. was Milton (b. 1846, d. 1929, buried in the Broomfield Twp. Cemetery). He was born in Montour County, PA and came to Broomfield Twp. in the 1880s and lived at Woodruff Lake. He made his living as a farmer and also ran a country store at Rolland Center, corner of Broomfield and Rolland, later in life. He married Phebe Lazarus (b. 1846, d. 1907), a housewife. She is buried in the Broomfield Cemetery.

Generation II of the Diehl family to live in Broomfield Twp. was Clark (b. 1878 in Pennsylvania, d. 1933). He is buried in the Broomfield Twp. Cemetery. He made his living as a farmer on the farm he bought in 1902 (which is still in the family). He married Gertie Burnside (b. 1879, d. 1904) ca. 1900. She is buried in the Broomfield Twp. Cemetery. He married second, Harriet Emily Foster (b. 1887, d. 1980) ca. 1910. She is buried in Broomfield Twp. Cemetery. After clearing his land Clark farmed, had dairy cows, and helped his brother Joe go around the country threshing for other farmers. He tore down his temporary home built in 1927 of shingles and built his beautiful stone house in the same year. He was a devoted father and doted on his four children.

Generation III of the Diehl family - Clark had four children: Ward, Bertha Phebye, Lon and Marjory Janet Diehl Hyder (b. Nov. 16, 1927) who is still living on the family farm which became a centennial farm in 2002. Marg made her living as a telephone operator before the kids were born, then was mainly a housewife rearing kids and after the kids left, she worked in the Milbrook nursing home and part time in the Remus and Mt. Pleasant dime stores. She married Albert Ray Hyder on May 27, 1947. He was born July 31, 1927 in Remus, Mecosta County.

Albert tested milk for a number of years, did odd jobs for a couple years, then farmed on the Diehl farm from 1952 until today with most land rented out and Albert and Margie maintaining a small garden. Albert continues as custodian at the Broomfield Twp. Hall. Both do a lot of volunteering and are members of the New Hope United Methodist Church.

Generation IV of the Diehl family. Margie and Albert had four children: Allen who made his living at Dow for 33 years and is now an ordained minister in the Free Methodist Church Between Lake City and Manton; Nancy Hyder now in Mount Pleasant and makes her living as a housekeeper at the hospital; Cathleen Hyder Van Orden lives in Mt. Pleasant and works at the hospital in admitting; Emily Kaye of Bronson is the assistant manager of the Shell station in Bronson. There are numerous grandchildren.

DIMENT-METHNER. Joan Lea (Methner) Diment (b. Feb. 3, 1930 in Wise Twp., Isabella County), the sixth of nine children born to William Methner (b. April 3, 1888) and Emma Vera (Gilbert) Methner (b. Sept. 22, 1896). They were married Dec. 25, 1916.

Father was a farmer and settled on a 40-acre farm in Wise Twp. In addition to farming,

he built many barns around the country. He also built the house which is still standing and is lived in by their second son's wife LaVern.

The children grew up in the Orr Community and attended the one room school called the Orr School. It was about a mile from the farm. The two boys were the oldest and did not attend high school. All seven girls graduated from the 12th grade. After high school, Joan found a job in 1948 at a factory and worked there for approximately 10 years. It was called Holly Carburetor in Clare, MI.

Joan married in 1951 to Richard O. Diment, who lived in Coleman, MI most of his life and went to the same high school. He was drafted into the Army that same year and served two years during the Korean conflict at Fort Benning, GA. Their first permanent home was on Murphy Street, Coleman, MI.

Dick returned to his job at Robinson Industries in Warren Twp., Midland County. In 1960 Dick was elected supervisor in the 1st Ward in Coleman and in 1968 appointed to the Midland County Register of Deeds. In the following election, he was voted in and held that position for 24 years, retiring in December 1992.

Joan was hired in 1971 in the Midland County Treasurer's Office and worked there until she retired 22 years later in February 1993. During their married years, three sons were born:

1) Thomas L. (b. Jan. 16, 1954) lives in Kenosha, WI, after serving 20 years in the U.S. Navy. He was married in 1974 to Patricia Wilson of Coleman, MI and they have two children.

2) Steven R. (b. Dec. 1, 1957) lives in Virginia Beach, VA and has served in the U.S. Navy since 1979. He was married in 1985 to Marina Bengania of the Philippine Islands. They have two children.

3) William V. (b. Feb. 26, 1960) moved to California after high school and worked there for about 20 years, moving back to Midland, MI in 2001. He is currently employed with J. Ranck Electric in Mt. Pleasant, MI. He was married in 1992 to Melinda Culberson of California. They have three children.

Dick and Joan have lived in the city of Midland since 1978. They are retired and spend winters in Ft. Meade, FL.

DOERFER-REID. Doerfer-Reid River Road between Lincoln and Meridian Roads has been important to the Doerfer and Reid families. In the 1880s, George Doerfer, then in his 30s, came from Ohio and bought 90 plus acres on the southeast corner of Meridian and River Road. George and Mary Doerfer had five children: Dora, Victor, Katherine, Julia and Carrie. George and his son Victor cleared a lot of the land. The family lived in a log cabin.

The George Doerfer family: George, Dora, Victor, Julia, Carrie, Mary. Probably taken in 1899 in front of their log cabin home.

Probably about the same time the Reids came from Canada and settled on Lincoln Road. Their son Joshua bought property on River Road about a mile east of the Doerfers. Their son Joshua married Louisa Gaugier and had eight children. Their oldest child was Imogene.

There was a one-room country school on the northwest corner of Meridian and River Road. Both Victor and Imogene went to that school but not at the same time, as Victor was older. It was called the Townline School.

All of Victor and Imogene's 11 children went to that school. At one time Alice Reid, Imogene's sister, was their teacher. The school kids were grand ball players. Another favorite game was "anti-i-over." Townline School is no longer a school building but is now used as a garage. This school went through the eighth grade and all of the Doerfer children completed the eighth grade at Townline School. Several went on to complete high school and some went on to pursue higher degrees.

The Doerfer house was getting small with all the young Doerfers growing. More room was needed so Victor bought an old house in Mt. Pleasant in the late 1930s, dismantled it and used the material to build four more rooms, and a large front porch, onto his home. The children all have very fond memories of the time they spent playing on that porch. Imogene and Victor also made good use of this porch sewing, reading and watching neighbors go by.

Electricity was installed in the house in the late 1930s or early 1940s, and with electricity there were no more kerosene lamps to clean and made household chores like ironing seem easy. Everyone also enjoyed listening to the radio. Electricity also meant indoor plumbing and not having to carry or hand pump water for daily use. The girls were all very happy to get rid of the scrub boards for the never ending laundry chores.

The typical grocery list included things like sugar, baking powder, yeast, flour and sweets for the children, as everything else was raised or made on the farm. Victor raised bees, so the Doerfers used honey as their main sweetener. A favorite treat for the children was taffy made with honey.

Both the Reid and Doerfer farms have been sold. There are still Reids that live on River Road and several Doerfers that still live in the area.

DOWNING-CHAMBERLAIN. Gabriel Daniel Downing (b. April 18, 1849 Troy Twp., Delaware County, OH) was the fourth child of William Downing and Catharine (Coonfare)

Downing. He married Eliza Jane Chamberlain on April 4, 1872 in Van Wert County, OH. The marriage was performed by C.B. Stiner V.D.M. John Chamberlain and Mary Mosher were Eliza's parents.

Gabriel owned a grocery store in Dague, OH about four or five miles south of Van Wert, OH. The story goes that too many relatives and friends living in the area caused his business to fail. So, he sold the business, packed everything the family owned into a covered wagon and moved to Michigan.

The family settled on a farm about seven miles east and north of Mt. Pleasant, in Chippewa Twp., Isabella County, just south of the Chippewa River on land that was mostly sand and wilderness. Charles, one of the children, stated he walked the entire distance from Ohio to Michigan behind the covered wagon, he was 10 years of age at the time.

This move to Michigan took place during the summer of 1894. They purchased the following land on July 28, 1894: 40 acres in Sec. 10, Town 14, Range 3, description NW of SW. Liber 64 - page 112. Andrew Turney and wife Charlotte being the Grantors. The 40 acres was purchased for $150.

One of their daughters, Bertha, being married did not make the trip to Michigan with her parents. She lived in the Celina, OH area. Eight children (six boys and two girls) did make the trip to Michigan. The three youngest were 3, 5 and 7 years of age. Eliza was pregnant at the time of the move and son Chancey was born that fall on Nov. 5, 1894, either in the covered wagon or in a small lean-to shed they had built. The log cabin Gabriel was building was not completed when this son was born. Three children were born to them in Michigan, the above mentioned Chancey, Millie May and Nella. Altogether this family had 14 children. Two children dying in Ohio before the move.

l-r: Gabriel Daniel Downing, Eliza Jane (Chamberlain) Downing and daughter Millie May

Names of their 14 children are in order of birth: Still born child, Rufus F. (Frankie), Minnie Elnora, Bertha Elmira, Josephine Elizabeth, Lemuel Vince, Sidney Verning, Elmer Charles, Thomas G., Fred Leroy, George Edward, Chancey William, Millie May and Nella.

Gabriel (d. June 13, 1917 Chippewa Twp., Isabella County) and Eliza Jane (d. Sept. 5, 1931 same Twp.) are both buried in the Chippewa Twp. Cemetery along with eight of their 14 children.

While there is no record of this early family doing great things in the county there are still many, many descendants in Isabella, Gratiot and Montcalm counties. These early families are what made our histories. Gabriel and Eliza

Downing are this writer's great-grandparents and she is proud to be a descendant of this large family.

DOYLE. Thomas Doyle (b. 1850, d. 1928) was born to Robert Doyle in Ontario, Canada about 1850-53. Robert was born in England and his wife (name unknown) was born in Ireland. Robert married and had a large family and died before 1840. Thomas worked his way to Michigan and bought land in Sherman Twp. in 1872. He met and married Ora Bly Southern (b. 1853, d. 1885) daughter of Thomas and Henritta Bly of Livingston County, MI. They lived in Saginaw where their daughter Hattie was born in 1875. They moved to Sherman Twp. where Ora's brother Winfield Bly had also bought land. Her mother and her child, Charles Southerland (b. 1872, d. 1922) by a previous marriage, also moved to Sherman Twp. John (b. 1877, d. 1901) and Victor (b. 1880, d. 1943) were born here.

Thomas married 2nd Margaret McGuire (b. 1869, d. 1887) of Odessa, MI. Their only child Mae Orrie (b. 1887, d. 1974) was born and Margaret died on the train coming home from visiting her parents with the new baby. Later in 1905, he married Jennie Burd Wooden Holton of Sherman, she had one son Gurdon Woodin. Thomas bought the estate of John Burd in about 1903. He cut lumber from his first purchase of land and built two houses, one barn and remodeled a house. These were all in Sherman Twp. and all are in good repair yet today (2002).

Charles, moved to Mecosta County where he lived the rest of his life.

Hattie married Chelsea Latham (b. 1869, d. 1931) of near Remus, they lived a short time near Remus, then moved to her father's place and they reared eight boys: Thomas, Claud, Elic, Carl, Gerald, Harold (Pat), Ted and Harley. The boys are all gone now but many of their families live in Isabella and Mecosta County.

John enlisted in the U.S. Army in 1889 and served in the Philippines where he was injured and was returned to the U.S. but no wonder drugs yet and he died of his wounds.

Victor worked at core mining in Michigan, Wisconsin and Minnesota. He married Laura Sparks there but later returned home alone and worked in the factory in Flint. He married Bessie Lee (b. 1900, d. 1991) of Sherman Twp., daughter of Jesse and Belle Lee. Later Victor farmed in Sherman and Coldwater Twp., and moved to his father's farm (1933) after his fathers death. Victor and Bessie had three girls: Arlene, Elinor and Mary; they have married and still live close.

Mae Orrie was adopted by George and Louisa Waight of Sherman Twp. This may of been one of the first open adoptions, as Mae lived with the Waights but was back and forth with her first family, remaining close with them all her life. She taught school and than was married to Allen Wolfe (b. Feb. 29, 1888, d. Dec. 21, 1936). He died just after his 12th birthday (as you will note he was born on Feb. 29, so he was 48 but had only had 12 birthdays). They had three children: Olydene, Beatrice and Ralph Lyle. They are all dead now but many of their children live in the western part of the U.S. Mae later married Benjamin Cotes of Illinois; they moved to California and most of her children also moved there.

Thomas never was in touch with his family, but it is believed they came from near St. Gregory's Mission in Ontario, Canada, but we are unable to locate this Mission at this time. Thomas always planted an orchard, grapes and berries wherever he lived. He cleared the lands that he bought. He was burning some of the brush he had cleared on the day the fire got away from him. His wife and hired girl saw it and grabbed pails of water and ran to him. He met the hired girl, took her pail and drank most of it, which rather startled the girl, but she soon realized he needed it. In a few minutes the three had the fire out with shovels and sand. The hired girl later became his daughter-in-law. Mr. Doyle looked like a slightly short Irishman with black wavy hair. He was a hard working man.

DUCKWORTH-DAVIS.
Gene Richman and Marydeana Davis Duckworth moved to Mt. Pleasant in 1955 to teach school. They had married in 1953 in Evanston, IL where they met while attending Northwestern University. Both completed BS and MA degrees.

Gene was born in Rittman, OH in 1929 to Max Leroy and Francis Lucile Wilmot Duckworth, their second son. The family moved to Jackson, Michigan where a sister was born. After high school graduation Gene enlisted in the Army Airforce and was in the military police during the occupation of Japan. He was discharged in 1949.

Gene was director of drama, debate and the radio/television program at MPHS as well as teaching speech and English. In 1965 he accepted a position at Delta College. He was chairman of the Humanities Division over 20 years, and was made a professor in 1978. Believing that service to organizations and community were important, he was active in Jaycees, Wabon Lodge 305, Royal Arch Masons 111, Commandery, OES 55, Presbyterian Church, the County Commission, County Building Authority, and the Republican Party. In his professional associations he served as president of the Michigan Speech Association, Michigan Education Association, United Nations Association-Michigan, and was a board member for the Michigan Education Association, the National Education Association, Michigan Association of the Professions, UNA-USA, Academy of Professional Educators, CMU Chapter Phi Delta Kappa, Chairman of the National Education Association International Relations and vice-chairman of the Michigan International Council. He traveled extensively and participated in international events with WCOTP. He received many awards from the various groups for his service.

Marydeana is the only child of Wilson Lorenzo and Gertrude Leota (Greenman) Davis. She was born in Flint in 1930. Wilson Davis was a civil engineer in the U.S. Corps of Engineers. Marydeana's parents retired to Mt. Pleasant in 1970 and resided there until their deaths. After graduation in 1952 Marydeana taught in Illinois

and Michigan until Annajeanelle was born in 1957. Although she did not return to teaching Marydeana worked as a volunteer. Organizations which benefited from her service were Girl Scouts, Jobs' Daughters, PTA, Zeta Tau Alpha, DAR, Eastern Stars, CAR, Retired School Personnel, GFWC-Mt. Pleasant, CMCH Hospital Auxiliary, Habitat for Art Reach, Presbyterian Church, Historical Society and the Genealogical Society. Her volunteer work has been commended by several groups.

Both Gene and Marydeana were active in the Mt. Pleasant Centennial and the U.S. Bicentennial.

Annajeanelle grew up in Mt. Pleasant and graduated from MPHS. She received an associate degree from Delta College and in 1977 married William George McInnis. They have two boys and a girl and live in Farwell, MI. Saramichelle (b. 1963) graduated from MPHS and attended Central and Michigan State where she received her BS. She later completed an MBA at Oakland College. She married Christopher Martin Duris in 1989. They have a boy and a girl and live in Watervliet, MI

Gene was killed in an auto accident in 1990. Marydeana continues to live in Mt. Pleasant.

DUHAMEL-ARMSTRONG.
The Duhamel-Armstrong family has made Isabella County its home since 1863 and members of the Duhamel family still reside in Mt. Pleasant and own and operate the family business.

Jacob Armstrong (b. 1832 near Liverpool, England) came to America in 1849. He married May Maisey in New York, and moved with his wife and two children to Michigan in 1863, settling in Chippewa Twp. Jacob served his country during the Civil War in the 14th Michigan Inf., Private, Co. A, 1864-65. One of his children, Frank Armstrong, married Merilla Taggart in Isabella County in 1899. In 1900 Frank and Merilla's first child, Grace, was born. Grace was followed by Harry.

Joseph and Martha Duhamel came to Isabella County with their children shortly after the turn of the century from Minnesota. They are believed to have come to Minnesota from Canada. One of their children, John, married Grace Armstrong in 1920. John also served in WWI. Grace and John lived in Grand Rapids for a short time and had one child, Robert Joseph Duhamel, before they separated.

Downtown clothing shop. Picture taken in 1928. Julia McKnight on left and Grace Duhamel on right. They were partners for a short while.

Grace then went to Flint to learn a trade. She attended beauty classes and returned to Mt. Pleasant to work, taking a job at a downtown

beauty shop. The beauty shop was later sold and the new owner expanded into retail clothing sales. The business moved to East Broadway street and Grace eventually became a partner in the business and then, working with her son Robert, bought her partner out. The new store was named Duhamel's and thrived in downtown Mt. Pleasant in the 50s and 60s.

During this time, Grace lived in the main Armstrong home on Broadway. The family also owned the large homes on either side of the house and, in the oil boom of the 20s and 30s, Grace rented rooms out to people. Her son, Robert, had six children of his own that spent much of their childhood there. Most of the space in those old houses has been converted to more modern apartments and over the years the houses have been home to many Central Michigan University students and professors, as well as to Mt. Pleasant residents from all walks of life.

The Duhamel family's original apartment house located at 512 E Broadway. This apartment house is one of three on East Broadway that the Duhamels still own and operate to this day. Picture taken in 1922. Grace (Armstrong) Duhamel on far right, her mother Merilla (Taggart) Armstrong is fourth from the right.

Grace Duhamel passed away in 1995 and her store hasn't been a fixture in downtown Mt. Pleasant since 1969. However, the family is still very much a part of the area. Her grandson, David Duhamel, and her great-grandson, Paul Duhamel, own and operate the property on East Broadway today and Paul is raising his sons, the 7th generation of the Duhamel-Armstrong family to grow up in Isabella County.

l-r: Paul Duhamel Jr., Paul Duhamel Sr., Corey Duhamel

ECKERSLEY-BROWN.
J. Dean and Betty L. (Brown) Eckersley moved to Mt. Pleasant in late 1946 from Ypsilanti, MI. After discharge from military service in late 1945 Dean had worked as a cost accountant for Kaiser-Fraser Corp. for several months before taking a job with Arthur E. Skeats, CPA, in Mt. Pleasant.

Dean was born June 14, 1919 in Lapeer County, MI, the son of John C. and Carrie H. Eckersley. His parents were both born and reared in Iroquois County, IL and moved to Michigan in 1915. They owned a farm in Mayfield Twp., Lapeer County, where they raised a family of six children, five of whom are still living. Dean grew up on the family farm and attended Misner School, a one-room schoolhouse, for the first eight grades. He then attended Lapeer HS graduating in 1936.

Betty (b. Oct. 24, 1922, Armada, MI), daughter of Neil F. and Clarice V. Brown, moved to Lapeer with her family at the age of 9 years. She then grew up in the city of Lapeer and attended schools there, graduating from Lapeer HS in 1940. She has one sister and one brother (now deceased).

After graduation from high school Dean worked for one year at Fisher Body, Pontiac, MI before attending Cleary College, Ypsilanti, MI where he studied accounting and business administration. While working for Fisher Body in 1936-37 he experienced early union organizing efforts and was forced to spend two nights in the factory as the result of the first sit down strikes. After attending Cleary College for one year he again was employed by Fisher Body and was drafted into military service before completing college.

After Betty's graduation from high school she was employed for some time by the local McClellans Five and Dime. She later worked for AC Spark Plug in Flint, MI during part of the WWII years as an inspector.

Dean and Betty were joined in marriage in Lapeer, MI on July 11, 1942. To this union was born Diane K. (Thomas) Bond (b. Aug. 25, 1944), Deborah L. (John) Skinner (b. Jan. 3, 1951) and Denise L. (Charles) Lenk (b. March 21, 1955). Both Diane and Deborah graduated from Central Michigan University in 1966 and 1972, respectively, with majors in elementary education. Denise attended CMU for one year then attended various colleges in pursuing a bachelor's degree in nursing. Seven grandchildren have been added to the family by their daughters families.

Dean entered military service in March 1941 serving until his discharge in October 1945. During his tour of service he served in the cavalry, military police and as a pilot in the Army Air Corps. Assigned to the 451st Bomb Group, 15th Air Force, as pilot of a B-24, he was shot down on a mission to the oil refinery at Blechammer, Germany on Dec. 2, 1944 and was a POW until May 1945.

During Dean's tour of duty overseas, Betty lived with her parents in Lapeer while taking care of baby Diane (b. Aug. 25, 1944).

Shortly after their move to Mt. Pleasant they joined the First United Methodist Church where they have both served on various boards and committees. During the years that the children were attending the Mt. Pleasant Schools they were active in PTA along with other school activities. Betty was a stay at home mother and homemaker, while rearing a family of three girls but was active in a volunteer capacity in several organizations among which were Child Study Club, Hospital Auxiliary and Women's City Club as well as being very active in her church.

Included among Dean's civic activities were the Jaycees, Chamber of Commerce, Lions Club and as a member of the City Commission for two terms in which he served in several capacities including mayor for two years. He also served on the boards of directors of Eagle Village, Inc. Foundation, Mid-Michigan Community College Foundation, and the Exchange Savings Bank (now National City Bank). In 1969 he was honored by being chosen by the Chamber of Commerce as the Outstanding Citizen of the year.

After working for the Skeats Accounting Firm for four years, Dean took a position as accountant and office manager for Gordon Drilling Co. where he was employed until 1959 when the company sold its assets and dissolved. He then joined with partner, G.R. "Rollie" Denison, in forming Lease Management, Inc., an oil producing, contract well operating and well servicing company, and was involved until 1979 when he retired from the company.

Since retirement they have both remained active in church and civic affairs. While spending their winters in Florida, they still remain residents of Michigan and maintain their home in Mt Pleasant.

ELKINS-SAGE. James Roy Elkins was born April 1, 1915 in Mecosta County to Roy Cleveland Elkins (b. 1886, d. 1944) and Amy Gertrude (Sample) Elkins (b. 1889, d. 1979).

His family moved to Champaign County, IL in 1916 and back to Michigan in 1926 to a farm in Fremont Twp. He attended grade school at Dewey Primary School in Illinois then Fisher School. Later he attended Riverdale High School where he played baseball, acted in the Riverdale Theater and played the French Horn in the Winn band. He left school after the eighth grade to help support his family.

Between 1934-36 he did a tour with the Civil Conservation Corp in northern Michigan. He was a farmer most of his life, he worked at Borden's dairy in Mt. Pleasant, hauled milk for a short time, and milked cows until his barn burned in 1955. He worked for Ferro Mfg. for 22 years until his death from a heart attack on May 4, 1970.

Lucille Vivian (Sage) Elkins (b. 1911, d. 1987) was born in Fremont Twp. to Marion Lewis Sage (b. 1873, d. 1958) and Iva May (Clark) Sage (b. 1882, d. 1950).

She attended grade school at the Davis School located near the Davis farm southeast of Winn, and later attended high school in Mt Pleasant. She stayed on the farm helping her parents until she married.

They met when he worked as a farm hand for her father. They were married June 5, 1937, in the home of Rev. George Dyer in Mt. Pleasant with her sister Verl and brother-in-law Ora Walkington in attendance. They lived in a rental house on her parents farm, later moving to a farm on Deerfield road.

She retired from Ferro Mfg. in 1973 with more than 30 years of service. She had a stroke in the spring of 1982 which left her unable to care for herself. She died from a massive stroke Dec. 10, 1987.

To this union was born:

Betty Ilean (b. March 10, 1938) md. Everet

Schafer, and they have five children: Christopher, Wendy, Randy, Cathy and Todd. She retired from the Davis Clinic in 1998.

Robert James (b. Aug. 25, 1939) never married and retired from Dow Chemical in 1994.

Barbara Jean (b. Oct. 31, 1940) md. Richard Recker. They have four children: Matthew, Rebecca, Michelle and James. She works for Mt. Pleasant Insurance.

Sally Anne (b. Jan. 11, 1942) md. Marvin Bellinger. They have three children: Phillip Scott, Sandra and Melissa. She retired from Central Michigan University 2002.

Cecil Bellinger family

Donald Lewis (b. Sept. 10, 1945) married and divorced Nora Kappler. They have one son Daryl. He retired from General Motors in 1999.

Richard Allen (b. Aug. 22, 1949) married and divorced Nancy Howle. They have one daughter Michelle. He then married and divorced Donna Chapman. They have two sons, Douglas and James. He is employed with Dow Chemical in Texas.

Mary Jane (b. 1943, d. 1944 from pneumonia) and Larry LeRoy died at birth in 1951.

EMBREY-DARNELL. Carl Edward Embrey was born May 10, 1912 in a log house that's located at 831 N. Rolland Rd. (southwest) of Weidman, MI. Carl's mother was Phebe (Losey) Embrey (b. 1893), daughter of Isaac and Liza (Leiter) Losey.

Carl's father Roy J. (b. 1886) was 14 years old when he moved from Rodney, MI, with his parents, John W. and Sarah (Fortner) Embrey, to the log house at 338 N. Rolland Rd. They had a butcher shop and farmed 120 acres growing check row corn, rye, oats, hay, navy beans and potatoes. Potatoes was the big crop back then (all or most hand planted). The tilling and cultivating was done with a team of horses. They had five or six milk cows, a flock of chickens and a vegetable garden.

Roy helped his father and others build the big stone house at 338 N. Rolland Rd. in 1910. Roy had time between building and farming to convince Phebe Losey to marry him in March 1911. They set up housekeeping at 831 N. Rolland Rd. (a log house, the second place south of Jordon Rd.) where Carl Edward (b. 1912), Gerald Wesley (b. 1915) and Leo Raymond Embrey (b. 1919) were born and reared.

Roy, Phebe and family lived in the log house until approximately 1933. The family lost four of their own in a short time: Roy's father, John Wesley (d. 1928), his brother Edgar (d. 1931), his mother (d. 1932) and his son Gerald (d. 1933). They continued to farm until approximately 1936 when Pure Oil drilled several wells on the property. Roy then became involved with the school system by serving as the Director of County Schools and later, a member of the Weidman School Board for many years.

Carl E. Embrey worked the farm with his father and brothers. He was about 16 when his father became very ill and with the help of his mother (Phebe) and the brothers, did all the farming during Roy's illness. Carl got his education in a one-room country school located at the bottom of Woodin Hill, just north of Ervin Dutcher Jr. on Rolland Rd. Carl graduated from Weidman High School in 1928. The high school was located just east of Coldwater Bridge on Weidman Rd.

In 1938 Carl married Daisy G. Darnell (b. 1918), the fourth of eight children born to Ray D. Darnell and Adelaide (Denslow) Darnell. She was born southwest of Weidman.

Daisy and Carl Embrey, 50th wedding anniversary, April 3, 1988

Carl and Daisy spent one winter in 1938 at the house on the corner of Wyman and Drew Rd., where their son Dennis Charles was born in 1939. They moved to 3228 N. Woodruff in Weidman in the spring of 1939. That same spring, Carl and Leo Embrey purchased the "White Rose" gas station from Russel and Mable Sides.

In 1941 Carl and Daisy's daughter Carolyn M. was born. That was the same year that the big fire destroyed the east side of Weidman.

In 1945 WWII ended and Leo returned to the States, the same year Carl and Daisy's son, Richard C. Embrey, was born. Leo and Carl operated the Embrey Bros. until 1955 when Leo sold out to Carl to purchase a hardware in Farwell. Carl operated the Embrey's Service until 1968 when Carl and Daisy retired. They spent the next 27 years traveling and spending their winters in Florida. Carl passed away Feb. 12, 1997.

EWING. Franklin and Audrey Ewing were reared in the Isabella area and started their young married life there. They were married on this writer's grandparents, Paul and Halena (Wixson) Cole's property located on West Coleman Road on Aug. 27, 1949. Writer's grandfather, Earl Howard Ewing, an Elder of the RLDS church, his wife Laura Hubbard

Frank and Pat Ewing on their wedding day, Aug. 27, 1949

Ewing, married them. They celebrated their 50th wedding anniversary on the same property they were married.

They had eight children: William Paul Ewing was born Aug. 29, 1950 in Clare Hospital. They moved to South Dakota where Franklin worked as a rancher. Laural Louise was born there on Sept. 10, 1951 and died two days later. Patricia Franklin was born in Pierre, SD on June 27, 1953. They moved back to the Isabella area, where Russell Howard was born May 14, 1954 in Mount Pleasant. Laura Lena, Connie

Frank and Pat Ewing, Aug. 27, 1999

Jean, Carol Ann, and Mavis Mary were all born in Saginaw, MI after they moved into Tuscola County.

William "Bill" married Sally Proffer (b. May 24, 1954) on Aug. 25, 1973. Bill served in the U.S. Army in Vietnam, Thailand, Korea and Germany. They have four daughters: Rebecca Lynn (b. July 3, 1975), Sara Ann (b. May 2 1977), Theresa Sue (b. April 4 1981) and Elizabeth Marie (b. Nov. 9, 1988).

Rebecca married Robert Druban (b. Sept. 28, 1971) on Oct. 14, 1996. They have two children, Finnigan Ewing Druban (b. March 22, 2000) and Aurora Ewing Druban (b. March 21, 2002).

Sara and her fiancée Bruce Skinner are planning a June 23, 2002 wedding. Both are West Point 2002 graduates.

Theresa is attending Grand Valley University, Grand Rapids and Elizabeth attends school in Vassar.

Patricia "Patti" married (divorced) Albert M. Legue (b. Jan. 1, 1951) on Oct. 3, 1971. They have four children: Audrey Jean (b. Sept. 10, 1972), William Andrew (b. May 18, 1974), Adrianna Franklin (b. Nov. 21, 1977) and Michael Paul (b. March 19, 1979).

Audrey Jean married (divorced) Colin Skelding. They had three children: Lee Michael (b&d. in December 1990), Ashley Carmen (b. Feb. 1, 1993) and Jacob Michael (b. Sept. 6, 1995). Audrey has a daughter Kaylin Morgan (b. June 6, 1997), who was adopted into the Abell family.

William Andrew married (divorced) Carrie (b. May 24, 1975) on Feb. 1, 1997. Their children are Skylar Marie (b. May 5, 1996), Katie Lynn (b. March 11, 1998) and Brandon Michael (b. March 15, 1999).

Adrianna has two children Tayvon Lee Legue (b. June 28, 1995), father Lee Smith, and Rozzalynn Angeline (b. Sept. 23, 1999, father Scott Tucker. Adrianna married Todd White Feb. 12, 2001.

Michael married Maria Scott on Oct. 4, 1999. They have a daughter Aubrey Jean born Aug. 20, 2000. Michael served in Enduring Freedom 2001 with the U.S. Airforce.

Russell Howard Ewing married (divorced) Denise Guiett, had one step-daughter Tonya. Russ served in the U.S. Army 82nd Airborne Division.

Laura Lena (b. Feb. 1, 1956) married (divorced) Wayne Smeaton. They had three children: Dennis Wayne Smeaton (b. May 23, 1979), Alycia Mae (b. Feb. 10, 1981) and Joseph Ishmael (b. Oct. 14, 1982 in North Dakota).

Dennis has a son Daniel Joseph Rosin Smeaton (b. Dec. 28, 1995). Dennis married Alison Kathleen Lolli (b. Jan. 10, 1981) on Sept. 21, 2000. They have a daughter Kaela Paige (b. March 22, 2002).

Connie Jean (b. Sept. 9, 1958) md. Charles E. Allen (b. Dec. 15, 1953) on May 5, 1984. James Martin Ewing (b. Jan. 27, 1981) and is attending Mount Pleasant Community College. Eric Cole Allen (b. March 17, 1986) is attending school in Edmore.

Carol Ann (b. Aug. 12, 1959) married (divorced) Aaron Rutan. They have two children, Melissa Ann (b. March 20, 1981) and Gregory Aaron (b. Dec. 22, 1984, he is living in Arizona with his father. Carol married Mark Szelogowski (b. Jan. 7, 1955) on May 17, 1997, and has three children: Amanda Mae (b. April 3, 1992), Joshua Mark (b. Feb. 19, 1995) and Jacob Joseph (b. Nov. 19, 1998). The children attend school in Essexville.

Melissa married Adam Bielski (b. Jan. 30, 1979) on Sept. 23, 2000. They have a son Maurice Joseph (b. Feb. 25, 2001).

Mavis Mary (b. Sept. 8, 1960) married (divorced) William Pailey Barlow. They have two children: William Franklin (b. May 10, 1982) attended Ford Automation 2002 and Jacquline Delores (b. Dec. 28, 1983) lives in Virginia and is expecting a baby in 2002 (father Marty Garbar). Mavis married (divorced) Russell Feldhouse (b. May 24, 1954) on July 31, 1992.

The parents, grandparents and great-grandparents of this group have volunteered for many different organizations. Franklin Ewing has done volunteer work for Saginaw County Youth Protection Council, Habitat for Humanity, where he worked with former President Jimmy Carter and the First Lady in Washington and Canada. He has helped with Christmas in July, building ramps for the handicap and was chosen Saginaw Man of the Year on Jan. 1, 1993.

Audrey Ewing was president of the Vassar Blue Star mother, women's leader of the RLDS Church in Juniata Branch. Both ran a Foster Home for multi-handicap children and worked at Camp Quality in Boyne City for kids and their siblings with cancer for several summers.

EWING-DRAPER. Earl Norman Ewing came to Isabella County as a resident in 1983 with his wife Betty Leona (Draper) Ewing from Saginaw, MI, where they resided for 43 years. Earl has been employed in Saginaw at the Wickes Boiler Co. for 10 years and the Saginaw Police

Department for 30 years, retiring in February 1983.

They had purchased property and a home in Isabella County, Gilmore Twp. on Littlefield Lake at 5103 W. Stevenson Lake Road in 1965 with the intention of moving there to live when Earl retired.

Earl (b. Jan. 29, 1925 at Lansing, MI) was the oldest of eight children of Earl H. Ewing and Laura A. (Hubbard) Ewing. He has seven brothers and sisters: Franklin, Russell, Paul, Walter, Velma, Duane and Doris.

Betty (b. July 30, 1923 at Bart, Taymouth Twp., Saginaw County, MI) was the oldest of six children born to William H. Draper and Mildred M. (Burleson) Draper. She had five brothers and sisters: Josephine, Darrell, Kathleen, Garland and William.

Earl (Norman) and Betty were married Dec. 26, 1945 at her parents home, near Burt in Taymouth Twp., Saginaw County, MI. They have two sons, Terry L. Ewing (b. Nov. 4. 1946) and Dennis Norman Ewing (b. Nov. 29, 1950), both born at Saginaw. Terry married Michelle Weber on June 24, 1967 at Rapid City, SD. They have two sons: Terry L. Ewing Jr. (b. March 28, 1968) and Cary Dean Ewing (b. Nov. 19, 1970). All live in the Saginaw and Bay City area. Dennis Ewing married Pamela Jean Lapan on Dec. 11, 1971 at Saginaw, MI in they live in the Saginaw area. No children.

Earl Norman Ewing enlisted in the U.S. Marine Corps in November 1942 and entered the service, in March 1943. He took basic training at the Marine Corps Recruit Depot at San Diego, CA. He left for overseas duty from San Diego on Dec. 6, 1943 for the South Pacific. He fought in two battles in the assault waves at Guam and Iwo Jima. He was in five assault waves in the re-capture of Guam. He was on the amphibian tractors which transported the troops into shore over the coral reefs. At Guam his tractor was hit by mortar fire and set on fire. His crew was not hurt. At Iwo Jima he was in the second assault wave on Green Beach at the base of Mt. Surabachi. After getting the assault troops ashore, they hauled supplies and ammunition in and wounded out for the next 11 days. On the 5th morning they hauled a load of 155mm shells into a battery at the base of Mt. Surabachi, and while there watched from about 400 yards away as the troops went up and raised the first flag on the top of Mt.

Earl Norman and Betty Ewing, Dec. 26, 1995, 50th wedding anniversary

Surabachi. He fought with the infantry on the front lines during the last days of the fighting until the island was secured. Earl spent 24 months in the Pacific Theater before returning to the States and was discharged from the Marines on Dec. 7, 1945 at the Great Lakes Naval Training Station in Illinois.

Earl and Betty are now both life members of the Veteran of Foreign Wars Post 3039 of Farwell, MI and are active in the Honor Guard and the Ladies Auxiliary. Earl also decorates the Veterans graves at Gilmore Twp. Cemetery each Memorial Day with a flag for each grave.

From October until May each year they travel to Rockport, TX where they have a home for the winter months. Earl is a volunteer tour guide for the past 10 years on the USS Lexington, a WWII aircraft carrier. This carrier is now a museum at Corpus Christi, TX.

Earl and Betty are now in their 57th year of their marriage.

EWING-HUBBARD. Earl Howard Ewing was working in one of the war plants in Saginaw, MI when, in the Spring of 1945, he decided to move to a farm he had purchased in Isabella County. The 80-acre farm was located 2-1/4 miles west of the Wood Store on Coleman Road. In 1946 the family suffered a disaster when their home caught fire and burned completely to the ground. At that time building materials were hard to get due to the war, so they decided to build a cement block home. Along with lumber harvested from the farm, a new house was completed in 1947.

Earl Howard was born in Hot Springs, SD on April 6, 1892. As a small child, Earl traveled from South Dakota to Illinois in a covered wagon, which today is hard to comprehend. His family later moved to Michigan. During WWI Earl served in the U.S. Army and was stationed in France. He met his future wife, Laura Adrianna Hubbard, in Lansing, MI.

Earl and Laura (b. Sept. 29, 1903, Howard City, MI) were married on April 25, 1924 in Lansing. During their lifetime they farmed, successfully reared eight children, and most of the time Earl was a minister in the Church of Jesus Christ. Laura faithfully supported her husband's endeavors. Their lives were not easy but were filled with happy times when the whole family would come together to enjoy fellowship with one another. The meals served on these occasions are still remembered all these years later. The eight Ewing children are:

1) Earl Norman (b. Jan. 29, 1925, Lansing) md. Betty Leona Draper on Dec. 26, 1945, and they had two children, Terry Lee Ewing and Dennis Norman Ewing.

2) Franklin William (b. Nov. 20, 1926, DeWitt) md. Audrey Delores Cole on Aug. 27, 1949, and they had eight children: William Paul, Patricia Franklin, Russell Howard, Laura Lena, Connie Jean, Carol Ann, Mavis Mary and Laural Louise, who passed away as an infant.

3) Russell Miles (b. March 31, 1928, DeWitt) md. Daisy Ewing in Shanghai, China on April 23, 1947. They have two adopted children, Bobby Lee and Linda Diane.

4) Paul Francis (b. Jan. 16, 1930, DeWitt) md. Julie Joanne Lamson on Aug. 23, 1952. They have two children, Deborah Anne and Michael Paul.

5) Walter Lavern (b. July 30, 1931, DeWitt) md. Isabel Maria Perea in Puerto Rico on April 7, 1956, and they have three children: Walter Earl, Eric Todd and Dulcie Dee.

6) Velma Jean (b. June 24, 1933, Corunna) md. Grant Kenneth Allen on Aug. 23, 1952, and they had two children, Steven Kenneth and Darcy Jean.

7) Duane Morrice (b. May 11, 1935, Owosso) md. Ruth Marie Driscoll on Dec. 10, 1955. They have six children: Douglas Mitchell, Norman Craig, Mark Steven, Sharon Marie, Darlene Ann and Glen Duane.

8) Doris Annette (b May 4, 1937, Chesaning) md. Harvey Hunt (deceased) on May 21, 1955. They had three children: Rickey Harvey, Randy Eugene and David Bradley. Doris later married Lee Hillacker in 1973.

The three older boys were away in the service at the time Earl purchased the farm in Isabella County. Norman was in the U.S. Marines, Frank and Russell were in the U.S. Merchant Marines. Later Russell and Paul joined the U.S. Army, Walter joined the U.S. Air Force, and Duane joined the U.S. Navy. All the boys served in one branch of the service or another. At this writing all are still living in various parts of Michigan.

Earl Ewing and his wife Laura successfully operated the farm until their deaths in 1955. Earl died in the VA Hospital in Saginaw, MI on Jan. 13, 1955, and Laura was killed in a car accident Feb. 19, 1955 in Ovid, MI. The family was devastated by the loss of both parents in such a short time. Regrettably, the farm was sold after the death of Earl and Laura.

As Walter reminisces back to the time they lived on the farm, one of the things he recalls was the harsh winters. The snow would often block all of the roads into town for days. His favorite pancake mix was Famo, which was made at the mill in Weidman. When he was in the U.S. Air Force he would purchase some to take back with him.

Woods Store was busy at this time and served as a meeting place for the local people. They attended school in Weidman through the 12th grade. It is hard for the young people today to believe that the school buses were painted red, white and blue, but they were. Another thing that was popular at that time were the free movie shows. Almost all of the towns in the area had free shows that were well attended by the kids from all over the county. All of the family has done well and are grateful life has treated them so kindly.

EWING-PEREA. Walter Lavern Ewing, first came to Isabella County in the Spring of 1945 when his father and mother, Earl Howard Ewing and Laura Adrianna (Hubbard) Ewing, purchased an 80-acre farm. The farm was located 2-1/4 miles west of Woods Store on Coleman Road.

Walter attended Weidman High School and graduated in 1950. After graduation he worked in Lansing, Detroit, and then Mt. Pleasant. He was employed by the Gase Baking Company for about one year when he enlisted in the U.S. Air Force in 1952. In the Air Force he was trained as an aircraft mechanic and served his first four years in Texas, Louisiana and Puerto Rico. In Puerto Rico he met his future wife, Isabel "Lelly" Maria Perea. They were married in the Base Chapel at Ramie AFB on April 7, 1956.

He separated from the Air Force for one year. During that year they lived in Mt. Pleasant, MI where he worked for Smale Chevrolet as a salesman, and later at Dow Chemical. Their first child, Walter "Wally" Earl Ewing, was born Feb. 3, 1957, Mt. Pleasant.

In May 1957 he re-enlisted in the Air Force, taking his wife Lelly and newborn son Wally with him. They spent the next 16 years in the Air Force and were stationed in Indiana, Virginia, Louisiana, Texas, Japan, Mississippi, Vietnam (by himself of course), Florida, Spain and Kansas. During this time they had two more children: Eric Todd Ewing (b. Dec. 14, 1958 in Hampton, VA) and Dulcie Dee Ewing (b. Jan. 4, 1962, England AFB, LA).

After a very enjoyable career in the Air Force they retired in May 1973 and settled in Shepherd, MI. For a year he worked at Morbark in Winn. Then he decided to attend Central Michigan University, where he earned a BS degree in community development and a master's of arts in educational counseling. Eventually all the rest of his family graduated from Central Michigan University.

His wife Lelly earned a BS in community development. Wally earned a BS in outdoor recreation and a MS in field biology. Todd earned a BS in community recreation and has taken master degree courses. Dulcie earned a BS in psychology, MA in counseling in higher education, MA in school guidance counseling, and is currently pursuing a doctorate of education degree in educational administration. This was perhaps the highlight of my life to see them all with excellent education and ready to cope with life.

He is also very proud that all three of his children served their country in the armed services. Wally was commissioned as an officer in the U.S. Army. He achieved the rank of major and retired from the Army in 1996. Wally is now a teacher at Fremont High School, and lives in Fremont, MI with his wife Elaine (Hughes) Ewing. He has two grown sons, Samuel Walter and Nathan Richard.

Todd was commissioned an officer in the U.S. Army and served six years. He achieved the rank of captain, resigned his commission and returned to Michigan. Todd is now the recreation director at the prison in Jackson, MI and lives with his wife Tammi (Sparks) Ewing and their two children, Timothy Jeremiah and Colleen Danica in Marshall, MI.

Dulcie was commissioned an officer in the U.S. Air Force, served four years, achieving the rank of captain, and returned to Mt. Pleasant after resigning her commission. She is now working at Central Michigan University as the assistant director for Institutional Diversity. She lives in Mt. Pleasant with her son Dylan Patrick Hand and husband Dr. Edwin Telfer, LtCol, USAF (Ret).

While Walter was attending CMU Lelly worked as a substitute teacher and school secretary. After graduating from CMU he accepted a position with the Bureau of Indian Affairs in Philadelphia, MS as a middle school counselor. After three years they transferred to Dover AFB, DE where he was employed as an education counselor in the Base Education Office. Lelly was employed as the assistant director of the Base Youth Center.

In 1984 they had a chance to return home to Michigan. They transferred to Wurtsmith AFB, MI and worked there until the base closed in 1993. Walter had the same position as he had at Dover AFB and worked in the Base Education Office. Lelly was employed as a preschool teacher and as the base family day care coordinator.

After retirement in 1993 they relocated to their present home outside of Mt. Pleasant, MI, and have become "Winter Texans" spending their winters in Rockport, X. Life has been good to them and they are very grateful.

FEDEWA, Peter, came from the Pewamo-Westphalia area of Clinton County, MI to Isabella County where he built a home and settled near Beal City, MI. He married Crescentia Kebelbeck on May 12, 1891 in Beal City. Their children were Frank, Anna, Catherine "Kate," Ferd, Albert, Mary, John and Eleanora "Norie." They lived on the family farm just east of Beal City. Peter died in 1931 and Crescentia in 1952. They are buried in the St. Joseph Cemetery, Beal City, MI.

Frank married Mary Doerr in 1919 in Beal City. Frank and Mary had seven children: Erwin, Estella "Stella," John, Elton, Grace, Francis and Dean. Frank and Mary are buried in the St. Joseph Cemetery, Beal City, MI.

FEIGHT FAMILY. Kurt Edward Feight (b. Oct. 6, 1959) is the son of Keith Edward Feight and Beverly Jean (Elson) Feight. Kurt has one sister, Sherrie Michelle (Feight) Carrigan (b. Feb. 10, 1962). Kurt is a 1978 graduate of Mt. Pleasant High School and a 1982 graduate of Central Michigan University. Kurt is a licensed insurance agent and part owner of Mt. Pleasant Agency, Inc. an independent insurance agency located at 119 S. Franklin Street. He has been in the insurance business since 1982.

Julie Ann (Bristol) Feight (b. March 24, 1959) is the daughter of Barry Bristol and Margie (Fulton) Bristol of Lansing, MI. Julie has three brothers: Barry "Chip" Bristol Jr., Brian Bristol and Scott Bristol, and one sister, Sheryl (Bristol) Dekett. Julie is a licensed real estate agent and property manager for Feight Apartments. She is a 1977 graduate of Lansing Sexton High School.

Julie and Kurt were married at the First United Methodist Church on Oct. 1, 1982 and have two daughters, Kelly Ann Feight (b. June 22, 1985) and Lisa Jean Feight (b. March 30, 1988).

Keith Edward Feight (b. Jan. 2, 1932) is the son of Glenn and Olive (Dickerson) Feight. Keith has two brothers, Richard Feight and David Feight. Keith graduated from Belleville High School, Belleville, MI in 1949 and attended Alma College for one year prior to enlisting in the U.S. Navy for four years where he served on the USS *Wisconsin* battleship and USS *North Hampton* cruiser. He graduated from CMU in 1956. He married Beverly (Elson) Feight in 1956 and they had two children, Kurt Edward Feight and Sherrie (Feight) Carrigan. In 1978 Beverly past away from cancer. In 1981 Keith married Patricia (Sublett) Feight.

Keith has many businesses in the Mt. Pleasant area including, Mt. Pleasant Realty, Inc., Mt. Pleasant Agency, Inc, Valley Travel, LTD, Apollo Oil & Gas Development, Inc., Merchandise Outlet, Inc. and Feight Apartments.

Patricia Lynn (Sublett) Feight (b. Aug. 31, 1950) is the daughter of Clarance Sublett and Jackline (Brien) Sublett. She is a graduate of Mt. Pleasant High School and attended CMU for three years. Pat has two daughters, Carrie (Jackson) Paden and Michele Jackson.

FIKE-METHNER. Lester Fike was the sixth child of Edwin and Carrie (Wotring) Fike. He was born in Wise Twp., Isabella County, Feb. 1, 1913 at the Fike Homestead where he spent his entire life. He attended Wise School and Coleman High School. He married Kathryn Methner, daughter of Edward and Daisy (Baughman) Methner, on March 29, 1936. Kathryn was born 1918 in Wise Twp. and attended the Orr School, Coleman High School and Central Michigan College.

Kathryn and Lester Fike, summer of 1985

In the spring of 1936, Edwin and sons, Lester and Dale, each priced the tools and livestock on the farm to start a partnership. Amazingly there were only a few dollars difference in each ones total. Lester and Dale bought one-half interest in the assets, their father keeping one-half interest, until his death six years later. Lester and Kathryn bought the 80 acres from the Fike Estate in 1942. Lester and Dale continued to farm together and rented over 200 acres from the neighbors. They did custom work—threshing, combining, silo filling, and corn shredding as well as preparing the land and planting many crops for the neighbors, including checking corn.

Kathryn served the youth of Isabella and Midland counties for over 25 years as a volunteer 4-H leader. Their daughters took many projects, winning many awards on the local level, as well as state. Lester and Kathryn also were active in Farm Bureau, Grange, and Home Extension. To help out financially and provide for a few luxuries, Kathryn worked for E.R. Simons Co. (Elevator) in Coleman for 28 years (1952-80). The extra income enabled the girls to take music lessons: Sharen (piano), Lovene (guitar), Lee piano and accordian), Lynn (piano and flute) as well as Kathryn (organ).

Lester enjoyed doing the Bear Dance with his brother Dale, or anyone interested. He was enticed to do the dance with his nephew, Nelson Cary, at his 50th wedding anniversary.

Lester and Kathryn raised dairy and beef cattle, pigs and chickens, having over 700 laying hens at one time, and harvested hay, corn, wheat, oats, navy and soy beans.

In the early 1940s, Emerson Fike came from West Virginia to make his home with Lester and Kathryn. After Edwin's death in 1941, Laurence Burke made his home with them until both boys went into the service.

Lester worked for Robinson Industries for a short time and the Coleman Farmer's Creamery delivering butter to Detroit.

Lester and Kathryn joined the Shepherd Church of the Brethren on Broomfield Road April 25, 1965. Lester died Jan. 3, 1989. Kathryn remained on the farm until 1997, moving into the Pere Marquette Senior Estates in Coleman. In July 1999, Kathryn sold the original 40-acre farm of Edwin and Carrie Fike to her granddaughter Rebecca and Mike Crampton and daughter Micca. This farm was certified as a Centennial Farm with the Michigan Historical Commission on June 25, 2001.

The Fike's have four daughters: Sharen (md. Ronald Geeck), Lovene (md. William Witkovsky), Lee (md. Frank McDowell) and Lynn (md. Brugger). There are 10 grandchildren and 16 great-grandchildren.

FIKE-WOTRING. Edwin Fike (b. 1875, Preston County, WV, d. 1941) was one of 13 children of Levi and Rebecca (Henline) Fike. In 1889, Levi moved his family to Lenawee County in southern Michigan, where Edwin met and courted Carrie Celesta Wotring (b. 1877, d. 1941), daughter of Jacob and Rebecca (Harsh) Wotring. They were married May 29, 1897. Their first child, Goldie, was born in Lenawee County. On Jan. 8, 1901, Edwin and Carrie purchased the original 40 acres in Wise Twp., Isabella County, which would become "The Fike Centennial Farm."

Edwin and Carrie prospered, adding more land until the farm consisted of 200 acres. Seven more children were born to Edwin and Carrie making it necessary to add to the original four-room house, adding four more rooms. Still later, the small four-room house occupied by Levi was moved across the driveway and attached to the main house in 1934. That part became the kitchen, bathroom, and back entrance for the family home.

Edwin was recognized throughout Isabella and neighboring counties for his horses and his skill as a horseman. He traveled around the community with his Percheron Stallions, Jandee (nicknamed Dan), Claude, and Jesse, and a Belgian Stallion, Sandy.

The entire family worked on the farm. In cold weather, when the cows had to be brought up from the pasture, the children remember getting their bare feet warm in the places where the

cattle had been laying down, before heading back to the barn. As early as 1915, Edwin was making a success of the land he had acquired. A newspaper clipping reports that his bean crop, sold to the Coleman Elevator Co., brought him the considerable sum of $1,622.40 off a 10-acre field.

All of the Fike children attended the small country school known as the Wise School, walking three miles most of the time, sometimes riding in a horse and buggy. Vernell remembers the morning when it was 26 degrees below zero and Edwin said it was too cold to take the horse out of the barn. Edwin and Carrie took great pride in taking their eight children regularly to Sunday School and church. For many years they were members of the Shepherd Church of the Brethren on Broomfield Road, Mt. Pleasant.

When Edwin died in 1941, the children had a private auction, with Lester and Kathryn buying 80 acres, (which included the original 40 acres), Goldie (and Rollin) Gross bought another 40 acres and Iva (and Allen) Weihls bought 80 acres across the road (the Wotring farm). The original 40 acres were purchased from Kathryn Fike in 1999 by her granddaughter, Rebecca and Mike Crampton and daughter Micca, who is Edwin's great-great-granddaughter and one of the fifth generation. This farm was certified as a Centennial Farm with the Michigan Historical Commission on June 25, 2001.

Edwin and Carrie Fike family

Their children are Goldie (Rollin) Gross (b. 1899, d. 1980); Ruth (Roscoe) Cary (b. 1901, d. 1989); Iva (Allen) Weihls (b. 1905, d. 1983); Vernell (b. 1908, d. 1983) md. Eva Hodson; Emma (Albert) Lowery (b. 1910, d. 1984); Lester (b. 1913, d. 1989) md. Kathryn Methner, Dale (b. 1915-) md. Dorothy Nurnberger, and Dora (Raymond) Pifher (b. 1918).

FOOTE-LIND. Lawrence E. Foote was born Feb. 16, 1931 in a farmhouse south of Brinton, Coldwater Twp., Isabella County to Eugene and Mary Jane Larrance Foote. Eugene Foote was born June 12, 1897 near Crystal Lake, Montcalm County. Eugene's father, Charles E. Foote, was brought at age 3 from Pennsylvania. He married Cora York, daughter of Charles E. York, a Civil War veteran, and Carrie Tubbs from western New York state. Eugene's parents moved to a farm on Beck Road, near Brinton, when he was 7, living in a log cabin before buying the Brinton Hotel and moving it to the farm.

Mary Larrance (b. Nov. 27, 1900 in Indianola, Vermilion County, IL) came to Michigan with her pioneering parents, Benjamin Cassius and Melissa Jordan Larrance. Three years after settling in the Traverse City area they relocated to land on Meridian Road, Gilmore

Twp., there draining swamps instead of fighting sand and forest fire. Mary lived in a log cabin until high school in Farwell where she boarded. At 17 she started teaching school. Later her father bought the Farwell Hotel and moved it to the farm.

Mary taught school in Brinton from 1920-22 where she met and was courted by Eugene. According to a letter written by Gene in 1922, he had swapped his car for 40 acres of "good" pasture, he still cared for her but could not come to see her so she was free to look for another. Mary again taught in Brinton, 1928-30 and in May 1930 they were married. They spent two years on the farm south of Brinton, one year on a farm at the West End of Broadway, Mt. Pleasant (now built up) before moving to the farm on South Meridian, where they lived until death. Lawrence, raised there, attended the Rhodes one-room school and graduated from Mt. Pleasant High in 1948.

At 17 Lawrence left home, worked for six months on a dairy farm near Loup City, NE, then a year on a dairy farm near Shelbyville, IN, returning home to work for six months for Hubscher in a gravel pit. During that time the Korean War started. In January 1951, at 19, he volunteered for the U.S. Army. He received his training at Fort Lee, VA and served as training cadre, training several companies, many of whom went to the front lines in Korea after the Chinese invasion. In July 1952 he was stationed in Munich, Germany with the 7th Army.

Upon discharge, starting in 1954 he attended Central Michigan University and farmed with Eugene, transferring in Fall 1956 to Michigan State University (MSU). In 1957 he traveled to Italy where he worked with farm families under the International Farm Youth Exchange. In 1958 he received a BS degree, and in 1959 an MS degree from MSU. Lawrence completed work on his doctorate in agronomy at the University of Illinois. During this time he met Sally Anne Lind of Danville, IL and they married Nov. 9, 1963. Sally was born Sept. 14, 1939 in Danville.

In June 1963, he became the agricultural engineer for Minnesota Highway Department, later becoming the Director of Environmental Services. He retired 33 years later on Aug. 6, 1996 as chief environmental officer. He worked on many projects, rest areas, landscape and environmental effects of transportation. During his tenure, MN/DOT won over 50 awards for environmental design and construction. In April 1997 he and Sally traveled to Washington DC where he received the first-ever award from the Federal Highway Administration for "Excellence in Environmental Leadership."

After rearing their four children: Will E. (b. 1965), Wade A. (b. 1966), Karl W. (b. 1969) and Ellen M. (b. 1970) and running a successful secretarial service from home, Sally began a second career with the Association of Minnesota Counties. She retired Aug 7, 1996 as special projects coordinator where she was responsible for planning local and district meetings as well as an annual conference for the county commissioners.

Will (in Minnesota) is married to Candace Gallagher and has two children, Dylan and Emma. Wade (in Maryland) is married to Carla

Lucas and has two children, Beth and Matthew. Kati (in Minnesota) is single while Ellen and her husband Andrew J. Hacker make their home in Indiana.

GARCHOW-GEECK.

Perry and Marie Geeck moved with their family from Clare County to Isabella County, Wise Twp., 7010 Chippewa Road, on Oct. 31, 1945. They purchased their 80-acre farm from Walter and Edna Wilt. This farm still remains in the Geeck family, part owned by grandson, Mark Geeck and part owned by grandson, Andrew Geeck.

Perry L. Geeck was born Nov. 14, 1903 in Clare County, Hatton Twp. Marie M. Garchow was born June 1, 1911 in Clare County. Both were graduates of Clare High School. They were joined in marriage July 2, 1929. To this union five children were born: William Phillip, Ronald Lavern, Eunice Marie, Perry Richard and Edward Frank.

Perry was a farmer in Isabella County for 30 years.

GEECK-FIKE.

Ronald Geeck was born May 31, 1931 in Clare, MI, the son of Perry and Marie Geeck. In 1945 they moved to Wise Twp., Isabella County where they had purchased 80 acres to start a dairy farm. They brought 30 head of cattle with them from Clare County. Ron attended the Orr School and graduated from Coleman High School in 1950. He helped on the farm, building the herd to 80 head.

Ron and Sharon Geeck with granddaughters Alicia and Kortney.

He painted with his uncle, William Garchow of Clare for about 18 months before serving in the Marines for two years. He returned to work for his uncle, and in 1961 he bought the business.

Sharen Fike, the daughter of Lester and Kathryn Fike, was born Dec. 7, 1938 on Battle Road in Isabella County, the same home where her father was born. Sharen attended school in Coleman, graduating in 1957 and graduating from St. Mary's Hospital School of Nursing, becoming a registered nurse in 1960.

Ron always wanted to farm so they bought 80 acres from Rellinger's in 1957, working very hard clearing the land and tilling, while still helping with the dairy herd along with painting. He raised navy and soy beans, wheat and corn. Later they bought 110 more acres and 120 acres from his brother Bill.

Sharen worked for Dr. James Clapperton, D.O. in Coleman as his office nurse, until 1961. Later she worked as a clinic nurse at the Midland County Health Department, Nursing

Homes, and Midland Hospital. In 1978 she started working in Home Health for many different agencies, currently working for Heartland Home Health Services.

In 1977 they sold their first house and built a chalet home near the farm pond back in the woods on Chippewa Road, doing the finishing work themselves. Because of Ron's accident in the barn in 1985 and the low farm crop prices, they felt it was best to sell the house and farm. Ron was able to keep painting, giving his sons, Jeff and Jon, more responsibilities each year. They formed a partnership in the 1980s.

In 1992 they moved to Battle Road. In 1996 they bought Ron's mother's home, living only one-half mile from where Sharen was born.

Ron and Sharen were married Aug. 20, 1960 at the Shepherd Church of the Brethren on Broomfield Road. Sharen was baptized in 1952 and Ron in 1961, both being very active in the church. They transferred their membership to the Living Word International Church of Midland in 1982. He is a Deacon and both are in the Ministry of Helps. Sharen's life-long dream of being a missionary nurse was realized in 2001 when they both served in Honduras, Ron painting classrooms and Sharen in the medical clinic.

Ron had a stroke in 2002 but with much prayer and hard work in therapy, he has achieved his goal to return to work.

The Geecks have three children: Jeffrey (b. 1961), Jeanette (Dan) Retzloff (b. 1965) and Jon (b. 1967). They also have two granddaughters, Alicia Geeck (b. 1992) and Kortney Geeck (b. 1996).

GIBSON-BAKER.

Andrew (sometimes spelled Gipson as on his marriage license) was born May 24, 1879 in Kinderhook, near Coldwater, MI to William Gibson (Ohio) and Amanda Hankus (Michigan), whose last name appears as Pottof on Andrew's death certificate. Andrews grandparents were William Gibson (Ohio), part owner of a dry goods/grocery store, and Sara Willet (Ohio); and Nicholas Hankus (Michigan) and Delie Peters

Andrew and Alma (Baker) Gibson

(Michigan). Andrew had two sisters, Elmyria (md. Robert Foster) and Mary, who died in early childhood in 1887. In 1884 Andrew's father William died in a logging accident. Amanda then married Levi Lawrence in 1898. In 1899 Amanda, Levi, Andrew and step-brother Frank moved to Edmore, then to a farm on the corner of Coldwater and Deerfield Roads west of Mt. Pleasant.

Andrew met a school teacher in Mecosta named Alma Grace Baker (b. July 1882 in Indiana). Alma's parents were James Albert Baker and Agnes Brockway who lived on a farm in Mecosta. Andrew and Alma married in Mecosta in 1900 and lived on Levi's farm where Andrew worked the farm. Levi also made and sold patient medicines and Amanda worked with herbs to heal the sick. Alma and Andrew had 13 children, all born in Michigan. They are as follows:

J.W. (b. 1901, d. 1992) lived and worked in Flint; Willard (b. 1903 in Mecosta, d. 1979) lived in Mt. Pleasant and worked Mt. Pleasant Lumber Co.; Lloyd (b. 1905, d. 1907); I.O. "Mike" (b. 1908, d. 1970), worked for Chase Dairy; Lyle (b. 1909, d. 1936) was paralyzed and in a wheelchair; Alva (b. 1911, d. 1998) lived in Mt. Pleasant, worked in and owned grocery stores in Mt. Pleasant; Eva May (b. 1912, d. 1913); Clayton (b. 1913, d. 1964) worked at Chase Dairy; Raymond (b&d. 1915); Gladys (b&d. 1916); Matilda Helen (b. 1919 in Mt. Pleasant) is currently living in Eaton Rapids; Karl (b. 1922 in Mt. Pleasant, d. 1987) served in Navy, worked for Michigan Con Gas Co. and lived in Clare; Kleland James (b. 1929, d. 2001) served in Army, lived and died in Utah.

Andrew and Alma lived at 1217 W. Lyons on Mt. Pleasant's west side, where he was a laborer at Riverside Cemetery and Alma was a practical nurse. Alma died April 14, 1946 in Ann Arbor and Andrew died of heart failure Dec. 8, 1966 at home. Both are buried in Pine River Cemetery west of Winn on Blanchard Road.

In 1913 Andrew and Alma moved their family by train to Jamestown (Indiana) to work the farm of a relative of his mother due to a family emergency on the farm. They were back in Isabella County two years later.

GILLETT,

Jesse Benjamin Jr. (b. July 16, 1865 in Washington, Macomb County, MI) was the first of two children of the second marriage of Jesse Sr. and Mrs. Elizabeth (Johnson) Howley. Jesse Jr. had eight half-brothers and sisters, but only one full sister Nellie (b. Oct. 30, 1867).

His father Jesse Benjamin Sr. was a fruit farmer on Sec. 5, Shelby Twp. in Macomb County, MI. Jesse Sr. moved to southern Tennessee to grow a vineyard on the hillsides.

Jesse Jr. married Lillian Carter Wrinkle (b. June 2, 1866) on May 5, 1886 in Bradley County, TN. They had one unnamed son (died at 1 day old); their other children were Chauncey Ray (b. Aug. 6, 1891); Benjamin Rollo "Roy" (b. Feb. 13, 1895) and Queena Mae (b. Oct. 27, 1896 at Birchwood, TN).

Jesse Benjamin Gillett Jr. was studying medicine as a preceptor with the doctor who delivered Queena. An affidavit signed by Jesse Gillett, M.D., attested that he assisted at her birth, when later, the courthouse at Birchwood, TN burned and a birth certificate became necessary.

After Jesse obtained his full medical license and graduated from the Chattanooga College of Medicine "summa cum laude," the family moved to Wixom, MI and then to Flint where they lived until 1910. Dr. Jesse Gillett had an office above police headquarters on Kearsley Street. The doctor was discouraged by the in-fighting and poor medical ethics of the time and moved to Weidman, MI where he practiced the rest of his life.

He obtained some distinctions; graduated "summa cum laude" in his medical school class; tutored human anatomy; delivered two sets of triplets in the home and all of whom lived (one set named the Simmer Triplets were the first set of triplets born in Isabella County).

It is said that he was the only doctor in Michigan that did not lose a patient in the terrible influenza epidemics of 1918-19. He practiced in Lakeview Hospital and was good friends with Dr. Dawson of Blanchard.

He was very innovative, he had a 1926 Chevrolet truck on which he built a frame with two cupboards, a Coleman gas stove and a double bed which he drove to Florida and lived in while there many times. He would take it on picnics and visits. He called it the Redwing.

Dr. Jesse Gillett and his motor home that he made and named the Red Wing for his trips to Florida.

Dr. Jesse Gillett married for a second time to a nearby much younger widow, Ina Gardner, with whom he spent the rest of his life. He died of a heart attack on May 27, 1942 at home in Weidman, MI.

GILLETT FAMILY. Reverend Jacques de Gylet (b. 1549 in Bergerac, Guyenne, France) was a Huguenot minister. He left France, went to Scotland and settled in England. His wife was Jeanne Mestre. They had two sons, William (b. 1574) and Richard (b. 1576). Reverend William Gylett, Rector of Chaffcombe, Somersetshire, England had 10 children. Jonathan (b. 1604) was #4 and came over on the ship *Mary and John* in 1630 with one of his brothers, Nathan. They landed at Nantasket, MA near Boston.

Roy and Olive Gillett, Naomi Bates, Martha Eckles, Jim Olson and Taylor Olson

Jonathan returned to England, married Mary Dolboir on March 29, 1634 and returned to Massachusetts. They had 10 children and lived in Hartford County, CT.

Josiah was #10. He married Joanna Tainter in 1676 and had 11 children.

Joseph (b. March 30, 1695) was #8 and he married Deborah Chappell and had nine children.

Richard (b. in 1741) was #6. He married Nelly Elliott and had six children. He married a second time and had six more children.

Benjamin was the first born on June 27, 1765 in Cairo, Green County, NY. He married Asenath Grimes and had four children.

Jesse was the first born on Dec. 10, 1810. He married twice, first to Anna Mook, then to

Mrs. Elizabeth (Johnson) Howley producing seven children and had three stepchildren.

Jesse Jr. was #5 and born July 16, 1865 in Washington, Macomb County, NY. He married Lillian Carter Wrinkle in Cleveland, TN and had three children: Chauncy Ray (b. 1891), Benjamin Roy (b. Feb. 13, 1895) and Queena Mae (b. 1896), all were born in Tennessee. Jesse Gillett was a medical doctor and came to Macomb County, MI in 1898. He practiced in Wixom, Flint and came to Weidman, MI in 1913. After Lillian passed away, he married a nurse, Mrs. Ina Gardner of Weidman.

GILLETT-RATHBURN. Chauncey Ray Gillett was born Aug. 28, 1890 in Birchwood, Bradley County, TN to Dr. Jesse Gillett and Lillian Carter Wrinkle Gillett. His family moved to Macomb County, MI when he was 8 years old. He lived in Howell, MI until he married at age 22 and was a machinist.

He married Edith Weidman Rathburn, daughter of Charles Orlando and Mary Elizabeth Weidman Rathburn of Weidman, MI in Mt. Pleasant, MI on Nov. 26, 1913.

Ray and Edith (Weidman) Rathburn

They had no children of their own, although they adopted a son Ernie and reared another son L.O. Rathburn. Chauncey is best known by his middle name Ray. They lived in Weidman where Ray went to work as a mail carrier.

Ray lived in Weidman and Palmetto, FL for most of his adult life. After Edith died, Ray married Daisy, a school teacher from Chattanooga, TN and lived in Palmetto, FL until his death on June 24, 1979. He and Edith are buried in Fairview Cemetery, Weidman, MI.

Ray was a member of the Masonic Lodge #424 of Weidman and he served in the Coast Artillery Corps from 1911-15.

GILLETT-WHEELER. Benjamin Roy Gillett was born Feb. 13, 1895 in Birchwood, Bradley, TN to Dr. Jesse Gillett Jr. and Lillian Carter Wrinkle Gillett. He came to Michigan when he was 3 years old to Macomb County. He lived in Pontiac and Flint where he worked as an upholsterer. He moved to Mt. Pleasant in 1924 where he married Olive Maria Wheeler (b. Aug. 2, 1905 in Putnam County, OH) in Alma, MI. Olive was the daughter of Alphon Wheeler and Rosabelle Eagleson Wheeler. He had a used furniture store/upholstery shop on West Michigan and lived upstairs over the shop.

They had five children: Betty, Naomi, Iva, Jesse and Eileen. All five children graduated from Mt. Pleasant High School and three went on to graduate from Central Michigan College. They moved to their house on the corner of Illi-

nois and Oak St. B.R. Gillett was a well-known upholsterer and took pride in his work. In the late 60s, they moved to Shepherd where they retired. They spent their winters in Palmetto, FL, where his brother Ray lived. Olive was a member of the United Methodist Church. One of their children, Naomi Bates, still lives in Isabella County.

B.R. Gillett and Olive, 60th wedding anniversary

Olive died in June 1997 at age 92.5 years and Roy died in December 1997 at age 102. Both are buried in Riverside Cemetery in Mt. Pleasant, MI.

GORDON-METHNER. Ruth Methner was born Oct 1, 1924 at home in Wise Twp., Isabella County. Her mother was Emma Gilbert (b. Sept. 22, 1896 in Isabella County) and father was William Methner (b. April 3, 1888 in Warren Twp., Midland County). They married Dec. 25, 1916 and lived in Isabella County at that time and until their death. Her father was a carpenter who built barns and homes around the area plus other counties of Michigan. He did farming and owned and operated a thrashing machine. They had the following nine children:

William Methner (b. June 11, 1918, d. Feb. 3, 1980), Lavern Methner (b. Jan 11, 1920, d. Jan 29, 1992), Velma Frances (b. Nov 11, 1921), Ruth (b. Oct. 1, 1924), Alta Mae (b. Jan 11, 1928), Joan Lea (b. Feb. 3, 1930), Dolores Ann (b. Aug. 20, 1932), Kathleen Nellie (b. Nov 30, 1932), Phyllis Pauline (b. May 15, 1935).

Ruth grew up in Isabella County, Wise Twp. and lived there until she was 19. She attended Orr School and Coleman High School. She had many memorial events during that time. They were a close family and played ball a good deal of the time. They also attended her father's ballgames. On the way home they would beg for a ice cream cone but never got an answer; but when they arrived in Coleman, he would pull into Merritt gas station and they then knew they would get their ice cream cone.

Another event was being very close to Floyd (Pat) Methner's family. Her father and Pat married sisters so they played together a great deal of the time.

Her first job with pay was pulling mustard out of Uncle Ed's field and she got 75 cents. She went to the 4th of July celebration and spent it all. Between the 10th, 11th and 12th grades she did housework in Midland.

Her first real job was working in the plant at Dow Chemical Co. in the Magnesium where they produced castings which they sawed, filed, sanded, worked on the lathe. They worked on window frames for the B-29 airplanes which were used in WWII. In 1960 she went back to Dow and worked in the office until 1983.

In 1944 Ruth married Robert Gordon, who was born and reared on the Cornwall Ranch in Clare County. He rode horses and drove cattle. The ranch had the Woodland Dairy and (Bob) worked and delivered milk in Coleman and at the high school—that was where she first met him. Bob and Ruth have three sons and one daughter:

1) Gregory Dean Gordon (b. Oct. 6, 1945) md. Maura Mecheat, lives in Palau and manages a DFS store.

2) John Jay Gordon (b. July 2, 1948) md. Pam Troug and divorced. He is a teacher in Waterford High School.

3) Michael Lee Gordon (b. June 7, 1951) md. Pam Glenn and is plant manager at Ford Motor Co.

4) Tracy Lynn Gordon (b. June 17, 1958) md. Tim Riley, lives in Saratoga Springs, NY and works for Skidmore College.

Bob and Ruth (Methner) Gordon family at Jessica's 5th birthday in 1988.

They attended Community of Christ Church all these years and she helps with the Soup Kitchen during the summer months. From November through May she lives in her home in Bradenton, FL.

Ruth has 10 grandchildren (which include a set of twin girls) and eight great-grandchildren.

GRACE, Jennifer L. (b. Sept. 25, 1975 in Grayling, MI), daughter of Dan and Agnes Grace of Mt. Pleasant. Jennifer has lived in the Mt. Pleasant area her entire life and graduated from Mt. Pleasant High School in 1994.

She attended Montcalm Community College where she first earned her licensed practical  nurse degree, then continued her education, graduating with a registered nurse degree in May 2000. She is currently working at Central Michigan Community Hospital as a staff nurse.

Jennifer lives in the Mt. Pleasant area with her son, Taylor Lee, who was born July 25, 1996. Jennifer was active in softball and soccer and also enjoys camping and being in the outdoors.

GRACE-GAMBLE. Ray Grace and Jo Ann Gamble met and were married in 1947 at the Lutheran parsonage in Remus, MI. The Reverend David M. Metzger performed their marriage.

Jo Ann (b. March 20, 1930, Boyne City, MI) was the daughter of Leon A. Gamble and Tressa (Brunges) Gamble. Ray (b. June 25, 1926, Isabella Twp., Isabella County, MI), the son of Loyd C. Grace and Ida (Huber) Grace. The house Jo Ann was born in is still standing in Boyne City. The house Ray was born in is located on Meridian Road, Mt. Pleasant, MI.

Ray farmed his folks farm before leaving for the service. He was in the Army and served overseas in the Pacific where he was wounded on Okinawa.

Ray and Jo Ann lived most of their lives in Mt. Pleasant. Jo Ann went to Longwood School, a one-room schoolhouse. The teacher was Mrs. John C. Williams who taught kindergarten through the eighth grade. Ray went to Townline School. His teacher was Mae Lyons West. She also taught kindergarten through eighth grade.

After their marriage Ray and Jo Ann bought a small home on Granger Street in Mt. Pleasant. They later built and lived in homes on Greenfield Drive, Bellevue Drive and Jordan Road, all in Mt. Pleasant.

Jo Ann and Ray were members of Zion Lutheran Church for many years then later transferred to Faith Lutheran Church on Preston Street in Mt. Pleasant. Ray was very active in the church and served on the church council as a member and later as its President. He was also an usher and was instrumental in the expansion of the church building project. Jo Ann was active in the Ladies Aid and baked many, many cookies for fellowship as well as cooking and serving for dinners in the church.

Ray worked for Hood Lumber Co., Millington Lumber Co., Cashway Lumber Co. and Erb Lumber.

Their children are Danny Lee Grace (b. Jan. 26, 1949) md. Agnes Toovey; Dr. William Raymond Grace (b. Aug. 1, 1950) md Marsha Klumpp; Sharon Sue Grace (b. July 11, 1953) md. Robert Ebner); Thomas Joseph Grace (b. Aug. 21, 1958) md. Judy McDaniel; Sandra Ann Grace (b. Jan. 30, 1963) md. Robert Chesebrough. There are 13 grandchildren and four great-grandchildren.

Ray had five brothers: Floyd, Harold, Howard, Earl and Joseph and one sister, Mildred Ruth, who died at the age of 2 from pneumonia and whooping cough. Jo Ann had two brothers, Leon A. Jr. and Robert, and four sisters: Patricia, Peg, Charlene and Kay Lynn who died of cancer at the age of 3.

Ray passed away on July 6, 1994 of prostate cancer. Ray and Jo Ann were married 46-1/2 years prior to Ray's death.

GRACE-HORN. Floyd Charles Grace was born Feb. 11, 1911 to Loyd C. and Ida (Huber)

Grace on the homestead on Meridian Road, Isabella Twp., Isabella County, MI. Floyd married Zerua "Zeke" Ellen Van Horn on Jan. 13, 1932 in Mount Pleasant, MI. Their children are Charlene Ellen Grace (b. Feb. 2, 1933), Lonnie George Grace (b. Feb. 9, 1935), Richard J. Grace (b. Sept. 10, 1936) and Carol Grace (b. March 31, 1939).

As a youth, Floyd helped on the farm on Meridian Road. He later became a bricklayer/mason and worked for Shepherd Lumber Co. for many years.

Zerua passed away June 12, 1980 in Mount Pleasant, MI. She is buried at Two Rivers Cemetery, Isabella County, MI.

Floyd then married Donna Darling on Aug. 1, 1980. Floyd and Donna cared for his mother, Ida, at her home until her death. Floyd passed away May 22, 1996.

GRACE-HUBER. Loyd Charles Grace was born Sept. 15, 1889 to Charles and Addie (Wood) Grace on the old homestead northwest of Mt. Pleasant on Meridian Road in Isabella Twp., Isabella County, MI. He married Ida Catherine Margaretha Huber on Aug. 21, 1910 in Isabella Twp., Isabella County, MI. Ida was the daughter of George Michael Huber and Johanna "Jennie" Barbara Wissmueller. They had the following children: Floyd C. Grace (b. Feb. 23, 1911), Earl L. Grace (b. Nov. 16, 1912), Howard G. Grace (b. July 4, 1914), Harold J. Grace (b. Feb. 11, 1916), Mildred Ruth Grace (b. July 6, 1919), Joseph W. Grace (b. June 19, 1922) and Raymond W. Grace (b. June 25, 1926). All of their children were born at their home on Meridian Road.

As a young man Loyd worked on his father's farm and also did some lumberjacking in the Isabella County area. He later took over the farming operation at the homestead and worked as a farmer until the late 1940s. At that time he sold the farm and moved to North Kinney Street in Mount Pleasant where he went to work at Central Michigan University as a janitor in the dorms.

When their youngest son Floyd was still a baby, there was a terrible storm (probably a tornado), which destroyed their home. Floyd was later found still in his cradle, safe and sound. The home was rebuilt after the storm and still stands, although it is now larger than the original home.

Loyd played fiddle and banjo and would gather in the summer with his friends, Bill Butah and "Irish" Ed Carey, on the front porch of their home in Mount Pleasant and play music for hours. Loyd also enjoyed playing cards, fishing and hunting.

Ida was an extremely good crocheter and her works are found throughout the world, as people would come from all over to buy them. She also had a very large Raspberry patch which was started at their home on North Kinney when they moved to Mount Pleasant. They were known far and wide for their berries and again, people would come from all over to buy them. Ida also loved playing cards, working in her flowers and loved to sit and hold her grandchildren and great-grandchildren for hours.

Ida and Loyd had all boys except for one little girl, Mildred Ruth, who died from whooping cough at the age of 3 years.

GRACE-HUBER. Theodore "Thea" Grace (b. Aug. 17, 1880 in Oakland County) was the son of Addie Wood Grace and Chas Grace. His parents moved from the Novi area where they had farmed. They moved to the Mt. Pleasant area in 1883 and continued to farm. Thea married Laura Margaretha Huber on Sept. 11, 1904. They had nine children plus three that died in infancy. Carl (b. March 9, 1905), William "Bill" (b. April 22, 1907), Elsie (b. Oct. 4, 1909), Edwin "Pete" (b. Nov. 17, 1911), Erma (b. May 20, 1914), Roy (b. June 21, 1915), Clara (b. March 2, 1917), Minnie (b. March 30, 1919) and Cecil (b. June 15, 1921).

John Schertel built the farm at Meridian and Baseline Roads in 1892. Schertel was a brother-in-law of Thea. The farm was sold to Thea and Laura in 1928. They farmed 360 acres which was considered a large farm in those days. Three of his sons continued to farm there until Carl and Edwin died. Shortly after that time, in September 1984, Cecil sold the farm.

Two of their sons never married, Carl and Edwin. William md. Aletha Welsh on Aug. 14, 1935, three children: Janet, Sharon and Shirley; Elsie md. Donald Meyer April 27, 1966 and adopted Garry; Erma md. Alton Cameron March 6, 1938, children: Melvin, Donna, Beverly and Richard; Roy md. Mary Cluley April 6, 1940, two children, Jim and Karen; Clara md. Ben Creech Feb. 24, 1937, children: Ben Jr., Robert, Cathy, Judy and Theo; Minnie md. Clifford Newell Feb. 15, 1942, children: Ted, Jim, Bill, Chuck, Clifford, David and Robert; Cecil md. Irene Allen April 12, 1978, they didn't have any children although Irene had children from a previous marriage).

Carl and Cecil both served our country in the U.S. Army. Cecil spent time in Korea during the Korean War. Thea died on May 3, 1952 and Laura died in 1961. The only living child of Thea and Laura is Erma Cameron who is 87 years young and resides in Mt. Pleasant, MI.

GRACE-MCDANIEL. Thomas Joseph Grace was born in Mt. Pleasant, MI on Aug. 21, 1958 to Raymond Wallace Grace and Jo Ann Louise (Gamble) Grace. Tom attended Mt. Pleasant Schools and graduated from Mt. Pleasant High School in 1976. While in high school Tom played in the Marching Band.

On April 23, 1982 Tom married Judy McDaniel in Grand Rapids, MI. Judy was born in Louisville, KY Sept. 8, 1951. She attended Indiana University.

They currently live in Baldwin, MI where they operate a video and pizza store and also have a floral shop. Tom is also a county commissioner.

Tom and Judy have two children, Adam and Eric.

GRACE-ROBISON. Howard George Grace was born July 4, 1914 to Loyd C. and Ida (Huber) Grace on the homestead located on Meridian Road, Isabella County, MI. He married Crystal May Robison on Dec. 19, 1936 in Mount Pleasant, MI. Crystal (b. Aug. 12, 1918), the daughter of Alfred and Minnie (Porterfield) Robison in Isabella County, MI. Their children are Arnold Grace (b. Aug. 26, 1937), Robert Lee Grace (b. March 4, 1940) and Patricia Ann Grace (b. July 7, 1941).

Howard worked on the family farm and later went to work at Harris Milling Co. in Mount Pleasant. Howard and his family relocated to Owosso, MI when Harris Milling moved their main operations there in 1950 and worked for them until his retirement.

Crystal passed away Feb. 11, 2002 in Ovid, Clinton County, MI and is buried at Hillcrest Memorial Gardens in Owosso, MI.

GRACE-SMITH. Earl Loyd Grace was born Nov. 16, 1912 to Loyd and Ida (Huber) Grace in Isabella Twp., Isabella County, MI. He had five brothers: Floyd, Howard, Harold, Joseph and Raymond, and one sister, Mildred, who died at an early age. Earl was married Feb. 23, 1933 to Beulah Smith who was born Feb. 8, 1912 in Wise Twp., Isabella County, MI to John and Maggie Smith. She had three brothers: Ralph, Rennie and Manly.

Earl and Beulah had two children, Bonnie (b. 1933) and Leroy (b. 1946). Bonnie married Ken Schaeffer on Nov. 27, 1952. They have two children, Kendall and Larai. Leroy married Gail Baker on Oct. 5, 1969. They also have two children, Karen and Aaron.

l-r: Beulah (Smith) Grace, Bonnie Grace and Earl Grace. In front: LeRoy Grace.

Earl was very active in community affairs. He had a team of heavy weight horses that he pulled at different fairs and celebrations. He was lay speaker in the Methodist Church at Rosebush, coached Little League, Pony League and Colt League baseball in Rosebush and Mt. Pleasant for 18 years. Earl was an avid fan of the Detroit Tigers and rarely missed watching or listening to a game. Both Earl and Beulah loved to fish and made many trips to Brimley, MI for their fishing vacations.

In 1940 Earl and Beulah purchased the Howard Kennedy farm west of Rosebush through the FHA at 3-1/2 percent interest. The annual payment on the farm was $325. Earl bought his first tractor in 1946, a Farmall H at the cost of $940. Earl had to give up farming in 1962 for health reasons, so the farm was sold and a home was purchased in Mt. Pleasant on North Kinney Street.

Earl worked for Central Michigan Community Hospital as the food purchasing agent for the kitchen until 1978 when he retired. Earl passed away on April 27, 1986 and Beulah died on Oct. 12, 1999.

GRACE-TOOVEY. Dan Grace, the son of Raymond and JoAnn (Gamble) Grace, was born Jan. 26, 1949 in Mt. Pleasant, MI. Dan has lived in Mt. Pleasant the majority of his life (time away while in military) and graduated from Mt. Pleasant High School in 1967.

Dan entered the U.S. Navy in October 1967 and served in the Submarine Service aboard the USS *Kamehameha* (SSBN-642) out of Guam. He was later transferred to Holy Loch, Scotland and while stationed there met and married Agnes Toovey on July 8, 1972. Their children are Jennifer Lee Grace (b. Sept. 25, 1975), Amy Lynn Grace (b. Feb. 21, 1982) and Robert Raymond Grace (b. April 7, 1984). Agnes was born June 13, 1950 to Robert Toovey and Agnes (Henvey) Toovey in Glasgow, Scotland.

l-r: Dan Grace, Agnes Grace, Robert Grace and Amy Grace. Picture taken Dec. 25, 2001 at Bill Grace's home in Cadillac, MI.

Dan has worked in the accounting profession for the last 30 years. He coached boys Little League and Pony League baseball and later coached girls Junior and Senior Division softball in Mt. Pleasant summer leagues. He also enjoys camping and playing golf.

Upon arriving in the U.S., Agnes entered the Clare Public School system to get her American High School diploma. She graduated from Clare Schools in 1974. Agnes has worked at Central Michigan University for 18 years, starting in food service and moving on to the auxiliary services area. She enjoys going for walks, swimming, and gardening during the summer months. Agnes has also been a volunteer for Hospice of Central Michigan for a number of years.

Jennifer Grace graduated from Mt. Pleasant High School and later from Montcalm Community College with her registered nurse degree. She is currently working at Central Michigan Community Hospital in Mt. Pleasant. Jennifer has a son Taylor (b. July 25, 1996). Jennifer enjoys camping with her son in northern Michigan.

Amy Grace is currently attending Central Michigan University and Saginaw Valley University where she is working on her degree in elementary education. She played on the girls basketball, volleyball and softball teams for four years at the high school level. Amy recently assisted the Junior Varsity Volleyball Coach with her team until she left for Orlando, FL where she is doing work/study at Disney World.

Robert is a senior at Mt. Pleasant High School and will be graduating in June 2003. He plans on attending Central Michigan University in the fall of 2003. Robert was active in basketball at the high school level through his sophomore year.

GRACE-TRUSSELL. Harold J. Grace was born Feb. 11, 1916 to Loyd C. and Ida (Huber) Grace at the homestead located on Meridian Road, Isabella Twp., Isabella County, MI. He married Laura Belle Trussell on April 15, 1939 in Rosebush, MI in the minister's home. Laura Belle was born Dec. 29, 1918 to Major R. and Ida (Braley) Trussell in Isabella County, MI. Laura's father was a farmer, auctioneer and also was employed at the Sugar Beet Factory in Mount Pleasant, where he was a boiler tender.

Their children are Barbara Jean Grace (b. April 29, 1940), Alvin Grace (b. March 30, 1943), Judy K. Grace (b. Sept. 28, 1944), Ruth Ann Grace (b. Sept. 13, 1945) and Linda J. Grace (b. Sept. 4, 1946).

Harold and Laura made their first home in Flint, MI where Harold worked in a foundry plant. In 1943 they moved to Rosebush where Harold worked as a farmer for over seven years until they moved to a small farm in Denver Twp., Isabella County. Harold then went to work for the Harris Milling Co. in Mount Pleasant where he worked for 25 years. At Harris Milling Harold packed Famo Flour, mixed feed and was also a foreman. After leaving Harris Milling, Harold went to work for Central Michigan University where he worked for 10 years until his retirement.

Laura still remembers, as a child, having to walk about four miles a day to school and back. There were times in the winter when the snow was so deep it was over the top of the fence posts and the children would walk on top of the snow to get to school. In the 30s moving snow was difficult and many times a bunch of neighbors would get together and shovel their roads open so they could travel about.

Harold and Laura later moved to Shepherd and lived next door to Harold's brother, Joseph Grace, until Harold passed away on April 1, 1984. Laura returned to Mount Pleasant where she still resides today.

GRACE-WOOD. One of the true pioneer families of Isabella County was Charles and Addie (Wood) Grace. Charles and Addie farmed their land in Novi, MI and cared for Charles' elderly father, Amasa Grace, who resided with them. Upon the death of Amasa, Charles and Addie sold the farm in Novi to Charles brothers and sisters and moved to Isabella County in De-

cember 1883. Upon arrival they purchased 85.12 acres of farmland on Meridian Road, Isabella Twp., Isabella County from H.G. Prindle. This farm would remain in the Grace family until the late 1940s when Charles' youngest son, Loyd, retired and moved into Mt. Pleasant.

Shortly after their arrival to Isabella County, tragedy struck Charles and Addie's household when their son, Roy Milton, contracted diphtheria and passed away on Feb. 27, 1884. Again, on Nov. 11, 1911, disaster came as their home was completely destroyed by a tornado. Fortunately, all were spared and a new, splendid home was built. This home still stands on Meridian Road.

Charles Grace's grandfather, Benjamin Walker Grace, fought in the Revolutionary War and was part of General Washington's Army. Benjamin's brother, Joseph Grace, was married to Mara Sargent who was friends with Martha Washington. Mara (Sargent) Grace was at the Battle of Bunker Hill and helped carry water and ammunition to the troops along with helping with the wounded. She has a memorial in her honor in Bradford County, PA where she is buried. Charles' father, Amasa, was a successful farmer and businessman in the Farmington, MI area. He ran a hotel, oxen team and a very successful farming operation. Charles brothers in Farmington were also successful businessmen as they ran a general store, two hotels and a livery in Farmington along with their individual farms.

It is therefore no surprise that Charles also had a successful farming operation for many years in Isabella County and eventually turned the farm over to his son, Loyd Grace. In their later years, both Charles and Addie remained on the homestead and were cared for until their deaths by their youngest son Loyd and his wife, Ida (Huber) Grace.

Charles Grace (b. Feb. 4, 1846 in Farmington, Oakland County, MI) and Addie Amelia Wood (b. June 23, 1847 in Franklin, Oakland County, MI) were joined in marriage Sept. 17, 1867 in Farmington, MI. They had the following children: Mertie Bell Grace (b. Oct. 29, 1871), Roy Milton Grace (b. March 26, 1873), Theodore Grace (b. Aug. 17, 1880); Mina Emm Grace (b. Oct. 9, 1885) and Loyd Charles Grace on Sept. 15, 1889).

GROSS-FIKE. Rollen A. Gross (b. 1899, d. 1976) was the eldest son of Herman and Elizabeth Glecker Gross. He was born in Fremont, OH and came to Michigan with his parents in the early 1900s to settle in Wise Twp.

Rollen married Goldie Fike (b. 1899, d. 1980) in 1921 and spent several years as a minister serving in Colorado, Kansas and several churches in Michigan before retiring from the ministry and moving back to Wise Twp. where they purchased a farm in Sec. 36 in 1941.

Seeing the need for tile drainage on the farm and many other farms in the community and county, Rollen and son Paul purchased a farm tile drainage machine and started the R.A. Gross & Son Farm Tile Drainage business. They purchased two new machines in 1952 and sons, David and James, joined in the business. In the early 60s Rollen became County Drain Commissioner for Isabella County and served until retiring in 1968.

The Gross children are:

Paul (b. 1923) md. Alta Methner. Their children are Phillip, Aileen Acker, Laura Dana and Timothy.

Ruth (b. 1924) md. William Simmons. Their children are Gary, Beverly Schepers and Dennis.

Naomi (b. 1926) md. Robert McClintic. Their children are Robert, Linda Winger, Patricia McCourt, Martha Stellow, Daniel Rebecca Anthony.

Rachel (b. 1927) md. Elmer Michell. Their children are David, Pamela Keller, Susie Jones and Tina (b. 1960, d. 1967).

Esther (b. 1928) md. Alvin Peacock. Their children are Roger, DiAnn, Edward, Ranetta Donovan, Douglas and Grieg.

David (b. 1930) md. Natelle LeDuc. Their children are Raymond, Bruce, Bruno and Glen.

James (b. 1932, d. 1975) md. Marilyn Schneider (b. _, d. 1986). Their children are James, John, Beth Smallwood and Mary Lynn Fletcher.

GROSS-GROSS. John (Johann) Gross was born Sept. 23, 1847 in Langenfeld, in the Eifel region of Germany. He was the son of Michael Gross and Maria Mueller Gross.

John sailed from Liverpool England aboard the S.S. Denmark and arrived in the port of New York on May 13, 1868. He was 20 years old and was accompa-

John and Gertrude Gross, Nov. 10, 1885.

nied by his father Michael (59), his brother John (Hans) (25), his sisters, Maria (21) and Maria (Anna) (17).

John and his family very likely spent some time in Westphalia, MI before settling on the Keweenaw Peninsula in Michigan's upper peninsula. John worked with his father and brothers in the copper mines until he and his brother John (Hans) left and settled in Nottawa Twp.

John married Gertrude Gross Nov. 10, 1885 at St. Mary's Catholic Church in Westphalia. Gertrude was the daughter of Michael Gross and Catherine Schaffer Gross. Gertrude was born Nov. 15, 1862 in Portland Twp., Ionia County, MI. Her father was born in Langenfeld, Germany. Her mother was born in the neighboring village of Acht, Germany. John and Gertrude were distantly related cousins. Their common ancestors were Peter and Christina Gross of Langenfeld, Germany, who were born in the late 1600s.

John and Gertrude settled in the southeast corner of Sec. 17 in Nottawa Twp. in the early 1880s. Over the years they owned and farmed several acres of land throughout Nottawa Twp. Of this union was born: Eva (Bernard Neubecker), John "Joe" (Ida Trierweiler), Rosina (Sister Mary Salvatore RSM), William (Gertrude Strauss), Michael (never married), Leo (Coletta Reamer), Charles (Alma Fox), Ernest (Anna Fox) and Minnie (John M. Schafer).

Gross Family, 1910. Back: Charles, Michael, Joseph, Rosina, William, Leo, Ernest. Front: Gertrude, Eva, John, Minnie

Tragedy struck the family on Monday, March 31, 1926 when their home was totally destroyed by fire. The fire started at 8:45 p.m. on the roof and undoubtedly was caused by a spark from the chimney. Fortunately, no family members were injured in the fire. They rebuilt their home, which still stands on Weidman road. This farm stayed in the family until 1972 when John's youngest son Ernest retired and moved into Beal City.

As founding members of St. Philomena Church, later renamed St. Joseph the Worker in 1960, they were entitled to have their name displayed in one of the stained windows in the church. Over the years they were very active members of the Parish.

John died March 4, 1937 and Gertrude died April 16, 1950. They were buried in St. Joseph's Cemetery in Beal City. Presently there are 627 descendents of John and Gertrude. Many have served in the armed forces, 320 of them still reside in Isabella County and the rest are scattered throughout Michigan and live in 17 different states.

GROSS-METHNER. Paul Gross (b. 1923), eldest son of Rollen A. and Goldie Fike Gross, was born in Cincinnati, OH where his father attended Bible College and later became a minister. Sisters and brothers are listed under Rollen A. and Goldie Fike Gross.

Paul, with his father and brothers, owned and operated farm tile drainage machines and worked throughout Isabella County. He married Alta Methner in Wise Twp. in 1949 and in 1951 purchased the Greenwald farm in Denver Twp., Sec. 2 where they now reside. They also purchased farms in Sec. 3 and 10 and in Wise Twp. farms in Sec. 25, 27 and 36. Four children were born and reared on the farm.

1) Phillip (b. 1952) lives in Kalamazoo. He married Cindy Allen (1974) and has two children, Brina and Bryan.

2) Aileen (b. 1954) md. James Michael Acker (Michael's Realty) and lives in Coleman. They have four children: Anne, Sarah, Michael John and William James.

3) Laura (b. 1957) md. Roger Dana (Dana Carpet) and lives in Coleman. Laura is employed at Central Michigan University. They have one daughter Liz. Roger has two sons from a previous marriage, Chad and Nicholas.

4) Timothy (b. 1961) md. Emily Porte and lives in Mt. Pleasant. They have three sons: Corey, Tyler and Cole. Tim attended Ferris State University, served in the U.S. Navy, and is employed at Dow Chemical Co. Emily is in management for Gordon Foods Service.

Paul attended schools in Kansas, Ft. Morgan, CO; Mt. Pleasant, MI and graduated from Alma, MI in 1942. He entered the U.S. Navy and spent three years in service making three trips to England, Scotland and Wales. He went through the Straits of Gibraltar to the Mediterranean Sea to Egypt, visited pyramids, then through the Suez Canal on the way to Ceylon (Sri Lanka) and on to Calcutta, visited Mosques then on to Australia, New Guinea, Philippines and back to the States. The war was over, so many servicemen were ahead of him to be discharged. He was sent to Japan on a minesweeper repair ship for six months.

Alta attended Orr School, a country one-room school in Wise Twp., Sec. 26. Graduated from Coleman High School in 1946, attended Northeastern School of Commerce, Bay City and was employed by Dow Chemical Co. in the Accounting Dept.

A childhood memory was listening to the church bells ringing from Wise, Salem and Coleman on Sunday mornings.

Parents of Alta, William and Emma Gilbert Methner were married Dec. 25, 1916 and lived on a farm in Wise Twp.

Mother, Emma Gilbert (b. Sept. 22, 1896, d. 1984), daughter of Henry and Frances Gilbert born in Wise Twp. Grandmother Frances was born in Canada. Grandparents resided on a farm, Shepherd Road, Wise Twp.

Father, William Methner (b. April 3, 1888, d. 1968), son of Fred and Pauline Methner. There were 18 children in the family. He was a carpenter and noted for building barns in the area. They reared nine children: William (b. June 11, 1918, d. Feb. 3, 1980), Lavern (b. Jan. 11, 1920, d. Jan. 29, 1992), Velma (b. Nov. 10, 1921), Ruth (b. Oct. 1, 1924), Alta (b. Jan. 11, 1928), Joan (b. Feb. 3, 1930), Dolores (b. Aug. 20, 1932), Kathleen (b. Nov. 20, 1933) and Phyllis (b. May 15, 1935).

GROSS-TRIERWEILER. Joseph Gross (b. 1888, d. 1970), the eldest son of John and Gertrude Gross, was born in Nottawa Twp. He was baptized John Joseph Gross at St. Philomena's Church. However, he used his middle name to avoid confusion with three other John Gross' in Nottawa Twp. (his father, an uncle and a first cousin).

Joseph and Ida Gross, wedding in 1918

As a young man, Joe helped clear the home farmland of his parents. He worked for the John S. Weidman Lumber Co. and logged around Trout Creek in Ontonagon County in Michigan's Upper Peninsula. He met his future wife, Ida, while working on her brother's farm in Westphalia.

In 1918, he married Ida Trierweiler (b. 1889, d. 1982), a daughter of Peter and Mary Trierweiler of Westphalia. They then purchased a farm near Beal City where they began their family. While farming, Joe also worked for the Isabella County Road Commission from 1934-42. In 1952, Joe and Ida retired from farming and moved to Mt. Pleasant. For 12 years, he performed janitorial and grounds work for the Davis Clinic.

The Gross' had nine children: Carl (b. 1919, d. 1968) md. Vivian Stewart (b. 1922, d. 1989); Herbert (b. 1920, d. 1999) md. Betty Kalahan); Eleanor md. Paul Esch (b. 1919, d. 1997); Stanley md. Rosanne Alvesteffer; Paul md. Bee Crockford; Joseph md. Theresa O'Brien; Hilary md. Beverly Hubble; Bernadette md. Bert Sunderman; Catherine md. Russell Hesch.

Joseph and Ida Gross, 50th wedding anniversary in 1968

Eleanor and Bernadette reside in Isabella County. Stanley resides in Holt, Joseph in Lansing, Hilary in Livonia, and Catherine in West Branch, MI. Paul resides in Castleton, NY. As of April 2002, Joe and Ida have 167 descendants.

Ida, a Blue Star Mother, proudly displayed her flag. Herbert, Paul and Stanley served in the Armed Forces during WWII; Joseph and Hilary served in the Army during the Korean Conflict; Carl was not accepted in the service for medical reasons.

Joe loved to whittle and play the banjo and fiddle. He was frequently asked to play at family gatherings and dances. Ida enjoyed sewing, especially crocheting and quilting. Ida was known as an excellent cook and baker, which often spilled over into helping her neighbors. When there were lemon pies at a potluck supper, the question was always asked, "Which one is Ida's?" and her pie was the first to disappear.

Devout Catholics, Joe and Ida were members of St. Philomena and Sacred Heart churches. She was a member of the Catholic Daughters of America and Joe was a member of the Catholic Order of Foresters.

GROVE-WILEY. Robert C. was born on the Westside of Mt. Pleasant, MI in 1932 to Henry F. and Mabel J. Wilson Grove. Henry F. Grove was the son of Joseph Grove, who served in the Union Army during the Civil War. Joseph settled in Deerfield Twp. in the 1890s. Mabel was the daughter of Thomas Henry Wilson, who settled in Union Twp. in the 1880s. Both of Mr. Grove's parents are deceased. Robert had one brother, Albert T., who also is deceased. Mr. Grove served in the U.S. Navy, on a destroyer in Korean waters during the Korean War.

In 1959 he married Wilda M. Wiley, and to this union was born one son, Robert C. Jr. Mrs. Grove was a registered nurse. She served her profession for many years before retiring. From 1967-77, she was the Director of Nursing at Central Michigan Community Hospital. Wilda is also deceased. Mr. Grove is retired and is a member of the Odd Fellows, the Son of Union Veterans of the Civil War, the Veterans of Foreign Wars and the American Legion.

GRUSS-THIESON. Peter Gruss was born in Neiderklin, Hesson land, Germany on June 29, 1854. He came to the USA at the age of 21 in

1875 and settled in Grand Rapids, MI and worked as a meat cutter.

Anna Marie Thieson (b. Dec. 8, 1863 in Leimbach, Germany) came to the USA with her parents at the age of 5 years. Her family settled near Big Rapids and later moved near Grand Rapids.

Peter and Anna were united in marriage on Jan. 13, 1885. They had eight children, but their first born died at the age of 11 months due to cholera.

Back Row: Fred, Emma, Elizabeth, Franklin. Middle: Peter, Joseph and Anna. Front: Marie and Margaret.

Peter and Anna came to Isabella County and homesteaded 80 acres in Deerfield Twp. on Vandecar road in Sec. 10, between Pichard and River Roads. They cleared the land and used the timber to build their home and farm buildings. Later they purchased 40 acres on the west side of the road in Sec. 9. In about 1908 they bought another 80 acres in Sec. 8 on the corner of River and Winn roads. They were good farmers, raising cattle, pigs, and chickens.

In 1917 Peter and Anna retired and moved to Mt. Pleasant. They bought a house on south Washington Street, leaving the farm work to sons: Joseph on the farm on River Road and Franklin on the home place. Anna Marie died Dec. 18, 1933 and Peter on Sept. 22, 1935.

GULICK-SCHLAEFLI.

The Schlaeflis came to Michigan from Switzerland in the 1800s. It was just a wilderness. They lived in Lincoln Twp. and settled, among relatives that had come prior to or with them and with friends in the area known as Isabella County. Although many hardships were endured, they persevered.

Their family's had come to America and settled in Pennsylvania and Ohio before learning of the beautiful and fertile land in Michigan.

Back, l-r: Sadie, Roger, Nettie. Front: Louisa, Joseph and Anna Gulick

Nicholas Jr. married Saloma Miser Aug. 19, 1859 and were blessed with four children: Edward (b. 1860, Ohio), Adeline (b. June 1862, Ohio); they moved to Coe Twp. where Louise was born in 1864 and Mary in July 1866. The name Schlaefli was changed to Schlaefley somewhere between immigration papers and employment and a more American way of speaking and writing.

On April 12, 1882 Louisa Schlaefley married Joseph Gulick. That marriage produced four children: Anna (b. 1883), Sadie (b. 1890), Nettie (b. 1888) and Roger (b. 1895), all in Deerfield Twp.

Anna married very young, her husband, Archie Wooden, a veteran of the Spanish American War, went berserk and murdered Joseph and Louisa and his own baby daughter in October 1902. Roger, then went to live with Edward Schlaefley, an uncle. Roger married Eunitha Hudnutt in the year of 1916. That marriage also produced four children: Dawn (Gulick) Maybee (b. 1918), Lorraine (Gulick) Long (b. 1919), Joseph Roger (b. 1922) and Ione (Gulick) Zody (b. 1924). Eunitha died in 1929.

Roger remarried in 1932, to a widow-lady by the name of Mildred G. Brown, who had three children: a daughter Ruth, and twin boys, Daryl and Hal. A daughter Roseann (Gulick) Donnelly was born in Mt. Pleasant in 1933. This rounded out the already crowded household to eight children. Joseph, after serving in the Marines in WWII, came back to Shepherd, only to be killed in a car accident in 1951. Roger farmed around Shepherd all of his life, with the exception of owning and operating the Sunoco Gas Station in Shepherd, in the late 1950s early 1960.

HAFER/HOUSE.

In 1879, George House and his wife Elizabeth (Chancellor) moved from Monroe County, MI along with their family of 10 children to the 160 acre farm northwest of what is now Rosebush, MI.

Son, Alexander John George, married Charlotte (Armstrong) on Oct. 27, 1885 of Farwell, MI and they had five daughters and one son. Alex House continued to farm on the homestead until his death in 1936. His wife died at the farm in 1952. The farm remained unoccupied until it was purchased by Arlo and Barbara House in 1966. They remain owners of the property.

Alex and Charlotte's second daughter Flossie (b. 1892) md. Roy Delbert Hafer of Delwin, MI in 1915. Roy's parents Joseph and Ida Hafer farmed and he had a repair shop. Roy's occupation for the first two years of the marriage was that of a fireman for the town of Mt Pleasant. The couple lived for a time above the firehall then located on the corner of Main and Illinois Sts. In 1920 Roy purchased the franchise for the Sinclair Petroleum Co in Mt. Pleasant and operated the bulk plant that was located on N. Lansing St. He later added the Pure Oil franchise and built a gas station on the corner of Mission and Pickard Sts. For the first year there was no electricity at the station as the line had not been brought that far north of town.

As a young woman Flossie taught school in Rosebush. The marriage was blessed with three sons: Roy Jr (b. 1917), Milan Lee (b. 1920) and John J. (b. 1923). Flossie died in 1978.

Tragedy struck the young family when 3-1/2 year old Milan was hit by a car on Mission St. in front of what is now Ric's grocery. Milan remained completely crippled and died at age 58.

Sadly, pneumonia claimed Roy Sr. in 1932. Flossie took over as owner of the fledgling Hafer Oil Co. It became a very prosperous business due to the oil boom east of Mt. Pleasant during the Depression era. Flossie and son Roy managed the company until his retirement.

Roy married Betty Warriner in January 1939. They had two daughters, Kay Love (Harry) and Marcy Kenny (Richard). Kay and Harry have one daughter Lacy. Both girls have worked for many years at Central Michigan Community Hospital. Betty died in 1987 and Roy died in 2000.

In 1943 John J. was drafted into the Army where he served honorably in Italy. Shortly before his military departure he married his high school sweetheart Mary (Heinlein). In 1945 he became the proprietor of Hafer Hardware located at the north end of Mt. Pleasant. The store was sold in 1981 at the time John J. retired.

The three children of that union all remain in the city of Mt. Pleasant. Mary Jay (Mayme) (b. 1946) is married to Jerry Card. Their children are John R. Fetterly (wife Christy) (b. 1965), Carrie Sue Fetterly (b. 1966) and Jeny Card (b. 1975). Mary is co-owner of an insurance agency located in Okemos, MI. She and her husband create and sell iron lawn ornaments and decorative pieces.

Molly Melinda (b. 1949) md. Cornell LaLone in 1967 and they have three children: Christopher (wife Cherie) (b. 1968), Curt (wife Leanne) (b. 1970) and Leigh Mary (husband Kraig Moeggenborg) (b. 1974). Cornell and Molly are the owners of MLT, Inc. a trucking company located in Mt. Pleasant, MI.

John Frederick (Jeff) (b. 1950). He and his wife Christine have two sons, Joseph (b. 1978) and Jeffrey (b. 1981). Jeff Sr. is a finance officer with a local auto dealership. Christine has been an employee of Isabella Bank and Trust for 28 years.

HALSTEAD-WOODIN.

Elijah Merritt Henry Halstead was born Nov. 31, 1838 in Michigan and died July 19, 1914 in Sherman Twp., Isabella County, MI and is buried in Forest Hill Cemetery west of Weidman. He enlisted for Civil War duty in September 1861 and discharged in December 1865 from Co. D, 18 Michigan Vol. Inf. I Division 5th Corps. Elijah and several of his relatives came to Isabella County from southern Michigan. His relatives included a sister Supreonia Halstead (md. John Gatehouse and later John Wolfe of Broomfield Twp.), Elmer, Palmer, Daniel Fred, Albert, Burt, Edward, Elizabeth, Euretta, Mary, Hiram, Bern, Medora and Abel.

He married Anna Augusta Woodin, daughter of Henry and Sarah (Rose) Woodin of Sherman Twp., and they reared five children:

1) Eudora (b. Feb. 19, 1868, d. Feb. 17, 1891) md. William Rosencrantz. They had one son William (b. 1890, d. 1965) md. Jessie Losey (b. 1890, d. 1988), no children.

2) Euretta (b. 1870 d. 1950) md. Amos Tinker (b. 1861, d. 1895), no surviving children. She became a nurse and was well-known

3) Gorden (b. 1878) md. Ethel Dell. They reared two children: (1) Clarence, a teacher, married Mabel Perkins. Their children were

Ernest, Gloria, Deloris, Gary, Eugene, Larry and Lyle. (2) Mabel, a teacher, married Art Wilson of near Lakeview.

4) Forrest (b. 1888, d. 1923) md. Hannah Hansen. They died in a house fire, no children.

5) Bessie (b. 1889) md. Emory Leiter of Sherman Twp. Their children were Lloyd, Oren, Clifford and Freeman. After clearing the land of lumber, Mr. Halstead also farmed, had a grist mill and raised sheep. His land was near a small town and the dogs from there attacked his sheep many times. Each of his children inherited 80 acres or more of land. His stone house still stands but has been uninhabited for many years.

HESCH FAMILY.
The Hesch family was a late arrival in Mt. Pleasant. In the summer of 1951, after the collapse of the family coal mining business due to faulty geology, Russell Jacob Hesch accepted a purchasing agent position with Dow Chemical. With the family still in Titusville, PA, Russ began work in Midland and house hunting within commuting distance. While visiting the Moose Lodge, he met Joe English, who convinced him that Mt. Pleasant was the place for the Hesch family.

In September 1951, Russell's wife, Eleanor (Southworth) and their three children moved into rental property on East Michigan before buying a home at 402 East High Street. Russ died unexpectedly in February 1954 and Eleanor accepted a position in the Registrar's Office at Central Michigan University. She worked in service to Central's students and faculty until her retirement in, the 1970s, after which she turned her interest to the Catholic Daughter's of America Chapter at Sacred Heart. Eleanor died in 1994 and was returned to Titusville, PA for burial with her husband.

None of the Hesch children remained in Mt. Pleasant. Barbara (Hesch) Schnoes (SHA 52') lives in retirement with her husband Paul in Bowling Green, KY. Russell Joseph (SHA 55') (yes, he is not a junior) married Catherine Gross, daughter of Joe and Ida (Trierweiler) Gross and is now retired in West Branch, MI. The youngest, John (SHA 59') and his wife, Mary Mikolaizik, of Flint have their retirement home in Rochester Hills, MI.

HILLS FAMILY.
The Herbert Hills family history started in 1891 with the birth of Herbert's father P.G. Hills. He was born in Lombard, IL, the son of Allen E. Hills, in a family of 12 children.

Herbert Hills

After a visit to his sister Florence in Mt. Pleasant, who was married to Sam Harris, the co-owner of the Harris Milling Co. on West Broadway, they together purchased the 39-acre farm from Sam Rosberry on what is now 1691 E. Broomfield Rd.

After establishing a herd of Holstein cattle, Proctor was married to Bertha Wheeler, the daughter of Homer and Alice Wilcox Wheeler on Jan. 1, 1916. This was in the house built by Homer Wheeler, which is the same place that Herbert lives today. Bertha was also born in the same house. The address is now 5297 S. Whiteville Rd.

Donald Hills was born on March 23, 1917, Herbert was born on his parents 5th wedding anniversary in 1921, and Mary Alice was born on May 18, 1925, she is now Mrs. Richard Aldrich of Rice Lake, WI.

Proctor G. Hills, Bertha Wheeler Hills, Donald Hills, Herbert Hills

All three children attended The Gulick School, which was on the SW corner of Lincoln and Deerfield Rd. and also graduated from Mt. Pleasant High School. Proctor Hills farmed for many years and was Union Twp. supervisor for several years in the 1920s. He later served as welfare administrator for Isabella County until his death in 1940. His name is on the cornerstone, which serves as the base for a glass top table in the courthouse lobby in Mt. Pleasant.

Donald Hills worked at Dow Chemical in the early 40s and served in the Merchant Marine and Navy during WWII. He married Eileen Thompson, the daughter of Bert and Opal Thompson of Coleman. They had three children: James, Kirk and Kay. Donald died in 1997 and is buried in Vernon Twp. cemetery north of Rosebush.

Mary Alice Aldrich taught school in Minnesota and Wisconsin for many years and is the mother of four boys: Ricky, Terry, Mickey and Gary.

Herbert started farming after attending Central in Mt. Pleasant for two years and after the death of his father. He married Marcille Price, the daughter of F.H. and Mary Price, in 1947. They had four children: Paula Leonard, Brad, Roger (now deceased) and Herbert Jr.

On May 29, 1961 the barn at 5297 S. Whiteville Rd. burned and a new one was built that summer. Bertha passed away the following year in March. The next year the property purchased in 1921 by Proctor and Bertha Hills was sold to settle the estate of Bertha. It was purchased from Homer Wheeler and located in Sec. 25 in Deerfield Twp. on Meridian and Blue Grass roads. It is now a developed subdivision known as Hiawatha Hills.

Marcille Hills went to work as a cook at CMU and held that position for 20 years. Due to health reasons, she now resides at Tendercare Nursing Home in Mt. Pleasant.

Herbert has been a farmer since 1940 and was elected Union Twp. trustee in 1970 and as a supervisor from 1972-76.

Herbert served on the committee that developed McDonald Park. There is a bronze plaque on the present park building commemorating the dedication services in 1976. He continues to serve as Union Twp. Trustee at this time. He continues farming on his own and hopes that in the future the farm can be passed on to yet another generation.

HOCHADEL-THERING.
Henry Thering of Clarence Twp., Erie County, New York State, purchased an 80 acre farm in Michigan at 3265 E. Beal City Road in Isabella Twp., Isabella County, Sec. 22 from David and Ennice Cotter for the sum of $2,100. Henry inspected the farm and in the fall of 1883 moved his wife, six of his children, farm equipment, furniture, tools and household supplies by railroad. The land transaction recorded at the Isabella County Courthouse of March 27, 1884 shows he later purchased 40 acres northwest and adjacent to the farm.

Henry Thering was born Bernard Heinrich Thering on Oct. 28, 1833 in Selm, Westphalia of the Prussian-German Empire. He immigrated to the U.S. on Oct. 18, 1854 to avoid being drafted into the Prussian Army. Henry landed in New York and followed the Erie Canal route to the Buffalo, NY area. Henry married Christine Hochadel on Jan. 8, 1857. In these years before 1883, Henry and family moved to Erie County, PA, then back to Erie County, NY. Henry worked as a railroad section foreman and a farmer.

Henry and Christine had eight children: Madaleine E. Thering Noll (b. 1857); Elizabeth Thering Handel (b. Oct. 10, 1862); Mary Thering Hirsch Setter (b. Nov. 2, 1864); Henry Thering (b. March 24, 1868); Rose K. Thering Barz (b. March 28, 1869); Benjamin Robert Thering (b. Feb. 22, 1871); William Thering (b. Dec. 23, 1875); Oliver Aloysius Thering (b. June 18, 1880).

When the big move to Michigan occurred, two married daughters, Madaleine Noll and Mary Hirsch Setter, stayed in New York. The other six children moved to Isabella County, MI where they were schooled, grew up, married, reared families and lived out their entire lives. Henry Thering left Germany with a very bleak future. He knew that if he stayed he would become a Prussian soldier, and not being the oldest son, he would not be inheriting the farm. His trade as a weaver was also being replaced by machinery during the industrial revolution.

In 1885, Henry's will divided all his worldly possessions equally between his children with his wife as the executor of the will. Henry died May 26, 1896, a devout Catholic. He left behind a devoted and loving wife and family of eight children, many grandchildren and a very productive 120-acre farm. He must have considered himself a very successful man.

Christine Elizabeth Hochadel born Christina Elisabeth Hochadel came from the town of Augsburg, Bavaria Prussian German Empire. She was born on Sept. 24, 1835. The Hochadel family immigrated to the United States in 1847 when Christina was 12. The family settled in Erie and Chautauqua counties of New York State. At age 21, she married Henry Thering and bore him 10 children, two dying as infants. After Henry's death, she moved in with her daughter Rose Barz and lived with her until her death on November 12, 1916.

HOWARD FAMILY.
Horton Howard moved to Broomfield Twp. to a farm at the west end of Halls Lake in 1916. He came to the area from Columbus, OH with his four children: Faber, Louise, Mary and Reva, after his wife Laura had passed away. Other family members who had migrated earlier to the area from Ohio were brothers: Edward Howard, Dan Howard and sister Eva Roberts. Eva and her husband owned the mill in Millbrook.

Faber served in WWI and later returned to Halls Lake where he and his wife Nellie continued to farm the family farm. About 1926 the family moved north to an area around Big Eldred and Little Eldred Lakes in Sec. 18 of Broomfield Twp.

Over the years as the family was growing up, the land was cleared of stumps, rocks were removed, and what was later known as the "Deep Gully" berry farm came into existence. Many of the area school children had memories of boarding with the Howard family during the summer and picking the strawberries and raspberries that were produced on the farm. Eventually the farm was turned over to sons Harry and Harold. Today the Harold Howard Farms is still producing strawberries.

Faber and Nellie reared six sons and three daughters: Ruth, William, Lester, Harold, Harry, Charles, Ray, Laura, and Mary Lou, who all attended Remus School. During WWII five of the sons were serving their country at the same time.

Today, three of the sons and several grandchildren are still living in Broomfield Twp. Lester married Betty Whitney and they have six children: Brian, Paula, Jim, Donald, Lou Ann and Doris. Lester is now retired from his dairy equipment business and still lives across the road from the old homestead.

Harold is farming on an adjacent farm and lives along M-20. He married Darlene Karcher and they have six children: Dar, Julie, Terry, Rick, Mari Kay, and Joni. He is known in the area for his strawberries and quarter horses.

Charles has a farm on the south side of the Twp. He married Alice May and they had one son Dan. Alice died of cancer in 1954. Later Charles married Linda Townsend and they had two children, Vera Lee and Charles L. Charles retired from the Michigan Department of Agriculture.

Harry married Donna Karcher and lived on the home farm. They had two sons, Denny and Gary. Harry was killed in a logging accident in 1963.

Faber was born July 16, 1897 in Columbus, OH and Nellie Irene was born Feb. 19, 1896 in Muskegon, MI. Children are Ruth (Nelson), b. May 3, 1916; William H. (b. May 4, 1921, d. Jan. 8, 1991); Lester Howard (b. Nov. 23, 1922); Harry E. (b. Aug. 22, 1924, d. May 1963); Harold A. (b. Aug. 22, 1924); Charles F. (b. June 14, 1927); Ray E. (b. October 1929); Laura (Edinger) (b. Nov. 11, 1934); and Mary Lou (Khars) (b. May 22, 1937).

HUMMEL-BELL.
Kenneth and Helen Hummel were married Nov. 10, 1932 in Shepherd, MI by the bride's father, W.H. Bell. Kenneth Rarden Hummel was born in Broomfield Twp. in Isabella County May 19, 1911 and Helen Louis Bell was born in Evart, MI Aug. 27, 1912. They lived their married life in Shepherd, MI.

As a young man, Kenneth helped his father on the farm west of Mt. Pleasant. The family moved to Shepherd in the summer of 1927 and Kenneth continued to help his father work and manage Hummel and Son Gas Station, located at the southeast corner of Wright Ave and First St. In 1945, Kenneth became manager of the Estee Elevator, soon to be named Frutchey Bean Co. Ken enjoyed working and helping farmers; he especially liked wheat and bean harvest.

Kenneth and Helen Hummel

Kenneth graduated from Shepherd in 1928 and Helen graduated from Alma in 1929. They were members of the Orchard Ave. Church of Christ, Salt River Masonic Lodge 288, Mason and Eastern Star; Kenneth was a member of the Shepherd IOOF lodge; Helen was always ready to help the various church functions and was admired by many for her poetry readings.

The Hummels had four children: Theodore William (b. Sept. 7, 1934); Myra Ann (b. Nov. 3, 1935); Suzanne (b. Nov. 17, 1938); and Cathy Jane (b. Jan. 7, 1950).

Both Kenneth and Helen served on the Shepherd Village Council; Kenneth as president for two terms, one of which was in 1957 during the Shepherd Centennial. He also served as village clerk and Helen served as clerk for several terms. They were active in the Shepherd Sugar Bush and Maple Syrup Festival. Ken was in charge of trailer parking for many years.

Ken was an avid deer hunter, fisherman and poker player. Helen loved her bridge and was well known by close friends and neighbors as the best bread maker and cherry pie maker in town. For many years they owned and enjoyed a cottage at Mecosta Lake in Mecosta County.

Ken died on Father's Day, June 15, 1975. In 1976 Helen moved to Sanford to be near her children and died July 25, 1986.

HUMMEL-RARDEN.
Theodore Robert Hummel (b. Dec. 18, 1885 in Broomfield Twp., Isabella County) and Myra Elnora Rarden (b. March 29, 1886 in Deerfield Twp., Isabella County) were married April 23, 1908 at Broomfield Zion Lutheran Church.

Theo was a farmer west of Mt. Pleasant and later worked for the Merritt Oil Co. in Mt. Pleasant. With his son, Kenneth, he owned and managed Hummel and Son Gas Station in Shepherd. Both Theo and Myra worked at Starr Commonwealth for Boys in Jackson, MI. Theo also worked at Central Michigan College in maintenance/custodial and Myra worked for the Glen Oren Store in Shepherd. Myra, along with Okla Baughman, Mae Gruber and Louine Slates, enjoyed helping people. They especially enjoyed dressing in centennial clothes for the 1957 Shepherd Centennial. The Hummels last position was as managers at the Isabella County Farm north of Shepherd.

Theo and Myra enjoyed returning to the Old Hummel farm on Coldwater Road for the family reunions; there they were joined by the Cooks and Leuders. In April 1958 for their 50th wedding anniversary, Myra and Theo were married again in the same church, by the same minister, with the same attendants as in April 1908.

The Hummels moved to Shepherd in 1927; all their children graduated from Shepherd High School. Their children were Clifford Robert (b. 1909 and died in infancy); Kenneth Rarden (b. May 19, 1911); Geraldine Irene (b. Nov. 1, 1912); Eileen Frederika (b. March 24, 1914); Berniece Margaret (b. Oct. 6, 1916) and twins, Joyce and Jean (b. Oct. 22, 1923).

Theo died April 1, 1962 and Myra died April 29, 1973.

HUTCHINSON-ORMEROD.
John and Isabella (Ormerod) Hutchinson were among the first permanent settlers in Broomfield Twp. They cleared the land, built their home and settled down to farm life at the western end of the Twp. They were married in 1860 in York County, Ontario, Canada and moved to Broomfield Twp., Isabella County approximately two years later. According to Isabella's obituary, which appeared in the June 11, 1909, *Central Michigan Times*, 12 children were born to them. Eight of the children survived to adulthood: Joseph, Wesley, Ernest, Clark, Edgar, Bertha, Lizzie and Maggie. Isabella died in 1909 and John died in 1915, they are buried in the Pine River Cemetery, Mecosta County.

One of the 12 children, Clark Blaine, married Florence McGregor on June 23, 1907 in Mecosta, MI. Five children were born to them: Orville "Blaine," Inez, John "Max," Lloyd and Marion.

It was stated in John Hutchinson's will that Clark was to inherit the farm and pay each of his brothers and sisters the sum of $200 as settlement of John's estate. This caused financial hardship for Clark and his family and in the 1930s lost the farm to foreclosure. Blaine married Thelma Pratt July 4, 1935 in Holt, MI. They had two children, Orval and Darlene. Clark and Florence, as well as Blaine and Thelma, are buried in the Mt. Hope Cemetery, Mecosta, MI.

HYDER FAMILY.
Albert and Marjory were married May 27, 1947 in the Remus United Methodist Church. They spent that summer on the Old Mission Peninsular at Traverse City, MI with Carl and Dorothy Richardson, living in tents and working in the cherry factory. In the fall the Hyders stayed at Old Mission and worked in the orchards. In the spring they moved to Grand Rapids

Albert and Marjory Hyder, May 27, 1947.

where Albert worked in the Joppins Dairy for a few months and then moved back to Remus to the Wilber Denslow farm.

Allen Lee was born in July 1948. In October while harvesting potatoes, the horses Albert was driving spooked and ran with Albert on the wagon. He was scraped pretty badly on his back. It took three hours, three times a day to dress his wounds. Marjory's mother moved in with them to help with Allen.

Nancy Marie was born in July 1949. At Thanksgiving Mom (Harriet Diehl) married

Charles Austin. In the spring of 1950 they bought the Clark Diehl farm in Broomfield Twp. where Marjory was born. Her father, Clark Diehl, bought the farm in 1902.

In 1950 Cathleen Ann was born and in 1952 Emily Kaye came along.

In 1953 Albert started working at Dow Chemical in Midland. He also worked for a year at the Gibson Plant in Greenville. He retired from Dow after working there 30 years.

Their family consists of four children, two sons-in-law, a daughter-in-law, 12 grandchildren and 12 great-grandchildren.

Albert and Marjory Hyder

They do a lot of volunteering and also are Mr. and Mrs. Santa Claus. Marjory taught Sunday school when her children were young. Albert likes to garden where he raises flowers and vegetables and welcomes visitors. They both help at church dinners, etc. and also in the neighborhood.

JEPPESEN FAMILY. The Levi J. Jeppesen family moved to Mt. Pleasant from Owosso, MI in 1954. Sons, Gregory C. and Richard Lee, graduated from Mt. Pleasant High School in 1968 and 1970.

Phyllis I. (Clarke) Jeppesen graduated from CMU Elementary Education and taught 30 years, 25 in Mt. Pleasant and six in Michigan Rural Schools.

Lee was a U.S. Navy Air Corps pilot in WWII, serving in the Reserve 28 years and retiring with rank of Commander, USNR. Lee worked in agri-business for 43 years.

Gregory graduated from MSU Engineering and has various manufacturing and business interests.

Richard graduated from WMU, served as an administrator in municipal government, and is marketing business development director for an international engineering consulting firm.

Gregory married Lisa Claudette Bernhardt and has three children: Shane Christian, Jesse Noelle and Skylar Levi.

Richard has two children, Amanda Marie and Nathan Jacob.

JOHN FAMILY. Maurice John (b. May 17, 1929, in Grand Rapids, MI) and Patricia (b. April 18, 1930, in Pontiac, MI) met at a mutual friend's home at ages 11 and 12. Then as childhood friends riding bicycles to go to Saturday PM movies (usually westerns) at 10 cents each, it was quite often with the neighborhood "gang." They "went steady" at ages 16 and 17 until there was parental interference. Each eventually married another. However as lives changed, some 30 years later, they finally were married May 29, 1976.

Maurice had Beth and Mike, ages 9 and 11, and an older daughter Elaine, that now (in 2002) has been at the CMU Registrar's office about 25 years. She has a son Matthew First, age 21, starting at CMU now.

Maurice and Patricia C. John

Patsy had Tammy and Suzy, ages 10 and 11, and a son Richard (Jerry) Carter and wife Cathy living in Mt. Pleasant. He served in Vietnam Special Forces and has three Purple Hearts. He went to CMU and is now a loan officer at Fairway Mortgage. They have no children.

Her oldest son Steve Carter and wife Kelly live in Camarillo, CA and own Security Systems Co. Their children are Theresa, Danielle, Nicole and Jeffrey, ages 6-18. Steve also has Steve Jr. by a former marriage. Steven Jr. is married to Stacy and they have a daughter Kaley, age 2, and live in Wilmington, NC.

Tammy and her husband Rick House live near Rosebush. She is a RN and is a Diabetes Educator at the Nimkee Clinic (Chippewa Tribe). Their daughter Trisha is 9 years old. Rick is a heavy equipment operator and truck driver for construction.

Sue and her husband Rick Lowe live near Shepherd. Both have worked at Delfield about 20 years. They have a son Carter age 2-1/2 and Sue's daughter Kristen Lovejoy, age 10.

Maurice's son Mike drives 18-wheeler trucks and has been all over the country. He and his wife Lori live in Saginaw. They have no children.

Daughter Beth was in the Navy eight years and now works at a clinic doing medical records. She has a daughter Jamie Aarhus, age 12.

Patsy is well known in Central Michigan as a painter of flowers, birds, portraits, and scenes of all kinds in oils, acrylics and water colors. She also taught painting in several towns in and around Mt. Pleasant, including Lansing, Grand Rapids and Arnie's at Houghton Lake.

Maurice retired at age 62 in December 1991 from a 35 year career as a builder-developer in and around Mt. Pleasant, after supervising the building of over 200 homes, several apartments, some commercial buildings, many remodels and additions and also developed five subdivisions. He was a Charter Member of the Central Michigan Assn. of Homebuilders in 1966, and became a life director of local, state and national assns. He is a full time Realtor with Coldwell Banker/ Mt. Pleasant Realty and 2002 is his best year yet. Maurice and Patsy sold their home of many years on Chippewa Trail and bought a Rosewood Condo in spring of 2002.

Maurice's father Maurice Sr. passed away in December 1989 at age 84, and mother Ellen also in July 2002 at age 100 years and 7 months.

JOHNSON-REED. Bessie Ann Reed (b. Feb. 18, 1891, d. Aug. 31, 1976) was the daughter of Mary L. (Prentiss) (b. March 28, 1863, d. Nov. 10, 1947, Mulberry, MI) and Charles Reed (b.

Nov. 9, 1852, d. May 16, 1906 Blissfield, MI) of Mulberry, Lenawee County, MI. Bessie was a bright teenager who enjoyed life to its fullest.

Bessie and Floyd H. Johnson were married Feb. 18, 1911 and they had three children: Mynard Johnson (b. April 14, 1926); Robert Johnson (b. Jan. 25, 1939) and Betty (Johnson) Larrance (b. Sept. 13, 1943). Floyd was from the Rosebush area and owned Johnson's Garage in Mt. Pleasant where they lived. Bessie was a homemaker and helped in the office of the garage.

Both of them did many acts of kindness for the people in the community. Bessie and Floyd would take people into their home for sometimes many months at a time. They would help people anyway that they could and enjoyed every minute of it.

At Floyd's garage they sold Ford-Lincolns, DeSoto, Rockne (named after Knute Rockne coach at Notre Dame) and Studebaker cars.

Floyd H. Johnson (b. Dec. 9, 1886, d. Jan. 14, 1947) had siblings: Harry Reed (b. Jan. 5, 1884, d. May 24, 1964) of Blissfield; Clara (Reed) Wilt (b. March 2, 1886, d. April 16, 1971) of Coleman; Edna (Reed) Brown (b. July 1, 1889, d. July 19, 1966) of Toledo; Charley Reed (b. July 1, 1893, d. Aug. 24, 1893).

JOHNSON-REED. Adah Irene Reed (b. March 1, 1908, d. Nov. 16, 2001) was the daughter of Harry and Emma (Wotring) Reed, Blissfield, MI. She graduated from high school and Lenawee County Normal in Blissfield and taught school at the White country school in Addison, MI.

Through the years Adah's family came to Isabella County to visit aunts, Bessie A. Reed (Floyd) Johnson of Mt. Pleasant and Clara Reed (Page) Wilt of Coleman. On one such occasion she met E. Lee Johnson (b. March 12, 1905, d. March 1, 1984) and they married on June 9, 1930. Adah became very active in the United Methodist Church up to and including being a district officer. Lee became owner of Johnson Motors.

Four children were born to this union: Duane (Marilyn) Johnson, Meredith (Johnson) Richter, Janice (Johnson) Aldering-Stewart, and Milan (Dorothy) Johnson.

Adah's siblings are Charles A. Reed (b. 1911) of Mt. Pleasant, Woodrow W. Reed (b. 1913) of Rosebush, Archie G. Reed (b. 1915) of Adrian, MI, and Bessie M. (Reed) Bourland (b. 1918) of Shepherd.

JONES-HALSTED. Euretta Estella Halsted was born Oct. 8, 1912 to Albert and Estella (Yats) Halsted. She was born on South Fancher St. in Mt. Pleasant, MI. Her family moved to Franklin Street on a berry farm for the first few years of her life. Her parents separated in approximately 1915. Euretta lived with her father and uncle, Fred Halsted. Euretta's father was away often and she split her time between Charlie and Hattie Swan and the Tinker family.

Euretta was 8 years old when she went to live with her mother, Estella Reef, who had remarried. At the time they lived in Owosso and Euretta believes she stayed there until she was 16. The dates are confusing because she went back and forth so much between parents. She attended Owosso Schools through the tenth grade.

Returning back to Mt. Pleasant, Euretta went to work for Thick's who owned a plumbing and heating shop where the Pickwick is now.

She was hired as a housekeeper. When Mrs. Thick found out Euretta couldn't cook, she got Euretta a job in Jim Ryan's household taking care of their children. Mrs. Thick also tried to convince Euretta to return to school. She even offered to pay her wages and clothing to go back, but Euretta was too proud and refused.

After 1-1/2 years with the Ryan's, she went to work for Fred and Dussie Warner who lived on Main Street. It was Fred who taught Euretta to cook as he was a cook for the Ellis'. She stayed there 3-4 years.

When Euretta was almost 21, she met Milo Jefferson Jones at a sleigh ride held at the Batchelders. Three years later they were married on Nov. 9. 1935. The service was held in Owosso at the Methodist Church. This was also the day Milo quit his job at the railroad. What a start— especially considering this was during the depression.

The Jones' set up household on the Chippewa River near Hiawatha Hills in a tent. They were there all winter. It was a very rough winter with lots of snow and very cold days. They had an old car to get to town with, but many times they would walk into town to get supplies because their vehicle would not get through the snow. Many times they would get stuck in town and stay with friends.

In April 1936 they purchased Kenneth and Florence Bundy's grocery at 1018 W. Broadway. The Jones' had been saving money since they met. Fifteen dollars a week from Milo and $3-4 from Euretta. They needed money to stock the store and went to Isabella Bank to borrow $1,500. They turned Milo and Euretta down. They then went to The Exchange Bank who did loan them the funds. Jones' Superette opened that year and Milo also started on the Mt. Pleasant Fire Department the same year.

Lynn Gary Jones was born to Euretta and Milo in 1939 and Kay Joy Jones followed in 1941.

In 1961 Milo retired from the Fire Department and the Jones' sold the store to Loigi Deni. They moved to Brimley, MI and stayed there until Milo died on March 7, 1987. Euretta sold their place up north and moved back to Mt. Pleasant in the fall of 1987 where she still lives.

Euretta's children, Lynn and Kay, also reside in Isabella County. Lynn married Veronica Jean Kirkey in December 1958. They have four children: Jeff, Dan, Jennifer and Scott. Lynn and Jean have 10 grandchildren. Kay married Raymond "Ed" Bissett in November 1964. Their children are Patti, Julie and Renee. Ed and Kay have six grandchildren.

JUDGE-TIGHE. In 1869 Thomas and Dorothy Judge settled on 200 acres of wild land in Sec. 11 of Fremont Twp. They emigrated here from Westport, Ontario, Canada. Thomas and Dorothy were both originally from Ireland, having come to Canada at very young ages. They met and later married in Kingston, Ontario.

Nine of their 12 children were born in Westport: James (b. Jan. 27, 1852), Thomas (b. Nov. 27, 1853), Mary (b. March 3, 1856), William (b. Oct. 13, 1857), Catherine (b. Sept. 15, 1860), John (b. Dec. 1, 1862), Dorothy (b. Dec. 16, 1863), Sarah (b. Nov. 27, 1866) and Charles (b. Feb. 14, 1868). The youngest three children: Anna (b. March 16, 1869), Celia (b. Feb. 27, 1872) and Daniel (b. Dec. 15, 1876) were born on the family homestead in Fremont Twp.

Originally living in a log house, the family built a double-brick home in 1882 at a cost of $4,000. This home is currently occupied by fourth and fifth generation direct descendants of Thomas and Dorothy Judge.

Seated: Dorothy and Thomas Judge. Standing, l-r: Charles, Daniel, William, Anna and Sarah Judge. Lillian Kane Hall is on bicycle. Picture taken in early 1900s.

Mr. Judge was a farmer and a lumberman. He was active in Democratic affairs and is listed as one of the prominent men in the early history of Isabella County. He was also very active in the affairs of Sacred Heart Catholic Church, serving as president of the very first church committee. He was instrumental in starting Sacred Heart Academy, arranging for the first group of Dominican Sisters to come to Mt. Pleasant to teach in the school.

Four of the Judge children, William, Sarah, Anna and Daniel, lived on the family farm until their deaths. William and Daniel continued the farming and lumbering which their father had begun. William never married. Daniel married Katherine O'Grady of Farwell in 1904. Ms. O'Grady was a teacher at the Hulse School in Fremont Twp. prior to her marriage to Mr. Judge. The couple had eight children: Dorothy (Loren Brooks), Thomas (Alice Trecy), twins— Marie (Albert Stangle) and James (Irene Lynch), Joseph (Margaret Fox), Kathleen (John Neyer), Raymond and Loretta (Ken Ruby).

Thomas, the oldest son of Daniel and Katherine, his wife Alice and their four children: Daniel (Terry Dutmers), William (Vicky Feltman), John (Beth Quillen) and Katherine (Rick Perkins) continued living in the original family home and farming the family acreage. Thomas and Alice lived there until their deaths. The family homestead is currently occupied by Thomas' son William (Bill), his wife and their daughter Kristin. Another son, John, his wife and their children John, Jason, Jeremy and Elisza, also occupy a home on the family farm.

Thomas Judge Farm

The Judge farm was recognized as a Centennial Farm in 1969.

KEENAN-ANDRES. The Keenans fled County Sligo in their native Ireland in the 1840s during the great potato famine. The elder Thomas Keenan (b. 1799), his wife Hanora, and their five children came to North America to settle in the "Province Of Canada." They selected a new home at the settlement of Read northeast of Bellevue, Ontario. The elder Keenans spent the remainder of their lives on their 100 acre Crown Grant.

One of the children, Thomas (the younger) married Mary Ann Donovan from the farm next door. One of their five children was Frank Keenan who was born in Canada in 1870 and baptized at St. Charles Church, Read. Thomas and Mary Ann moved their family to Michigan in 1881. They purchased a farm in Lincoln Twp. Isabella County. The children attended the nearby Pine School. As parishioners of Saint Charles Catholic Church in Mt. Pleasant the Thomas Keenan family helped with the construction of the newly named Sacred Heart Church in 1888. In 1890 they sold the Lincoln Twp. farm, moving to a 40 acre farm on what today is the northeast corner of High and Isabella Road. Soon after the move the Keenan and Son meat business was started. The business prospered in a frame building at 126 South Main Street. In 1903 Thomas and son Frank built a brick structure which is still in use today.

Frank Keenan continued in the meat business after his father's retirement in 1912. When Frank retired 28 years later in 1940, he sold the business and the building. Frank had married Helen Dorherty in 1894. Helen's family came from Duro near Peterborough, Ontario to Deerfield Twp., Isabella County in 1885. Frank and Helen were parents of four sons and three daughters. In 2002 daughter Marguerite celebrated her 102nd birthday and daughter Katherine her 97th birthday.

John Keenan, the fourth son, was born in 1905 and died in 1984. He married Elizabeth Hudson of Shepherd in 1931. They resided in Mt. Pleasant where John managed the State of Michigan Liquor Store. Elizabeth died in 1988. Their only child, Hudson, graduated from Mt. Pleasant High School, Central Michigan University and acquired a MS from Michigan State University. He then served in the Army Engineers in Europe.

Hudson married Ann Andres of Maple Grove Twp., Saginaw County in 1958. Ann and Hudson are both retired science teachers. Ann is a graduate of Central Michigan University and has acquired additional degrees from CMU. Ann taught chemistry and physics at CMU and chemistry at Mt. Pleasant High School. Hudson taught the majority of his teaching career in the earth sciences at Mt. Pleasant High School. Both have a long interest in the cultural and natural history of Michigan.

Their four children are graduates of Mt. Pleasant High School. Three are graduates of Central Michigan University and one is a graduate of Michigan State University. Kieran is located in Wheaton, IL; Kevin (Cathy) resides in Syracuse, NY; Brendan lives in Auburn Hills, MI; Brigid (Greg) Gotham and children, Nicholas and Chelsea, live in Nashville, TN.

In 1999 Ann and Hudson visited the Keenan farm site in County Sligo, Ireland where today Keenans still reside on lands left by Thomas and Hanora some 160 years ago.

KELLER, Roy D., born May 12, 1930 on the original homestead in Isabella Twp. His great-granddad William D. Keller (b. 1850, d. 1926) and great-grandmother Eliz. A. Keller (b. 1857, d. 1925) bought the farm in 1882 and built the house and barn that are still there.

William D. Keller (age 65), Eliza (Wagner) Keller (age 58) and grandson, Roy C. Keller (age 7). (Photo taken in 1915)

After their deaths his granddad Walter E. Keller owned and farmed it, then his dad Roy C. Keller owned it. Upon his parents death the farm is now owned by Roy D. Keller.

Roy D. is married to Phyllis S. Randle Keller and they have one son and five daughters. One daughter lives on the homestead in the original house and the rest of the family lives in different parts of the country.

Roy went to Jordan School, a one-room school, through the eighth grade then to Mt. Pleasant High School. He served in the U.S. Army and after being discharged worked pipeline construction. He is now retired from Operating Engineers Local 324.

KIRKEY FAMILY. In the years from 1879-81, several families moved from Marmora, Ontario Canada to Denver Twp. in Isabella County. One of the families was headed by my great-grandfather Charles A. Kirkey. He was from a family of 10 children (Jean-Baptiste, Peter, Simon, Francis, Louis, Eleid, Joseph, Julienne and William were the others). His lineage went back to Cornwall, Ontario; Montreal, Quebec; Cahors, France; and Guyenne, France.

The family settled in Denver Twp. in the area of Leaton. Farming was the occupation of choice. Charles was married to Mary Connors who was from Ireland. Their union produced seven children: Eliza, Catherine, Joseph, Will-

iam, Charles, Mary and Margarette. The Catholic church St. Charles named for my great-grandfather is presently at Leaton and was built on land once owned by my great uncle and his wife, Joseph Kirkey and Agnes Rose. My aunt Josephine Kirkey was the first baby baptized at St. Charles. My great-grandfather was the first funeral at St. Charles. Charles was my grandfather and was married to Philomena Rose. The Rose family was headed by James Rose and Anne McCravey both of whose lineage goes back to Ireland. James brought his family to Denver Twp. from Owen Sound, Ontario, Canada.

My grandparents were engaged in farming. They had 10 children: Charles, Marie, Leo, Walter, James, Ann, Joseph, Agatha, Joseph and Lillian. James Francis was my father. In about 1910, the family moved from Denver Twp. to Union Twp. My grandfather was still farming as well as working on the railroad and lumbering. Later he worked for Dowell in Mt. Pleasant and was a carpenter specializing in cabinets. Some time in the 1920s the family moved to Mt. Pleasant.

My father attended school first in Leaton and later in Mt. Pleasant. He worked for a short time in Detroit but then returned to Mt. Pleasant to start his own electrical business. His business location ultimately ended up at 221 S. Main. He was the electrical contractor for many buildings at Central Michigan University as well as building in Mt. Pleasant.

I, William C. Kirkey, was born in 1931. My mother was Glady Brindstetter. I lived in Mt. Pleasant until I went away to college. After graduation I married Judith Raymond of Jackson, MI. My career as an electrical engineer took us to many parts of the United States. Some of those areas were in California, Utah, Alabama and Maryland. We have three children: Timothy, Elizabeth and Andrew. We also have three grandchildren: Kalleigh, Alexis and Megan. We moved back to Mt. Pleasant five years ago. *Submitted by William Kirkey.*

KLASHAK, Mary was born Aug. 12, 1837, in Einswald, Germany. (This was taken from data recorded by the Reorganized Church of Jesus Christ of Latter Day Saints at the time of her baptism on April 5, 1896. Because this information was handwritten, it was difficult to determine the correct spelling of the place of birth. The record did not indicate her parents' names.)

From information Emma Methner Ouderkirk (Mary's granddaughter) shared with me, Mary was married two times. Her first husband's surname was Hoeft (given name is unknown) and the family lived in East Prussia near Berlin. Mr. Hoeft was the son of a very wealthy man; however, he was a gambler and drank heavily which caused his death at an early age. Pauline Laura Hoeft was born Feb. 21, 1864, and her father died a short time after her birth.

Mary Hoeft's second husband's surname was Klashak (again his given name is unknown). Three children were born to that union, all were born in Germany:

1) August Andrew (b. Aug. 19, 1865, d. Jan. 15, 1958) md. Barbara Frank in Detroit. They had one son Joseph. The family settled in Coleman in 1881.

2) Gustav (b. Jan. 21, 1875, d. August 1931) md. Loretta Heimsch on Feb. 6, 1900. They also settled in the Coleman area and had three children: Emma, Minnie and Frederick "Fritz."

3) Emma Anna (b. Oct. 5, 1868, d. July 3, 1947) md. Augustus John Rose on July 5, 1886. I believe Mr. Rose was from Saginaw County. Early in their marriage, the Roses moved to Seattle, WA. I believe they made this move by railcar. Seven daughters were born to this family: Flora, Paulina, Rebecca, Minnie, Clara, Florence, Pearle.

A little history: In 1880 Pauline's paternal uncle, John Hoeft of Detroit, loaned her $42 for her passage to America. After her arrival in Detroit she worked for Joseph Methner who owned a dairy farm in East Detroit. She repaid her uncle for the passage, then re-borrowed it and sent it to her half-brother, August, so he could come to America. Pauline and August worked and saved until they had enough to bring their mother, Mary Klashak, and the other children, Gustav and Emma, to America. Mary's husband had died sometime prior to Pauline's coming to Detroit.

Following is the information regarding Mary's death as it appeared in the Coleman newspaper:

Mary Klashak was born in Germany, Aug. 12, 1835, and came to America Nov. 4, 1888, and was baptized in the Latter Day Saints Church in 1896 and died at the home of her son, Gustav Klashak, April 13, 1915. She leaves to mourn two sons and two daughters, Mrs. F. Methner of Coleman, Gustav and August Klashak of Coleman, and Emma Rose of Seattle, WA; 23 grandchildren and 13 great grandchildren.

It is my understanding from conversations with my mother Emma Ouderkirk that her Grandmother Mary always lived with her children. From Emma's account, her grandmother could not use her left arm and hand very well during her last years. She would use her right hand to open her left hand, place a potato in the left hand so she could peal potatoes; this was one way she could help her family. *Submitted by Emma Jean Ouderkirk Valley, great-granddaughter of Mary Klashak.*

KLASHAK FAMILY. Mary Klashak (b. 1835 in Prussia) came to America in 1888. Her daughter, Pauline Hoeft, came from Germany in 1880 and worked to save passage for Mary who also worked and saved money for passage of August and Emma Klashak. They then all worked for passage for Gustave.

Gustave came to America in 1889 and married Loretta Heimsch settling in Isabella County in 1896. They had three children: Emma (b. 1899), Minnie (b. 1901) and Frederick (b. 1906).

Gustave and Loretta purchased the farm on East Isabella County Line in 1903 from Frances and Anna MacNamara for $375 and moved into the log home that existed at that time on the property and purchased an additional 40 acres in 1908.

Gustave removed stumps and improved the property for farming. The Klashaks built a new home on the farm in 1912 a barn in 1915 and other buildings as they could get cash to pay for them.

Emma died of appendicitis in 1914 and Minnie became a teacher in Coleman and Beaverton Schools.

Frederick "Fred or Fritz" assisted Gustave with farming and subsidized his income by carrying mail as a rural carrier. He married Louise Braun in 1927 and they had four children: Alpheus (b. 1929), Doreen (b. 1933), Eleanor (b. 1935) and Carol Ann (b. 1943).

Gustave Klashak

Gustave passed away in 1934 and Fred continued farming and carrying mail. Loretta, Gustave's widow, passed in 1939. Fred purchased an additional 68 acres from the Neier estate in 1951 adjacent to the other 80 acres and continued farming. Louise passed away in 1975, and in 1976 Fred leased the land to other farmers and entered retirement.

Fred remarried in 1976 to Anita Grant and he subsequently passed away in 1986, leaving his interest in the farm to the children.

The farm was divided into three parts. Eleanor was married to Lester Fike (deceased) and still resides on the original 40 acres. Carol Ann and Bill Randall (her husband) own the 68 acres of the Neier acquisition at East County Line Road and Old U.S. 10.

The original log home succumbed to old age and the remnants were removed in 1953, All of the buildings constructed by Gustave and (Fritz) are still standing and serviceable in addition to a small house built in 1930 by Fritz as a residence.

Eleanor (Klashak) Fike and her son Paul and family continue to reside at the original farmstead. *Compiled by Alpheus Klashak.*

KLEINHANS-DENIKE.
William Franklin Kleinhans and Mary Elizabeth Denike Kleinhans and son William Dean moved to Mt. Pleasant from Cadillac, MI on Nov. 7, 1950.

Bill was born in Lee Twp., Midland County to Everett and Murty King Kleinhans on Nov. 7, 1916. He attended the Gordonville Grade School and graduated from Midland High School. After farming for six years he continued his education studying insurance business courses at several colleges. He became a life insurance underwriter for The Gleaner Life Insurance Society and commemorated 60 years of selling for them with a celebration with their executives on April 9, 2001 at the Adrian, MI home office. He had held state and local offices in various insurance organizations.

Mary was born Jan. 17, 1924 to Salyer and Eunice Killion Denike in Boon, MI. After graduation from Mesick High School, she attended Ferris State College. She then worked at The National Bank of Detroit in Detroit, The Cadillac State Bank and The Gleaner Life Insurance Society.

Bill and Mary were married in The Boon Baptist Church on Aug. 18, 1945. They had four sons: William Dean (b. Oct. 20, 1947), Robert Eugene (b. Aug. 12, 1951), Kevin Lynn (b. Oct. 19, 1954) and Mark Alan (b. Sept. 17, 1959). William was born in Cadillac and the other sons in Mt. Pleasant. They now have six grandchildren.

Bill and Mary Kleinhans with children: Billy (13), Bob (9), Kevin (6) and Mark (1-1/2).

The family was active in the Mt. Pleasant First United Methodist Church and participated in Cub Scout leadership roles and activities.

Both have held national and local offices in the Gleaner Life Fraternal Arbors. Bill and Mary have traveled in most of the states and several foreign countries.

KLUMPP-ESSIG.
Matthew Klumpp was born July 6, 1844 in Schonegrund, Germany. His father was Johann Ulrich Klumpp and his mother was Anna Maria Schmalzle. We believe he immigrated to the U.S. in 1865. He met Sophia Barbara Essig (b. April 7, 1856 in Kuppingen, Germany) and they married April 9, 1874 in Rogers CORNERS, MI. They had 16 children and moved from Washtenaw County to Mt. Pleasant in 1899. Matthew died Sept. 5, 1909 and Sophia died June 13, 1929. They had 16 children:

1) Louise Barbara (b. Oct. 28, 1874, d. May 10, 1963) md. Robert Alexander McNutt and had five children: June, Wilbur, Celia, Lena and Oscar.

2) Clara Ann (b. Feb. 13, 1876, d. Jan. 20, 1928) md. Loren C. Scramlin. They had three children: Alice, Marvin and Darvin. She later married George Willett.

3) Christina Sophia (b. Oct. 19, 1877, d. March 17, 1963) md. Benjamin Thomas Kinsey and they had 10 children: Raymond, Gladys, Oris, Benjamin, Frederick, Lucena, Robert, Thomas, Lloyd and Walter.

4) John Frederick (b. Dec. 27, 1879, d. Aug. 24, 1948) md. Maude Belva Johnson and they had 10 children: Alvy, Alton, Othel, Clayton, May, Marie, Elizabeth, John, Bertha and Betty.

5) Martha Maria (b. Oct. 15, 1881, d. Sept. 19, 1959) md. Jacob Michael Koengeter and had three children: Edna, Rupert and Alton.

6) Elizabeth Regina (b. Oct. 29, 1883, d. July 16, 1972) md. John Beaton Fraser and they had two children, Ernest and Esther, and they adopted Helen's son Henry.

7) Kathrine Julianna (b. June 4, 1885, d. Feb. 6, 1977) md. Wesley L. Merrill and had two children, Stuart and Glen.

8) Mayti Amanda (b. Feb. 9, 1887, d. March 9, 1887).

9) Otto Edward (b. Aug. 23, 1888, d. Oct. 28, 1969) md. Mable Ethel MacDonald and had 13 children: Marjorie, Alfred, Sophia, Helen, Dorothy, Robert, Randall, Charles, George, Katherine, Viola, Bonnie and Alice.

10) Matthew (b. Aug. 25, 1890, d. Oct. 20, 1964) md. Mathilda Willimine Steer and they had three children: Arthur, Lucille and Lawrence.

11) Salmona Emma (b. Jan. 28, 1892, d. Jan. 31, 1892) died shortly after her birth.

12) Earnest Michael (b. Feb. 2, 1893, d. Jan. 23, 1981) md. Leila Dora Johnson and they had eight children: Kenneth, Orville, Elsie, Earl, Marl, Ronald, Dale and Herbert.

13) Helen Rosenia (b. Nov. 24, 1894, d. Jan. 7, 1915) md. Issac Burmaster and they had one child Henry.

14) Edward Benjamin (b. July 21, 1896, d. July 24, 1918) never married.

15) Olga Bertha (b. March 16, 1898, d. Aug. 19, 1923) md. Ernest Ethan Courser and they had one child Louise.

16) Walter Jacob (b. Dec. 17, 1899, d. June 8, 1991) md. Vivian Grace Richardson and they had four children: Stanley, Shirley, Kendall and Marlin.

Klumpp-Essig Family. Back, l-r: Martha, Elizabeth, Clara, John, Louise, Christine, Kathrine. Center: Otto, Edward, Matthew Sr., Sophia, Earnest, Matthew Jr. Front: Olga, Walter Helen

An extensive record of the descendants of Matthew Klumpp is published every five years and is available at the Clarke Historical Library on CMU's campus. As of the 2000 printing, over 2,000 descendants are recorded, many who remain in Isabella County. The book also contains many photographs and Matthew's paternal ancestors back to 1580. *Submitted by Maxine Klumpp Kent.*

KLUMPP-MACDONALD.
Otto and Mable (MacDonald) Klumpp lived all of their lives in Isabella County. Otto Edward Klumpp (b. Aug. 23, 1888, d. Oct. 28, 1969) was the 9th of 16 children of Matthew and Sophia Klumpp. Mable Ethel MacDonald (b. Feb. 18, 1894, d. Feb. 2, 1978) was born in Mt. Pleasant.

Otto and Mable were farmers for most of their lives. Later in life they moved to Orchard Street in Shepherd. They had 13 children:

Klumpp-MacDonald Family. l-r: Alfred, Sophie, Katherine, Robert, Marjorie, Helen, Otto, Randall, Bonnie, Mable, Russ, Viola, Alice, George.

1) Marjorie Ethel (b. Jan. 11, 1916, d. May 25, 1996) md. Edward John Schafer and they

had seven children: Edward, John, Ruth Ann, Donald, Gerald, William and Robert.

2) Alfred Otto married Ruth Catherine Klumpp and had three children: Terry, Maxine and Donna. Alfred and Ruth adopted Cheryl and Cindy, daughters of Katherine.

3) Sophia Marie married Ralph Stowell and they had five children: Roger, Janice, Judith, Michelle and Russell.

4) Helen Betty (b. May 21, 1921, d. Aug. 9, 1987) md. James Arthur Scott and they had six children: Patricia, Caroline, Paula, Thomas, Barbara and Vicki. Helen later married Lloyd Arthur.

5) Dorothy Mae (b. Feb. 6, 1923, d. March 18, 1944) md. Richard Gary Sprague and they had two children, Sally and Peggy.

6) Robert Elwin married Renelda Helen Schafer and they had eight children: Douglas, Richard, Theodore, Dorothy, Sandra, Penelope, Gregory and Karen.

7) Randall Richard (b. June 26, 1926, d. Oct. 22, 1966) md. Betty Lou Nutter and they had five children: Linda, Rodney, Juanita, Jolene and Dianne.

8) Charles Russell (b. Feb. 9, 1928, July 8, 1997) md. Shirley A. Fitchett and they had two children, Judy and Theresa. Russ later married Pauline L. Lynch and together they had a son Mark.

9) George Matthew (b. Sept. 27, 1929, d. Aug. 14, 1971) md. Kay Anderson and they had three sons: David, Wayne and James.

10) Katherine Emojene married Gerald A. Griffeth and they had five children: Larry, Cheryl, Sheilah, Cynthia and Kimberly. Katherine later married Kenneth Allen Dickey.

11) Viola Jean married Norman Joseph Schafer and they had seven children: Pamela, Deborah, Michael, Patrick, Mary, David and Jeanette.

12) Bonnie Lou married Gale G. Zingery and they had three children: Mark, Michael and Laurie.

13) Alice Jeanette married Bernard Anthony Faber and they had two children, Bruce and Beverly.

KLUMPP-SCHAFER.
Alfred and Ruth (Schafer) Klumpp have spent the majority of their lives in Isabella County. Alfred Otto Klumpp (b. 1918) was the second of 13 children of Otto and Mable (MacDonald) Klumpp. Ruth Catherine Schafer (b. 1921) was one of seven children of Anthony and Matilda Schafer.

Alfred enlisted in the U.S. Navy in 1940 and Ruth went out to California where they were married July 18, 1942 in San Francisco. Alfred was shipped overseas 12 days later and served aboard the USS *New Mexico* for the next 30 months. When he returned from overseas, they lived at the naval base in Fallon, NV and then returned to Mt. Pleasant. They lived for a brief period at 210 Bennett Street, then purchased a 120-acre farm and built their dream home at 3200 E. Broomfield Road. This property was later purchased by CMU and they moved to a older farm on West River Road while they built their final estate on the wooded corner at 2075 West River Road, "Klumpp's little corner of the world." They enjoy this serene surrounding. Al has always enjoyed planting a large garden and sharing his "crop" with his friends and neighbors.

Alfred first worked for McKillip Electric, then at Leonard Refineries as an electrician from 1948-71. He was maintenance supervisor for the Isabella County building for 10 years. Al also served in the Naval Reserve for 26 years and retired as senior chief petty officer. Alfred was very active in the Moose Lodge, held several offices, received numerous awards and attained the highest level of recognition, the Pilgrim degree in 1988. He was also active with the Isabella County Fair Board for more than 15 years. They both worked with the Commission on Aging's Gold Key Volunteer Program. Ruth held various bookkeeper positions on military bases and back in Mt. Pleasant. She also did taxes, provided daycare in her home and was active with the Catholic Daughters and the Moose.

Klumpp-Schafer Family (1994). Back, l-r: Dave Ahler, Carla McCreery, Mike McCreery, Jeremy Tubbs, Mike Kent, Dave Kent. Second Row (standing): Cheryl McCreery, Chris McCreery, Maxine Kent, Jason Tubbs. Third Row (seated) Donna and Heath Ahlers, Ruth Klumpp, Al Klumpp, Cindy Ludwig, Tony Fox. Front Row: Brad Ahlers, Angie Fox. Insert below: Terry Klumpp (1982).

Ruth and Alfred have five children.

1) Terry Lee (b. Feb. 10, 1948, d. Aug. 13, 1986) attended Ferris State College, served in the Naval Reserve and worked for CMU. He was active with the Boy Scouts.

2) Cheryl Lea married Michael McCreery and they have two children, Christopher Michael and Carla Lea. Chris married Emily Hayes in April 2001.

3) Maxine Ann, married Tom Tubbs and had two children, Jeremiah Edward and Jason Edward. Maxine and Tom were divorced and Maxine later married Michael Kent and added stepson David Michael to the family.

4) Cynthia Jean married Mike Fox and they had two children, Anthony Edwin and Angela Jean. Cindy and Mike divorced and she later married Phil Ludwig.

5) Donna Jean married David Ahlers and they have two sons, Bradley John and Heath Joseph.

KOESTER FAMILY.
Children of C.A. and Loretta Koester: Garold Henry (b. 1951) attended Michigan State University, where he received his degree as a doctor of veterinary medicine and is in partnership in the Airport Animal Clinic in Cadillac. He married Sandra Farnan of Shepherd on June 14, 1973. They have a son Benjamin

Patrick (b. 1976) who obtained a bachelor of science degree in chemical engineering, at the University of Michigan (UofM) in 1998, received a master's degree in human genetics, UofM, 2000, received a master's degree in physics, 2002, and is currently in Ph.D. program in physics at UofM. Their daughter Erin Rose is in her senior year at UofM, majoring in environmental engineering. Another son, Kevin Anthony, is a sophomore at Ferris State University, majoring in education/history.

Carol Ann (b. 1953) received her education at Michigan State University, majoring in psychology and is now the office manager for Clawson Container Co. at Clarkston. She married Andrew Abid of Farmington on Oct. 4, 1975. They have one son Joseph (b. 1983). They reside in Walled Lake, MI. Joseph is a sophomore at Michigan State University majoring in biology. He also plays the guitar and sings in his band, Life Line.

At 50th wedding anniversary in 2000. Front: C.A. "Dick" and Loretta Koester. Standing l-r: Patrick, Jack, Betty Lou, Rosemary, Carol and Gary Koester.

Patrick William (b. 1955) graduated from Michigan State University, majoring in animal husbandry. He is the manager of Greenstone Farm Credit Services in Mt. Pleasant. On April 16, 1977 he married Magdalene Scully of Mt. Pleasant where they also reside. Their daughter Tara Michelle (b. 1978) graduated from the University of Michigan in 2000. She is employed at Harper Associates of Farmington Hills as a medical office recruiter. She plans to marry Greg Kopacz in May 2003. Their son Mark Edward (b. 1981) is in his third year at Western Michigan University, Kalamazoo. His major is business accounting. Another son, Eric Michael (b. 1984) is a freshman at Michigan State University. His interests are in veterinarian medicine.

Rosemary Kathryn (b. 1958) is a graduate of Central Michigan University and Lansing Community College. She is currently employed as a systems analyst for the state of Michigan. She married Daniel Klodt of Gladstone, MI on Sept. 14, 1991. They have son Nathan (b. 1999) and they reside in Grand Ledge, MI.

Elizabeth Louise (b. 1960) attended Michigan State University and graduated as a registered nurse from North Central Michigan College, Petoskey, MI. Thereafter, she obtained a bachelor's degree from the University of Michigan. She was employed at the Sparrow Hospital, Lansing for several years then took employment at Pioneers Hospital in Meeker, CO; later was a home health care nurse and currently is the public health nurse for Rio Blanco County, residing in Meeker. She married Gary Moyer

Sept. 6, 1986. They have three daughters: Kelly (b. 1988), Jessica (b. 1996) and Jamie (b. 1998).

Annette was born June 21, 1962 and died the next day, June 22.

Jack Norbert (b. 1964) graduated from Michigan State University, majoring in crops and soil science. After graduating in 1987, he was employed by the U.S. Department of Agriculture for a short time. He then chose to be a loan officer for Production Credit Association, later named Farm Credit Services, presently Greenstone Farm Credit Services, working in Lakeview, Alpena and currently in Alma. He resides near Shepherd, MI.

KOESTER-MOEGGENBORG.
Celestine (Dick) A. Koester of the Village of Shepherd, Coe Twp., was born Jan. 3, 1924 in Putnam County, OH to William, son of Christopher and Elizabeth (Hilvers) Koester, and Rosa (Beining) Koester, daughter of Henry Sr. and Mary (Dulmer) Beining. Dick's parents, of German descent, were natives of Putnam County. His father (b. 1889, d. 1948) was a farmer by trade. His mother (b. 1889, d. 1974) was a homemaker. The seven children of this family were Richard, Lucinda, Albertha, Ambrose, Celestine, Hilarious and Rosemary.

C.A. "Dick" and Loretta Koester

Mr. Koester married Loretta T. Moeggenborg (b. 1926) on Feb. 11, 1950 at the St. Vincent de Paul Catholic Church, Shepherd, MI. Loretta's parents were Bernard Henry (b. 1885, d. 1953) and Mary A. (Dickman) (b. 1886, d. 1946) Moeggenborg. B. Henry was a native of Germany, coming to America in 1886 at 14 months of age. He was the son of Barney and Elizabeth (Knipper) Moeggenborg. They sailed from Bremen, Germany, March 10, 1886, arriving in Baltimore April 1, 1886. Naturalization papers were finalized in October 1893. They settled in Cincinnati, Hamilton County, OH, where Barney worked for a dairy for several years. Another son, K. Ben (b. 1887, d. 1957) was born here. They then moved on north to Putnam County, OH. As the sons grew up and married, there was a need for more land to farm and land was cheap in Michigan. They took their belongings and journeyed by train, arriving in Forest Hill. They purchased two 80-acre farms in southern Coe Twp. Later, B. Henry purchased several farms just across the road in Gratiot County where he spent his remaining years.

B. Henry moved to Isabella County, MI in 1908 with his first wife, Wilhelmina (Kamphaus) who died in 1918 in the flu epidemic. He then married Mary A. Dickman in 1920, whose husband Anthony Beining died of diabetes. Mary A. was born in Putnam County, OH, the daughter of William and Anna (Spielbrink) Dickman. The children of this family were Clara, August and Carl by Wilhelmina, and Monica Beining, and later family consisting of Mathilda, Catherine, Bernadine, Leo, Loretta, Theresa and Julia Ann.

After their marriage, Koester moved to Forest Hill, MI where he managed a dairy and beef farm for Albin Rademacher for six years. His family then spent two years farming the old Struble farm located four miles east of Shepherd. In 1958 they moved to the Shepherd Farm (one mile north of Shepherd) where he farmed and managed the successful beef and cash crop farm until his retirement. He survived a 1958 plane crash piloted by Dr. Lee Hileman, owner of the Shepherd Farm, while on a cattle buying trip to northern Michigan.

Koester has been involved in various organizations including the Gratiot-Isabella intermediate School Board, Michigan Cattlemen's Association Board of Directors, First Midland Bank and Trust Board, Shepherd State Bank Board, CoAmerica now Firstbank Board, Isabella Livestock Producers, Michigan and National Cattlemen Associations, Knights of Columbus, Parish Council and on the board of the Family Independence Agency. Mrs. Koester served as a 4-H leader for many years, was involved in the 4-H Council, St. Vincent de Paul Rosary Altar Society, Parish Council, Shepherd Area Historical Society and the Soup Kitchen. They are members of St. Vincent de Paul Roman Catholic Church, Shepherd, MI.

KRUSKA FAMILY.
Michigan natives, but new to Isabella County, Paul and Jan Kruska moved to Mt. Pleasant in 1976 seeking a better way of life. Paul was born Aug. 7, 1950 in Ludington MI to parents, Lee and Gen (Mach) Kruska. Lee was born in Manistee, MI on Aug. 26, 1914. He moved to Ludington in 1932. Genevieve was born in Chicago, IL on July 15, 1919. Lee and Gen met at an "arranged" social event and married April 3, 1949 in Chicago. Gen reared four sons and one daughter: Ralph (b. April 11, 1951), Michele (b. Dec. 5, 1952), Russell (b. April 10, 1954), and Edward (b. July 11, 1956).

Janet was born May 4, 1951 in Detroit, MI to parents Paul and Amy (Fardig) Lytikainen. (Father) Paul was born in Hancock, MI on Aug. 30, 1921 and moved to Detroit in 1924. Amy was born in Detroit on Dec. 3, 1924. Amy and Paul married in November 1948 and had two sons, Paul (b. May 23, 1954) and Rob (b. Aug. 12, 1957). The family moved from Detroit to Taylor, MI in 1956. Amy died in 1973. Father Paul married Charlotte Strauss in 1976. Paul died in 1999.

Paul Kruska had an idealic childhood growing up in Ludington. He graduated from Ludington High School in 1968 and attended Ferris State University, graduating from there in 1973 with a BS in pharmacy. Following Jan (met at Ferris) to the Detroit area after graduation, he settled in Pontiac in 1973 to work at Pontiac St. Joseph Hospital. Married April 26, 1975, Paul and Jan lived in a mobile home until 1976 when they moved to Mt. Pleasant. Mt. Pleasant was chosen as the future home for two reasons—a job opportunity and "escape" from the big city. Mt. Pleasant was almost equal distance from both parents in Ludington and Detroit).

Janet lived in a Detroit flat until she was 5 years old and moved to a "new" suburb, Taylor. Grandma Fardig lived with them and two uncles and their families were neighbors.

Janet graduated from Taylor Kennedy High School in 1969 and Ferris State College in dental hygiene in 1972 and worked in the Fisher building in Detroit for Dr. Christl until 1976.

In Mt. Pleasant, Paul and Jan rented a house on Mission Street (now Stadium Mall) and purchased the home at 1520 S. Bamber Road in August 1977. Janet found work with Dr. H Benjamin Loseth in April 1977. Retiring for child rearing, she rejoined the office in 1987 and worked part-time including through the buy-out of the office by Dr. Ken Egger in 1999. Paul's first employment in Mt. Pleasant was with Gould Drug Co. In 1978, a pharmacy job occurred at Central Michigan Community Hospital and Paul has been there since.

Phil, Paul, Jan and Jeff Kruska

Son Jefferey was born in July 27, 1978 at Alma Hospital and graduated from Mt. Pleasant High School in 1996. He spent four years in U.S. Marine Corps and afterwards worked in Mt. Pleasant. Son Philip was born June 24, 1981 at Alma Hospital. He graduated from Mt. Pleasant High School in 2000 (editor of yearbook), and attends Central Michigan University.

Jan and Paul have been active members of Immanuel Lutheran Church since 1978, Mt. Pleasant Optimist Club, Mt. Pleasant Area Historical Society (charter members), AIM, and active since 1980 in Christmas Outreach.

LAWRENCE-MESLER.
Andrew Lafayette Lawrence was born Oct. 20, 1856 in Kalamazoo, MI, son of George H. and Mary (Kent) Lawrence. Andrew came to Sherman Twp. in 1872 and acquired 80 acres of forest land and cut trees to build a log house where he, his mother and half-sister lived. He worked for lumbermen in the forests around there.

In 1890 he married Cora Adelade Mesler (b. Sept. 6, 1871 in Lenawee County), daughter of William and Emily Roseltha (Sutherland) Mesler. They lived in the log house he had built and his mother lived with them until her death in 1893. Eleven children were born to them in this little log house: Sidney Andrew (b. 1891, d. 1968) md. Mary Nettie Graber (b. 1901, d. 1999);

Herbert James (b. 1892, d. 1969) md. Frances Fackler (b. 1893, d. 1967); Orren Lyle (b. 1894, d. 1948) md. Dorothy Delo (b. 1900, d. 1982); Edna Lena (b. 1895, d. 1983) md. first, Erie Monroe (b. 1890, d. 1939) and second, George Merrihew (b. 1885, d. 1973); Mable Katherine (b. 1897, d. 1906); Lorena Inez (b. 1899, d. 1937) md. Ira Lee Quick (b. 1896, d. 1995); Leora Mary (b. 1902, d. 1926) md. James O. Kent (b. 1883, d. 1944); Jimmie Albert (b. 1904, d. 1957) md. Una Smith (b. 1911, d. 1972); a stillborn in 1906; Elsie Roseltha (b. 1907, d. 1997) md. first, Ivan Abell (b. 1906, d. 1939) and second, George Bolinger (b. 1892, d. 1973); and Ruby Bertha (b. 1911) md. Dewey Kirvan (b. 1903, d. 1984).

Cora helped clear the ground, planted garden and took care of the food for the family. Andrew left for work before daylight in the morning and didn't get home until after dark at night. They had cows and chickens which Cora took care of along with taking care of her family. There were still bears in the woods at that time. The cows roamed the woods and she kept bells on them so that if they didn't come home at milking time she would go into the woods to look for them, often carrying a baby on each hip. She never did encounter any bears. Cora baked 32 loaves of bread a week, made the butter, canned the vegetables and fruits and did a lot of cooking and baking to feed her children. She also made all of the children's clothing, including the boys pants and shirts. Cora assisted her neighbors in many ways through the years, by helping the women during illnesses and with childbirth, and providing food when needed.

In 1912 they had a barn raising. All of the neighbor men came and there was one carpenter who directed the work of putting up the frame for a large barn with a basement.

Andrew held the office of commissioner of highways and was treasurer of school district No. 2, (Sherman Twp.) for 27 years. He died Feb. 12, 1928.

Cora purchased a large country school and a church building that were for sale in 1930. Her daughter Elsie's father-in-law, George Abell, who was a carpenter, helped the Lawrence brothers tear these buildings down and save the lumber to build a new house. Mr. Abell, with what help the brothers could give him, built the new house, five rooms downstairs, three bedrooms upstairs and a full basement.

Cora didn't have very long to enjoy her new house. She died Oct. 9, 1936. Her oldest son Sidney and his family continued to reside there.

Andrew, Cora, Sidney, Herbert, Mable, Leora, Jimmie and Elsie are buried in the Forest Hill Cemetery.

LEE, Jesse (b. 1875, d. 1971), son of Sherman (b. 1833, d. 1910) and Fannie (Parmelee) Lee (b. 1852, d. 1929), was born in Ionia County, MI. Sherman was born in Yates County, NY, and his folks moved to Seneca County, OH with their first three children, including Sherman and having lost the first child in New York. In Ohio four more children were born. Sherman and his first wife Margaret (Bretz) moved to Ionia County and another child was born who only lived a few days and the mother died also.

Sherman then married Fannie Parmelee, of Ionia County. They had four children in Ionia

County and the family soon moved to Millbrook Twp. in Mecosta County, only two of these children lived. Jesse moved back to Seneca County when he was in his teens and worked in the Glass factory and stone quarry. He married Belle Clark (b. 1877, d. 1939), daughter of Jacob and Mary Jane Clark.

Sherman had moved to Sherman City and wrote what a wonderful place it was, so Jesse, his wife and two daughters, Pearl, and Bessie, moved to Sherman City and Jesse said all he saw was sand and sand burrs. He settled on a farm on Denver Road about two miles south of Sherman City. There their oldest daughter died of appendicitis, a daughter Vola died of pneumonia and twin boys died at birth, but Hazel, Avery, Willis, Albert, Mary and Lloyd were born.

In about 1922 their house burned and they moved to a farm in Coldwater Twp. Bessie and Hazel had married by then, so just the four boys and Mary moved to Coldwater Twp. In 1939 Belle died, later Jesse moved to Clare County with his son Albert. Later in 1968 he moved back with his daughter Bessie. When she married Tom Latham they moved to Remus. Jesse died there in 1971. He and Belle are buried in the Sherman City Cemetery.

Jesse was very interested in medicine and very helpful with animals. He was often called to help with sick. He was also good with home remedies for humans. There had been doctors in his family who served in the Revolutionary War and all other wars. One Dr. Joshua Lee was well-known and many studied with him during the Civil War Times. Jesse never lived near these people, but did inherit a very thick dictionary of medicine that he must have studied. He was known to fall off roofs, and would stand on his head while a helper wrapped his ribs tight. He was a tall man, not 6 foot, only 5'11 and 1/2 inches." His grandchildren miss him, and were very privileged to have such a wonderful Grandfather. He lived during a great time in our history, he heard William Jennings Bryan talk with that big booming voice and remembered the headlines of the Wright Brothers first flight and saw on TV the men land on the moon.

LEITER, Charles Edward "Ed" (b. Nov 20, 1861 in Horsehead, NY, d. _ 1939 in Sherman Twp.) moved to Sherman Twp. with his family before 1870. He remembered walking from Horsehead to Sherman Twp. with his dad, Charles Henry, by way of Ionia where his youngest sister was born. Charles Henry (known as Henry) moved his family. His father Martin also came before 1885. When Henry was treasurer of Sherman Twp., he collected taxes of as little as 34 cents from one farmer.

Edward Leiter was of Swiss descent. The first Leiter in U.S. was Jacob (b. 1706) in Maryland, then Christian (b. 1736) in Pennsylvania, another Jacob (b. 1772), Martin (b. 1809), Charles Henry (b. 1835), then Charles Edward (b. 1861).

Charles Henry md. Martha Goodenough and their first four children were born in New York, Liza was born in Ionia County, and the last three in Isabella County. The children were Rosa md. Frank Losey, Charles Edward md. Emma Jane Losey, Ira md. Viola Denslow, George md. Minnie Mull, Liza md. Issac Losey,

LJ(Jay) md. Mertie Goodenough, Cassie died very young, and Oscar md. Ethel.

Charles Edward md. Emma Jane Losey and their children were Emory (b. 1888, d. 1963), md. Bessie Halstead; Mary md. Rubin Hine; Amy md. Edward Darnell; Nellie md. Harry Paterson; Morris md. Carmel Schedelle; Howard md. Ruth Cornell. Most of these children lived in Isabella County and are buried in Forrest Hill Cemetery west of Weidman.

LOSEY, Joseph (b. 1830 in Pennsylvania, d. Sept. 4, 1894 in Sherman Twp.) and his brother Stephen came to Sherman Twp., Isabella County from New Jersey (where their ancestors served in the Revolutionary War) by way of Tioga, PA to Jackson County, MI and Coe Twp., Isabella County near St. Louis where their last child Emma Jane was born. He married Mary Ellis (b. 1832, d. Oct. 14, 1889). Their children are as follows:

1) Franklin (b. 1857, d. 1942) md. first, Caroline Carr and second, Rosa Leiter. Their children were Jessie, Charlie, and Joe or Joseph, who died very young.

2) Cynthia (Tint) (b. 1860) md. Frank Sherman.

3) Isaac (Ike) (b. 1862, d. 1946) md. Liza Frances Leiter (b. 1868, d. 1972). Their children were Pearl, Bessie, Basil, Phoebe and Fillis.

4) Zoe E. (b. 1864, d. 1913) md. Bailly Darnell. They adopted a son Ray.

5) Emma Jane (b. 1868, d. 1949). Their children were Emery, Mary, Amy, Nellie, Morris, Howard.

Stephen (b. 1827, d. Aug. 10, 1895) md. Alvina Brand (b. 1837, d. 1893) served in the Civil War before he came to Michigan. They had seven children: Albert, Lewis, Lelia, Nancy, Calvin, Hiram and Valalia.

The brothers settled in Sherman Twp. before 1870, were farmers and operated threshing machines; others became carpenters, building many local houses and barns. Ike was a well-known "fiddle" player; he, and later a neighbor Emery Dell, played for all the "happenings" in the neighborhood.

The brothers, wives and most of the children are buried in the Forrest Hill Cemetery west of Weidman.

MARSHALL FAMILY. Robert James "Rob" Marshall II was born July 9, 1970 in Livonia, MI to Robert James "Bob" Marshall and Judy Ann Robertson. Bob (b. Nov. 30, 1946 in Detroit, MI) and Judy (b. March 21, 1948 in Colorado Springs, CO) had three other children: Teri Ann Marshall (b. Feb. 17, 1967); Lori Lynn Marshall (b. April 25, 1968); and Tami Jo Marshall (b. Oct. 18, 1972). Bob and Judy divorced in 1975.

Judy then married Carl Eugene Canfield from Leslie, MI on June 29, 1979. Carl's four daughters came to live with the family: Shaun Marie Canfield (b. Feb. 19, 1972), Sheri Lee Canfield (b. July 22, 1974), Rebecca Lynn Canfield (b. Aug. 25, 1976), and Melissa Kay Canfield (b. March 23, 1977). Two children were born to Judy and Carl: Keli Erin Canfield (b. Sept. 18, 1980) and Travis Eugene Canfield (b. June 8, 1982). Rob spent his childhood in Perry, MI. He attended Perry Public Schools and graduated in 1988. He loved being part of a large, busy family. He loved sports and was active in Boy Scouts. He received his Eagle Scout Award in May 1988. He currently attends Central Michigan University to pursue a career in secondary education with a math major and a physical education minor.

David Arnold Brant (b. Aug. 14, 1942 in Alma, MI) and Kathlene Kay Thurlow (b. Sept. 28, 1944 in Saginaw, MI) had six children: Eugene David Brant (b. May 15, 1967), Robert Anthony Brant (b. Jan. 12, 1969), Deanna Jane Brant (b. April 24, 1970 in Mt. Pleasant, MI), Ryan Daniel Brant (b. April 1, 1974), Sarah Lynne Brant (b. May 14, 1975) and Christine Louise Brant (b. March 24, 1980). They resided in Shepherd Michigan.

Deanna Jane Brant spent her childhood on the family "farm" (a few horses, ducks, dogs, and cats.) She enjoyed participating in 4-H. She attended Shepherd Public Schools and graduated in 1988. She then attended Central Michigan University and graduated Cum Laude with a bachelor of science degree in elementary education with an early childhood education major and a reading minor. She taught for Chippewa Hills Public Schools for three years until the birth of her children.

Rob and Deanna met on Feb. 12, 1988 in East Lansing, MI. They were both attending a church youth dance. Rob asked Deanna to dance, and they began to date. They attended senior prom together. Rob served a two-year mission for his church to the Netherlands and Belgium. He returned in August 1991, and the two were married in Chicago, IL Feb. 12, 1992. They built a ranch-style house in 1994 and currently reside there. They have

Rob and Deanna with sons Caleb and Kyle.

two children: Caleb Carl Marshall and Kyle David Marshall, identical twins who were born Dec. 29, 2000 in Mattoon, IL. They are wonderful, enthusiastic children. The family enjoys camping, gardening, being outdoors and swimming. The family also enjoys activity in their church, The Church of Jesus Christ of Latter-Day Saints.

Rob received his builder's license in the fall of 2002, and is self-employed. His business name is Precision Builders. He is busy working and attending college. Deanna is happy to have the opportunity to be an at-home mother. Future plans include conclusion of college for Rob, a teaching position, and construction work in his spare time. Deanna plans to return to teaching when her children are older.

MCCONNELL FAMILY. When Raymond McConnell (b. 1831, d. 1916) arrived in Isabella County in 1886, his family had already been in America for over 50 years. His parents, John and Bridget McConnell, were among the first to settle near Streetsville, Peel County, Ontario (now Mississauga). By the time Raymond inherited his father's farm in 1880, he had been married

for 17 years to Mary Joan O'Donnell (b. 1843, d. 1913), and they had a family of 10 children (plus two who had died young).

Even then Peel County was beginning to get crowded, so they decided to move to central Michigan so there would be land available for all four sons to have farms. Upon arrival, he bought for $2,000 the NW1/4 of the SW1/4, the NW1/4 of the SE1/4, and the NE1/4 of the NW1/4 of Sec. 31, Wise Twp. Raymond and Mary Joan retired to Clare around 1897, but their sons (and daughters) did indeed farm the land, and many still do.

The McConnell's eldest child was a daughter Mary Ann (b. 1865, d. 1938) who married Cornelius O'Sullivan (b. 1869, d. 1933). As mentioned before, Joseph, Daniel and Elizabeth married three of the Battles: Anna, Mary Agnes and Francis respectively (my father had so many aunts and uncles when growing up they would be distinguished by their husband's name - thus Aunt Mary Pat was Mary Battle, wife of Patrick, and Aunt Mary Dan was Mary McConnell, wife of Daniel).

James McConnell (b. 1873, d. 1963) was known as J.D. and md. Anna Murphy (b. 1877, d. 1949); Isabelle (b. 1875, d. 1953) md. Joseph Crowley; Raymond (b. 1880, d. 1960) md. Mary O'Connell (b. 1885, d. 1956) and Therese (b. 1884, d. 1920); Thomas Maloney (b. 1880, d. 1951). Two of the sisters became nuns, Anna became Sister Mary Amanda (b. 1877, d. 1939) and Catherine (b. 1879, d. 1918) was Sister Mary Raymunda.

MCDONALD, Douglas Allen (b. July 29, 1962) graduated from high school in 1980, enrolled at CMU the following fall and earned his degree in accounting in May 1986. Doug spent four years with the accounting firm, Shoemaker and Doerr, before starting his own accounting practice in downtown Mt. Pleasant. Doug resided on East Bennett Court in Mt. Pleasant with Sherry Ann (Mayer) Doerr and her daughter Heather Ann. They built their current residence in Mineral Springs, west of Mt. Pleasant, in 1997. Doug and Sherry have supported Heather's outstanding high school cross-country career by attending many of her state and Midwest running events. They enjoy their cottage on Lake Mecosta, outdoor activities, and nights out with friends. Heather will graduate from Sacred Heart Academy this year and is considering many college opportunities at some of the country's best schools.

MCDONALD. The history of the Edward Joseph McDonald family is a story filled with love, family loyalty and togetherness. The McDonald family story began on July 13, 1930 when Edward Joseph McDonald was welcomed into the world as the youngest child of Joseph Harold McDonald and Edna Irene (Salchert) McDonald. Ed was reared on the family farm at 60 North Lincoln Road in Isabella County. Ed attended Sacred Heart Academy until he joined the U.S. Air Force at the age of 16. He served a total of seven years in the Air Force during the Korean War.

On Sept. 28, 1957, he married Harriet Kay Dowell (known as Kay). Ed and Kay built a new home at 10 North Lincoln Road where they be-

gan to raise the first eight of their nine children. In 1971, they purchased their current home at 2245 North Winn Road in Beal City. Ed worked as a laborer for many years for various construction companies in the mid-Michigan area. He is currently working part-time for Krapohl Ford in Mt. Pleasant. Ed enjoys attending his grandchildren's sporting events. He also spends a great deal of time assisting his children with their seemingly perpetual home improvements.

Kay graduated from Mt. Pleasant High School in 1956. She attended beauty school until starting their family in 1958. She was employed by St. Joseph the Worker church and school for 15 years, as well as, for area families and businesses as a housekeeper. She enjoys sewing and scrapbooking in the winter, but loves the summer when you will find her in her yard working in flowerbeds at 6:00 a.m. nearly every day. She also enjoys her grandchildren's sporting events and activities.

Ed and Kay's greatest joy are their children and grandchildren. Ed and Kay's children were all graduates of Beal City High School. They were all involved in many activities through the years. Together, the Edward J. McDonald family shares a loving bond that will outlive their history in their children and grandchildren.

MCDONALD, Edward Leroy is known as "Pete" by family and friends. He was born Sept. 13, 1959 and graduated from high school in 1977. Pete met his future wife while working for his aunt Marguerite Rice, at her party store on west Remus Road. Pete and Peggy Lynn "Peg" Crowley were married July 17, 1981 at St. Joseph the Worker Church in Beal City.

Pete began his carpentry job at CMU, and Peg her job at K-Mart in 1980. Pete has been employed at CMU for 23 years. Peg left her management position at K-Mart in 2000. They enjoy camping with their children Kay Lynn (b. May 16, 1985) and Brian Patrick (b. June 5, 1989). They camp every summer in Chapleau, Ontario, Canada, which has become a family tradition. Pete enjoys hunting and fishing.

Brian, following in his Dad's footsteps, got his first buck and turkey in 2002. Kay Lynn will graduate from Mt. Pleasant High School this year. She excels at softball and hopes to play at the collegiate level next year

MCDONALD, Eric Scott, known as Scott, was born Jan. 31, 1961 and graduated high school in 1979. Scott met his future wife while building a new dairy facility for her father. Scott married Debra Kay Haupt on Dec. 3, 1983 at St. Joseph the Worker Church in Beal City. Scott and Deb spent 11 years working on the John Haupt family farm. Deb also operated an in-home day care for several years.

Scott and Deb have three children: Jason Scott (b. Feb. 1, 1985), Kyle Joseph (b. June 17, 1986) and Jodi Ann (b. May 10, 1988). They all attended Beal City High School, their alma mater. They all enjoy the Beal City athletic events, 4-H and outdoor activities.

Scott changed occupations in 1991, when he joined his brother Joe at the House of Cabinets. In 1996, the growing cabinet manufacturing part of the business became Pinnacle Cabinet Company. Scott is a partner with brothers,

Fred and Joe, in the expanding company. In 2000, Deb also joined Pinnacle as the office manager.

MCDONALD, Frederick Kelly was born Jan. 31, 1965 and graduated from high school in 1982. He enrolled at CMU the following fall and earned his bachelor of science degree in political science. He worked in Minnesota and Ohio until he returned to the Mt. Pleasant area to manage a joint venture selling building supplies.

Fred met his wife, Lisa Kay McLaughlin, while she was employed by a local radio station. Fred and Lisa have two boys, Jack Edward (b. April 24, 1998) and Samuel Frederick (b. Aug. 2, 2001). They live at 503 North Lansing Street in Mt. Pleasant, where they have made numerous improvements to their home. Fred enjoys golf in the summer and activities with his family, Fred is a partner with brothers, Joe and Scott, in Pinnacle Cabinet Co. in Mt. Pleasant. Lisa is a speech pathologist with the Gratiot/Isabella RESD.

MCDONALD, Gregory Mark was born July 3, 1966 and graduated from high school in 1985. Gregg met Linda McLellan through a mutual friend, and they married on August 11, 1988. Greg worked for Beal City Service until he started his current job at Randell Manufacturing where he has remained for 13 years.

Greg and Linda reside at 751 North Gilmore Road near Beal City. They have three children: Bradley James' (b. Sept. 6, 1988), Tyler Justin (b. Nov. 27, 1990) and Morgan Taylor (b. Jan. 22, 1993). The children attend Beal City schools where the boys are active in sports. Morgan keeps the family entertained with her great sense of humor. The family likes camping and spending time on their boat fishing. Linda has worked for the Isaella County Medical Care Facility for eight years.

MCDONALD, Jennifer Ann was born Nov. 18, 1968 and graduated from high school in 1987. Jenny went on to further her education at CMU. She earned a bachelor of applied arts degree in journalism and political science in May 1992. She worked for the Student Book Exchange in Mt. Pleasant during college.

After college, Jenny pursued her journalism career at the *Isabella County Herald* for a short time before returning to the Student Book Exchange for another four years as a manager. She is currently employed by Central Michigan Community Hospital as a Human Resource Generalist.

Jenny met Duane Patrick Reid in 1998, and they married Sept. 16, 2000 at Sacred Heart Church in Mt. Pleasant. Jenny and Duane reside at 1745 South Lincoln Road in a home originally built by John and Leona McDonald on land that bad been part of the McDonald centennial farm that was established in 1888. They are expecting their first child on August 28. Duane works for Pinnacle Cabinet Co. and has been able to put his woodworking skills to good use at home.

MCDONALD, John Sr. and his wife Catherine (Kane) McDonald were born in Westport, Ontario, Canada. They came to Isabella County in 1870 and purchased 80 acres of land in Union Township, it being the E1/2 of the SE1/4 of Section 8.

They were the parents of nine children: Ann married Patrick Carey and lived in Union Township; Michael was a farmer and later an employee of Tice Ice Co. in Mt. Pleasant; James was an employee of Wick's Boiler Co. of Saginaw (his grandson James became president of General Motors Corp.); John Jr. was a farmer; Cecelia was not married and remained at home most of her life; Thomas was a conductor on the Ann Arbor Railroad; William was a dentist in Mt. Pleasant; Edward became a priest; and Loretta was a school teacher.

At the time the family came to Isabella County, most of the land was covered with forest and a large part of it was an Indian Reservation. The nearest mill at which the settlers could get their grain ground into meal and flour was at Isabella City about a mile north of what is now the city of Mt. Pleasant. It was built by the U.S. Government for the Indians. The government also had a school for the Indian children on the E1/2 of Sec. 9. The McDonald children attended school here with the Indians until a school was later constructed on the corner of Pickard and S. Lincoln Roads. The Indian school was moved across the road to what is now the Ronald Ervin farm.

The story is told that shortly after they came to Isabella County, Catherine became seriously ill and wanted to see a priest. There being no priest nearer than Saginaw, and as they had no horses at this time since oxen were used to farm and clear the land, a neighbor and relative living a short distance south of Sec. 16 volunteered to go to Saginaw and get a priest. The story is told that John Garvin, also known as "Beaver John," ate his breakfast at home early the next morning, set out on foot and ate his supper in Saginaw that evening. He returned the next day with the priest in a horse and buggy.

John McDonald Jr., was born in Westport, Ontario, Canada on July 8, 1867. He married in November 1899 to Anna Diehl in Sacred Heart Catholic Church in the corner of Franklin and Illinois streets, which had just been completed. They were the parents of nine children: Joseph, Fred, Elizabeth, Cecelia, Marguerite, Mildred, Ann Louise, Frances, and Evelyn. They all graduated from Sacred Heart Academy in Mt. Pleasant. The seven girls graduated from Central Michigan Normal, now Central Michigan University, with teacher certificates and became teachers. John Jr. died Dec. 25, 1920 and Anna died July 8, 1949.

MCDONALD, Joseph H. was born Sept. 17, 1900 on a farm in Union Twp., Isabella County, the elder son of John and Anna (Diehl) McDonald. A brother Fred, his son John, and grandson Gary have resided on that farm. Joseph attended the McDonald School at the corner of Pickard and Lincoln Roads. He graduated in 1918 from Sacred Heart Academy in Mt. Pleasant. There were eight other children in the family: Brother Fred and sisters Elizabeth, Cecelia, Marguerite, Ann, Mildred, Frances and Evelyn. The sisters graduated from Central Michigan University (Central Michigan Normal) and taught school in various Michigan cities.

On Oct. 6, 1925, he married Edna Irene Salchert (b. June 27, 1904), the daughter of Michael and Mae (Perry) Salchert. Joseph and

Edna lived in several homes in the Mt. Pleasant area before purchasing a farm at 60 North Lincoln Road. Joe farmed and worked for the Tice Ice Co., the Sugar Beet Factory and the Mt. Pleasant Home and Training School until the time of his death on July 3, 1945.

Edna worked for Waterman's Clothing Store, Ferro's, Mt. Pleasant Home and Training School, Lee Equipment and Orens before moving to Florida in 1971. She returned to make her home at 209 East Maple Street in Mt. Pleasant in 1977. Edna died Jan. 9, 1994.

Marguerite Josephine was born on April 16, 1926, Elizabeth Eileen on Nov. 8, 1927, Barbara Jean on April 6, 1929, and Edward Joseph on July 13, 1930. The children attended the Whiteville School which was located on Jordan Road in Isabella Twp. and later Sacred Heart Academy and Mt. Pleasant High School. The family was members of the Sacred Heart Parish in Mt. Pleasant.

Marguerite, graduated from Sacred Heart Academy in 1944, and began working at Kroger. She has been employed at various jobs through the years and most recently self-employed. She was owner and operator of the old Van Zandt Store (Rice's Party Store and the Barn Door on West M-20 at Coldwater Road). On Dec. 15, 1944, Marguerite married Roderick Rice; he was employed by Dow Chemical until the time of his death in 1969. Children: David Leo (b. Aug. 11, 1949), Teresa Mae (b. July 7, 1951), Gary Lynn (b. Sept. 10, 1952), Mark Harold (b. July 22, 1954), Nicholas Lee (b. July 14, 1958) and Carol Irene (b. Oct. 18, 1959). Gary Lynn was killed in an automobile accident while serving with the Navy in California. Elizabeth Eileen graduated from Mt. Pleasant High School in 1946 and began working at Ferro's. She was employed by the state of Michigan for many years and is now retired. On April 12, 1947, she married Stephen Rau, a self-employed farmer until 1969 when he became a laborer for Marchiando-Rau Construction until he was disabled by a stroke in 1975 and died Nov. 3, 1992. Stephen J. (Joe) (b. Nov. 1, 1948), Marjorie Ann (b. July 1, 1950), William Edward (b. June 4, 1951) and Mary Kaye (b. Sept. 20, 1952).

Barbara Jean attended Mt. Pleasant High School and later worked at Ferro's. On Nov. 24, 1951 she married Earl Oplinger, a farmer in Sherman Twp., Isabella County. They have lived and farmed the same place since 1951. Kenneth Earl was born Aug. 16, 1952 and Edward Sterling June 15, 1954.

Edward Joseph attended Sacred Heart Academy and enlisted in the U.S. Air Force at the age of 16. He spent the next seven years in Texas, Alaska, Korea, Michigan and Florida. On Sept. 28, 1957 he married Harriet Kay Dowell and lived at North Lincoln Road for several years. The family now resides in Beal City. Edward has worked as a laborer for many construction companies in the area. Edward and Kay remain in their Beal City home acquired in 1971.

MCDONALD, Joseph Harold (named for his grandfather) was born on March 30, 1958 and graduated from high school in 1976. Joe continued his education at Central Michigan University (CMU) to pursue his interest in music. He soon changed career directions towards construction.

Joe met Jennifer Jean Korcsmoros at CMU, and they were married on Aug. 11, 1978 at St. John Vianney Church in Flint. Joe and Jenny will celebrate their 25th wedding anniversary later this year. Joe started his own construction business at 20-years-old, and Jenny worked at Post Pharmacy until their son, Andrew Joseph, was born on July 18, 1982. Two years later, their daughter Shannon Marie was born on May 5, 1984. Between the birth of their two children, Joe and Jenny settled into their current home at 510 South Franklin Street in Mt. Pleasant.

In 1988, Joe and Jenny purchased the House of Cabinets from its founders, Harold Franke and J. Milne Witbeck and continue in the kitchen and bath business some 15 years later. Andy and Shannon are both graduates of Sacred Heart Academy, following a legacy of some 100 plus years of McDonalds at that Isabella County institution. They are currently pursuing careers at work and school.

MCDONALD, Matthew Brian was born Sept. 30, 1963 and graduated from high school in 1981. Matt earned a bachelor of science degree in secondary education from CMU in 1988, and a masters in athletic administration in 1994. He worked along side CMU baseball coach Dean Kreiner as a graduate assistant and remains in coaching to this day. Matt has held teaching and coaching positions at Saginaw Novell and Fruitport. He is currently the head football coach at McBain High School.

Matt met his wife, a sister of one of his students, in McBain, and proposed marriage with flowers and candlelight in the high school gym. Matt and Nicole Dana Stahl were married on May 13, 2000, at the Northland Community Church in McBain. Nicole is a professor of psychology at Cornerstone University in Grand Rapids. Matt and Nicole live in Cadillac with their daughter Kennedy Nicole, born August 2, 2001 (a date of birth she shares with her cousin Sam). Child number two is due this summer.

Matt enjoys golf in the summer, is active at the state level in high school sports administration, helps with baseball activities at CMU and has enjoyed success with his teams, including a state runner-up football championship title in 2001. The entire McDonald clan gathered to watch him and nephews Jason and Kyle (of Beal City) earn runner-up state titles in back-to-back games at the Pontiac Silverdome.

MCDONALD, Michelle Martha (b. April 8, 1972) graduated from high school in 1990 and enrolled at CMU the following fall. She earned a bachelor of applied arts degree in journalism in 1994. Shelly dated her future husband through high school and married Darin Edward Spayd on Aug. 17, 1991, at St. Joseph the Worker Church in Beal City. Shelly and Darin have two boys, Justin Edward (b. Nov. 21, 1993) and Michael Glenn (b. Aug. 25, 1995). The boys attend Shepherd schools.

Shelly worked at the Student Book Exchange near campus while attending college. She worked for the *Isabella County Herald* as a sales representative for one year and then began working for the House of Cabinets. Shelly now works part-time for Pinnacle Cabinet Co. while pursuing a teaching certificate at CMU. She is anx-

ious to begin a teaching career allowing her more time to spend with her boys. Shelly enjoys scrapbooking, music and photography. She has begun to develop an interest in portrait photography.

Darin works as a machinist for Bandit Industries near Blanchard. The family enjoys outdoor activities and sporting events.

MCGUIRE FAMILY. While James Battle's parents did not survive to join their son in Michigan, his wife Julia's did. Patrick (b. 1808, d. 1883) and Bridget Burke McGuire (b. 1810, d. 1881) were among the founders of what became St. Henry's Parish, although they are both buried in Mount Pleasant. Their seven children all had farms in northern Isabella County and there are many descendants still living in the area.

Their eldest child was Bridget (b. 1832, d. 1926). Unfortunately, her marriage resulted in tragedy when her husband Henry Hamel (b. 1849, d. 1894) died as a result of a farming accident less than a year after their marriage. John (b. 1837, d. 1911) md. Cecelia Mahon (b. 1848) and Julia md. James Battle. Patrick (b. 1842, d. 1918) never married; Michael (b. 1844, d. 1935) md. Roseann Cox (b. 1845, d. 1927), Hugh (b. 1850, d. 1930) md. Catherine Crowley (b. 1861, d. 1950), and Dominic (b. 1854, d. 1932) md. Margaret McKenna (b. 1863, d. 1908).

MCINTYRE, John was born April 26, 1826 in Kircubbin, County Down, Ireland and was the son of William J. and Martha Ann (Dunlop) McIntyre. The English Lord's took his parents farm away from them because it had peat on it. This was a time of great trouble and distress in Ireland so his father and mother emigrated to Canada in the 1800s, but Martha Ann died on the way over and was buried at Port Hope, Canada. His sisters came too and lived with an aunt in Canada until they married. One sister, Mary, was left in Ireland. She married Samuel Rose Allen on May 5, 1856 in Grausha Townland, County Downs, Ireland.

John was brought over by a lawyer named Crabb who paid his way over. John had to work for him a number of years to pay for his passage. While he lived in Ireland he was a jockey until he had a bad fall from his horse, hitting his head. He had sleeping spells afterwards and would go to sleep while talking to you and when he woke up, go right back to talking as if he had never stopped. He married July 20, 1869 to Margaret M. Inman who was 14 years old. She was a daughter of Thomas Inman who was born in Cork, Ireland, and Elizabeth Hill who was born in Balentemple townland, County Wicklow, Ireland and who emigrated to Canada and later moved to Sanilac County, MI.

Neither John nor Margaret could read or write. In Canada John bought a farm and built up a large herd of livestock; then he signed a note for a neighbor and lost them all. Soon after, he moved to Peck, Elk Twp., Sanilac County in October 1886, where Margaret's brother John Inman, wife and 15 children lived and farmed. There he signed another note for someone and lost everything again.

They moved to Rolland Twp., Isabella County in November 1892. There they got a Mrs. Comstock to do all their paper work. John loved

animals and would sit with a sick one night and day. He was a farmer in Rolland Twp. and lived to be 104 years old, 10 months, 17 days, Luce County Death Certificate, died March 8, 1931, Newberry at a daughter's.

Margaret (Inman) McIntyre was born in Ireland and died March 2, 1914, Rolland Twp. and is buried on her brother John Inman's lot, Peck, Elk Twp. Cemetery, Sanilac County, MI. She was the one that was the "work horse" and made the children work.

Back row: John William, Samuel A., Maggie and Martha J. Courser (d. 1901), Margaret and John McIntyre. Photo taken before 1901.

Their children were Martha J. McIntyre (b. Oct. 29, 1872, Goderich, Canada); John William McIntyre (b. 1874, Goderich, Canada), md. Lillian Beard; Samuel A. McIntyre (b. 1875, Goderich, Canada) md. first, Kristena Larsen and second, Lovina Pettinger; Jane McIntyre (b. Goderich, Canada) md. Charlie Steinbarn; Maggie Margaret McIntyre (b. 1880, Goderich, Canada) md. Oliver Ohls; Sarah McIntyre (b. August 1882, Goderich, Canada) md. Morgan Smith; Thomas McIntyre (b&d. soon after birth, 1889, Sanilac County.

MERRIHEW-PENNINGTON. George Theron Merrihew, the eldest son of Hiram Elmer and Victoria (Huguelet) Merrihew came to Sherman Twp., Isabella County, when he was 4 years old. He was born Dec. 26, 1885 at his parents' home in Olive Twp., Clinton County, MI. George's parents were farmers who loved to build, adding a stone house, a round roof barn and an octagonal barn to their property. George had three brothers: Orrie Jourdan, Otto Wilmer, Theodore Edwin, and three sisters: Lena May, Edith Belle and E.V. (Eva). George passed away in 1972 in Isabella County.

George and Effie Merrihew

Effie Lee (b. June 12, 1890) was the daughter of Millard and Luella (Woodin) Pennington of Sherman Twp., Isabella County. Effie had two brothers, Floy and Elwin, and one sister, Sadie. Effie was a co-owner of the Chippewa Ranch for Boys and Girls, as well as Woodin's Mill in

Drew, MI, until her death at age 48, in January 1940.

George and Effie were united in marriage on March 12, 1914 in Mt. Pleasant, MI. They resided at their farm and raised registered shorthorn Durham cattle. The couple had nine children: George Keith, Reva May, Aletha Lucille, Theron, Zelpha Irene, Gale and Dale (twins), Audrey Marie, and Roland.

METHNER-BAUGHMAN. Edward Methner (b. March 4, 1894 in Wise Twp., Isabella County) was the 10th child of Fred and Pauline (Hoeft) Methner. There were nine older and 10 younger siblings.

On April 29, 1917 he and Daisy Baughman traveled by horse and buggy to Beaverton, MI where they were married by Rev. Pendelton. They bought the William Matier farm in Wise Twp. in the 1920s.

Ed was a "Jack of all Trades." Besides farming their 40 acres, and yearly raising 1,000 chickens for eggs, he was one of the first in Isabella County to purchase a threshing machine and steam engine. Summers would find him threshing for area farmers, some as far away as Beal City. The steam engine gave way to a tractor and eventually to the new fangled "pull" combine, which he continued to use harvesting for $5 an acre. Ed was also a carpenter, building his own home and helping build several barns. Many times he could be heard in his shed as he heated iron and welded broken plowshares or cultivator teeth. Nothing was thrown away unless he absolutely could not fix it.

As a young adult Ed was the catcher for the Methner Brothers Baseball team, made up entirely of his brothers.

No one is sure how much schooling Ed had, for he always said "I went to school two days, and those two days the teacher wasn't there," but he was a math whiz—often figuring bushels per acre, or the price of 15 dozen eggs in his head. Ed died Jan. 24, 1955.

Daisy Violet Baughman was born Sept. 22, 1899 near Findley, OH, and came to Michigan with her parents, John and Mary Ann (Davidson) Baughman and her siblings in 1906. They first lived in Midland County, then bought a farm in Wise Twp. about two miles from the Methner homestead. Daisy attended the Loomis school. She was active in the community as a Home Extension leader and a 4-H leader for 19 years. She was active in the Wise Presbyterian Church ladies aid, and later in the Shepherd Church of the Brethren. She worked about 10 years in the fabric department of Oren's Department Store in Mt. Pleasant. In 1961 Daisy sold the farm to a niece, Kathleen Methner Dennis and her husband Don. She bought a mobile home and lived on her daughter Kathryns farm. In 1967 she married Charles Spencer of Shepherd. They continued living in her home and bought a home in Florida where

Edward, Daisy and Kathryn Methner, 1921

they spent their winters. Charles died Dec. 14, 1977. Daisy made her home with her daughter Kathryn Fike until her death in 1995.

The children of Ed and Daisy were Kathryn Virginia (b. Nov. 21, 1918) and Isabella Louise (b. Feb. 11, 1930). Kathryn married Lester Fike and they lived on the Fike homestead over 50 years. Isabella entered St. Mary's School of Nursing in Saginaw and graduated in 1951. She married Peter Dominguez and remains in the Saginaw area.

METHNER-DAVIS. John Albert Methner was the second son of Frederick Frank Methner and Adelia Hopkins. He was born June 15, 1876 in Wayne County, MI. Mary S. Davis was born Feb. 25, 1877 in Grant County, WV, the first child of Ines Davis and Chloe Hawk, Grant County, WV. John A. Methner was 9 when he moved to the Coleman area, Midland County, MI with his father, stepmother Pauline Hoeft, and older brother Frank. While growing up in Coleman, John learned farming and lumbering skills. In the summer of 1896, he made his way to Grant County, WV, seeking employment in the lumber industry. "William McKinley was elected president in the fall and times were hard," John said.

John Albert Methner and Mary Susan Davis Methner, ca. 1900.

He married Mary Susan Davis on June 3, 1898, in Petersburg, WV. John's desire for good farming land and Mary Susan's homesickness and illnesses in her family caused them to move back and forth between Coleman and Maysville, WV. One move was made by railroad boxcar. All the household goods, farm implements, and livestock were loaded on board the train. One member of the family was allowed to ride in the boxcar to care for the animals. John farmed in Sec. 26 of Wise Twp., Isabella County, beginning about 1911. After Mary's death in 1926, John continued to farm there until he moved to Beaverton, MI, about 1936. He lived in Beaverton until his death, June 23, 1963. John and Mary had the following children:

1) Pearl (b. 1898, d. 1986) md. Gabriel Kitzmiller. They resided near Elk Garden, WV and reared 13 children.

2) Arthur was born in 1899 and died in infancy.

3) James (b. 1901, d. 1989) md. Leona McKibben and lived in Beaverton where he operated a grocery store, the Gem Theater and an oil business.

4) Nellie (b. 1903, d. 1979) md. Truie L. Miller and they had one son Richard L. Miller who lives in Ann Arbor, MI. She was a flight instructor from 1946-57 and operated Miller Flying School, Midland.

5) Ross (b. 1903, d. 1904) was a twin brother to Nellie.

6) Otis (b. 1907, d. 1946) md. Ella Prout and they resided in Remus. Their children are Modred of Blanchard, Clarence of Honor, Mary Lou Jones and Ann Jane Trudeau of Mount Pleasant.

7) Myrtle (b. 1909, d. 1928) lived in Detroit.

8) Violet (b. 1913, d. 1999) md. Willis C. Landon of Mt. Pleasant and their son Thomas lives in Boyne City.

9) Evelyn (b. 1916, d. 1945) md. Scott Wengert. Their daughter Sandra Wengert Martin resides in Beaverton.

10) Virginia (b. 1921, d. 1999) md. Fred Hooper. Their children are Larry Hooper and Pamela Hooper Kory, both of Beaverton.

John was a good-natured, hard and able worker, a good farmer and a barn builder. He was a spell-binding storyteller of his experiences working on a cargo ship in Lake Michigan with Burt Galloway, his jumping trains to West Virginia seeking work, and his lumbering adventures in West Virginia. John said, "The best cup of coffee I ever had was made in an old tin can under the Western Maryland Railroad Bridge over the Potomac."

Mary Susan is remembered for her nursing and midwife service to families in the Coleman and West Virginia areas and her West Virginia cooking.

METHNER-DIEHL. LaVern Gilbert Methner was born to William Methner and Emma Vera (Gilbert) Methner on Jan. 11, 1920. He had one older brother Bill, and seven younger sisters: Velma, Ruth, Alta, Joan, Dolores, Kathleen and Phyllis. He lived in Isabella County on N. Wise Road, Clare, MI.

Vern attended the Orr, one-room school, one mile from where he lived, throughout 8th grade. He was a

Lavern Methner, 1938

quiet, inquisitive and intelligent young boy who loved to play baseball along with his brother. They were very active in following the Methner Brother (Vern's Dad and Uncles) baseball team. In fact, in 1938 Vern and his cousin Roy Methner went to California to try out in the big league. They failed but had a great experience and fun trying.

In 1942 he was drafted into WWII along with his cousins, neighbors and friends. He served in New Guinea and the Philippines as a medic. When Vern came home he would have reoccurrence of Malaria fever that he had contacted while in the service. Vern taught us many things when he came home from the war. A few things I remember most was the correct way to make a bed, the correct way to bandage a wound and how to wrap packages the right way. Whenever I'm putting clean sheets on the bed, I'm always reminded of him.

After the war, Vern began doing all my father's farming (dad was a full time carpenter), and then began buying his own land. He was well known in the farming community for the clean, straight rows of crops he would plant and harvest. He did all his own work never hiring. This included fixing all the machinery and tractors.

He married Doris Diehl of Isabella County in 1966. They had one girl and two boys: Donna, Daniel and Allan. The boys are married and live nearby, and Donna lives with her mother at the Methner homestead farm. They have four grandchildren. Vern died Jan. 29, 1992.

METHNER-EPLETT. Henry Methner (b. April 16, 1906) was the youngest son of Fred and Pauline Methner. He was born on the family farm in Wise Twp., Isabella County. During his youth, he and his brothers had many responsibilities on the family farm - care of the animals, planting and harvesting crops, and a myriad of other activities related to farming. He attended Andersonville and Orr country schools prior to attending and graduating from Coleman High School in 1924. Members of the class of 1924 did not receive their diplomas that year due to a fire at the school. Many years later (actually after his retirement) Henry and others in his class received their diplomas at a special ceremony along with that year's graduating class.

After high school, Henry received an associate's degree from Graceland College (Iowa) and a BA degree from Michigan Central College (Mount Pleasant) in 1934. He received a master's degree in education administration from Michigan State University in 1957. He began his teaching career in Iowa and Missouri after graduating from Graceland, then returning to Michigan, he taught at Frederic, Pinconning, Rapid City, Charlevoix, Traverse City, Mason, Rosebush and Pickford. In addition to teaching he also was a coach, driver's education instructor and school administrator.

Henry and Betty Methner, fall of 1970.

Henry married Elizabeth Ann "Betty" Eplett (b. March 2, 1907), the daughter of Henry and Anna Eplett of Ironwood, MI, on Sept. 27, 1940. She, too, was a teacher. At the time of their retirement in 1971, Henry and Betty had 40 and 33 years, respectively, of teaching experience. They thoroughly loved teaching and many young people were blessed to have them for their teachers.

Reminiscing, Henry would tell about the country schools and his teachers keeping 50 children occupied in those one-room facilities. He loved baseball and was on the school team which was successful in beating every other school team in the area. Later Henry would be part of the Methner Brothers baseball team.

Because of the distance to Coleman from the farm, he and his youngest sister Fern were allowed to take a horse and buggy (no school buses then) to attend high school in Coleman. But during basketball season Henry had to walk the four miles to and from Coleman for the evening practice sessions.

During the summer, the Methner brothers managed to find time to practice and play baseball in the Five-County League. The team won the championship two consecutive seasons and had a reputation for winning - often coming from far behind to make a stunning win.

After retirement Henry and Betty spent many happy years in Pickford, MI, and Clearwater, FL. They were always busy with community and church activities, golf, fishing, hunting, and visiting friends and family. Henry died May 3, 1993, in Sault Ste. Marie, MI, and is buried in Pickford, MI. His wife Betty continues to divide her time between her homes in Pickford and Clearwater. She is very active in the Pickford Presbyterian Church and a Methodist Church in Clearwater, Delta Kappa Gamma (an international teachers society), senior citizen groups, and many other activities in Michigan and Florida. She continues to enjoy her friends and family members throughout country. *Submitted by Elizabeth A. Methner.*

METHNER-FALCONER. Leroy Harold Methner was born March 3, 1919 in Wise Twp., Isabella County, MI. His father Floyd "Pat" was born June 11, 1898 and his mother Leila Barbara Gilbert Methner was born June 24, 1900 also in Wise Twp.

Leroy was the oldest of Floyd and Leila's children. He had four brothers: Floyd Jr., Kenneth, Dean and Sheldon, and four sisters: Norma, Alma,

Roy and Marian Falconer

Helen and Sandra. They all attended Andersonville School and Clare and Coleman high schools.

Roy and his dad were both avid baseball fans and played either together or on separate teams. At one time Roy hoped to be a professional ball player and traveled to California with two of his cousins to a baseball school after graduating from high school.

Roy married Marian Falconer in 1940 and shortly after, they settled on 40 acres on Wise Road, Isabella County. Roy and Marian were farmers raising a small herd of milk cows and cash crops. He also traveled with threshing machines from farm to farm to harvest grain and beans. Their children were Connie Jean (b. Nov. 16, 1940), Deanna Kay (b. Jan. 3, 1942), Cheryl Lee (b. June 22, 1945), Scott Jay (b. Nov. 17, 1950), Shelly Renee (b. Oct. 7, 1957) and Kerry Ellen (b. Feb. 23, 1960).

Marian Falconer Methner was born Jan. 5, 1922 in Alma, MI. Her parents were Earle and Lurah Falconer. Earle was born March 13 1893 in Flinn Twp., Sanilac County to Helen Scott Falconer and Arthur Falconer. He was an Elder

in the Reorganized Church of Jesus Christ of Latter Day Saints, ministering in various communities in central Michigan throughout his life. Lurah was born June 26, 1886 in Gratiot County to Aaron Boyer and Immogene Krisher Boyer. Lurah's mother died when she was 6 years old. Her aunt and uncle, Loren and Cora White, adopted her at age 7. Coral Jean, Marian's older sister, was born July 7, 1920 in Alma, MI. The Falconer's moved to Midland when the girls were very young where they lived for the next 16 years.

In 1945 the couple bought a farm East of Coleman on Alamando Road, Geneva Twp., Midland County. At that time Connie transferred from Orr School to Alamando School. Connie and Deanna both attended this one room schoolhouse about a mile from their home until consolidation and they were bused to Coleman Community Schools.

In 1960 they decided to expand their farming and bought a farm in Sanilac County. Roy intended to work both farms and moved his family to Peck, MI. In 1961, Roy became sick and passed away. Cheryl graduated from Peck Schools and Shelly attended kindergarten there. The family then moved back to Coleman and Kerry started kindergarten in Coleman. The two oldest girls were attending Graceland College in Lamoni at this very difficult time.

In 1969 Marian moved to Mt. Pleasant where Shelly and Kerry both graduated from Mt. Pleasant High School. Marian has lived one block north of the high school for the past 25 years and her home has been a gathering place for her children's families. She has 11 grandchildren and nine great-grandchildren. Marian remains healthy and active volunteering several hours a week for local organizations.

METHNER-FALCONER. William Vernell Methner, son of William and Emma Methner, was born June 11, 1918 in Wise Twp., Isabella County. Two of the Methner brothers, William and Floyd, married sisters, Emma Vera and Lelia Barbara Gilbert. Their first sons, William Vernell and Leroy Harold, married sisters, Coral Jean and Marian Lucille Falconer.

The children from these two double cousins were related to everyone alike except the Methner grandparents. William and Leroy, along with other Methner cousins carried on the Methner ball team.

William Vernell Methner married Coral Jean Falconer on March 26, 1940 and died Feb. 3, 1980. They had two sons, and one daughter: Gary Lee, Terry Lynn and Pamela Jean. Coral Falconer Methner married second, Richard Blackmore on March 28, 1984 in Florida.

1) Gary Lee Methner (b. Sept. 24, 1940) md. Lola Condit Dec. 22, 1962 in Anchorage, AK. Their children are Bradly Alan, Douglas Gary and Stephen Michael.

a) Bradley Alan Methner (b. March 3, 1966) md. Pamela Freeman on July 5, 1994 in Seattle, WA. Their children are William Daniel Methner (b. Oct. 27, 1995) and Carly Marie Methner (b. Oct. 23, 1997).

b) Douglas Gary Methner (b. Feb. 27, 1968) md. Lori Devary Dec. 28, 1996 in Bloomington, IL. Their children are Joshua Douglas Methner (b. Dec. 5, 2001) and Nicholas Grant Methner (b. Dec. 5, 2001).

c) Stephen Michael Methner (b. March 4, 1970) md. Sarah Mowry July 3, 1993 in Seattle, WA. Their children are Catherine Hope Methner (b. Jan. 5, 1997), Scott Mowry Methner (b. Feb. 3, 1998), Andrew Methner (b. Sept. 28, 2000) and Stewart James Methner (b. Dec. 16, 2001).

2) Terry Lynn Methner (b. Jan. 4, 1942) md. Claudis Lorraine April 7, 1967 in Midland, MI. Their children are Christopher John and Tony Daniel.

a) Christopher John Methner (b. April 1, 1971) has a child Marc Christopher Methner (b. June 25, 1998).

b) Tony Daniel Methner (b. Aug. 30, 1972) married and divorced in 1991. He has a child Jesse Ryan Methner (b. June 25, 1991). Tony Daniel Methner married second, Leyla, on Sept. 17, 1999.

3) Pamela Jean Methner (b. March 2, 1944) md. Kenneth Schlafley Aug. 14, 1965 in Midland, M1. Their children are Wendy Lynn, Shelly Jo and Heidi Ann.

a) Wendy Lynn Schlafley (b. June 30, 1967) md. Gary Dean on Dec. 16, 1996 in Lawton, M1. Their children are Abigail Ruth Dean (b. April 18, 1998), Isaac Russell Dean (b. Jan. 28, 2000) and Jonah Richard Dean (b. Jan. 19, 2002).

b) Shelly Jo Schlafley (b. June 3, 1969) md. Donald Kasik on Sept. 26, 1992 in Midland, MI. Their children are Jeremy Michael Kasik (b. April 10, 1996), Jacob Kenneth Kasik (b. June 22, 1998) and Joel Steven Kasik (b. Feb. 19, 2002).

c) Heidi Ann Schlafley (b. May 11, 1973) md. William McGraw on Feb. 17, 2001 in Midland, MI. Their children are Levi Hunter Schlafley-Gromaski (b. Oct. 5, 1997), Thomas Jay McGraw (b. Sept. 4, 1999) and Cole Michael McGraw (b. Nov. 20, 2001).

METHNER-HOEFT. In 1851 Franz Methner (b. 1817, d. 1896) left Germany with his family and settled in Detroit. His oldest son Frederick Frank (b. Nov. 4, 1844) was 7 when they arrived in America. Franz worked for logging companies clearing Michigan at that time and Fred joined his father in that work as he grew to adulthood.

On Aug. 14, 1872, Fred married Adelia Hopkins at St. Louis, MI, and records indicate he was a farmer. The family moved to Detroit where sons Frank and John were born. In 1875-

76, Fred was a partner in a milk company, and in 1884 he was a foreman for the George C. Weatherbee Co. (broom, brushes and basket manufacturer). During the mid-to-late 1870s the marriage dissolved and Adelia moved back to Gratiot County. Sons Frank and John stayed with Fred in Detroit.

Pauline Laura Hoeft (b. 1865, d. 1934) also was born in Germany (near Berlin). In 1880 she emmigrated to the United States and settled in Detroit near her paternal uncle. She worked for Joseph Methner (brother of Fred) who owned a dairy farm in East Detroit. Fred and Pauline were married in 1883 and lived in the Detroit area until 1885 when they moved to Warren Twp. near Coleman. Fred worked for Peters Lumber Mill and, as land was cleared, he farmed. In his later years he owned a meat market in Coleman. Eight children were born while they lived in Warren Twp.

Frederick Frank and Pauline Methner

In 1893, 20 acres of land were purchased in Wise Twp., Isabella County; additional purchases increased that farm to 260 acres. Nine children were born during the time the family lived there (presently owned and operated by Jack MacDonald, a great-grandson of Fred and Pauline).

In 1909 forty acres were purchased in Sec. 26, Wise Twp. The title for this property is from the federal government and is signed by U.S. Grant, President of the United States. A house, barn, and other buildings were built and an orchard planted. In 1912 the family moved into this home, which was always referred to as the "home Place." (Additional acreage purchased increased the farm to 160 acres.) In 1935 Joseph purchased the farm; his son Eugene bought it in 1959 and operated it until 1970 when it was sold to Shirley Methner Dennis and her husband who owned and operated it until the end of the 1990s. The farm is no longer owned by a family member.

Fred and Pauline were baptized in the Reorganized Church of Jesus Christ of Latter Day Saints in 1893 and 1894 respectively. Several of their children also became members of the church. Following are the Methner children:

1) Frank (b. 1874, d. 1944) md. Edna Baker Blasdell, their children: William, Ralph, Leon, Marlin and Joyce Methner; Pearl Blasdell; and Elva Blasdell Hubbard.

2) John (b. 1876, d. 1963) md. Mary Davis, their children: Pearl Methner Kitzmiller, Arthur, James, Nellie Methner Miller, Ross, Clarence, Myrtle, Violet Methner Landon, Evelyn Methner Wengert and Virginia Methner Hooper.

3) Annie (b&d. 1884).

4) Otto (b. 1886, d. 1945) md. Elsie Spore, their children: John and Hulda Methner McDonald.

5) William (b. 1888, d. 1968) md. Emma Gilbert, their children: William, LaVern, Velma Methner O'Connor, Ruth Methner Gordon, Alta Methner Gross, Joan Methner Diment, Delores Methner Anthony, Kathleen Methner Dennis, Phyllis Methner Simon.

6) Caroline "Carrie" (b. 1889, d. 1949) md. Eugene Burton, their children: Otto, Norman, Samantha Burton Johnson, Oren, Caroline Burton Bissonnette, Beulah Burton Thompson, Edith Burton King, Roy, Arlene Burton Townsend, Dorothy Burton McClure and Robert.

7) August "Chub" (b. 1890, d. 1963) md. Jennie Rose, their child is John.

8) Fritz (b. 1891, d. 1948) md. Essie Avery, their children: Genevieve Methner Phillips, Pearl Methner Livingston, Harold, Fritz and Edith. Fritz married second, Jessie Rilett.

9) Albert (b&d. 1893).

10) Edward (b. 1894, d. 1955) md. Daisy Baughman, their children: Kathryn Methner Fike and Isabella Methner Dominguez.

11) Joseph (b. 1895, d. 1985) md. Rosella Seibt, their children: Joseph II, Elton Eugene, Janice Methner Allison Orth, Gerald and Ronald.

12) Susie (b. 1897, d. 1960) md. Thomas Dowd, their children: Gerald, Russell, Pauline Dowd Galsky Eakins, and Dorothy Dowd Moore.

13) Floyd "Pat" (b. 1898, d. 1969) md. Lelia Gilbert, their children: LeRoy, Norma Methner Powell, Floyd, Kenneth, Dean, Alma Methner Tice VanAekst, Helen, Sheldon, and Sandra Methner Moore.

14) Walter (b&d. 1899).

15) Jason "Jake" (b. 1900, d1 1979) md. Mina Swan, their children: Edith Methner Wiltse, Betty Methner Ranck, Alice Methner Christopher, Geraldine Methner Geiling, Shirley Methner Dennis, Franklin, Jane Methner Johnson, Donald, Albert, and Mary Lou Methner Bolt.

16) Emma (b. 1902, d. 1995) md. Benjamin H. Ouderkirk, their children: Daryl, Emma Jean Ouderkirk Valley and John.

17) Elmer "Ike" (b. 1904, d. 1982) md. Letha Herring, their children: Clarend and Cleland.

18) Henry (b. 1906, d. 1993) md. Elizabeth "Betty" Eplett.

19) Alta Fern (b. 1907, d. 1933) md. Delos Baughman.

20) Hulda (b&d. 1909).

The Methners were known for their generosity and kindness; their home was always open to people in need or those who wished to join the happy family gatherings. They worked hard individually and collectively and yet had time for music and fun. The Methner household was filled with music - piano, trumpet, trombone, violin, saxophone, accordion and piccolo were played by the children.

The 12 sons had a baseball team, The Methner Brothers, during the early 1920s which won the county pennant two years in succession.

Fred died at his home in Wise Twp. on April 29, 1925, and Pauline died July 24, 1934. They are buried in the Coleman Cemetery. All of Fred and Pauline's children are deceased at this time; however, there are many, many grandchildren living in Michigan and throughout the USA, and several of their descendants do live in Isabella County at this time.

In the mid-1970s the Methners in Michigan made contact with relatives in Germany. In 1977 a group of 20, including Henry, Betty and Daisy (Ed's widow), attended the Methner Reunion in Lunaberg, Germany. Since that time some of the German cousins have visited Michigan and attended the family reunion held annually in Mount Pleasant and several Methners have returned to Germany to visit and attend reunions.

METHNER-RILETT. Fritz Methner, the sixth child of Frederick and Pauline Methner, was nicknamed "Slippery" because of his ability to steal bases while playing baseball with the Methner Brothers team. He was born Nov. 18, 1891 in Warren Twp., Midland County, MI. He spent his young, formative years doing routine farm work; however, at age 14 he ran away from

Fritz Methner Sr.

home and ended up in California where he joined a circus. After two years, Fritz returned home.

After his return to Michigan, Fritz worked for his half-brother Frank in the meat and grocery business in Coleman for several years. In 1913 he married Essie Avery and they had five children. During the early years of their marriage, he operated two different farms, one of which had a peppermint still.

Fritz later gave up farming and from 1930-45 he ran his own meat and grocery store. In 1937 he married Jessie Rilett. After leaving the grocery store, Fritz went into semi-retirement and sold fish throughout the countryside to old friends and acquaintances. In 1948 Fritz was killed in a tragic traffic accident on his way back to Coleman with a load of fish.

When the Methner Brothers Baseball Team was formed (around 1915), Fritz played third base and acquired a reputation for his skill in defending the base. Fritz and Essie had the following children:

1) Genevieve (b. 1914, d. 1993) md. Beryl Phillips. Their two children are Pauline Phillips Bussa and Patricia Phillips Shaw.

2) Pearl (b. 1918) md. Jack Livingston, their two children are Donald Livingston and Linda Livingston Kukla. Pearl and Jack reside in Traverse City.

3) Edith (b. 1919, d. 1920).

4) Harold (b. 1921, d. 2001) md. Viola Plamondon, their children are Carol Methner Nelson, Gail Methner, Darlene Methner Burkett and Vicky Methner Thompson.

5) Fritz Jr. (b. 1925) md. Shirley O'Dell. Their children are Sandra Methner Mixon, Diane Methner Frownfelter, Raymond Methner and Dawn Methner Pope. Fritz and Shirley presently reside in Indian River.

MOORE FAMILY. Francis Moore was born in Ontario, Canada. He married Anna Moffit and moved to Wise Twp., Isabella County in 1890 where they homesteaded on Wise Rd. Austin, who was 4 years old and Roy 2 years old, came

with them. Both boys worked on the farm and attended Wise School, a half mile south of their home. Roy later moved to Detroit. Austin married Florence Ranck in 1910 and they reared four children on the farm: Bernice (b. 1911, d. 1999), Charles (b. 1916, d. 1995), Murray (b. 1922) and Anna (b. 1925). All of the children attended local schools, and all took jobs elsewhere except for Charles who farmed at that location all his life.

Moore Family ca. 1928/29. Francis, Charles, Murray, Anna Jane, Helen, Florence, Austin, Anna L., Bernise and Laura.

Charles married Lena Myers in 1940 and she joined him on the farm. Their children include Shirley, Linda and David. Both Linda and David live on the same farm. In 1974 David married Jo Ellen Meister and they have five children: Molly (b. 1979), John (b. 1980), Robin (b. 1983), Joshua (b. 1984) and Christina (b. 1985).

The village of Wise was located east off of Wise Rd. along the railroad tracks south of Vernon Road. The railroad through Wise provided a link to Mt. Pleasant and Coleman.

When supplies were needed Francis would walk to the railroad carrying a flour sack or burlap bag to bring home flour, sugar and other necessities. The Moores built their one room log cabin, cutting logs from their 40-acre farm, squaring the logs with adz and chinking the cracks between the logs with mud. To wallpaper the interior they bought newsprint from the paper office.

During the winter Francis cut lumber for the lumber company to earn money to plant a summer crop. One day while he was gone, a lone Native American Chippewa Indian walked into the cabin without knocking and sat down by the fire. Anna was there with her two small boys and of course they were frightened, but the man recognized that they were afraid of him and told them he would not hurt them. He just wanted to get warm.

As a young boy Austin planned to ride his bicycle to Coleman. He asked a neighbor if she needed anything from town. The neighbor's reply was "a 50-pound sack of flour would be good." So Austin wrestled a 50-pound bag of flour five miles on his bike.

Charles grew up thinking he could do most anything. When he was 8 years old he convinced Francis that he was old enough to plow. His father Austin had already told him he was too young. Grandpa Francis said if he could plow a straight line and handle the team of horses, he was big enough to plow by himself. Charles tried it and plowed a furrow straight enough to satisfy both his father and grandfather. By the time he was 10 years old he could take the team of

horses and spend the day working on a thrashing crew.

NEELAND FAMILY. In 1833 Robert Neelands was born in Peel County Ontario. He received his education training in the public schools and grew to manhood in close touch with nature on the farm. At 43 years of age he disposed of his interests there and came to Isabella County in 1877. He purchased 100 acres of unimproved land in Sec. 10 Isabella Twp. and in due time cleared and put in condition for tillage. He made all of his first improvements with his own hands and a common chopping ax.

He built a brick home in 1903 and a barn 44' x 66' was built 14 years prior to that. He was a Republican on state and national affairs but in local affairs voted for the best qualified candidates. He had a firm abiding faith in Christian religion. He was a faithful member of the Methodist Episcopal Church in Rosebush. He served as class leader and one of the trustees.

His domestic life, which was a happy one, dates from the year 1874 when he was united in marriage to Margaret Caesar whose birth occurred in Peel County, Ontario in 1840 and terminated in 1900 by her death. Three children were born to Robert and Margaret, namely Leuella, Edwin J. and Ollie. Robert died in 1921.

In 1915 Edwin purchased the farm from Robert. Before Edwin was married he added five more rooms to the house. This gave them 10 rooms. He also put carbide lights and a bathroom in the house - very modern for the time. He married M. Lucille Loomis in 1915. There were four children born to this union: Frank, Florence, Mary Jane and Agnes. Edwin died in 1948 and Lucille in 1972.

Frank married Goldie Flegel on June 27, 1937. Frank had been farming with his father and the first five years of his married life he lived with his father's family. He was able to purchase a little four room house and moved it on 20 acres he had purchased from his father in 1942. Frank and Goldie had three children: Robert, Nita and Ruth. Frank purchased the farm from his mother after the death of his father. In 1949 Frank traded houses with his mother. Frank purchased two more parcels of land which made the total acreage of 180.

Robert married Shirley Tice in 1959. They built a basement house on one of the 40 acre parcels. They lived in the basement until 1965 at which time Robert and Frank traded houses. Robert and Shirley moved to the brick house and Frank and Goldie moved to the basement on which they moved a house. Robert farmed with his father.

In 1970 Robert purchased the farm and machinery. Robert and Shirley had three sons:

Randall, Edwin and Ronald. Edwin purchased 51 acres adjoining the family farm. Randall is a social medical councilor and minister. Edwin works for Dow Corning. Ronald works for Morbark. Robert and Shirley are active in the township as clerk and dept clerk. They are also active in their church, Central Michigan Free Methodist.

NEYER, Edna Fern (b. May 15, 1915, Detroit, MI), daughter of William Martz and Edna Floy Fish. They courted and were married in Van Wert, OH. They moved to Detroit, MI where her father found work at the Ford Motor Co.

At the age of 11, Edna and her sisters, Eliza and Niada, and brothers, Bill and Ford, moved from Detroit to Harrison, MI. The trip in a Model-T car took two days.

Going to school in a one-room schoolhouse out in the country was very different from city life. They walked two and one-half miles to their one-room schoolhouse carry-

Edna Fern Neyer, June 1933

ing their lunch in a peanut butter pail. When their little brother Rod started to school, they pulled him in the wagon.

Edna attended Hayes Agricultural High School in Harrison and graduated in June 1933. At the age of 19, she began training as a nurse's aide at McArthur-Strange Hospital in Mt. Pleasant, MI.

During this time, Edna met Frank Arthur Neyer who lived in Beal City, MI. His father and mother were Jakob and Agatha "Jenny" Neyer who emmigrated to America in the year 1908 from Burs, Austria. Frank was one of eight children: Matilda (Neyer) Leik, Anthony Neyer, John J. Neyer, Frances Neyer, Mary Anne Neyer, Frank Neyer, Hedwig (Neyer) Quillen and Agnes (Neyer) Engler.

On Dec. 30, 1939, Frank and Edna were married in Sacred Heart Catholic Church in Mt. Pleasant, MI. They set-up housekeeping on the family farm near St. Philemonia's Catholic Church in Beal City, MI.

Frank planted several crops including sugar beets. In Europe, WWII was raging. One cold frosty morning in October, young German boys who were prisoners (POWs) were brought to Frank's farm to harvest the sugar beets. They were only 17 to 19 years old. Agatha, Frank's mother, was very moved knowing that the prisoners' mothers back in Europe had to be worried if they would ever see them again and if they had food to eat. Agatha and Edna decided to make the boys a large pot of Austrian soup and took it to them in the fields. The guard was very kind and allowed them to give the prisoners the soup and to talk with them in their German language. The boys told them of their families and how they missed them and where they lived. They were so grateful for the kindness shown to them. At the end of the day, they were loaded on a truck and taken elsewhere to work. Edna and Agatha often talked about this event

wondering if the German prisoners made it back to their families. They shared many other happy times together talking of life in the Austrian Alps and cooking Austrian food.

Frank and Edna had six children: Mary Ann (Neyer) Woltz (b. 1940), David Arthur Neyer (b. 1938), James Terrance Neyer (b. 1944), Virginia Eileen (Neyer) Withey (b. 1947), William Joseph Neyer (b. 1951) and George Timothy Neyer (b. 1955).

Edna is now a widow. Her husband Frank died May 5, 1983. She lives in the Winchester Towers and enjoys being with her many friends there. On May 15, 2002, she celebrated her 87th birthday. She is blessed with 14 grandchildren and many great-grandchildren. She is a devoted member of Sacred Heart Catholic Church.

NEYER FAMILY. Jack is the oldest son of John J. Neyer and Kathleen E. "Judge" Neyer. Our families were early residents of Isabella County. The Neyers came from Burs, Austria in 1878 and settled on an 80-acre farm just north of Beal City, which is now owned by the Weber family.

The Judges came to Westport in Canada in 1837 from Ireland, then moved to a 160 acre farm just east of Winn in 1868 which is now owned by Bill Judge. Jack was born in Mt. Pleasant in 1937 and grew up on a farm just east of Beal City now owned by Fred Zeien. He graduated from St. Philomena grade school in Beal City in 1951 and in that year his family moved to 517 S. Washington St. Mt. Pleasant. Jack's high school years were at Marmion Military Academy in Aurora, IL, and his college years at St. Thomas College in St. Paul, MN.

His military service was with the USAF where he was stationed in Madrid, Spain. While in Spain, he met his wife Cora Doyle who was from Dublin, Ireland, and working in Spain as a governess for a Spanish family, teaching their children English. Jack and Cora were married in Dublin, Ireland at St. Joseph Church on Berkley Rd., May 7, 1960. They returned to Mt. Pleasant that same year, when Jack's tour of duty finished!

They are the parents of one son John H. Neyer who is a graduate of MPHS and MSU. John is presently employed with his father's company Coldwell Banker Mt. Pleasant Realty & Assoc. as a sales associate. John is married to Meredith Rodman of Charlotte, NC. She is a graduate of University of North Carolina, Wilmington, and has a degree in teaching. John and Meredith have a daughter, Emma Elizabeth (b. May 1, 2002).

Jack Neyer is the president of Coldwell Banker Mt. Pleasant Realty & Assoc., the leading real estate firm in Isabella County. He has been in the business since 1964. Jack and Cora have been very involved in the community over the past 40+ years and love the central Michigan area. They make their home at 415 E. Chippewa, Mt. Pleasant.

NEYER FAMILY. Jacob Neyer came from Austria to Michigan with his parents in 1878 at 10 years of age. He lived with his parents on what is now the Weber farm one mile north of Beal City. He helped clear the land and farmed with oxen. He married Agatha Jenny in Austria

in 1903. To this union nine children were born: Matilda Neyer, Anton Neyer, John Neyer, Frances Neyer, Mary Neyer, Frank Neyer and Arthur Neyer are all deceased; Hedy Neyer Quillen, wife of Pat Quillen of Mt. Pleasant and Agnes Neyer Engler, married to Matt Engler of Mt. Pleasant.

John J. Neyer family.

John Neyer and wife Kathleen Judge Neyer lived in the Mt. Pleasant, Beal City and Winn areas all their lives. They were married in 1936 at Sacred Heart Church, Mt. Pleasant. John went to Beal City schools and worked on his parent's farm for the first 22 years of his life. He was in the cattle and trucking business for over 15 years. He also owned gas stations in Midland, Bay City, Traverse City, Ionia and Mt. Pleasant. In 1942 John became active in oil exploration and drilling in the Coldwater Oil Field. He was also very involved in the oil trend in Jackson and Calhoun counties as well as Niagaran development in St. Claire County.

John and Kathleen had six children: John F. "Jack," Rosee Neyer McFarlane, Robert J. "Bob," Patricia "Patty Neyer Gostola, all of Mt. Pleasant; Kenneth D. "Ken" of Traverse City and Jane Neyer Bacon of Petoskey. John and Kathleen are now both deceased.

NICHOLSON, Herbert J. (b. Aug. 5, 1869 Jackson County, MI), son of William M. and Margaret Ann (Riker) Nicholson who came to Jackson County, with his parents, George and Cynthia (Locks) Nicholson, from Erie County, PA. Herbert moved to Isabella County in 1880 with his parents. He worked in the mills in Shepherd when he was 18 years old and married Millie Cora Johnson on April 10, 1890. (*Isabella County Enterprise*).

Herbert J. and Millie Cora Nicholson. This picture was made in the 1940s because my husband's mother sent it to him while he was overseas. He went over in 1942 and returned in June 1945.

Millie had moved from Clinton County in the Spring of 1880 with her parents, Adelbert and Rhoda Jane (Ennest) Johnson. Millie (b. Oct. 24, 1872) had a twin sister, Chili Dora Johnson, who went back to Clinton County to be raised by an uncle and aunt. After their marriage they lived near Caldwell (Two Rivers now) in a house on the banks of the Chippewa River.

Early in 1900 he moved to Tennessee because of ill health. In a covered wagon drawn by horses, taking what furniture he could, and his wife, a 4-year-old son and a 2-year-old daughter; his sister and her husband, Mert and Emma Brooks, and their young children. In Tennessee Herb bought a farm sight unseen. They found the weeds and brush so high they had to cut their way through with a scythe. Millie was homesick and wanted to come home, so they sold everything and came back by train. They had returned to their old home in Deerfield Twp. by May 31, 1901. Herb and Millie were Adventists. Millie was known for the pretty quilts she made.

On Oct. 5, 1916 the carpenters began work on a big, beautiful cobblestone home across the road on a hill with the Chippewa River at the foot of the hill. This home still stands today though it has passed out of the Nicholson Family.

Herbert was a farmer, a stonemason, an inventor and a road contractor. He raised potatoes and sheep, hauling potatoes to Weidman and Mt. Pleasant with horse and wagon to sell. In 1921 and 1922 he started building roads, grading and graveling, using his own equipment pulled by horses. The first road he built was the Airline road west of Weidman.

In 1923 and 1924 he built roads in Hillsdale County, near Pittsford, MI. On Jan. 29, 1931 an oil well was put down on Herbert Nicholson's property. It caused a lot of excitement from the article in the *Isabella County Times*. "Scores of persons from Mt. Pleasant were flocking to the area of the Nicholson well…"

Herbert died Oct. 21, 1951 and Millie died Sept. 8, 1961, both died in Mt. Pleasant and are buried at Two Rivers Cemetery. Millie and Herb had a little girl, Mabel Bell, who was the apple of their eye. She was born Jan. 24, 1891 and died July 3, 1895 of dysentery (Isabella County Birth And Death Records) and is buried at Two Rivers Cemetery. They had a female child born July 29, 1892, stillborn; male child born Oct. 17, 1893, stillborn (Isabella County birth records); son Floyd (b. March 28, 1896) and daughter Lula Mae (b. Aug. 4, 1898).

OLSON-WALLACE.
Nanacy E. Wallace was born June 5, 1936. Due to a job transfer from the Gaylord Alpine Center to the Mount Pleasant Regional Center, she made the move to Mt. Pleasant in June 1983. It took two days to find a place to live while she stayed at what is now the Budget Inn. She selected an apartment at University Arms. Her youngest daughter

attended Pullen Elementary. Her two older daughters were already grown and living in Honor and Indian River. After two years they decided to purchase a house, and after being there a few years she remodeled the house, squaring it out and adding an upstairs bedroom. During this time her daughter attended West Intermediate and MPHS

Being a recently divorced parent, Nanacy and a lady friend went to area singles dances, it was a good time. Nanacy and her daughter started a business selling Amway but discontinued after six months due to unforeseen circumstances. About that time her future husband, Gerald Olson, asked her for the first date. Five months later on Aug. 22, 1994 they were married at Sacred Heart Church, and she moved in with him at Stevenson Lake. By this time her daughter had graduated from high school and was going to college.

While attending Sacred Heart Church, she served as a Eucharistic Minister from the late 1980s until 2001, then quit due to health problems.

She retired from the Regional Center in 1997, after 20 years of being a state employee. Currently she has six wonderful grandchildren and is expecting one more any day now! She also has two adult stepchildren, both recently married who live in Minnesota and Illinois.

OUDERKIRK,
Daryl Murray, son of Benjamin H. and Nora (Mogg) Ouderkirk, was born April 11, 1923 at the family home north of Rosebush on Irwin Road, Vernon Twp., Isabella County, MI.

Daryl's mother Nora was the only daughter of Malcolm A. and Deda (Prout) Mogg. Nora, like her mother Deda (called Dettie), died in childbirth. Prior to Nora's marriage, she was employed

Deda "Dettie" Prout Mogg, wife of Malcom Mogg, mother of Nora and grandmother of Daryl M. Ouderkirk.

by the Rosebush Post Office. (Information about Benjamin is recorded separately in this book.)

Daryl's great-grandparents were George and Elisabeth Mogg and they were married in Hannarsville, Nelson Twp., Ontario, Canada. In the 1870s the family moved to Lapeer County and later to Isabella County, MI. Daryl's great-grandfather William Henry Ouderkirk along with his grandfather John Henry Ouderkirk moved from New York State to Vernon Twp., Isabella County during the winter of 1876-77.

In 1925 Daryl's father married Emma Pauline Methner. The family continued to live on Irwin Road in Vernon Twp. Daryl first attended a country school near the family farm and after the family moved to 1701 West Lyons Street, Mount Pleasant, he attended Murphy School.

In 1936 and just before Daryl's

Seated: Nora Mogg, daughter of Malcolm and Deda "Dettie" Mogg, md. Benjamin H. Ouderkirk on Nov. 10, 1920. Standing is Pearl Prout, cousin of Nora, married Merrill Dunn. Picture taken June 10, 1917 (Nora was 19). Nora is Daryl M. Ouderkirk's mother.

13th birthday, the family moved to West Branch, MI, where he attended West Branch Public Schools. Daryl was talented in music. He played the trumpet (he was in the high school band) and had a beautiful singing voice. He was a member of the Reorganized Church of Jesus Christ of Latter Days Saints.

Daryl joined the Civilian Conservation Corps when he was 17 and during that time he helped plant trees and participated in other conservation efforts on state lands north of West Branch.

Daryl married Emma Jean Sharrow (b. 1924, d. 1981) on June 21, 1942, at Saginaw, MI. They resided for a short time in Gaines and then West Branch. Not too long after their marriage, Daryl became a driver for Alger Trucking and they moved to Detroit. He loved machinery and was very mechanical. He was very good at handling the large steel-hauling trucks which he drove between Detroit and Chicago.

WWII was in full force in the

Daryl Murray Ouderkirk, age 20, late 1943, San Diego, CA.

spring of 1943 when Daryl enlisted in the U.S. Navy; he received his basic training at Great Lakes Naval Station. He played trumpet in the Navy band while stationed at Great Lakes.

Daryl and Jean's daughter Sally Ann was born in West Branch on June 15, 1943, just a few weeks before Daryl entered the Navy. Daryl saw his daughter only once-when he came home on furlough at the end of his boot camp training.

After his furlough Daryl spent a few months at the naval station in San Diego, CA, then was sent to Pearl Harbor, HI. While stationed in Hawaii, he went into submarine training and served in the USS S-28 as a third class petty officer/machinist mate. On July 4, 1944, the S-28 was reported missing and Daryl was classified as missing in action. Later in the year his status was changed to lost at sea. The S-28 was an old submarine in 1944, actually a year older than Daryl, and was being used for training purposes. Forty-nine other young men lost their lives with Daryl.

Daryl and Jean's daughter Sally Ann married Gary James Graniti on May 19, 1962, in Detroit, MI. Sally is vice president of operations and human resources for DiHydro Service Inc. They have three children:

1) Vincent James Graniti (b. Aug. 14, 1963) md. Lisa Jones (b. Feb. 9, 1965); they reside in Alma and have a son Vincent T. (b. April 2, 1991).

2) Donna Marie Graniti Taube (b. Jan. 28, 1966) has a son Joshua (b. June 2, 1991) and they reside in Clinton Twp.

3) Craig Allen Graniti (b. June 24, 1968) resides in Sterling Heights and has two children: Tyler (b. Dec. 17, 1991) and Kayla (b. Jan. 29, 1993). *Submitted by Emma Jean Ouderkirk Valley.*

OUDERKIRK,
William Henry's ancestor, Jan Janse Ouderkerk, has been difficult to trace to the exact date of his arrival in the New World.

What records are available lack detail; however, the earliest reference to our family in the Dutch Colony is by J. Silk Buckingham, a British traveler, who made a tour of the North American Colonies in 1637-38. In speaking of Beverwyck, he says: "It is stated that a Dutchman of the name of Ouderkerk was the first person christened in this church and the last one buried at the sound of its bell." If the date of that reference is accurate, the Ouderkerk referred to is probably an ancestor of Jan Janse.

William Henry (b. March 19, 1829 in New York State) md. Lucinda C. Haggart (b. 1834, d. 1873) at Gloversville, NY in 1852. Their children were:

1) Ida (b. 1854, d. 1927) md. a man whose surname was Vrooman. They had three children: Samuel, Ralph and Lucy.

2) Mary Alice (b. 1856, d. 1933) md. James H. Bellinger and they had a large family including William, Jim Henry, Vilo, Regina and Archie.

3) John Henry (b. 1860, d. 1935) md. Della May Tracy June 17, 1891 (See Ouderkirk-Tracy for more information).

4) Charles William (b. 1864, d. 1935) md. Lillian (surname is unknown). They also had a large family including Cecil, Edward, Ray, twins that died at birth or shortly thereafter, and Alice.

William Henry spent his early years in New York State. He and his family had moved from New York and were in Lena, IL, by 1856. Lucinda was not a strong healthy woman and the family returned to New York shortly before her death in 1873.

In the winter of 1876-77, William and his oldest son, John Henry, came to Michigan. In February 1877, 40 acres in Vernon Twp., Isabella County (at the southeast corner of North Crawford and Irwin Roads) were purchased from Johanna David Seiter. William was a carpenter and he and John built a log house and later frame home on this property.

For many years William was blind in one eye (blinded by a stray bullet) and in 1889, while clearing his land, he was struck by a wood chip in his sighted eye which resulted in his being totally blind.

William spent the remainder of his life with his son John and his family on their farm. His grandson Benjamin remembered his grandfather with a long white beard and told how his grandfather helped his mother (May) by holding and rocking the babies while she did her house work.

He was a Republican and his son John told his children about the time when he was a small boy and they were in Illinois, and his father held him up in a crowd so he could see President Abraham Lincoln during one of Lincoln's tours.

William died Feb. 6, 1908, and his body was returned to Gloversville, NY, so he could be buried alongside his beloved wife in Prospect Hill Cemetery. *Compiled by Vilo Ouderkirk Wiltse and Emma Jean Ouderkirk Valley.*

OUDERKIRK-METHNER. Benjamin "Ben" Ouderkirk, the fourth child of John and May (Tracy) Ouderkirk, was born April 4, 1898, in the family home north of Rosebush on Irwin Road, Vernon Twp., Isabella County. He attended Lynch School (located on the Horning Place). As a youth and a young adult he worked with his father and brothers on the family farm.

On Nov. 10, 1920, Ben married Nora Mogg (b. May 16, 1898, d. April 11, 1923) and they built a house across the road from his parents' home. A son, Daryl Murray, was born on April 11, 1923. After Nora's death Ben returned to his parent's home and his mother and sisters helped him care for his infant son. For the next two years he farmed and one winter worked in a logging camp in the Upper Peninsula.

Benjamin H. and Emma Ouderkirk, 1976.

On Aug. 23, 1925, Ben married Emma Pauline Methner (b. Nov. 23, 1902), daughter of Fred and Pauline Methner. She was born in Wise Twp. and attended Andersonville and Orr Schools. During her youth she helped her mother and sisters with the many duties necessary to run a large and busy farm home. The Methner family was very musical. Emma took piano lessons and became an accomplished pianist. At age 14 she began playing the piano at church and continued to play the piano and organ until she was in her late 80s. For a short time prior to her marriage, Emma worked for her brother Frank in a dry goods and grocery store in Beaverton.

After Ben and Emma were married, they moved into Ben's house in Vernon Twp. and operated his parents' farm. In 1930, the family moved to Mount Pleasant and built a house at 1701 West Lyons. Daryl attended Murphy School on the west side of town.

The depression years were difficult for all; however, Ben was able to find enough work to provide for his growing family: Emma Jean (b. March 4, 1933) and John Benjamin (b. Sept. 30, 1935) were born at the home on West Lyons. During that time Ben and his brother Roy worked for the oil company unloading pipe. Also, he owned a truck with which he hired out to haul beets, wood, etc.

In March 1936 the family moved to West Branch where work opportunities were better because of the new oil fields in that area. Ben built a little house at 2280 South Dam Road which was his and Emma's home until their deaths.

Ben was ordained to the priesthood in the Reorganized Church of Jesus Christ of Latter Day Saints (now Community of Christ) and was pastor of the West Branch congregation from 1942 until 1963. He was a self-sustained minister. For many years he worked in the oil industry and retired in 1963 from Total (previously was Leonard Oil Co. and before that Roosevelt Oil Co.).

Daryl attended West Branch High School and joined the Civilian Conservation Corps. He married Emma Jean Sharrow on June 21, 1942 and daughter Sally Ann was born June 15, 1943. Daryl was in the U.S. Navy and lost at sea on

July 4, 1944. Sally married Gary J. Graniti and they have three children: Vincent, Donna and Craig, and four grandchildren: Vinnie, Joshua, Tyler and Kayla. Sally and Gary reside in Rochester Hills, MI. (See Daryl Murray Ouderkirk for more information on his family.)

Emma Jean graduated from West Branch High School and Northeastern School of Commerce (Bay City). She married Ray Valley and they have one son Martin (b. Jan. 16, 1965) He and his wife Dawn have three daughters: Morgan, Lane and Jordan. Emma Jean retired in 1997 from the Michigan Department of Agriculture where she was executive secretary to the Commission of Agriculture. Emma Jean's family resides in Haslett, MI.

John graduated from West Branch High School, Graceland College (Iowa) and Michigan State University. He was a section manager for the Michigan Department of Transportation Planning Division where he worked for 37 years. After retirement in 1993 he and his wife Patricia moved to Loudon, TN. Children in his family are:

1) Jon Mark (b. June 11, 1957) resides in Arcadia, MI with his wife Victoria and children: Joni, Jeanne, Tom, Jon and David.

2) Valeri May Peck (b. Nov. 26, 1963) and her husband Pat and son Joshua reside in Ann Arbor.

3) Andrea Brush (b. Sept. 27, 1965) and her husband James reside in Lansing.

Ben died in West Branch on Oct. 27, 1986 and Emma died in Lansing on Sept. 11, 1995; they are buried in Brookside Cemetery, West Branch, MI. *Submitted by Emma Jean Ouderkirk Valley.*

OUDERKIRK-TRACY. John Henry Ouderkirk (b. Dec. 3, 1860 Lena, IL) was the third child of William Henry and Lucinda (Haggart) Ouderkirk. The family returned to Gloversville, NY, where his mother died in 1873. John's schooling was limited to three years of formal education. He began work in the mills as a water boy at an early age.

During the winter of 1876-77, he and his father moved to Michigan. They purchased 40 acres located at the corner of North Crawford and Irwin Road, Vernon Twp., Isabella County, from Johanna David Seiter. John and his father built a log house and later a frame house. They cleared the land and began farming. (Information about William Henry is in another section of this book.)

John met and courted Della May Tracy and they were married June 17, 1891, at Mount Pleasant, MI. Reverend D.B. Davison performed the ceremony and witnesses were Laura Hooper and Bessie Davison.

John and May (Tracy) Ouderkirk wedding picture, June 1891.

John and May lived in the farmhouse that John and his father had built. A large round-roofed barn was built in 1913. During John's lifetime the farm was increased to 160 acres. In 1917 the house was remodeled and bricked on the outside, a hot water furnace was installed, a bathroom and kitchen with hot and cold running water were added. This was a joy to the whole family and their home was one of first in rural Vernon Twp. to have those "modern" conveniences. John and May had the following 11 children:

1) Lena Alice (b. 1892, d. 1964) md. Harry Maybee, a farmer, and they spent most of their lives in Isabella County. They had five children: Edra, Merle, Edith Erma, Malcom and Milan.

2) William Tracy (b. 1894, d. 1908).

3) Roy Nathan (b. 1896, d. 1985) was in WWI. He married Pearl Wiltse and they owned the Tracy farm for many years. They worked at Mt. Carmel, KY, for 20 years. Their children are Inez, Dorothy, Dale and Vale (twins), Agnes (died at birth), Nora and Foster.

4) Benjamin Harrison (b. 1898, d. 1986) md. Nora Mogg (b. 1898, d. 1923) and their son Daryl was lost at sea during WWII. Ben married Emma Methner in 1925 and their children are Emma Jean and John. (See Ouderkirk-Methner for more information).

5) Archie Richard (b. 1901, d. 1916).

6) Karl Edward (b. 1902, d. 1983) md. Thelma Yager and they had two sons, Richard and David (David lived only one day). Karl farmed the home place until he retired, then Richard took over the farm.

7) Mabel Lucinda (b. 1904, d. 1979) md. E. Lloyd Jones. He was a contractor and they lived in Midland. Their children are Mildred (died in infancy), Lorna, Donna, Barbara, Laurence "Larry" and Kathryn.

8) Mildred May (b. 1907, d. 1990) md. LaVerne Simpson who was employed by Dow Chemical Co. and also sold real estate. Their children are Corrine, Durwood "Bud" and Kenneth.

9) Edna Elizabeth (b. 1909, d. 1995) md. Orval A. Graham; he was a barber in Rosebush and Mt. Pleasant. Their daughters are Emogene (died at birth), Jean Ann and Monalee.

10) John Laurence (b. 1911, d. 1927).

11) Vilo Pearl (b. 1918) md. Wilbur Wiltse who worked in retailing. They reside in Mount Pleasant. Their sons are Wilbur Garth (b. 1937, d. 1964) and Leon (b. 1939).

While he had little opportunity to attend school, John believed in the importance of education and served on the Lynch School District Board. He was a Republican. During the early years of the last century, he joined the Methodist church. In the 1920s May joined the Reorganized Church of Jesus Christ of Latter Day Saints and, while John did not join with her, they were deeply religious and shared a strong faith. John died May 5, 1935 in his home in Vernon Twp., Isabella County.

A few years after John's death, May left the farm and lived with Vilo and Wilbur Wiltse, first in the house across the road from the home place and later in Mount Pleasant. During the last years of her life she had her own little house which was located on the Wiltse's property on Cross Lanes in Mount Pleasant. Through the years from 1935 until 1953, May would spend a week or two each year with each of her children; she also traveled to Colorado to visit friends and family there.

May was an avid reader and her favorite hobby was crocheting. Those who were privileged to receive one of her beautiful crocheted gifts cherish them and marvel at the many hours she devoted to creating these masterpieces.

May died on Oct. 23, 1953, at Mount Pleasant, MI. John and May are buried in Cherry Grove Cemetery, Clare, MI. *Compiled by Vilo Ouderkirk Wiltse and Jean Ouderkirk Valley.*

PENNINGTON, Elwin Sanford was born July 3, 1896 at Drew Rd. Weidman, MI to Millard and Louella E. Woodin Pennington and he died March 22, 1979 at the ranch in Williamson, GA. His wife Ethel was born Oct. 8, 1896 and died June 27, 1974 at their winter home in Ocala, FL.

Ethel and Elwin Pennington, parents of Dorothy Adams.

Elwin was reared in Sherman Twp. where he worked on the family farm. He graduated from high school, then attended Ferris State (Big Rapids) where he graduated with a degree in banking. In 1916 Elwin met Ethel G. Holmes at a Methodist Church Social and they were married Aug. 8, 1917 at her parents home in Mt. Pleasant.

They both entered the Normal School (now CMU) and graduated with teaching certificates. Both taught in country schools in Isabella County. In 1927 the family moved to Flint, MI where both Ethel and Elwin taught school. Being Depression years in 1930, all wives lost their jobs because the school board decided that only one person (the husband) in a family could be employed.

Ethel and Elwin had three sons and a daughter: Wendell S. (b. Dec. 13, 1918), Kenneth (b. 1920, d. 1922), Dorothy Eileen (b. Aug. 28, 1922) and Stanley (b&d. 1923). The family remained in Flint until 1940 when they returned to Sherman Twp., Weidman as permanent residents.

Ethel and Elwin had begun a children's camp around 1936-37 using the Woodin homestead as the main house. The camp, Chippewa Ranch, developed into a thriving business and continued to operate until 1972. The camp became a co-ed camp in the early 40s. The entire family participated in the operation of the business.

Elwin and Ethel had a very busy, active life, living in Georgia much of the winter and returning to the business of camp in summers. They had nine grandchildren, truly loving each and everyone of them.

PENNINGTON, Millard F. (b. Oct. 24, 1860 in Carter County, KY), son of John W. and Mary (Bailey) Pennington, died Aug. 26, 1933 in Sherman Twp. Isabella County.

Millard rode to Michigan from Missouri with his brothers: Steve, Jim and Nate, in search of work. Approximately 1878-79 they arrived in Sherman Twp. where they were employed by Henry Woodin in the lumbering business, Woodins Mill, at Drew, MI. The men bunked in the house and also other outbuildings. They took their meals at the house prepared by Sarah Woodin and daughters, Anna and Louella. Millard and Louella were married in 1882 at her parents home.

Louella (b. Aug. 10, 1860) was

Louella E. (Woodin) Pennington and Millard F. Pennington.

the daughter of Henry and Sarah (Rose) Woodin. She died June 9, 1937. Four children were born to Louella and Millard: Floy (b. 1883, d. 1945), Sadie (b. 1885, d. 1926), Effie Lee (b. 1890, d. 1940) and Elwin Sanford (b. July 3, 1896, d. March 22, 1979 at the ranch in Williamson, GA).

Millard was a farmer and also an outstanding horseman. He served as Grand Marshall at the Isabella County Fair for several years with his horse, Guess.

Louella was a full-time homemaker, a caring Grandmother and Mother.

PETERS, Coleman C. (b. March 25, 1910 in Cheboygan, MI), lived in the Cheboygan area until about 1935 when he moved to Mt. Pleasant, MI. He attended the First Baptist Church where the pastor, Rev. Richard Elvee, introduced him to one Ms. Kathleen M. Childs.

About 1926 Kathleen moved with her parents, Mr. Arthur and Minnie Childs, from North Bradley in Midland County to Mt. Pleasant. She graduated from Mt. Pleasant High School in 1933 and went on to attend Central Normal College.

Coleman and Kathleen dated and on Oct 24, 1936 they were married at the First Baptist Church in Mt. Pleasant. The first of their six children, Douglas Coleman Peters was born March 29, 1938.

Coleman worked for a local radio repair and also started to repair radios in his home in the evenings, which led to the beginning of his own, radio repair business.

In 1939 Mr. C.W. Campbell approached Coleman about buying his five-story building at 107 N. Main St. Mr. Peters purchased the building, which had businesses on the first floor and in the basement, and apartments on the top four floors. Coleman started his own radio shop at that time in a section of the ground floor.

Later when the Giant Super Market moved into the ground floor, he moved his radio business to the basement. Coleman and Kathleen lived in the downtown building until 1958, and reared their six children there.

Peters Family, front: Coleman, Steve, Susan, Kathleen. Middle: John, David, Doug. Back: Marilyn.

Later, they moved to 522 East Broadway, where Coleman eased out of his radio and television business and started Peters Real Estate Co. Coleman Peters passed away Dec. 15, 1971 and was laid to rest at the Mt. Pleasant Memorial Gardens.

Coleman and Kathleen's children all graduated from Mt. Pleasant High School and are as follows:

1) Douglas Coleman Peters (b. March 29, 1938) graduated in 1956. He married Darlene Kimmer of Albion, MI and they reside in Colorado Springs, CO.

2) John William Peters (b. May 29, 1940) graduated in 1958. He married Leslie Osmus of San Diego, CA, where they also reside.

3) Marilyn Kathlene (Peters) Blodgett (b. Dec. 11, 1941) graduated in 1960. She resides in Orange, CA.

4) David Arthur Peters (b. Dec. 5, 1944) graduated in 1963. He married Sharon Bellaire of Grand Haven, MI and they reside in Norton Shores, MI.

5) Susan Jean (Peters) Doom (b. March 6, 1952) graduated in 1970. She married Martin Doom Jr. and they reside in Port Huron, MI.

6) Stephen Phillip Peters (b. May 5, 1953) graduated in 1971. He married Sherry Carr of Farwell, MI, where they also reside.

Kathleen M. Peters still maintains her home on East Broadway in Mt. Pleasant and lives there when she is not on the road visiting or staying with one of her six children. *Submitted by John Peters.*

PHELPS, Frederick M. "Fritz" III and wife Marion moved to Mount Pleasant in 1970 where Fritz accepted a position in the physics department at Central Michigan University. He graduated from Carleton College, MN, has an MS from the University of Michigan, and a PhD from the University of Alberta. Marion earned a BSN from the University of Michigan. Their three children are Frederick M. IV, Dorothy Louise and Richard Alan.

The Phelps family were founding members of Mount Pleasant Community Church in 1980 and are members today. They participate fully in the ministry of the church which is the center of their lives.

Fritz has been scoutmaster of Troop 628 at the church for 30 years. Marion has been troop advancement chairman as well as district advancement chairman and president of University Dames. Both Fred IV and Rick are Eagle Scouts. Dorothy was active in Girl Scouts. This whole family worked two summers at Bear Lake

Scout Camp and the boys at several other Boy Scout Camps through the years. Dorothy worked on Girl Scout Camp waterfronts and managed the Shepherd, MI city pool two summers.

Fred IV is married to Liou Li Li and they have three children: Frederick M. V, Rachael Xinyan and Kaile. They live in Kazakhstan. Fred attended Kalamazoo College, University of Utah and Oxford University. He holds a PhD in mathematical biology. Li Li holds a BS from the National University of Singapore.

Dorothy is married to Andrew Paul Gellai and they have two sons, A. Paul Jr. and Matthew John. They live in Tucson, AZ. Andy holds a bachelor's degree from Rochester Institute of Technology and works for IBM. Dorothy earned a BS from CMU and a master's degree in teaching the deaf from Smith College. For several years she taught the deaf at the Clarke School, Northampton, MA.

Richard and Emily live in Mount Pleasant where Rick is director of music for Mount Pleasant Public Schools. Rick holds a bachelor of music education from CMU, a master of New Testament from Reformed Seminary, and a master of conducting from University of Cincinnati College Conservatory of Music. Emily graduated with a degree in business management from Clearwater Christian College, FL.

PRIDGEON, Stanley Dale (b. 1934 in Isabella County), son of Stanley Ivan and Tessie Elizabeth (Sisco) Pridgeon, lived in a home in Sherman City between the Sherman City Church and Dr. Rondot's home and office. His father Stanley Ivan drove for Dr. Rondot in the winter time when he went to make home visits. His family moved to Weidman in 1939 where he attended Weidman Public School. When Stanley was 16 years old his family moved to Barryton, MI where he graduated in 1952 from Barryton

Stanley Dale and Joyce (Carr) Pridgeon, May 2001.

High School. After graduation he worked in his Uncle George McClain's Chevrolet Garage for a short while, then worked for the state of Michigan in the Lewis Cass Building in Lansing. He also worked for a short while at Fisher Body in Lansing.

In 1955 he married Joyce Ann Carr (b. 1936) at Barryton Methodist Church. Joyce was born and lived on a farm on the Michigan/Ohio line in Lenawee County, MI. She is the youngest of nine children born to Glenwood Faye and

Nellie Elizabeth Carr. Joyce and her parents moved to a farm at Barryton, MI in 1952 where she attended Barryton High School and graduated in 1955. She worked part time at Loos Pharmacy in Barryton while attending high school.

Stanley and Joyce lived in both Lansing and Barryton a short time after their marriage. In 1958 they moved to Mt. Pleasant where they have lived for 45 years. They have lived the last 31 years in their 115-year-old home.

Both are interested in the history of Mt. Pleasant and Michigan. They are charter members of the Mt. Pleasant Area Historical Society. In their travels they enjoy the Upper Peninsula and the history of the lumbering days and exploring ghost towns.

Stan worked for the state of Michigan Mental Health Dept. for 32 years as a care giver for the developmentally disabled and also in a supervisory role to other state employees. He is a licensed practical nurse. Joyce worked for the Mt. Pleasant Public School System and the Michigan Dept. of Mental Health. Joyce owns a craft business called the Country Mouse.

They have two children who graduated from Mt. Pleasant High School: Deborah Joyce Pridgeon (b. 1956) is a library assistant at Veterans Memorial Library, and Gregory Pridgeon (b. 1958) works for Central Fire Protection and is married to Jacqueline Anne Shepperly from Manceola, MI. She is employed in the Admissions Dept. at CMU. Both Gregory and Jacqueline are graduates of Central Michigan University. Gregory served in the U.S. Navy for four years.

Since Stan's retirement 15 years ago, his love of music (mostly old time gospel, country and bluegrass) has been his passion. He plays guitar and mandolin and volunteers many hours singing and playing at nursing homes, senior centers, community events, music festivals, jamborees and where ever he is asked to entertain. He plays with a musical group called the Waybacks. In December 2002 at the age of 68 he recorded his first CD and Cassette. Stan and Joyce are members of Mt. Pleasant First United Methodist Church. For many years they toured the United States by motorcycle, but now enjoy traveling in their motor home to many places and enjoy spending winters in Florida.

QUINLAN, John Bernard (b. June 22, 1897 on the family farm in Isabella Twp.) was the oldest son of William J. and Inez (Teeters) Quinlan. He went to the Whiteville School until he was through the 8th grade, then entered Central State Normal School in Mt. Pleasant. With only a six week course, he took a teachers examination and received his 3rd grade

John Quinlan, Aug. 10, 1980.

certificate to teach in the rural schools of Wise, Jordan and Whiteville. The Normal had two certificates-one for rural elementary which took two years and advanced rural elementary which took two years more.

He signed up to teach at the Russell School about 15 miles west of Mt. Pleasant. One day he lifted the lid of his desk and saw the name of Owen Barrett who had taught there at one time. Owen Barrett was the first man killed in action from Isabella County in WWI.

Thinking he would be drafted, Bernard signed up along with 300 others from the area. About that time, there was a popular book called *"Over the Top."* It told how terrible it was in the muddy trenches and going over the top. A flu epidemic broke out in their training camp and four from his company died. Bernard also got the flu and never got the chance to go over the top.

He finished school and headed for Pontiac, his first teaching job. He got his life certificate in the early 30s and became principal at McPhee Junior High in Alpena. Knowing if he wanted a better position, he would need two more years of school. However, before he could finish, the depression hit and he ran out of money, just 12 months short of graduating.

He decided to go to Flint where there were jobs in the auto plants. He began a new career at Fisher Body. His brother Bill also worked there. When the first sit down strike in the nation began in Flint, they were part of it. They entertained the strikers with their music, Bernard on the violin and Bill on the banjo.

When Bernard was 40, he married Barbara McKay and settled down in Flint. His brother Bill and wife Alda lived nearby. The brothers would get together and play for dances. During WWII, they composed a patriotic tune and had it patented.

When his parents died, he and his sister Lenore bought the family farm and kept it until 1988 when they could no longer keep up the repairs. Bernard retired in 1962 from Fisher Body and he and his wife made many trips with the Senior Citizens. He also found time to write a memoir for his family. He died March 3, 1992, well loved by all his nieces and nephews.

Exerpts From All In A Lifetime
by John Bernard Quinlan

My father finally purchased a farm across the road from my grandfather William Henry Quinlan. Grandpa helped him to get the farm and he moved the Joe Troutman's house from across the road. He had a carpenter by the name of Jack Regan build a small stable and some repairs were done to the house. Later he dug a basement, had a stone wall built and moved the house over the basement.

Grandpa Quinlan lived in a log house a long distance from the road. When he built the house, he didn't know where the road would be as they hadn't completed the exact survey for the road. There were just Indian trails through the woods. Later Grandpa built two barns near the road and made a stile over the fence which led to the log house.

My dad bought another 20 acres across the road, with a lot of good timber of beech and maple. In the winter Dad would cut down trees and cut them into stove wood. Then he would load up the sleigh and haul them to Mt. Pleasant. He would park the load on Main St., blanket the horse and wait for some buyer to make him an offer. They would usually wait until evening to get a better price as they knew he

would be anxious to get home before dark to do his chores. The wood would sell for a dollar to a dollar and a half a cord, hauling it to the buyer's wood shed. He would then park the team in Jockey Lane and head for Kenny's grocery for groceries and coal oil. If mother ran out of coal oil before he returned, she would make what she called a "bitch." This was some cloth wrapped around a button and placed in a saucer of lard. She would light the cloth and it would burn like a candle. Dad would always bring back a bag of stick candy with barber stripes.

Dad was busy clearing the land on the 20 acres across from his 40 acres. He and Uncle Walt Carpenter bought a used buzz saw and drag saw. This was driven by horse power. They even built a shanty for the hired hands to live in. Some of the trees they cut down were birdseye maple about three feet in diameter.

When I was 4 or 5, Grandpa Quinlan went out to Washington and Idaho to stake out a claim. He held an auction sale and sold off all his stock. He and a fellow by the name of Claud Parrish took off for the west to seek their fortune. This was around 1905. He paid a lawyer $200 to stake out his claim. He and his partner Parrish spent five years out there, working the harvest fields, panning for gold and built a cabin on the claim.

While Grandpa was homesteading, Grandma Quinlan rented a house in Mt. Pleasant. She did dressmaking and was also a cook at the Bennett House. The girls went to the Catholic school. My dad rented the family farm on shares and he and his cousin Jack Reid worked both farms. When Grandpa found out that his claim was on railroad property, he returned to his farm in Isabella Twp. and started again from scratch. He built a new house with seven rooms. One Sunday morning in 1912, he was awakened by a light shining in his bedroom window. He looked out and saw his barns all afire. Lightning had struck and everything was lost except for an old horse who had gotten loose. In 1914, he had a new circle roof barn built with a new basement. He painted it red with white trim and had his name lettered on the front. It was built by the Quick Brothers who were not as quick as the name implied as it took all summer.

In 1925, Grandpa fell from the haymow and broke his leg. It was such a bad break, that the bone was protruding through the flesh. The snow was so deep, it was impossible to get out with the car. They hauled Grandpa out to the pavement in the old Ford, pulled by a team of horses. Dr. Pullen set his leg and Grandpa stayed in town at his brother Charlie's place until his leg healed. In April 1930, at the age of 87, Grandpa died of a heart attack. He is buried in Calvary Cemetery.

RATHBURN-GILLETT.
Queena Mae Gillett was born Oct. 27, 1896 in Birchwood, Bradley County, TN to Dr. Jesse Gillett and Lillian Carter Wrinkle Gillett. She grew up in Flint and worked as a bookkeeper. On Dec. 24, 1919 at age 25 she married Merle Weidman Rathburn (b. April 13, 1897), son of Charles Orlando Rathburn and Mary Elizabeth Weidman Rathburn. They were married at the Weidman Methodist Church and resided in Flint for most of their married life. Merle and Queena spent many winters in Palmetto, FL with both of her brothers and their wives.

Merle died March 8, 1980 and Queena died Aug. 12, 1982, both are buried at Sunset Hills Cemetery, Flint, MI.

Their children are Barbara Jean (b. March 28,1924, d. 1952); Lillian Ellen (b. Nov. 27, 1926, d. Dec. 25, 1950); Robert Jesse (b. Oct. 21, 1928) and Patricia Mae (b. Feb. 26, 1932).

RAU, Stephen, the third son of Louis and Albina (Boge) Rau, was born in Beal City, MI on Jan. 17, 1922. Steve's parents lived in Beal City where they farmed and the children attended school.

On April 12, 1947, Stephen married E. Eileen McDonald in Sacred Heart Church in Mt. Pleasant, MI. Eileen (b. Nov. 8, 1927) is the second daughter of Joseph and Edna (Salchert) McDonald. Eileen's family lived on a farm at 60 North Lincoln Road, and she attended the Whiteville School and graduated from Mt. Pleasant High School in 1946.

In 1947, Steve and Eileen purchased the farm from Eileen's mother and continued to farm the land until 1954. Eileen's father Joseph McDonald died on July 3, 1945. In March 1954, Steve and Eileen purchased a farm from Michael and Anna Dobais at 1532 West Pickard Road (The Page Place) and in 1957 an adjoining 80 acres was purchased from Marvin Coughlin.

Steve continued to farm until 1969 when the farm was rented to Aloy Schumacher and Sons. At this time, Steve began working for Marchandio and Rau as a laborer. As the result of a stroke, Steve was forced into early retirement on May 16, 1975 and died on Nov. 2, 1992.

On December 22, 1977, Steve and Eileen moved to 2930 Michigan Street in Winn, MI. They had built a very pleasant two-bedroom home. They had wonderful neighbors and were close to St. Leo's Catholic Church. After Steve's death, Eileen built a house on the farm, where she currently resides.

Eileen was employed by and retired from the state of Michigan after 25 years of service at the Mt. Pleasant Regional Center for Developmental Disabilities (1957-83). After retiring, Eileen worked part-time for Central Michigan Guardianship as secretary until 1988. In 1988, she signed a contract with the Department of Social Services to be a private guardian-conservator. In 1992, she was appointed to the Social Services Board for Isabella County, she also volunteers for the Commission on Aging in the MMAP and holds the treasurers position for the State Retirees Association, Chapter #20.

All four of their children attended St. Joseph the Worker School and graduated from Beal City High School. They are as follows:

1) Stephen Joseph "Joe" (b. Nov. 1, 1948) graduated from high school in 1966 and attended

Ferris State College. He married on Nov. 30, 1974 to Denise Isenbarger of Troy, MI and they were divorced in 1986. In 1987 he married Debbie Chapman of Mt. Pleasant. They have one son Craig (b. June 2, 1988). Debbie has three children from a prior marriage: Missy, Jessica and Donald. Joe and Debbie currently live in Ravenna, MI. Joe is a self-employed trucker and hauls for K-Mart. Debbie works for the Bissell Corporation in Grand Rapids. Craig is a student at Ravenna Junior High School.

2) Marjorie Ann (b. July 1, 1950) graduated from high school in 1968 and from Michigan State University in 1972 with a degree in human ecology. On Sept. 16, 1972 she married Phillip Roberts of Flint. Phil graduated from Ainsworth High School in Flint and from Michigan State University with a degree in civil engineering. Phillip is the owner of Paller-Roberts Engineering in Culver City, CA. Marge owns Needlepoints West, a needlework store in Westchester, CA.

Marjorie and Phil have lived in Los Angeles, CA since they were married and have a son Michael and a daughter Sarah. Michael graduated from Westchester High School in Los Angeles, CA and has attended Arizona State University, Santa Monica Community College and is now attending El Camino College. Sarah graduated from St. Bernard High School in Playa Del Rey, CA and attends the University of Colorado in Boulder.

3) William Edward "Bill" (b. June 4, 1951) graduated from high school in 1970 and from Bailey Technical School in St. Louis, MO in 1971. On Aug. 10, 1973, he married Arylea Ann Davis and they live at 1588 West Pickard Road in Mt. Pleasant. Lea graduated from Chippewa Hills High School in 1972 and Mid-Michigan Community College in 1983 with a degree in nursing. Bill is a self-employed machinist and travels to farms in the area and repairs machinery for local farmers. As a registered nurse, Lea has worked for Hospice and is currently working for Mid-Michigan Health Care Systems at Clare Hospital located in Clare, MI.

Bill and Lea have three sons: Christopher Allen (b. Aug. 27, 1974), Kevin Stephen (b. Aug. 8, 1976) and Kyle William (b. Oct. 3, 1985). Chris graduated from Beal City High School in 1992 and Michigan State University with a construction management degree in 1999. He currently works for R.C. Hendrick & Son, Inc. in Saginaw, MI. Kevin graduated from Beal City High School in 1995, is an operator, welder, mechanic and currently works as a carpenter. Kyle is a 10th grader at Beal City.

4) Mary Kay (b. Sept. 20, 1952) graduated from Beal City High School in 1970 and from Northern Michigan University in 1973 with an associates degree in retailing in 1983 and a bachelors degree in business data processing. Mary Kay is single and has spent most of her career working for national consulting and accounting firms. She has lived in Washington, D.C.; Dallas, TX; and Lansing, MI. She is currently employed by the IBM Corp. and resides in Mecosta, MI on School Section Lake. *Submitted by Eileen Rau.*

REED, Charles Amos (b. March 14, 1911), son of Harry (Emma Wotring) Reed of Blissfield, MI. He was a graduate of Blissfield High and was very active in baseball, basketball and football.

Charles and his brother Woodrow raised white faced cattle for 4-H and won many ribbons. They traveled to Chicago in 1929 for competition.

His grandmother Reed had never seen a football game. Chuck and his siblings decided to take her to one. There were no bleachers, just a rope that spectators stood behind. On one occasion the players went beyond the rope, hitting his grandmother and knocking her to the ground. She just missed the bumper of a car with her head. Fortunately she was unhurt, but that finished her for sports.

Charles worked in New York for six years as a truck driver for Butler Transport. They took trucks and cars to the New York and Baltimore docks for exporting.

In 1943 he came to Mt. Pleasant for a vacation and eventually returned to stay in the area. He worked at various jobs: American Cleaners, Dow, Johnson Motors, and Taylor Brothers for 27 years.

He met Vera Mae (Wright) Donoghue who was born in Detroit. She went to Ferris State College and got a degree in accounting. She worked for Roosevelt Refinery, Leonard Pipe Line, Osceola Pipe Line, Floyd's Shoe Store, Vic's Grocery and Ric's Grocery.

Vera had three sons by a prior marriage when she and Charles were married on June 9, 1951. Glen Donoghue (b. 1936), Dennis Donoghue (b. 1938), and Patrick Donoghue (b. 1941). Together Vera and Charles had three children: Martin Reed, Dianna Reed and Mary Ann Reed (b&d. 1957).

Vera Mae (Wright-Donoghue) Reed was born Dec. 10, 1914 and died Sept. 14, 1999. Her grandmother Mary L. Reed was born March 28, 1863 and died Nov. 10, 1947. Siblings: Woodrow Reed (b. 1913) of Rosebush; Archie Reed (b. 1915) of Adrian; Bessie Marie (Reed) Bourland of Shepherd; and Adah (Reed) Johnson (b. March 1, 1908, d. Nov. 16, 2001).

REED FAMILY. Joseph Daniel and Callie Mae Bitler were married in Ohio and moved to Michigan where Joe spent several years working as a lumberjack while Callie reared their 10 children on a farm East of Harrison. Later Joe built the house at 414 Elizabeth St. in Mt. Pleasant where they lived until their death.

Doris was the only one of the family to graduate from Central. She worked her way through by cleaning houses. For a while she lived with and worked for

Woody and Doris Reed

the Dr. Pullen family. She taught school for several years until a parent saw her in a bar. It was just not proper for a teacher to be in a tavern on a weekend even though she was in her mid-20s and with friends. Doris worked in the county welfare office and then went into social work. She took classes at U of M but stopped six credits short of a master's degree because she wanted to continue to work with children, not just sit behind a desk in an office.

In 1936 Woodrow Reed came to Mt. Pleasant from Blissfield to work for his uncle Floyd Johnson who owned the Studebaker garage on the corner of Michigan and College streets. Woody saw Doris working in the county welfare office when he went to the bank.

Woody got a friend to get him a date with Doris. They dated for four years. By that time Doris was working in Lansing for the Department of Social Services. They knew he would be called up again in the military because of Pearl Harbor, so Doris made the arrangements and they were married in Mason on Dec. 13, 1941. Woody was stationed in Hawaii for most of WWII.

Upon their return to Mt. Pleasant, they lived with Doris' mother to care for her until a fatal house fire next door in 1949. Woody and Doris built a new house at 408 Elizabeth and lived there until 1958 when Callie died. They bought 10 acres of land at 3325 Isabella Rd. so that their daughter Susan could have her horse at their own place. Doris and Woody stayed there until the city wanted to run the city limits through their backyard in the early 1970s. They sold that home and moved to 5442 E. Rosebush Rd., a half mile from Susan's home.

Susan had married Robert Walton in August 1965, and they had five children: Trevor, Amy, Wendy, Hedlun and Dallas. The Walton family operated a dairy farm and later changed to a cow/calf beef herd and hay production just east of Rosebush.

When Doris and Woody retired from their respective jobs at the State Home and Training School they began spending winters in Zephyrhills, Florida. Doris enjoyed her family and friends. Woody became an avid shuffler. Doris suffered a heart attack in Florida and died the day after their 57th wedding anniversary. Woody will celebrate his 90th birthday on Jan. 11, 2003 and is still an avid shuffler.

RICE-WESTPHAL. George Chauncey and Lillian (Westphal) Rice came to Isabella County after reading in a local paper of land available in Isabella County and with the monetary help of Lillian's father, Frederick Westphal, Brighton, MI, purchased 40 acres in the center of Sec. 30, Deerfield Twp. in 1891.

In 1901 Chauncey and Lillian purchased a long 40 lying to the north of the original purchase. In 1915 they purchased another long 40, giving them a total acreage of 120 acres with the land extending to what has now become Broomfield Rd.

When they first came to their property, there was not any Broomfield Road bridge over the Chippewa River. In order to cross the river, they had to find a shallow spot and then cross. The roads were not on the section lines and a winding trail led them to their property where there was a log cabin.

Although the cabin was small, the family stayed there having to carry their water up hill from a spring just east of their property. After purchasing the last 40 acres that had a better log cabin, the family moved into it. One advantage of the new property was a spring about 1/4 miles away, but carrying water from there was much easier due to a more level ground.

Their two sons, Floyd (b. Sept. 27, 1893) and Lester (b. Feb. 21, 1895) helped with the farm work and cleared the land of stumps. In the winter the boys attended the Stoney Brook School in Sec. 29. Lillian picked blackberries on the land, took them by horse and buggy to Mt. Pleasant and sold them for 5 cents a quart and paid off the mortgage.

The boys grew up and Floyd went into military service during WWI, while Lester stayed home to do the farming. When Floyd came back from service, Lester purchased Floyd's interest in the family farm. Lester built a stone house on the north end of the property near Broomfield Rd., just in front of the log cabin, and the stone house still stands.

"Rice Centennial Farm."

Floyd married Perelie Brown in August 1917 and they had three children: 1) Maxine (b. March 28, 1920) md. Ernest Kalis and they live in Lansing; 2) Roderick (b. Aug. 19, 1922, d. Sept. 22, 1967) md. Marguerite McDonald and she lives in Sec. 20, Deerfield Twp.; 3) Beverly (b. Aug. 30, 1924) md. Leo Delong (now deceased) and she lives in Sec. 18, Deerfield Twp. Floyd and Perelie divorced and later in life Floyd married Alta Taylor. They had no children. Floyd died in November 1956.

Lester continued living on the farm and married Lennie Ball on Nov. 25, 1925. They had two children, Herbert Eugene (b. Dec. 22, 1929) and Phyllis Arlene (b. Oct. 17, 1932). Lester and Lennie divorced about 1947 and in 1956 Lester married Gladys Akin Wilson. They had no children.

The Rice homestead is currently owned and occupied by Herbert E. Rice and his wife Janet A. (Green) Rice. Herbert and Janet purchased the property from Lester's estate in 1965. They received the 100-year centennial farm certification in 1991.

RICE-GREEN. Herbert Rice, son of Lester and Lennie (Ball) Rice, was born on the family farm in Sec. 30, Deerfield Twp. that was originally purchased by his grandparents. He attended the "Little Brick" school on the northwest corner of M20 and Littlefield Rd. That school later merged with the Weidman School, where Herb graduated from in 1948. He was in the Army for two years during the Korean Conflict. He began working for Michigan Bell Telephone, Clare, MI, in September 1955, which later became Ameritech and he retired in September 1990 with 35 years of service.

In the summer of 1954 he met Janet A. Green at the Lake Roller Rink, Lake, MI. Janet was the daughter of Russell and Grace (Schlader) Green, Midland, MI. Her father was the owner of R.B. Green Plumbing and Heating Co., Midland. Janet was born in Midland, attended Midland Public Schools, graduating in 1954. She attended Central Michigan University in 1954 and graduated in 1976 with BS in education. Janet started working for the Social Security Administration, Mt. Pleasant office in March 1979 and retired in July 1998 with over 19 years of service.

Herb and Janet married April 2, 1956, at the First United Methodist Church, Midland, and they have three children: Daniel Herb, Stephen Russell and Joy Grace, all born in Mt. Pleasant.

Rice Family, August 1998. Back, l-r: Joy (Rice) Master, Dan Rice, Stephen Rice. Middle: Neil Master Jr., Marlene (Boehm) Rice, Bonnie (MacGregor) Rice. Front: Janet Rice holding Neil Jacob Master III, Herb Rice holding Rebecca Master, Alison Rice.

Daniel Herb (b. Jan. 22, 1958) was active in the Boy Scouts and graduated from Chippewa Hills High School, 1976, and Ferris State University in 1981 with associates degree in welding technology. He works for a contractor of Ford Motor Co., Dearborn Plant. He married Marlene Bloem in November 1996 and they live in Sylvan Lake, Oakland County, MI. Marlene works for Oakland Co. in Computer Dept. Daniel has a daughter Danielle (b. Oct. 7, 1978) from a previous marriage. Danielle married Richard Holland (b. Sept. 6, 1997) in Camden, Benton County, TN. Danielle and Richard have two children, Thomas Larris Holland (b. June 4, 1998, Tennessee) and Elizabeth Anne Haley Holland (b. Jan. 31, 2000, Mt. Pleasant, MI). Danielle works at the Hot-an-Now, Mt. Pleasant and is attending Mid MI Community College and Richard works at the Kroger store, Mt. Pleasant. They live in Mt. Pleasant.

Stephen Russell (b. Sept. 20, 1959) was active in the Boy Scouts, later graduating from Chippewa Hills High School, 1978, and Central Michigan University, 1983, BS in computer science and MS in administration, 2000. He works for Hitachi Data Services. Stephen married Bonni Macgregor April 22, 1989 in Pontiac, MI and they have a daughter Alison Taylor (b. Oct. 22, 1992, Traverse City, MI). They live in Sanford, MI.

Joy Grace (Rice) Master (b. April 4, 1967) was active in 4-H as a youth. She graduated from Chippewa Hills High School in 1985 and Ferris State University in 1989 with an associates degree in ornamental horticulture. She married Neil Jacob Master Jr. on Feb. 10, 1990, Mt. Pleasant, MI. She works for Central Michigan University, Grounds Dept., Neil is a full-time farmer, farming about 500 acres. They live in Sec. 21, Deerfield Twp. on farm purchased from a cousin of Joy's, Fred Rogers estate. They have two children, Rebecca Arlene (b. Dec. 17, 1994 at home) and Neil Jacob Master III (b. April 24, 1998, Alma).

Herb and Janet purchased the family farm in 1965 and it became a centennial farm in 1991. The farm has been farmed by the Rice family since 1891. Herb, Janet, Dan and Stephen enjoy deer and turkey hunting on the family farm. They are members of the First United Methodist Church, Mt. Pleasant.

RICHARDSON-STAPLES. Asa P. Richardson (b. April 29, 1797 in Vermont), son of Josiah and Sarah Richardson, was employed in lumbering and farming and also locating lines in the wilderness of the Pine-Tree State. Asa married Jane Staples (b. June 25, 1806), daughter of Noah and Ruth (Bradford) Staples, on Feb. 26, 1824 in Kingfield, ME. Asa and Jane came to Sec. 30, Fremont Twp., Isabella County in 1868. Their children are as follows:

1) Polly (b. Nov. 18, 1824) md. Henry Fuller.
2) Seth Staples (b. Oct. 31, 1826) md. first, Emily Taylor and second, Mary McEwen.
3) Caroline (b. Jan. 6, 1829) md. Charles Greenlear/Greenleaf Richardson.
4) Fidelia (b. May 18, 1831) md. first John Edgar and second, Phineas Allyn.
5) Silas Barnard (b. July 18, 1833) md. Catherine Hess.
6) Lucy Jane (b. March 1, 1835) md. Mark Curtis.
7) Fanny H. (b. Feb. 28, 1837) md. Harrison A. Cragin.
8) Cyrus Leland (b. Oct. 24, 1838) md. Elizabeth Mitchell.
9) Louisa Victoria (b. April 27, 1842) md. Leonard Vickery.
10) Charles Wallace (b. Dec. 3, 1844) md. Eliza Ann Inman.
11) Mandana Griffith (b. Oct. 8, 1847) md. James Ferguson.
12) Sarah deAlbra (b. Jan. 7, 1849) md. John Richards.

Asa died March 30, 1879 and is buried in Union Twp., Isabella County. His wife Jane's date of death is unknown. Asa and Jane's family remaining in Isabella County: Charles W., Silas Barnard, Seth Staples, Caroline B. Richardson, Poly Fuller and Louisa V. Vickery.

Seth Staples Richardson (b. Oct. 31, 1826 in Franklin County, Kingfield, ME) md. Emily Taylor on April 20, 1853. She died of consumption April 5, 1857. Two years later he married Mary McEwen (b. May 8, 1839).

Seth worked at lumbering and farming in Maine until age 26 when he moved to Lorain

Seth and Mary Richardson, parents of Cena Richardson Zufelt.

County, Grafton, OH. Seth and Mary Richardson came to Isabella County in 1868 and homesteaded 40 acres, subsequently purchased 120 acres more. Seth was township treasurer two terms, highway commissioner for two terms and school officer for 13 years in succession.

Children of Seth and Mary Richardson: Charles H. (b. Nov. 10, 1861, d. Feb. 9, 1886 of diphtheria); Eliza Jane (b. Dec. 26, 1863, d. 1912) md. Thurlow Courser; Emma (b. Oct. 12, 1865, d. Nov. 6, 1885 of diphtheria); George Wallace (b. Aug. 3, 1868, d. Nov. 21, 1885 of diphtheria); Mary Lois (b. Dec. 18, 1870, d. 1935) md. Luther Riggle; Cena Alice (b. Dec. 21, 1873, d. Dec. 5, 1957) md. Grant Zufelt (See Zufelt biography).

Seth died Dec. 17, 1903 and Mary died Sept. 25, 1915, both are buried in Union Cemetery, Fremont Twp., Isabella County.

RIFE-BONDURANT. Nello Franklin Rive was born in Charlottesville, VA in 1891 to Joseph and Birdie (Bacon) Rife (see Bacon, Birdie). When he was very small his mother and her sister May took the train, leaving their brother Bret and father William. They came back to the area of Monroe, MI and he was reared here and there, including lumber camps in central Michigan where his mother worked as cook's helper.

Sometime in here, when he was 14, he lived with Aunt May and her husband Otto Miller and worked in a machine shop in Muskegon. When he was about 18 he went back to Virginia to find his father and also found Anzonetta Earle Bondurant. They were married Dec. 10, 1910 and returned to Two Rivers (Caldwell) MI, where they lived in various places - wherever he could find work.

Their daughter Virginia B. was born Oct. 20, 1911 in his mother's house which was on the north side of the cemetery. When Virginia was about 7 years old, Anzonetta took her and went back to Virginia to visit her family. Their daughter Ruth P. was born while they were visiting. When Ruth was about three months old they returned to Michigan.

In about 1920 the family purchased 40 acres in Sec. 30 of Deerfield Twp. and lived there for the rest of their lives. Gradually adding more land until there was 200 acres. They raised their daughters and also two granddaughters, Rosemary and Phyllis, daughters of Virginia who had married Anthony T. Wollangur, and when they separated the little girls went to live with "Ma and Pa."

Life was not easy, the farm provided enough to keep them all going with a lot of hard work, done with horses until 1945 when Nello bought the second tractor to come on the market since the WWII. Everything except the land was paid for in cash. "If you can't pay cash you can't afford it."

The original house was a 16 x 24' two-story with a cellar, heated with the Home Comfort wood range and a wood stove in the living room (only in the winter). A new kitchen was added in 1936, and electricity finally arrived in 1938. There had been a radio which ran from a battery charged by a home made windmill. Electricity changed all that. Now water could be raised by turning a switch instead of pumping or starting a gasoline motor, but it still had to be carried into the kitchen in pails. In 1947 the old house was torn down and the family lived in the new garage while the new house was being built. It had four bedrooms, hot and cold running water and, wonder of wonders, a bathroom.

Nello died in 1951, only 60 years old. Part of the farm was sold and is now a hole in the ground from gravel excavation. The other 120 is still owned by the family. Anzonetta E. lived on the farm except for the last few years of her life. She died in 1980. Both of them are buried at Two Rivers Cemetery.

RILEY-SCHOFIELD. Hugh Kelley (b. August 1888) and Beulah Belle Schofield (b. 1895) were married in Isabella County Oct. 27, 1914. Beulah's parents, Mary and James Schofield, were originally from Pennsylvania. Hugh's parents were William and Margeret Kelley Riley from Hubbardston, MI.

Hugh and Beulah Riley

The Rileys owned a farm on Denver Road in Nottawa Twp. They lived one mile east of the Yuncker School, a one-room school that the older children attended. Hugh and Beulah, as other families in the area, had large vegetable gardens as well as many crops. They worked the land and reared their children in Isabella County. The family attended St. Philomena Church in Beal City, presently St. Joseph the Worker Church.

Hugh and Beulah had 10 children: Howard (b. March 1916), William (b. August 1918), Mary (b. November 1920), Patrick (b. November 1922), Genevieve (b. June 1924), Glen (b. March 1928), Herbert (b. February 1930), Donald (b. July 1932), Gilbert (b. May 1934), Bernard (b. November 1937).

Four of Hugh and Beulah's children served in the U.S. Armed Forces: Patrick, Herbert, Gilbert and Bernard. All the children attended Beal City Schools and most lived in Isabella County.

Hugh Riley died in 1952 and Beulah died in 1977. The Rileys were honest and hardworking people, proud of their heritage and proud of their family.

SANDERS, Floyd Jaklen (b. April 17, 1909 in Fremont Twp., Isabella County, MI) was the seventh child of William Henry Sanders (b. 1874, d. 1916) and Lucy Ann (Hutchins) (b. 1878, d. 1939). Floyd had two brothers, James Leverna (b. 1898, d. 1899) and Lloyd Levena (b. 1904, d. 1984) and six sisters: June (Locke) (b. 1915, d. ?), Sadie M. (Baun, Zufelt) (b. 1900, d. 1997), Marie M. (Coyer) (b. 1904, d. 1973), Margie Irene (b. 1906, d. 1908), Rozella Eliada (Maltby)(b. 1911, d. 1997), and Nora Euginia (b. 1913, d. ?).

On June 21, 1928 Floyd married Jessie May Rufner (b. Nov. 9, 1911 in Jennings, MI). She was the daughter of John Leslie Rufner (b. 1884, d. 1954) and Lesta Olive (Blakley) (b. 1885, d. 1963). Jessie had four brothers and sisters: Merle J. (b. 1909), Leola Leora (Kennedy, Leinaux) (b. 1914), Hazel Luceil (Fortin), and Harold Leslie (b. 1919, d. 1920). On their wedding day Floyd tried to start the car and the crank broke breaking his arm.

Floyd and Jessie Sanders

Floyd worked for a time with the Gorham Brothers Co. in Mt. Pleasant. Floyd was later a brine truck driver for the city of Mt. Pleasant and plowed the airport when needed. He was late for work one winter day and got his hand wrapped in a chain and lost two fingers. He had to go to Saginaw where the doctors were only able to save part of one finger.

Floyd and Jessie had four children: Richard Melvin (b. 1929), Carold "Sandy" Arthur (b. 1934), Stanley Lewis (b. 1934, d. 1989), Ruthann (Anderson, Barnes) (b. 1940).

When the Reorganized Church of Jesus Christ of Latter Day Saints had a bake sale they would request Jessie's baked goods. The family lived on the west side of Mt. Pleasant, MI. Floyd died young of a heart attack on Sept. 20, 1954.

Jessie married James Louis Strait on Dec. 28, 1957 and lived for many years on Main St. Mt. Pleasant. They opened a restaurant called The Coffee Cup on Main St. in the 1960s. Grandpa Strait loved to cook with pimentos. Grandma loved to hug her grandkids and collected glass figurines. Following James' death, Jessie married Clarence Geitman of Weidman. In 1969 Jessie was severely burned in a gas explosion at their house. Following a divorce Jessie married Howard Moffett, who preceded her in death. Jessie passed away September 20, 1991.

SANDERS, William Henry (b. July 1874 in Grand Ledge, Oneida Twp., Eaton County, MI) was the oldest child of Sylvester Sanders (b. 1852, d. ?) and Ettie Jane (Rendall) (b. 1856, d. 1880). William had three sisters: Mirty May (Foote) (b. 1877, d. ?), Lena F. (Luce, Bruce) (b. 1880, d. 1962), and Eta Jane (b. 1880, d. ?).

On Feb. 6, 1897 William married Lucy Ann (Hutchins), who was born Sept. 24, 1878 in Fremont Twp., Isabella County, MI. She was the

William Sanders with children, Lloyd and Sadie ca. 1903/4

daughter of Admiral Nelson Hutchins (b. 1844, d. ?) and Mary Martha (Peffer) (b. 1850, d. 1936). Lucy had eight brothers and sisters, James Leverna (b. 1898, d. 1899), Sadie M. (Baun) (b. 1900, d. 1977), Lloyd Levena (b. 1904, d. 1984), Marie M. (Coyer) (b. 1904, d. 1973), Margie Irene (b. 1906, d. 1908), Floyd Jaklen (b. 1909, d. 1956), Rozella Eliada (Maltby) (b. 1911, d. 1997), Nora Euginia (b. 1913, d. ?), and June (Locke) (b. 1915, d. ?).

On Aug. 11, 1916 the *Isabella County Enterprise* reported William's death as follows:

SUDDEN DEATH Will Sanders died under peculiar circumstances. Will Sanders, who lived in Chippewa, just north of the county farm, died very suddenly Monday forenoon and under circumstances that are said to be unusual. Mr. Sanders was laying a new floor in his granary, and along toward noon was taken sick. He laid on the floor and began to jerk and shake, when his boy asked him if he was cold, "No, I'm hot," he replied. Then he began to moan "oh, dear, oh, dear." The family called on neighbors to phone for a doctor, but before the neighbors who were notified arrived at the Sanders home he had died. Mr. Sanders had been well, ate his usual breakfast with the family, but the symptoms surrounding the death indicate poisoning.

The cause of death is listed as strychnine poisoning in the county record. Lucy sold the farm and moved back to the Winn area. Lucy passed away Jan. 4, 1939.

SANDERS-KAGE. Ann Jeanette Sanders was born Sept. 3, 1932 in Pontiac, MI to Lloyd and Loretta Sanders. She married Lowell Kage

on January 22, 1955, in Rochester, MI. They have four daughters: Angela, Kathleen, Christine, Julie Ann, and five grandchildren.

Left: Lucy and Mary Sanders. Right: Lloyd Sanders.

Lowell and Jeanette graduated from Central Michigan College in 1954. In 1963 they settled in Waterford, MI where Lowell taught high school industrial arts. Jeanette and Lowell now reside at Higgins Lake, MI. Jeanette's fraternal family was very much a part of Isabella County's history.

Lloyd Sanders and children, 1942.

Lloyd Sanders, son of William and Lucy Hutchins Sanders, was born on March 10, 1902 in Isabella County, the third eldest of nine children. Of the nine children Sadie, Lloyd, Mary, Floyd, Rozella and June survived. Several branches of the Sanders family owned farms in Isabella County.

Lloyd used to tell how he would warm his feet in the "cow patties." He liked to relate about the time the family was settled in the wagon to go into town when his mother, Lucy saw some debris in the yard. She made all of them get out of the wagon and spend the rest of the day cleaning up the yard. Lloyd broke a rib when he fell from the haymow in the barn. Lucy and Mary worked in the mill in Mt. Pleasant.

William Sanders' death was thought to be caused by Lucy poisoning him with arsenic. It was never proven, but Lucy did spend some time in an institution. As a result of this incident, the youngest member of the family, June, was adopted and raised by William's sister Myrtie Sanders Foote. We think this incident may have caused several rifts in the family,

After William died on Aug. 7, 1916, Lloyd became restless and decided to venture out into the world. He went to Flint, MI, to work in the coal yard of a railroad. Then he went to Lansing, MI where he found employment in the Reo manufacturing plant. This plant was later to become Oldsmobile a part of General Motors. Lloyd's roaming took him out west to Minnesota where he worked harvesting wheat crops. In 1926 he went to Pontiac, MI, where he hired into Pontiac Motors automobile plant. He retired from Pontiac Motors in 1963.

Lloyd married Loretta Brisbois in Detroit, MI, on Nov. 26, 1930. They raised three children: Ann Jeanette, Daniel Lloyd and Allan Gregory. Loretta, her three children, 11 grandchildren, and 19 great-grandchildren survive at the time of this writing. Lloyd passed away on Jan. 28, 1984. His wife Loretta will reach her 99th birthday in September 2003.

Jeanette's cousin, Ruth Ann Sanders Barnes, lives in Mt. Pleasant and they visit each other often. Ruth is Floyd Sanders' daughter. It has been only recently that Ruth and Jeanette have renewed family ties. In doing so, they have been able to learn more about their family history. Their wish is that the family history will continue to grow and be passed on to future generations.

SCHMIDT, Ernest A. was born in 1903 in Reese, MI, son of Karl and Theresa (Bauer) Schmidt. Karl and Theresa migrated from Austria and Bavaria respectively in the 1870s. Ernest's siblings were Frederick (bachelor), Otto (bachelor), Frank (md. Mary Bogemann), Herman (md. Mabel Humpert), Emma (md. John Tilmann), Charles (md. Irene Faber), Elizabeth (md. Leo Neubecker), Amelia (md. Julius Martin).

The family moved to the farm on the corner of Weidman and Vandecar Rds. by train in the early 1900s. The farm remains in the family to this day, owned by Charles' widow.

Ernest worked on the family farm and also did carpentry, working on many local barns. He worked for a period of time for the Liquor Control Commission in Mt. Pleasant after the Prohibition in the 1930s. In 1941, he

Ernest and Henrietta Schmidt

was elected Nottawa Twp. Supervisor, a position that he held until his death.

In 1938 he married Henrietta L. Boge, daughter of Henry and Pauline (Schafer) Boge. Henry migrated to this area from Germany in the 1880s. Pauline was the daughter of Michael and Clara (Mutz) Schafer. Michael was one of three brothers who were the first settlers of the Beal City area. Henrietta was a housewife and also worked for a number of years in food service at Central Michigan University.

Ernest and Henrietta purchased a neighboring farm of Karl and Theresa's in Sec. 23, Nottawa Twp., on Vandecar Road in 1941, where they spent their life together rearing their family. Seven children were born: Donald md. Virginia Mead and was killed in 1966 in Vietnam, Richard md. Karen Kelley, Patricia md. Ron Kraus, Jean (deceased, 2001) md. Michael O'Connor, Allen md. Ann Marsh, Ruth md. Wayne Barrett, and Judith md. Ted Van Berlo.

In the early 1950s a tornado destroyed many barns in the area including a tool shed and roof of their barn. Ernest helped rebuild some of these barns, his own among them.

In February 1972, their century-old farmhouse was totally destroyed by a fire. It was later replaced by a mobile home.

Henrietta died in December 1986 and Ernest died in June 1987. The buildings were sold to Mike Yuncker and the farmland to Fox Dairy Farms.

SCUTT/SKUTT/SCHUTT. The Scutts came from New York State to Middlebury and Owosso Twps. in Shiawassee County in Michigan. They settled in Isabella Twp., Isabella County around 1890. The first Scutts were Martin M. and Mary Jane Huntley Scutt. The other member of the family that traveled north to Isabella County was son Martin Eugene Scutt. Martin M. was a farmer.

Martin Eugene Scutt married Mary Ellen Matthews in 1893. They lived in Vernon and Isabella Twps. Mary Ellen was the daughter of Ephraim and Helena Louderbeck Matthews. Mary Ellen's parents came from Ohio before 1880. They also lived in Isabella Twp. Martin was a laborer-farmer, also, did some milk hauling and some threshing. They had a family of nine children: Irving, Lawrence, Lloyd, Cecil, May, Mildred, Bernice, Gertrude and Norris.

Irving Wesley was the one that stayed and reared a family. He married Sarah Florence Marshall in 1915. Sarah was the daughter of Thomas Edward Marshall Sr. and Margaret Lucretia Jerore. Sarah's parents came from Canada to Vernon Twp., Isabella County. Irving was a milk hauler-laborer and did some threshing. Irving and Sarah "Sadie" had a family of 11 children: Velma, Roland "Ronnie," Esther, Lorne, Lyle, Junior Irving "Jr.", Kenneth Alvin "Alvin," Donavon, Veronica, Dale and Leslie Wayne "Wayne."

Donavon took over the milk hauling business. Don had the business from 1948-66. In the mean time Don married Veronica Ann Daniel, the daughter of George John Daniel Jr. and Lois E. Cross from Bennington Twp. in Shiawassee County, MI. After the sale of the milk route, Don went to Midland and worked at Dow Corning for almost 23 years before retiring in 1990. Don and Veronica had four children: Lynette, John Wesley "Wesley," Cheryl and Eugene "Gene." Veronica was a 4-H leader with the Isabella-Denver 4-H Club for about 20 years.

SEITER-SEXTON. Leon Lowell Seiter (b. March 2, 1939 in Rosebush, MI) was married to Ann Elaine Sexton on Aug. 24, 1963 in South Rockwood, MI. Ann Elaine Sexton was born in Wisconsin.

Mr. and Mrs. Leon L. Seiter on their wedding day, Aug. 24, 1963.

Leon was employed in Detroit and Cleveland by the Ford Motor Co. He is a country and gospel music singer and song writer. He has written and recorded many songs. On June 30, 2000 Leon was taken into the Michigan Country Music Hall of Fame.

The children of Leon and Ann Elaine Seiter are Geoffrey Benjamin (b. Nov. 6, 1964 in Trenton, MI); Gregory Leon (b. Nov. 5, 1966 in Monroe, MI); Robert Lee Hess Seiter (b. Sept. 3, 1984 in Mt. Pleasant, MI (adopted 1989) and William Joseph (Billy Joe) Hess Seiter born Sept. 7, 1985 (adopted 1989).

SEITER-WAGER. Floyd Benjamin Seiter (b. Dec. 7, 1914 in Isabella Twp., Isabella County, MI) was the fifth child of Jacob and Minnie Seiter. He attended a one-room school and graduated from the eighth grade in 1929. He graduated from Clare High School in 1933; from Spring Arbor Junior College with an associates in arts degree, June 1, 1936; from Central Michigan with a

Floyd and Bessie Seiter.

bachelor of arts on June 14, 1952 and a bachelor of science June 5, 1954. He received his master of arts from the University of Michigan Aug, 17, 1957.

Floyd married Bessie Wager in Saginaw on Aug. 24, 1935. Bessie Wager (b. Aug. 4, 1914 on a farm in Isabella Twp., Isabella County near Rosebush, MI) was the fifth child of Norman and Minnie Wager. Her father was a minister and moved to Ontario, Canada when she was a small child. She attended one-room schools in Ontario and graduated from the eighth grade in 1925.

Her folks moved back to Rosebush and she graduated from Mt. Pleasant High School June 18, 1931. She received her bachelor of science degree from Central Michigan University on June 14, 1954 in Mt. Pleasant. She received her master of arts degree from the University of

Michigan on Feb, 1, 1958. She had majors in biology, music, English and speech.

On March 2, 1939 our son Leon Lowell Seiter was born. He attended the same country school his father had attended until it closed because of consolidation. He then attended the new elementary school in Rosebush. In 1943 Floyd began working in the Dow Chemical plant in Midland. He worked in the main lab until 1954, then decided to become a teacher.

Bessie taught in Hemlock from 1952-54. We both taught in New Haven High School in the English and science departments from 1954-58. Our son Leon graduated from high school in 1957. We transferred to Riverside, CA and taught for one year and moved back to Michigan. Bessie taught biology in Flat Rock High School and Floyd taught biology, chemistry and physics at Airport Community High School in Carlton, MI. They both retired from teaching in 1977.

They were active members of the Free Methodist Church in Mt. Pleasant. Bessie was very good at playing the piano, church organ and accordion. For many years we held Bible schools in different churches through summer vacations. There was a Free Methodist Church in Gilmore Twp. that had been closed for many years. We were asked to open it and hold Sunday school. We opened and held Sunday school there for five years. We organized a quartet and held church services through out Michigan and Ontario. Bessie for many years directed the choir, played the church organ and sang at many weddings and funerals.

We heard of an organization called the Michigan Antique Phonograph Society and were asked to join. They published a monthly magazine called *"In The Groove"* which Bessie wrote many articles for. It now has a membership of more than 1,100 scattered through the whole world. We also belonged to the Michigan Audubon Society and at one time held a state office in the organization.

Bessie was very much involved in "The Women's Christian Temperate Union." For several years she was president of the local chapter. Each year they sponsored a program for school children in grades 1-12 to do coloring sheets, posters and essays. The local chapter has had winners in all divisions including the state and nation.

We also belonged to a rock and mineral club in Clare. We learned to cut and polish rocks and collect fossils. We have a large collection of fossils from many countries of the world.

We became interested in tracing our family ancestry back to Germany. Our book was finished and published in 1972.

We both became interested in collecting antiques. Bessie collected celery vases, all of which were manufactured before 1900. She also collected antique talking and singing dolls. The first in her collection was made by Edison in 1890. The second was made in France in 1895. Bessie wrote a book on talking and singing dolls and her book was published in 2001 after her death.

SEITER-YOUNG. Gregory Leon Seiter was born Nov. 5, 1966 in Monroe, MI. His parents were Leon Lowell Seiter and Ann Elaine (Sexton) Seiter.

Gregory married Krisdon Louise Young on Aug. 25, 1989 in Mt. Pleasant, MI. Krisdon was

born in Ohio July 3, 1968. The children of Gregory and Krisdon Seiter, all born in Akron, OH, are Sarah Michelle (b. March 13, 1993); Katherine Louise Seiter (b. Sept. 27, 1995); Jacob Patrick Seiter (b. March 19, 1998) and Elizabeth Ann Seiter (b. July 10, 2002).

Krisdon and Gregory Seiter

SHILLING FAMILY. The year was 1870. A covered wagon left Athens County, OH and headed for Michigan territory. In the wagon were Solomon and Margaret Shilling and all of their worldly possessions. The wagon followed a dirt trail to 80 acres of property located in Coldwater Twp. of Isabella County on the corner of Coleman and Coldwater roads. Here the family was to begin a new life amid virgin forest, in an area where the closest store was 20 miles away, where there was no school for their children, and no shelter until they were able to build a house.

The wagon must have been fairly crowded for it also carried their seven children. From oldest to youngest, they were Louisa (Mrs. Henry Boger), John, George, Mary, Milton, Rose and Emma. Four more children were born later and they were Alvia, Orra, Artimicia and Artiminda.

The move to Michigan was a new start for the family in the aftermath of the Civil War. Solomon had served his own time with the Union Army and returned a second time to take the place of a neighbor's son. Eighty acres of virgin timberland had been claimed under the Homestead Act of 1862. When ownership had been established by living on the land, Solomon and his brother-in-law, Washington Brown, walked to Ionia, the nearest seat of government. There they made application for ownership of the property.

A deed dated June 15, 1877 and signed by President Rutherford B. Hayes was given to establish ownership. The deed is still in possession of the Shilling descendents as is the property. The homes of Maggie (Mrs. Martin) Boger and Harry and Virginia (Boger) Herman are located on the original 80 acres. While Solomon and Washington were making their trip on foot to Ionia, they witnessed a fight, which ended with one man being murdered. They were required to return to Ionia at a later date to testify in court.

To shelter his family, Solomon built a sturdy two-story log cabin with logs cut practically on the spot. With the help of a man named Byron Bailey, the logs were hand-hewn, fitted together at the corners and chinked with mortar made of limestone and sand, some of which is still intact. The shaved shingle roof lasted until 1933. Solomon Shilling was a master craftsman and the house that he built is still standing.

Margaret Shilling was called "Granny" by everyone who knew her. Her skills as a nurse and mid-wife were in frequent use by the pioneer families. When necessary, she spent several days away from home nursing a sick person and caring for their families.

Solomon Shilling (b. Oct. 26, 1837, d. Feb. 18, 1895) and Margaret Shilling (b. March 14, 1838, d. Aug. 22, 1923) were the grandparents of Martin Boger and the great-grandparents of Virginia (Boger) Herman, Pauline (Boger) Estes and Ruth (Boger) Turnbull.

SILVERBERG FAMILY. Arthur (b. 1929) and wife Frances (b. 1932) were both born in Poland. Holocaust survivors they came to New York after WWII, married and settled in Detroit. They moved to Midland approximately 1959 and subsequently to Mt. Pleasant in late 1963 or early 1964. They started the Dart store approximately 1960 which became Arthur's Catalog Showroom in 1974.

Their three children are Susanne (b. 1953), Steven (b. 1955) and Annette (b. 1957). Susanne is married to Robert Pinzur and living in Buffalo Grove, IL with three daughters, Geri, Jamie and Carly. Steven lives in Mt. Pleasant with wife Janet and sons, Daniel and David, and daughter Stephanie. Annette is married to Robert Roth and residing in Crystal Lake, IL and has one daughter, Sydney. Arthur and Frances are now fully retired and full time residents of Boynton Beach, FL where they now watch the "snowbirds" come and go. Susanne, Steven and Annette are all graduates of Mt. Pleasant High School, 1971, 1973 and 1975 respectively.

SIMON, Phyllis Pauline (Methner) was born May 15, 1935 in Isabella County, Wise Twp. in Mt. Pleasant, MI. Her mother was Emma Vera Gilbert (b. Sept. 22, 1896) and her father was William Methner (b. April 3, 1888). They were married on Dec. 25, 1916. Phyllis has two brothers and six sisters: William Vernell Methner (b. June 11, 1918), LaVern Gilbert Methner (b. Jan. 11, 1920), Velma Frances Methner (b.

Phyllis as Coleman's first Homecoming Queen in 1952.

November 1921), Ruth Doris Methner (b. Oct. 1, 1924), Alta Mae Methner (b. Jan. 11, 1928), Joan Lea Methner (b. Feb. 3, 1930), Ann Delores Methner (b. Aug. 20, 1932), Kathleen Nellie Methner (b. Nov. 30, 1933) and Phyllis Pauline Methner (b. May 15, 1935).

They lived on a 40-acre farm in Isabella County and attended the Orr country school. She graduated from 8th grade, then went to Coleman High School, graduating in 1953. She was elected Coleman's First Homecoming Queen the fall of 1952. (Since then there have been quite a few from the Methner family that have had that honor.)

During her years in school, she started babysitting at 10, and helped do spring cleaning for neighbors. They didn't make much during those days, and sometimes nothing, but they had good experience and it taught them never to turn any job down if you wanted to have a good reputation.

Her first real job was at Dow Chemical immediately after graduation in 1953 as a file clerk. She had several jobs during the 34 years she worked and ended with the title of a Michigan Division Plant Scheduler.

Phyllis met James Simon of Coleman in 1953 while he was in the Korean Conflict. After he was out in 1954, they married June 4, 1955. James also worked at Dow Chemical for 35 years as an operator. In January 1986 they both retired with full benefits.

James and Phyllis Simon and Tammy Ann.

They had one child, a daughter Tammy Ann Simon (b. April 20, 1961). She married Kim R. Haller of Coleman on Oct. 25, 1986 and they have two children, Kelsey Lynn Haller (b. March 30, 1993) and Dylan James Haller (b. Oct. 24, 1995).

Jim and Phyllis are both active members of the VFW Post 1071 in Coleman. After their retirement in 1986, they now take care of their grandchildren, Kelsey and Dylan, while both parents work at Dow Chemical in Midland.

SKINNER, George Wallace was born July 27, 1883 in Constantia Center, Oswego, NY to John and Roanna (Pitts) Skinner.

George Skinner's story is a spirited and adventurous account of early Michigan life in the lumber camps and is a composite of fiction, fact and personal experiences. The author told of his urge to write the tale for posterity and of his working on it in spare moments while he was employed by the Flint Sash and Door Co. in the early 1930s. The rough manuscript was written on strips of packing paper used to cushion layers of window glass shipped into the factory. On evenings his daughter, Thelma Alvira, typed the notes on "an old beat-up typewriter." "I never revised one word." A stenographer in the factory office where she worked offered to type it over. When she had finished the 30,000 word script he asked her what he owed and she said $5.00.

Subject matter for the "Axe-Thrower of the Tittabawasse" was gleaned from 15 years of work as a lumberjack in camps at Marion, Mancelonia, Pellston, Kalkaska and Vanderbilt. Some of the book's characters are patterned after lumberjacks he knew in the camps. He saw and felt the drama in logging life and stored it in his memory for future recording. It was rugged and exciting, with a few rough characters in every camp. Most were farmers who worked their land during the summer and turned into lumberjacks to support their families during the winter. They usually lived within 40-50 miles of the camp and would go home every three or four weeks for visits. Wages for common labor was $1.00 per day.

After the logging years George and Elizabeth led a varied life in hotel and store operations in Brinton. Later George and Elizabeth traveled west with three kids: Mary, Bennett and Thelma. They ended up in Centraila, WA where they worked in factories and also did some farming. Harold Raymond Skinner (b. Jan. 23, 1923) was 10 months old when the family moved back to Michigan.

In 1935 the Skinners moved to Coldwater Twp. from Flint buying 80 acres of land. During 1945 (WWII) while Harold was in the service, George and Elizabeth put in 20 acres of apple orchard known as Towers Estate.

On June 26, 1947 when Harold married Esther Alice Miller of Farwell he received 20 acres of the original land purchased by his parents. They planted more trees and berries. In 1952 and 1954 Harold purchased all but 10 acres of the original land from George and Elizabeth.

When Elizabeth died on June 17, 1959 the remaining 10 acres was given to Thelma. George married Connie Roe of Weidman Feb. 29, 1960 and lived with her until his death on Oct. 23, 1969 at the age of 86 years. He was buried in the North Brinton Twp. Cemetery, beside his wife, Elizabeth Jane (Hamilton) Skinner.

SLOCUM, Ervin Lowell, a farmer and carriage maker, was born Jan. 30, 1847 in Canadea Twp., Allegany County, NY. When still an infant he moved with his family to Lyndon Twp., Cattaraugus County, NY. Ervin married Ellen Jones on Feb. 14, 1869. In the fall of 1879, Ervin and Ellen moved with their three small children from their home in Fairview, Cattaraugus County, NY to the farm community of Calkinsville (now Rosebush), Isabella County, MI. There he purchased 40 acres of land, which was covered with timber and had to be cleared before he could commence farming. A house had to be built in which to live and much hard work lay ahead for this young family. About the year 1898, Ervin moved his family to Wise Twp., Isabella County, which is where he remained and where he died Aug. 17, 1926. Ellen died Feb. 9, 1926.

It is not clear whether or not Ervin and his wife and children were ever able to make a visit back to New York to see their families. Money was a scarce item and more babies were added to the family as the years passed, aside from the fact that it was nearly impossible to leave a farm for any length of time, except in winter, and then the children would have been in school. In the spring of 1882, Ervin's family including his parents, his sister Denise, and four brothers: Alvin, Almeron, Delbert and Emmet, all migrated to Dakota Territory where they settled near the town of Howard, SD.

There, each took themselves a homestead, which consisted of 160 acres each. This was open prairie country which did not require clearing as the land in Michigan did, but the sod had to be broken before crops could be planted. From the time of their arrival in Dakota Territory, they were determined to convince Ervin to move his family there also, where they could all have farms near each other. The year that Ervin finally made up his mind to make plans to move to Dakota Territory, the crops on the lands already settled by his family were destroyed by locusts. At that point, Ervin decided to remain in Michigan.

The original letters sent by relatives from both South Dakota and New York to Ervin and Ellen's family can be found at the Clark Historical Library at Central Michigan University in Mt. Pleasant, MI.

To Ervin and Ellen Slocum were born Richard and Jennie (who both died of scarlet fever in 1875 before the rest of the family left New York to move to Michigan), Newton, William, Elizabeth "Libbie," Howard, Ervin, Albert and Alfred (twins), Lillie and Sherman.

William Slocum was a school teacher. William had retinitis pigmentosa, a rare eye disease which was introduced into the family by William's mother Ellen. When he was going blind, the school sent a letter to his home informing him that they were letting him go. His wife intercepted the letter, went to the school, and talked them into letting William keep his job. William continued to teach school and was later made principal of the school. It is not known if William ever found out about the letter.

Albert Slocum was a veteran of WWI, entering service on March 31, 1918 and serving in the 324 Field Artillery. He received his training at Camp Custer, MI and Camp Humphreys, VA, embarking for overseas on June 15, 1918. He was in the Meuse Argonne, Verdun Sector, and Verdun Offensive. After serving 14 months he was discharged at Camp Custer on June 2, 1919.

Howard Slocum (named for Howard, SD) also had retinitis pigmentosa. He attended school near his home and helped on farms during his youth. In 1923 he became totally blind following a severe attack of measles, although he could distinguish light and dark up to the last. Howard supported himself and his family for many years by weaving rugs and making brooms. In about 1939, Howard decided to do his bit to help relieve the acute wartime manpower shortage by taking a job as a carpenter at the Midwest plant in Owosso, MI. So well did he carry out his duties, consisting largely of making shipping cases, that other employers became "sold" on the capabilities of blind workers with the result that several other sightless persons were given jobs.

Sherman Slocum was a farmer and lived and reared his family in the house where he was reared and where he died Feb. 21, 1970. Sherman also had retinitis pigmentosa. He married Lulu Faye "Faye" Arnett in Rosebush on April 7, 1920. To Sherman and Faye Slocum were born Leona (who died a few days after birth), Mildred, Ralph, Doris and Kenneth.

Mildred Slocum md. James Seaman and had children: Karen, Randy, (twins) Janet and Judy, and Scott. Ralph md. Theresa Fitzpatrick and to them were born David, Monica, Deborah, Beverly and Jeffrey. Doris md. Rodney Martz and they adopted Nancy as an infant and Paul was born to them. Kenneth md. Janet Hart and to them was born Daniel. *Submitted by Deborah A. (Slocum) Thompson.*

SMITH FAMILY. Alvah B. was born May 6, 1881 in Webster Twp., Wood County, OH to Jacob Smith and Margaret Caris Phillips Smith. Alvah came to Isabella County with his parents as a young boy in the late 1800s. They settled on 80 acres in Union Twp. on the corner of Meridian and Deerfield Rds. The 1910 census shows Alvah as having the Smith family farm in his name with his parents residing with him.

There were two churches in the area of the family farm, the Gulick and Coomer Methodist where most of the social life of families would take place. When Alvah was in his teens, he met a neighbor girl, Teresa Wheeler, daughter of Homer Wheeler and Helen Clark. Teresa was born on Jan. 10, 1885 in Isabella County. They would both attend church suppers and services and before long were spending time with each other. Teresa attended the Maple Hill country school and went on to Central Normal getting a teacher's certificate in 1904. She taught in several different country schools around the state. Teresa and Alvah were married on June 23, 1906 at the home of her father, Homer Wheeler. Teresa and Alvah had seven children, two dying as young boys.

Alvah and Teresa Smith

Carl Homer (b. Sept. 2, 1908) and his wife Ida lived in Isabella County on the original family farm until he retired from Central Michigan University and moved to northern Florida. Helen Margaret (b. Nov. 15, 1910) md. Lendy Davis and later Gerald Elliott and spent her adult life in Grand Rapids, MI. Winifred Alice (b. Sept. 18, 1915) md. George O. Sponseller and resided on Crawford Rd. in Union Twp. of Isabella County. Chancey (b. July 11, 1917) md. Vangie Spitsbergen and they retired to Houghton Lake, MI after his retirement from Central Michigan University. Shirley May (b. May 14, 1920) md. Robert Layman and they lived for many years in Gratiot County. They retired to Montana and later to South Dakota where they resided with their daughter Lynette.

Alvah and Teresa built their second home on Deerfield Rd. after returning from a short stay in California where Alvah worked in the lumber industry of the redwoods. Their home became a haven for wildlife and held impressive flower gardens nurtured by Teresa. Alvah passed away May 4, 1959 and Teresa on Oct. 27, 1980. In her later years of life, Teresa was an avid gardener and opened her pond and yard to hundreds of elementary school children for education. Both Alvah and Teresa are buried in Riverside Cemetery in Mt. Pleasant beside their two sons, Irving and Eugene.

SMITH FAMILY. Among the farm families who came to Michigan in the late 1800s was Jacob Smith and wife, Margaret Caris Phillips Smith. They came to Isabella County along with four other families in 1886 from Ohio. Jacob and Margaret came with their young son Alvah and settled on 80 acres in Union Twp. of Isabella County on the northeast corner of Meridian and Deerfield Rds. Jacob was the son of Samuel Smith and Margaret Ream, born Jan. 25, 1846 in Crawford County, OH. Margaret Caris was born Sept. 5, 1843 to Daniel Caris and Elizabeth Murray. Margaret was a widow with three children: Valerie, Burr and Julius, when she married Jacob Smith on Sept. 25, 1873 in Bowling Green, OH.

Most of the 80 acres that they owned was wooded. It took several years of clearing to get it ready for crops, a garden and fruit trees. The lumber they cut was used to build a barn for the livestock and a shed. Jacob and Margaret remained on the farm in Isabella County the rest of their lives with their son, Alvah and his wife, Teresa Wheeler, and children. Margaret died Sept. 17, 1928 and Jacob on March 2, 1931 and were among the first to be buried in the vault located at Riverside Cemetery in Mt. Pleasant, MI. Family members remember Jacob lying in bed and speaking in German when he was elderly and sick.

SNYDER, Freeman Max was born May 27, 1922 to James Kellogg and Rachel Mae Moray. Max, a third generation farmer, was born on the farm of his grandparents, Charles Wesley and Malinda A. Robbins, in Fremont Twp. near Winn. Freeman Max had seven siblings: Harold Moray, Inez Malinda, John Wesley, Wilma Francis, Pearl Louise and Jim Ray. Mable (Moray)

Max and Ann Snyder

Sipfle, Rachel's aunt, served as mid-wife for all seven of the Snyder babies. All of the Snyder children attended the Davis School, a one-room schoolhouse that adjoins the Snyder Farm. All but two still survive (John died in childhood and Jim died in St. Louis, MI in 1982). Harold Snyder (Max's brother) ran a successful Radio/TV repair business in Winn for many years. Harold was the oldest licensed electrician in the state at the time he gave up his license at age 84. Inez attended business college, Louise attended nursing college and Wilma owned and operated several small businesses in the Lansing area.

Max has lived most of his life on the Snyder Centennial Farm originally owned by his great uncle and great aunt, George W. and Emma (Robbins) Fox. Max moved to Lansing in 1947 were he met and married Ann Annis on Aug. 6, 1949. Max missed farming and rural life so he returned to Winn in 1951 to work the family farm. Max drove a school bus for the Shepherd School System and for Central Michigan University for 17 years, retiring in 1984.

Ann was born June 17, 1926 in Lansing Twp. to Clinton and Cleo (Gibson) Annis. She graduated from Sexton High School in 1945 and received her BS in science from Anderson University in Anderson, IN in 1949. While at Anderson University she was among nine women in the nation to win scholastic honors. She earned a MA from Central Michigan University funded by a Science Institute Fellowship while teaching full time and rearing her family. She taught science and English at Shepherd High School from 1957-84.

In retirement, Max and Ann pursued volunteer work for the Meals on Wheels Program and at the Masonic Home. Max joined the Masons in 1949, has a life membership at the Salt River lodge in Shepherd, and was a member of the Cedar Valley Lodge until its closing. They were members of the Order of the Eastern Star Coe Chapter of Shepherd and Ann was given the Rose Medallion Award in 1993. They are a members of the Winn Methodist Church and also attended the Central Michigan Free Methodist Church

Ann returned to our Lord Sunday, Aug. 27, 2000 at the Isabella County Medical Care Facility in Mt. Pleasant.

They had two sons, Robert Max and Donald Allen. Bob married Terie Lynn Taylor and had a daughter Jessica Laine. Don married Kim Cosby and had two daughters, Tiffany Marie and Christine Ann. Don remarried in 1996 to Nancy Heiss. *Submitted by Bob Snyder.*

SOWLE-BUGBEE. William Francis "Sid" Sowle was the eldest of four (surviving) sons born to Sidney E. and Mary Agnes West Sowle. (see Sowle-West). He was born July 1, 1909 in Boyne City, MI. Soon thereafter, his family moved to Mt. Pleasant, where he resided for most of his life.

He attended Sacred Heart Academy where he was active in football and other school sports. Upon graduation in 1926, he married Elizabeth (Liz) Bugbee, daughter of George and Elizabeth Bugbee of Mt. Pleasant.

After he was married, Sid worked at Dow Chemical in Midland, MI. During the Depression, Sid and Liz went wherever jobs were available. These included the Oldsmobile plant in Lansing, his Uncle Jason's grocery store in Detroit, and the Chris Craft boat factory in Algonac. When they later returned to Mt. Pleasant in the early 30s, he worked at the Mt. Pleasant Lumber Co.

Counter-clock wise from top: William F. "Bill" Sowle Jr., Elizabeth "Bette" Sowle Blake, Margaret Stribley Sowle, Elizabeth "Liz" Bugbee Sowle, William Francis "Sid" Sowle Sr. and Ruth Anne Sowle

During these years, Liz gave birth to four children, all of whom died at birth. Then in 1931, they were blessed with the birth of Elizabeth "Bette" Elaine; shortly after in 1933 William "Bill" Francis Jr. was born; three years later, Ruth Anne was born.

In 1946 Sid purchased Sowle Mayflower Moving and Storage from his father, and continued to operate it until his retirement in 1976.

Liz and Sid were very active in the community, and entertained frequently. Theirs was a very close knit family, spending much time to-

gether going on picnics, traveling on short excursions, and visiting with relatives and friends. The family was often seen at church, social and community activities.

Both Liz and Sid were very strong supporters of Sacred Heart Academy. Sid was a charter member and sponsor of the Sacred Heart Academy Foundation. He also was a Fourth Degree member of the Knights of Columbus. Liz was a charter member of the Sacred Heart Parish Junior League.

Liz actively supported Sid in his work and community service. He became president of several organizations, including the Michigan Movers and Warehouseman's Association, the Michigan General Tariff Bureau, the Sacred Heart Academy Athletic Association, the Sacred Heart Parish Council and the Sacred Heart Academy Foundation. He was also a member of the Rotary, the Elks, and the Mayflower Warehouseman's Association.

His efforts and membership of the Mt. Pleasant Senior Housing Commission also helped produce the Riverview Apartments in downtown Mt. Pleasant.

When Sid retired in 1976, he and Liz purchased a travel trailer and toured all of the contiguous States and most of the Canadian Provinces. They spent their winters in Florida and the southwestern states.

Elizabeth "Liz" Bugbee Sowle and William Francis "Sid" Sowle Sr.

In addition to their own children, Liz and Sid were the proud grandparents of Karen, Kathleen (md. Jack Cotton) and Kevin (md. Kathleen Turnbach), children of Elizabeth (Bette) Blake; Elizabeth (Betsy md. Jack McNeill) and William F. (Bill) Sowle III, children of Bill and Margaret "Peg" Stribley). They also had three great-grandchildren: Sarah Elizabeth, daughter of Betsy (Jack) McNeill; and Sean and Daniel, sons of Kevin (Kathy) Blake.

In 1986, Liz and Sid celebrated their 60th wedding anniversary with many friends and relatives.

For the last several years of their life together, Liz was incapacitated, which curtailed their retirement activities. Liz died in 1994. Sid remained active up until the time of his death in 1999. Both Liz and Sid are buried in Calvary Cemetery in Mt. Pleasant.

SOWLE-STRIBLEY. William Francis "Bill" Sowle Jr. was born Jan. 30, 1933 in Mt. Pleasant, MI. Except for a two year period when he was in the Army, stationed in Germany, he has resided there all of his life.

Bill's parents were William F. "Sid" Sowle Sr. and Elizabeth "Liz" Bugbee Sowle. His fa-

ther Sid was born in Boyne City, MI on July 1, 1909. His mother Liz was born on Dec. 8, 1908 in Bay City, MI. His parents were married shortly after they graduated from high school in Mt. Pleasant (SOWLE-BUGBEE)

Bill attended Sacred Heart Academy in Mt. Pleasant and graduated in 1951. He then attended Central Michigan College of Education now Central Michigan University, where he enrolled in the first ROTC program at Central, graduating in 1955 as a Distinguished Military Graduate and receiving his commission as a second lieutenant in the Army Artillery. While at Central, he was on the track team and was active in various campus organizations.

Following graduation from Central, Bill served two years in Germany in an atomic cannon (280mm gun) battalion. When he returned to Mt. Pleasant in 1957, he joined his father in the family business, Sidney Sowle & Son Moving & Storage. (see Sowle Mayflower). He continued to serve in the Army Reserve until 1969, when he resigned his commission as a captain to devote full time to the family business.

Margaret Ann McGrath Stribley was born Nov. 22, 1934, in Mexico City, Mexico. She was the daughter of Francis McGrath and Sarah Margaret Pratt. She lived the first 10 years of her life in Mexico. During that time, her mother married Frederick Frank Stribley, a second class gunners mate in the U.S. Navy. After WWII the family moved to Ypsilanti, MI, where Margaret attended high school. Margaret went to the University of Michigan, graduating in 1957 with a BS in nursing. After graduating, she went to work in the psychiatric unit of the University of Michigan Hospital for a year.

l-r: William Francis Sowell III, Margaret Stribley Sowle, William Francis Sowle Jr., Elizabeth Sowle McNeill.

Bill and Margaret "Peg" married on Sept. 27, 1957, at St. John's Catholic Church in Ypsilanti, MI. They resided at 701 N. Kinney Blvd. in Mt. Pleasant for 34 years until they moved to 3902 E. River Road.

Bill and Peg have two children, Elizabeth Margaret "Betsy" Sowle and William Francis "Bill" Sowle III. Betsy married John "Jack" McNeill in 1989 in Taunton, MA. Their daughter Sarah Elizabeth was born in 1991. Their son William married Elizabeth "Betsy" Goss in 2000 in Bloomington, IN.

Bill was active in his church, Sacred Heart Parish, and in many community organizations. He was a scoutmaster for many years and served as Grand Knight of the Mt. Pleasant Knights of Columbus. He was president of the Mt. Pleasant Lions Club, Sacred Heart Church Council, The Michigan Movers & Warehouseman's Association, and the State YMCA of Michigan. His honors included being named Sacred Heart Academy's Alumnus of the Year in 1979, Mt. Pleasant Citizen of the Year in 1980, and Michigan Mover of the Year in 1993. He was the first President of the CMU ROTC Alumni Association at Central, and was inducted into the ROTC Hall of Fame in 2002.

He is currently president of Sidney Sowle & Son, Inc. Moving & Storage in Mt. Pleasant, MI.

SOWLE-WEST. Sidney Edgar Sowle was born April 6, 1873 in Eaton County, MI. His mother was Angie Arnold Sowle and his father was William Sowle, both of Michigan. Sidney's brothers were Robert, Jason and Roscoe, and his sister was Tresah.

Sidney grew up in Eaton County and moved at about age 18 to work in the logging camps in northern Michigan. Following this, he worked on the transcontinental railroad out as far as Wyoming. Then he returned to Brinton, MI, where his parents had moved. It was there that he met his future wife, Mary Agnes West, who was teaching in a rural school near Brinton. Mary Agnes was the daughter of William and Mary Ann West, who were prominent Mt. Pleasant citizens, residing at 601 N. Kinney for many years. Mary Agnes was a graduate of Central Michigan Normal (now Central Michigan University). Sidney was a horse trainer and operated drays for hire during those days.

Sidney and Mary Agnes were married in Mt. Pleasant, then moved to Boyne City, MI, where he worked in the lumber industry. His first son, William Francis "Sid" was born 1909 in Boyne City.

The small family moved back to Mt. Pleasant, where Sidney trained teams of horses. He also operated horse drawn wagons for hauling various products, including household furniture. During the following six years, three more sons were born: Harold, Theo "Ted," and Donald. Unfortunately, the family then suffered the loss of a boy (Sidney) and a girl (Thelma), who both died in infancy.

The Sowle family were members of the Catholic Church, attending Sacred Heart Parish in Mt. Pleasant. Their children attended Sacred Heart Academy.

The Sowle family moved to Midland in 1918, where Sidney worked at Dow Chemical. As a result of a work related injury, they returned to Mt. Pleasant in the summer of 1920, where he started the moving business, using horses and wagons. (see Sowle Mayflower).

Sowle Family. Top, l-r: Donald, Harold, Theo "Ted," and William "Sid." Bottom: Sidney E. and Mary Agnes.

Sidney and Mary were not only blessed by their four surviving children, but they also had 16 grandchildren: Elizabeth "Bette," Bill and Ruth Anne, children of William Francis; Tom, Dave, Jack, Suzanne, Mary Jane, Jennifer and Colleen, children of Harold; James, Janet, Peter and Steve, children of Theo; and Lisa and Mary Ann, children of Donald.

Sidney died in 1953 and Mary Agnes in 1968, both are buried in Calvary Cemetery in Mt. Pleasant.

SPICKERMAN, Bishop W. was born 1859 in New York to Harvey and Martha (Winchester) Spickerman, with siblings, Jane and Peter. He moved as a child to Clinton County, MI where he lived with his grandparents, George and Jane Winchester. As a young adult, he moved to Isabella County, purchasing acreage in Sec. 7 of Denver Twp. In 1886 he married Emily Augusta Prout, daughter of Thomas and Mary (Poulten) Prout. They had three sons: Frank Albert (b. 1889), Curtis Milo (b. 1893) and Allen Edward (b. 1895). Emily died in 1926 and Bish in 1944.

In 1912 Frank Spickerman married Anna Kreiner, daughter of Hubbard and Anna Kreiner of Denver Twp. Frank and Anna were active in their church and worked 40 acres of the family farm until Frank's death in 1954. Anna moved to Mt. Pleasant where she lived until her death in 1985.

In 1914 Curt Spickerman married Hattie Gladys Walter from Wise Twp., daughter of Chester and Alice (Dilley) Walter. They owned 40 acres of the Spickerman farm. Curt and Hattie were well-known local musicians. Their one child, Alice Elfreida "Freida" Spickerman, was born in 1915. In 1932, Freida married Theodore Graham of Rosebush. Ted died in an auto accident in Saginaw County in 1947. Freida then married Walt Moore and resided in Farwell, MI with their four children. Curt died in 1954, shortly after his brother Frank's death. Hattie then lived with Freida in Farwell until her death in 1978. Freida passed away in Farwell in 1992.

In 1915 Allen (Allie) Spickerman married Sarah Ellen (Sadie) McDonel, daughter of James Ervin and Julia Ann (Mitchell) McDonel from Leaton. Sarah was from a family of four children; her brothers being Elwood, Cloyce and James C. McDonel. The family eventually changed the spelling of the name to "McDonald." Sadie was the third generation of family from Wood County, OH to reside in Isabella County. Her grandparents, Dewitt Clinton and Sarah (Whitney) Mitchell had also moved from Ohio to Denver Twp. Allie and Sadie lived on 80 acres of the family farm in Denver Twp., residing for a period in Saginaw and Flint, MI. Allie and Sadie had one child, Harvey Ervin Spickerman, born 1920 in Denver Twp. During retirement, Allie and Sadie built a house on the Spickerman farm, residing there until Allie's death in 1964. Sadie moved to Clare where she resided until her death in 1978.

Bishop's grandson, Harvey Spickerman married June Maxine Russell of Wise Twp., daughter of Henry and Lena (Barrus) Russell, in 1940. Their children were Allen Henry, Wayne Franklin, and Danny Lynn. Harvey passed away in 1984 and June in 1997. Wayne and Dan continued to live on the Spickerman farm as adults and reared families there. Wayne moved his wife and three sons into the house built by his grandparents, living there until his death in 1985. Wayne's wife Karen still owns and resides at the Spickerman property. There are currently sixth-generation Spickerman residents in Isabella County.

SPONSELLER FAMILY. Arthur Sponseller was born March 31, 1887 in Isabella County, the son of George Sponseller and Harriett McMacken. The Sponsellers along with other families from Ohio came to Isabella County to settle in the late 1800s. Arthur and his siblings, Frederick, Raymond, Lydia and Myrtle were raised in Union Twp. on Deerfield Road. Their children all attended the Gulick country school and as the three boys grew into manhood, they all worked on the family farm which still remains in the Sponseller family.

Arthur was married to Ivah Way on Nov. 20, 1911 in Lincoln Twp. by Rev. George W. Kiffer. Ivah was the daughter of Orville Way, originally of Ionia County and Florence Walling of Shepherd. Arthur and Ivah had three children, one dying in infancy. Maxine (b. Sept. 1, 1913) md. Wilbur Pierpont of Winn, MI and they spent most of their married life in Ann Arbor, MI. Maxine and Wilbur had two children, Ann and James. George Orville (b. April 30, 1916) md. Winifred Alice Smith on June 4, 1938 and they had five children: Sue Ann, Lester, Kirkwood, George and Kay.

Ivah Way Sponseller passed away on Feb. 18, 1954 and is buried at Riverside Cemetery in Mt. Pleasant, MI. In his later years Arthur lived with his son George on the family farm, until his health failed and then he resided in a nursing facility in St. Louis, MI until passing away on Sept. 2, 1971. He is also buried in Riverside Cemetery in Mt. Pleasant.

SPONSELLER FAMILY. George James Sponseller and Sherry Sue Braun were both born and reared in rural Mt. Pleasant. George is the son of George Orville Sponseller and Winifred Alice Smith of Isabella County, MI. George (b. Sept. 28, 1949), the fifth child of George and Winifred, was reared on the Sponseller family farm located on Crawford Road, just south of what is now the campus of Central Michigan University. He attended

George and Sherry Sponseller

Fancher Elementary School, Mt. Pleasant Junior High School and Mt. Pleasant Senior High School.

He was employed at Dow Chemical Co. of Midland, MI after his graduation from high school. In November 1968, George enlisted in the U.S. Army and served with the 4th Co., 12th Battalion, 199th Light Infantry Brigade. He served for 13 months in the Vietnam conflict.

After returning from the service, George attended Central Michigan University and returned to work at Dow Chemical Co. He later worked for the city of Mt. Pleasant in the Water Department and in 1984 began his own wholesale business called S.D.S. Energy Systems which specialized in exterior home improvement products. After selling the business in 1997, he began work as a salesperson for another wholesaler.

Sherry Sue Braun Sponseller (b. July 7, 1949 in Mt. Pleasant, MI) is the daughter of John C. Braun and Gala B. Welsh. Due to her father's death in May 1949, Sherry and her mother resided with her grandparents, Wesley and Florence Welsh, on their family farm, which was located on East Pickard Road. She attended Kinney Elementary School, Mt. Pleasant Junior High School and Mt. Pleasant Senior High School.

After graduation from high school, Sherry attended Central Michigan University. She worked in the accounting department at Dana Corporation for 16 years, then joined George in working at their own wholesale business for several years. She currently is a staff accountant with Central Michigan Newspapers located in Mt. Pleasant.

George and Sherry were married Jan. 1, 1969 in Mt. Pleasant and resided there while working and rearing a family. Michelle Lea Sponseller (b. Aug. 30, 1969) graduated from Northwood University and is currently working in marketing for a manufacturing risk assessment company in the Ann Arbor area. Brian Edward Sponseller (b. May 12, 1973) graduated from Central Michigan University and resides in Grand Rapids, MI where he is continuing his education to become a teacher in the field of special education. Brian was married on Oct. 19, 2002 to Jill Hartley. Jill is a speech pathologist in the Kent County school system.

SPONSELLER FAMILY.

George Orville Sponseller was born April 30, 1916 to Arthur Sponseller and Ivah Way Sponseller of rural Isabella County. George was reared on the Sponseller family farm in Union Twp. of Isabella County. He attended Mt. Pleasant High School and after graduation in 1934, George went on to attend Central State College where he was active in basketball.

On June 4, 1938, George O. Sponseller and Winifred Alice Smith, daughter of Alvah and Teresa Smith, were married by Rev. Charles MacKenzie at the home of Winifred's parents on Meridian Road. Winifred had attended the Maple Hill School and after graduating from the eighth grade, attended ninth grade at the training school and graduated from Mt. Pleasant High School in 1933.

In June 1938 after their marriage, George and Winifred opened a country store and Mobil gas station on the corner of Millbrook and South Mission Roads. The living quarters were two small rooms in the back with the store in the front and two gas pumps in the driveway. In 1940, the business was moved across Mission Road into a store building that had been moved in from Sherman Twp. and a house moved in from the Buckeye Oil Field. The Sponsellers had a very good business, as Mission Road was now Highway 27 for travelers heading "up north." The surrounding area was still heavy with farming and family pressure forced George and Winnie to sell the store in 1946 and move to a farm on Deerfield Road and later to take over the larger family farm on Crawford Road from George's parents.

It was on the family farm that George and Winnie reared their family of five children:

1) Sue Ann (b. Oct. 7, 1939) md. Peter Cotton and lived in California, Texas and several other states before returning to Mt. Pleasant.

2) Lester A. (b. Oct. 9, 1942) md. Judie Pelsma. Lester and Judie spent most of their married life in the Illinois area.

3) Kirkwood (b. April 23, 1946) md. Nancy Priestap and stayed in the Mt. Pleasant area working as a building contractor.

4) George James (b. Sept. 28, 1949) md. Sherry Braun. They lived in the Mt. Pleasant area where George owned and operated a wholesale building supply company.

5) Teresa Kay (b. June 24, 1956) md. Richard Rieck. They reside in the Traverse City area where Richard owned a manufacturing company.

In the early 1960s, George drove school bus for the Mt. Pleasant Public Schools until his retirement in 1975. George passed away Dec. 24, 1977. Winifred still resides on the family farm which is a gathering place for family and friends. She is an active member of the United Methodist Church and the Coomer Methodist Church. Winifred is a member of the Mt. Pleasant Fiber Guild, the Mt. Pleasant Historical Society and the county extension group.

TAYLOR,

Cyrus Claud (b. March 6, 1883 in Fremont Twp., Isabella County, MI) was the oldest child of John Henry Taylor (b. 1858, d. 1910) and Ella Adresta (Sanderson) (b. 1862, d. 1944). C.C. had two sisters, Ada Violetta (Smith) (b. 1891, d. 1960), Teresa Leota (Hapner) (b. 1899, d. 1985), and one brother George Loren (b. 1888, d. ?).

Lillie and C.C. Taylor

On June 1, 1904 C.C. married Lilie Fern (Sickels) at Mt. Pleasant, MI. Lilie was born June 11, 1886 in Pleasant Lake, Angola County, IN. She was the daughter of George W. Sickels (b. 1855, d. 1908) and Minerva Ann Mead (b. 1859, d. 1953). Lilie had two sisters, Minnie M. (Haenke) (b. 1879, d. ?), and Alice Elnora (Sanderson) (b. 1881, d. 1948).

The Taylors lived near Weidman, MI where on March 13, 1908 they had twins, Doris Fern (Anderson)(b. 1908, d. 1985) and Donald Claude (b. 1908, d. 1992).

Word has been received from Ann Arbor that Cecil Taylor also had to remain there and received treatment on account of having his hand in the dog's mouth which bit Mrs. Taylor.— *Isabella County Enterprise* Oct. 22, 1915

Lilie passed away Dec. 14, 1949. C.C. then married Merle Evelyn (Spicer) (b. 1985, d. 1975). C.C. passed away Aug. 17, 1975.

THEUNISSEN FAMILY.

Lucile Vedder Theunissen was one of the "Vedder Girls" included under the Jesse Vedder family history included in this volume.

Hendrik H. Theunissen (b. April 7, 1896) was a native of South Africa. His parents were Elizabeth and Jacobus Theunissen. He had two sisters, Elizabeth and Nelie, and two brothers, Koos and Carel. In 1918 he came to the USA to study dentistry at the University of Michigan. He met Lucile, was married in 1924, and never returned to his native land.

Lucile was active in community and social affairs in Mt. Pleasant. She was a charter member of the Women's Hospital Auxiliary, on the Board of Directors at Mt. Pleasant Country Club, an officer in the Tourist Club, and a long time member of 1st Presbyterian Church. She loved to play bridge and golf, to garden, and to travel. Lucile died in 1989 at the age of 88.

H.H. Theunissen Family. Lucile, Bill, H.H., Bruce.

Lucile was teaching in Lansing when she met "H.H." who was a graduate student in the School of Dentistry in Ann Arbor. On June 21, 1924 they were married. Their eldest son William was born on June 29, 1925 in Coloma, MI. In 1928 Lucile and "H.H." moved to Mt. Pleasant where he established a very successful dental practice that was to last through 1971. A second son, Bruce, was born on Aug. 5, 1929.

Hendrik, better known as "H.H." or "Tennie," had a large clientele of dental patients who were loyal to his work. He was a champion golfer (winning the Mt. Pleasant Country Club title four times), president of the Country Club twice, member of the Mt. Pleasant School board for 15 years where he acted as secretary, charter member of the Central Michigan College Athletic Booster Org. and the teams' dentist for many years, an avid bird hunter and fisherman, a gardener, a follower of all sports, president of the Rotary Club, and an extremely knowledgeable historian. He died in 1971.

The coverage of Lucile and Tennie's eldest son Bill and his family follows this write-up.

Younger son Bruce graduated from Mt. Pleasant High School as valedictorian, followed by graduation from Central Michigan College in 1951. His personal likes included sports, music, reading and card playing. At Central Michigan College he lettered in golf and was the school's sports information director for a short period. Bruce married Marilou Galloway in 1950.

His first major employment was with Whirlpool Corporation. Later, Bruce resigned this position and entered the Presbyterian Theological Seminary in Pittsburgh. Bruce became extremely dedicated to the helping of people/ groups who were in need and this led to his acceptance as executive director of a combined ecumenical/community action position in Germantown, PA. This was followed with similar leadership positions in Tulsa, Dallas, and Houston.

Marilou was always a person who centered her life on "others," environment, church work, womens' issues and community involvement. She was a registered nurse. Bruce and Marilou were the parents of two daughters, Karen and Mary. They lost a daughter, Renee, in 1958. The couple was divorced in 1988 and Bruce later married Oeita Bottoroff, a lady equally dedicated to civic and church work.

THEUNISSEN FAMILY. Dorothy, better known as Dottie, was sixth of seven children born in 1930 to Glapha and Arnold Eddy. After graduation from Ionia High School. she attended and graduated from Central Michigan College in 1952. She met Bill at Central and they were married in 1950. They had four children: Michael, Chris, Richard and Lorraine. There are 12 grandchildren. Dottie loved golf (twice MPCC champion), all sports, gardening and travel. From the time the children were old enough to travel, the family vacationed a month each summer camping across the USA. Dottie and Bill made a practice of attending the Summer Olympic Games.

Wm. Theunissen Family, 1995. Back: Lorraine, Michael, Chris, Richard. Front: Bill and Dorothy.

William "Bill" (b. 1925) was the son of Lucile and Hendrik Theunissen. They moved to Mt. Pleasant in 1928. His brother Bruce was born in 1929. Bill earned 13 varsity letters in high school and was valedictorian. He served 27 months in the U.S. Navy in WWII. Upon discharge, he graduated from Central Michigan College in 1947, competing in golf, basketball and baseball. After obtaining a master's degree and doctorate, Bill returned to Central Michigan College as faculty member in 1948. Among the duties was coaching three sports, including 10 years as varsity baseball coach. In 1962 he was appointed Dean of the School of Health, Physical Education and Recreation. Later he served as Dean of the School of Education,

Health and Human Services. Bill retired in 1986. Bill was an 11 time champion at MPCC, an avid trout fisherman and camper, gardener, photographer and sports fanatic.

Dottie and Bill were active in the lst Presbyterian Church, MPCC, Chippewa Valley Audubon Club and Isabella Child Development Center. Bill was president of the Rotary Club and received Mt. Pleasant's "Outstanding Citizen Award" in 1981. The M.U. baseball facility is named "Theunissen Stadium." He was elected into both the MPHS and the CMU Athletic Halls of Fame. Dottie received the Rotary Club's "Distinguished Citizen Award," Mt. Pleasant PTA's Special Award, and was chairperson of the Mid-State Substance Abuse Advisory Council. She was president of the Tourist Club and active in the local chapter of PEO. Rotary International honored both with its Paul Harris Fellow Award.

The eldest son Michael (b. 1953) graduated from MPHS and CMU. He married Michele Sauter and they had two daughters, Tiffany and Stefany, and one son Nathan. Mike worked with construction and served on the State Board as president and the National Board as officer. In 1998 he married Joanne Chappell, who worked at First Bank and did exhibition art.

Chris (b. 1955) graduated from MPHS and CMU. He married Barbara Bowen. Chris was an independent builder until joining the MPHS faculty in 2000 as Director of the Vocational Education Building Program. Barb was a teacher and later became president of National City Bank. They had three sons: Craig, Steve, Daniel, and one daughter, Victoria.

Richard (b. 1957) specialized in food services in high school and since has worked at Jon's Drive-In. He married Maxine Straus and they had two children, Melissa and Justin. Maxine works in the health care profession.

Lorraine (b. 1958) graduated from MPHS and CMU. She worked for the Dept. of Natural Resources and later as a respiratory therapist. Lorraine married Dale Karolak, who works in the computer business. They have Ryan and Lorraine. Another daughter, Jessica, died in 1988.

TINKER. The character of Euretta Holsted Tinker was well known by those acquainted with her. As a grand niece, I knew at a very young age that she never spoke a bad word about anyone, although the lack of a good word would often speak volumes! She was a daughter of Elijah Holsted, and one of five children (Forrest and Gordon older and Eudora and Bessie younger.

Elijah enlisted in the Civil War in September 1861 and was part of Co. D, 16 Michigan Volunteer Infantry. He had been a blacksmith by trade near Saginaw. I've heard he had been a prisoner of the Confederacy, and when he returned home his hair was snow white.

The younger daughter, Bessie, married Emory Leiter, therefore, becoming my grandmother. To their union was born four sons (living) and probably three who died in infancy. There was Lloyd, Oren, Clifford and Freeman. Bessie died long before I was born, so my only memory of a grandmother was Euretta. She was known as "Rettie" to others, but to my dad and uncles she was "Auntie," and I was 8 or 9 when I realized that wasn't her name.

Her marriage to Amos Tinker ended in tragedy as he was killed when a tree being felled crushed his buggy. Life was surely hard for her at that time. She took a correspondence course in nursing, going to Chicago for the final study and exams. From then on, she spent most of the time going from one home to another nursing the sick or injured. She would drop anything to rush to a patient (I've seen it happen in the midst of dinner dishes) and stay until she was no longer needed.

l-r: Bessie Holstead Leiter and Euretta Holstead Tinker.

She had a deep and abiding faith in God, and lived as Christian a life as anyone could. I was 14 when she died, and I still miss her. She hummed nearly all the time, and until I started writing this, I had never thought of where my habit of doing the same came from.

Euretta Holsted Tinker (b. Oct. 28, 1870, d. March 9, 1950) and Bessie Holsted Leiter (b. Oct. 27, 1888, d. June 13, 1932) were both gentle and caring people, and I am sure the world is a better place because of their existence. *Contributed by Donna Leiter Houghton.*

TRACY-WARDWELL-GARDNER. Cyprian "Tip" Tracy was born in New York State on Dec. 12, 1833. His father was born in Connecticut in the late 1700s and his mother was born in New York State.

Della Wardwell was born in New York State on March 10, 1834. Both of her parents were born in New York State. Della married a man whose surname was Gardner and they had two children, Lemuel "Lem" and Augusta "Gustie." Birthdates of these children are not known and the date of their father's death is not known.

Cyprian married Della Wardwell

Standing: May (Tracy) Ouderkirk. Seated: Lena (Ouderkirk) Maybee and Della (Wardwell) Gardner Tracy holding Edra May Maybee, 1916.

Gardner on Feb. 3, 1867, in Lincoln Twp., Isabella County, MI. Benjamin A. Smith, Justice of the Peace, officiated; witnesses were Betsy Wardwell and A. Bellenger (recorded in Libre of Marriages, p. 67 on Feb. 9, 1867, at 4 p.m.)

Cyprian and Della received title from the federal government to 80 acres of land located in what is now Vernon Twp. The government title is signed by U.S. Grant, President of the United States.

Della and Cyprian had two children: 1) Della May was born June 14, 1873, in Vernon Twp., Isabella County and died Oct. 23, 1953, in Mount Pleasant, Michigan. (See Ouderkirk-Tracy for more information about her.) After Della May's marriage, she discontinued using her first name and went by May. 2) Harry was born May 4, 1878 in Isabella County and died Aug. 11, 1946.

Cyprian was an engineer for the railroad. He was away from home a great amount of time; therefore, much of the work on their home place was Della's responsibility. She was a resourceful person, a good neighbor, and the midwife and helper in her neighborhood all the days of her life.

Cyprian Tracy died of diphtheria in Mount Pleasant, MI, on July 7, 1882, and Della died in Vernon Twp., Isabella County, on July 19, 1925.

May told her children about seeing bear and wolves around her home when she was a child and about walking to school through the woods knowing these wild animals were around. She liked school and reading and spelling were her favorite subjects. There were readers for each year of school for about six years; thereafter, the children read from the Bible. During her married life, May used her reading skill to read to her blind father-in-law and her children and grandchildren.

May helped farm with oxen and saw the day when tractors were used over the same farmland. She and her husband John were known as good neighbors to all around them. Her daughters learned well at her hand to be homemakers and excellent mothers. Her sons were diligent and conscientious workers in the fields of their choices and devoted to their families. She taught her children to enjoy beauty in the sunsets, stars and earth. She taught them to pray and trust in God.

Harry stayed with his mother until her death. He farmed the place from the time he was able until it was sold to Roy Ouderkirk on Sept. 6, 1927. He never married.

Roy Ouderkirk and his family lived on the "Tracy" place for several years. Roy's children walked to school over the path their grandmother had made many years before them. Roy sold the farm to his son Dale in 1951 and he sold it to Joseph Fancovic in 1958. *Compiled by Vilo Ouderkirk Wiltse and Emma Jean Ouderkirk Valley.*

VEDDER FAMILY. Orie and Jesse Vedder moved to Mt. Pleasant in 1912 from North Star, MI. They arrived with four daughters: Rhea, Lucile, Verna and Cordie. Orie (b. Dec. 18, 1872 in Grove City, IL) was the daughter of Charity and Calvin Kryder. She came to Gratiot County at age 5 years. Orie had a brother Shirley and a sister Cordie.

Arriving in Mt. Pleasant in 1912 she was active in the Eastern Star and the 1st Presbyterian Church. Following Jesse's death she opened her home at 909 S. College (University) to men roomers from the nearby college. Orie never learned to drive an auto but she loved to travel. She died March 23, 1960 at the age of 87.

Jesse (b. May 17, 1869 in Hillsdale County) was the son of Sarah and Clark Vedder and one of six children. He met Orie and they were mar-ried Oct. 26, 1893. He moved his young family to Mt. Pleasant in 1912 for the purpose of giving his daughters the benefit of the excellent schools there. He was the proprietor of a flourishing feed barn at the northwest corner of the intersection of Franklin and Michigan streets. This was convenient for the Catholics who could stable their horses there while they attended church across the street. Jesse died of a stroke on June 28, 1922 at the age of 53.

Jesse Vedder Family, 1917. Back: Verna, Jesse, Orie, Cordie. Front: Rhea and Lucile.

The eldest of the Vedder girls was Rhea (b. Nov. 10, 1894), unmarried, Rhea taught school in Detroit until her retirement when she returned to Mt. Pleasant to live with her mother. Rhea did extensive traveling throughout North America and died in 1961.

Lucile (b. Jan. 28, 1901) graduated from Mt. Pleasant High School in 1917 and from Central Michigan Normal School in 1919. She married Hendrik H. Theunissen on June 21, 1924. They had two boys, Bill and Bruce. Her family and her life are further described under the Theunissen Family history.

Verna (b. Jan. 14, 1904) graduated from Mt. Pleasant High School and later from Central Michigan Normal School. She taught school and later acted as a hospital secretary in Marquette, MI. Verna married Wallace Kemp in 1924. In 1959 Verna and Wallace bought a farm on E. Millbrook Rd. in Isabella County. Following Wallace's death in 1964 Verna moved in to Mt. Pleasant. She died in 1998. The Kemps had two children, Hildegarde and Joe.

Cordie (b. Aug. 5, 1906) graduated from Mt. Pleasant High School and Central Michigan Normal School. She did office work in Detroit prior to her marriage to Elwin Dunn in 1928. In 1934 the couple returned to Isabella County and settled on his father's farm on Walton Rd. Elwin died in 1978 and Cordie in 1988. They had three children: Richard, Robert and Dorothy.

Orie and Jesse Vedder raised four beautiful and delightful daughters. The couple were solid citizens of Mt. Pleasant.

WALLACE-BENCHLEY. Jo Anne Marie Wallace-Benchley (b. Oct. 11, 1975, Petoskey, MI) lived in Indian River with her parents, George and Nancy Wallace, and her two sisters, Elaine and Jackie. When she was about 3, Elaine moved out, her parents divorced, and Jackie later moved in with her dad. When Jo Anne was 7 years old, her mom got a job transfer from Gaylord to the Mt. Pleasant Center as an accountant in 1983, so Jo Anne and her mother moved to Mt. Pleasant.

Jo Anne spent summers with her father up near Traverse City, where she loved being near the lakes and going fishing.

They first lived in an apartment on Eastwood Avenue. Her very first friend made in this town was Jason Darrow, across the street. They used to swim in the pool and also collect stickers (he had a much better collection than mine!) Once she got in trouble at school, putting tacks on Mrs. Stengren's chair (she and Jo Anne still keep in touch sometimes) and giving her band teacher a handful of jalapino jelly beans that she got from Heather Bruer!

In 1985 they moved across town to a little house on Woodworth street. There she made a lot of new friends. They used to walk down to Island Park together, but it was not as nice as it is now. They used to swim down at the dams, too. On really hot days, I think nearly every kid in town was down there!

In the fall of 1989, her mother bought a lottery ticket and jokingly said that if she won, she would buy Jo Anne a horse. Well, she got four out of five numbers, and Jo Anne got the horse, which she still has today!

Jo Anne graduated from MPHS in 1993, then started taking college classes. She got a little sidetracked, taking a great horse-related job at the YMCA near Evart.

She lived in Rosebush from 1994-98. After that, she lived in an old house near Barryton for awhile. She recently discovered that particular property was first inhabited in the late 1800s by people named Adam and Margarette Pfaffenbach by tracing old plat maps and censuses.

l-r: William Benchley, Jo Anne and their children; Jackie with Steve; Jo Anne's nephews, Joshua and Kyle; maternal aunt Anita Sweeney, and Nancy Wallace-Olson, 2001.

Jo Anne currently lives in Oil City with her two daughters, Leah and Relin, one son named Ben and her husband William Benchley. They live on 40 acres on the Chippewa River. Her husband is a truck driver and builder, and Jo Anne is working full time on finishing her degree in nursing.

WALLING, William Henry was born on Jan. 17, 1831 in Gouverneur, NY to William Walling and Polly Smith. William was married to Anzolettie Brayton in Hartford, NY on Feb. 10, 1860. William spent his childhood on the family farm in New York and later learned the trade of shoemaking. William and Anzolettie left New York in 1866 and headed west to Michigan where land was cheap and settled in Coe Twp. of Isabella County along with his brother-in-law, A.J. Gibbs. He owned a quarter section of the township which he cleared and farmed for 25 years.

William and Anzolettie sold their farm and moved into Salt River (Shepherd) where he owned a grocery store for another 25 years. He was an active man in politics serving as the first drain commissioner of Isabella County, was a local school officer and a justice of the peace. Both William and Anzolettie were very active members of the Baptist Church and were Prohibitionists.

William H. Walling

William and Anzolettie had three children: 1) Florence Ada md. Orville E. Way of Ionia County; 2) Charles Henry md. first, Hallie Stahlman and second, Anna Seeley and resided in the Shepherd area; 3) Hazel. William passed away March 4, 1912 and Anzolettie passed away March 27, 1926, both are buried at the Salt River Cemetery in Shepherd.

WELSH FAMILY. Edward D. Welsh and Eleanor Crooks Welsh settled in rural Isabella County in approximately 1887 purchasing a farm on the southeast corner of Baseline and Meridian Roads. Edward, son of Edward Welsh and Martha McClelland, was born Nov. 1, 1836 in Canada West now known as Ontario. He lived in Waterloo County, Ontario until moving to Michigan after a severe economic depression hit the farmers of Ontario.

Eleanor Crooks Welsh was born March 12, 1835 in Co. Fermanagh, Northern Ireland, the daughter of Robert Crooks and Ann Barton. Eleanor, with her family, immigrated to Canada in approximately 1840 and spent her childhood in Waterloo County, Ontario.

Edward and Eleanor Welsh

Edward and Eleanor were married on July 11, 1861 in Hawkesville, Waterloo County, Ontario. They resided on a farm in Peel Twp., Wellington County, Ontario. Upon arriving in Isabella County, they rented land until they found the farm they wanted to purchase. Edward and Eleanor had seven children, all born in Ontario.

1) Henry Albert Welsh (b. July 24, 1862, d. March 27, 1947) md. Mary Melissa Harrison.

2) George A. Welsh (b. Feb. 20, 1867, d. Aug. 5, 1867 as an infant).

3) William James Welsh (b. June 26, 1868, d. March 12, 1895).

4) Wyman Welsh (b. Aug. 28, 1871, d. March 6, 1953) md. Mabel E. Gibson.

5) Annie J. Welsh (b. Sept. 13, 1873, d. May 9, 1956) md. first, Charles F. Allen and second, Edward Cameron.

6) Edgar D. Welsh (b. March 21, 1878, d. Oct. 28, 1895).

7) George Wesley Welsh (b. Aug. 24, 1879, d. Dec. 8, 1967) md. Florence Ruby Knowles.

All of the children with their spouses resided in Isabella County and were farmers.

Edward was active in the local politics of Union Twp. Isabella County where he resided. Edward and Eleanor lived out their years on the family farm until their deaths. George Wesley Welsh and his wife Florence stayed on the farm and cared for Wesley's parents in their aged years. Edward passed away on Feb. 16, 1925 and Eleanor on Feb. 29, 1924, both are buried in the Woodland Cemetery in Rosebush, MI.

WESLEY GEORGE WELSH FAMILY. Wesley George Welsh was born on August 24, 1879 in Wellington County, Ontario Canada to Edward D. Welsh and Eleanor Crooks. He along with his brothers and sister came to Michigan with their parents in the early 1890s seeking inexpensive farmland in Isabella County. They settled on 125 acres in Union Twp.

on the corner of Baseline and Meridian Roads.

Wesley along with his siblings attended the Townline country school and as he grew into manhood, he was the one who chose to stay on the family farm and care for his aged parents. A young woman came to live at the farm and help with domestic chores and care for Wesley's mother who had broken a leg in an accident with a horse and buggy. Florence Knowles was that young woman who was destined to become Wesley's wife. She was living in Wise Twp. with her uncle, William Badgley, and through friends, the arrangement for her help was made. Wesley and Florence were married on December 27, 1910 in Hungerford Twp., Hastings County, Ontario at the home of her father, William H. Knowles.

Wesley and Florence raised their three children on the farm in Union Twp. Aletha Winifred was born on January 21, 1914 and married William Grace, a neighbor boy from across the road. Edward Knowles was born February 29, 1916 and died from Bright's disease on February 24, 1936. Gala Beatrice was born on February 16, 1918 and married John C. Braun III on June 4, 1947 who preceded her in death on May 24, 1949. She later married Lloyd Casner on November 25, 1964.

Wesley and Florence remained on the original Welsh farm until 1942 when they sold it and purchased another on Jordan Road. This farm was given to their daughter, Aletha and her husband William. Wesley and Florence rented for about one year until they found another farm that suited them. They finally settled on 60 acres in Union Twp. on the northwest corner of Pickard and Isabella Roads which he nicknamed "Christian Hill". Wesley continued farming for another twenty-five years until passing away on December 8, 1967. Florence sold the farm to Hood Lumber Company and spent the remaining years

of life with her daughter, Aletha and her husband William at their home at Coldwater Lake until her death on August 12, 1971. Both are buried at Riverside Cemetery in Mt. Pleasant. Their farm on Pickard saw many changes from Hood Lumber Company to Erb Lumber Company and now the site of Appleby's Restaurant, Mid-Michigan Health Park and the Cinema Theatre.

Wesley was very active throughout his life in the Republican Party and held various public offices in Union Twp. Florence and Wesley were members of the First Baptist Church and Wesley worked as an insurance adjuster for Michigan Mutual Insurance Company.

WEST-HENNESEY. One of the oldest families still having direct descendents here in Mt. Pleasant was the William West family. William Horace West (b. July 12, 1849 in Kingston, Ontario, Canada) was the son of Mr. and Mrs. John West. William married Mary Ann Hennesey in 1875 in St. Mary's, Ontario. Mary Ann was born July 16, 1852 near St. Mary's, Ontario, Canada.

Both Mary Ann and William's parents had migrated from Ireland. William had several brothers and sisters. One brother was ordained a Catholic priest, and later, as a Monsignor, was a parish priest near St. Mary's. William was a farmer, as were several of his brothers.

When William and Mary Ann West first moved to Michigan in 1880, they settled in Isabella County near Leaton. The country was wilderness, and they worked diligently to clear land for the log cabin they built and resided in. During that time, William supported his family by farming. He started with an 80 acre tract of wooded land on Sec. 25, Isabella, and by the time he and his family moved to Mt. Pleasant, his farm size had increased to 240 acres.

In the early 1900s, Mary Ann and William retired to their new residence at 601 North Kinney Blvd. During this time, the Wests accumulated several properties throughout Mt. Pleasant. William and Mary Ann had eight surviving children:

Front, l-r: Hazel West, Mary Agnes West Sowle, Mary Ann Hennessy, William West, Margaret Lawler West, Ethel McKenzie West. Back: Tom West Sr., Sidney Sowle, Anna West, Allen Moss, Alice Therese West, Fred West, John West, George West.

John married Margaret "Maggie" Lawler, and they had a farm west of Rosebush, MI.

Thomas was a teacher, first teaching in Brinton, MI. Early in his career, he became the first superintendent of Schools in Mackinaw City, MI. Later, he moved to Detroit, where he taught for many years, and during the summer ran the athletics and parks system on Belle Isle. He retired to a farm near Howell, MI.

Alice Therese (b. 1879, d. 1961) was a telephone operator in the early 1900s in Detroit. After her father's death, she returned to the family home at 601 North Kinney Blvd., where she resided until the death of her mother.

Anna (b. 1878, d. 1921) moved to Chicago where she was a nurse, working mostly with premature babies. Her husband was Allen Moss, who had immigrated from England.

Mary Agnes married Sidney E. Sowle and settled in Mt. Pleasant. (see Sowle-West for more information).

George was a farmer and lived all of his life in the Leaton area. He married Ethel McKenzie (b. Sept. 21, 1887, d. 1947).

Frederick West (b. 1890, d. 1966) md. briefly. He served in WWI in France. After the war, he returned to Mt. Pleasant and was a security guard at what was then the State Home and Training School. He lived at the family residence on North Kinney Blvd.

William J. (b. 1883, d. 1903), at the age of 20, was scalded while working on a steam engine.

In the mid-1940s, following the death of their mother, Frederick and Therese moved from their Kinney Blvd. residence to another property at 615 North Lansing. They lived there until their deaths.

William West had been a prominent citizen of Isabella County for many years. As mentioned, he was a successful farmer in the Leaton area, and when he moved to Mt. Pleasant he was able to travel extensively. He died in 1922.

Mary Ann West was, on the occasion of her 90th birthday, described the local paper as "a lovely lady." She died in 1945.

Both William and Mary Ann are buried in Calvary Cemetery in Mt. Pleasant, along with four of their children: William J., Anna, Therese (Alice) and Frederick.

WESTBROOK FAMILY.

The current (2002) Jack R. Westbrook family of Mt. Pleasant has its roots in the early 1930s movement to Mt. Pleasant by an entourage of Westbrooks from Ohio and West Virginia who joined the number of oil and gas explorationists who came to Michigan following the 1928 discovery of the Mt. Pleasant Field between Mt. Pleasant and Midland in Midland's Chippewa Twp.

Four brothers: George (Lilly); John (spouse unknown); Orville (spouse unknown) and Walter Scott (Vada) Westbrook came to the Mt. Pleasant area along with a cousin, Oakey Westbrook, and their offspring. Orville returned to West Virginia in short order and John moved to California in the late 1940s.

The rest of the original Westbrook 1920-1930s migration stayed in the Central Michigan area and a great deal of confusion remains today from similarities in names. Oakie Westbrook, for instance, named his sons Jack, Robert and Scott, while (Walter) Scott Westbrook's son H.H. named his eldest son Jack Robert. Rufus (son of George) Westbrook named his son George and nobody liked to use "Junior" or "Senior" or "I" and "II" or the 1st, etc. So today the question "Are you any relation to Westbrook is likely to be answered with the question "Which one?"

The children of Walter Scott Westbrook were the late Howard Hood (Jean) Westbrook of Mt. Pleasant and the late Gwen (Dominic) Tragna of South Haven, MI.

The children of H.H. Westbrook are Jack Robert (Mary Lou) and James P. Westbrook of Mt. Pleasant.

Jack R. Westbrook, now retired, was managing editor from 1973-2001 of the Michigan Oil & Gas News magazine, published at Mt. Pleasant, while Mary Lou Westbrook, also retired, was a financial advertising copywriter for Ray F. Cline Marketing 1974-2001.

The children of Jack R. and Mary Lou Westbrook are Lydia Jean Westbrook of Houston, TX; Collette Marie (John) Wilson of Holland, MI; Steven Joseph (Kelley) Westbrook of Brunswick, ME; Paula Geralyn Westbrook-Kordas of Tustin, CA and Mary Geralyn (Don) Scott of Jacksonville, NC.

The Jack R. Westbrooks have lived at 501 North Fancher Street, Mt. Pleasant, since 1968.

WHEATON FAMILY.

Daniel/Ashe-don-qua-be Whedon/Wheaton/Ke-Che-Me-gis. Ashe-don-qua-be means almost reaches the clouds. He was born abt. 1821, Saginaw County, Taymouth Twp. and died Aug. 27, 1911 Burt, Saginaw County and is buried Wheaton Indian Cem. Seymour Rd. Burt, MI.

His mother was Sophia Nay-Naw-We-Go-Zhe-Go-Quay (b. abt. 1807 and his father was George Ke or Key Che-Me-Gis/Whedon. Both parents were born, lived and died in Saginaw County.

Brothers and sisters: Samuel G./Wain-daw-nuh-quot Whedon (b. abt. 1830-1836); Nathan Ke-Wainze/Whedon (b. abt. 1827-1830); Susan Whedon (b. abt. 1840-1842); George Whedon (b. abt. 1852-1861); Mary Whedon (b. June 27, 1852); Margaret Ke-che-me-gis (b. abt. 1840; Peter Whedon (b. abt. 1838).

He was born and grew up in Taymouth Twp. Saginaw County. The family hunted, fished and farmed along the Flint River on which they used to trade from Saginaw to Flint and beyond.

He received 40 acres of land on the Mt. Pleasant Reservation under the 1855 Treaty on March 4, 1872. We believe he stayed there until about 1878 when he returned to his ministry and teaching in Saginaw County.

He was married Dec. 21, 1856, Saginaw to Louise/Jane/Lucy/Ke-she-ge-waw-no-quay Fisher (b. abt. 1823 in St. Charles, MI. Louise died April 10, 1927, Taymouth Twp. and is buried in the Wheaton Indian Cemetery. Her parents were James Fisher and Waw-say-che-waw-no-quay/O-gaw-aw-no-quay.

Children of Daniel and Louise are George (b. abt. 1861), Peter (b. abt. 1862), Joseph (b. abt. 1866), Susan/Ne-saw-me-qua (b. Oct. 28, 1869), John D. (b. abt. 1871), Thomas/Kaw-gay-waw-been Whedon (b. May 19, 1874), Julia (b. abt. 1877), David (b. abt. 1884, Kate, Daniel, James, Harry, Eldon.

He went to the Indian Mission School (later known as Cazier Station) in Pe-won-o-go-wink on the Flint River.

He and his brothers, Nathan and Samuel, became interested in the Methodist religion. After being urged by the local pastors and teachers in 1850 and 1851, he attended the Wesleyan

Seminary in Albion, MI. That is when he acquired the name Daniel D. Whedon after a University of Michigan Professor who was teaching there.

He returned to Taymouth Twp. and became a pastor and teacher to his people in the area. An Indian church was first built on E. Verne Road outside of Burt and then was moved 1-1/2 miles to Seymour Road where Daniel owned land. He donated land to the church and for an Indian Cemetery (now called Wheaton Indian).

He has had writings about him and his family by Fred Dustin which are at the Saginaw Hoyt Library. There were many articles in the Saginaw newspapers over the years (Saginaw Courier-Herald Sept. 4, 1911 "Carrier of Gospel Among Own People Was Daniel Wheaton").

WHEELER,

R. Dale Wheeler Jr. was born June 25, 1961 in Mt. Pleasant to Ronald D. Wheeler and Barbara M. (Findley) Wheeler. Janet P. (Wiltse) Wheeler was born May 10, 1962 in Mt. Pleasant to Leon E. Wiltse, and Shirley M. (Elkins) Wiltse.

Janet and Dale were married Oct. 10, 1981 in Mt. Pleasant. They have two children: Amy Ann Wheeler (b. April 28, 1984 in Mt. Pleasant) and Justin Dale Wheeler (b. Nov. 21, 1987 in Saginaw, MI).

Janet works at the Mt. Pleasant Center as an RCA. Dale works with his dad for Ronald Wheeler Construction.

WHITEHEAD FAMILY.

Edwin (Edward) Benjamin Whitehead was five years old when his mother Sarah (Lockwood) passed away. He had a younger brother Ernest who was less than a year old and was being reared by their widowed father. Edwin's father met and married a teacher, Florence, two years later. Between age eight and 14 he would gain four stepsisters and a stepbrother.

Edwin grew up in Isabella and worked with his father George on the

Delia (Goffnett) Whitehead

family farm. He met his future wife Delia Frances Goffnett around 1899. She was born in Lockport, Erie County, NY on Feb. 11, 1879 to Jacob and Maryann Josephine (Tatu) Goffnett. Both sets of Delia's grandparents had been born and reared in France before immigrating to the United States.

Edwin and Delia were both members of the Catholic Church in Mt. Pleasant. Father Thomas J. O'Connor at the Mt. Pleasant Catholic Church married them on Nov. 27, 1900. They purchased a farm just north of Shepherd where they farmed and reared four daughters: Laura Mary (b. Sept. 19, 1901); Anna Lucille (b. April 16, 1907); Florence Vesta (b. Jan. 28, 1909) and Vergal Marie (b. March 4, 1911). They also had a son George Wayne (b. July 7, 1914).

In their senior years unable to continue farming they moved in with their eldest daughter Laura in the 1930s. Laura had met and married Thomas Leo Campbell on Feb. 24, 1924.

They purchased a small home still located at 4268 Bloomfield Road, Mt. Pleasant Route #4.

Edwin passed away on May 19, 1945 of a heart attack at the age of 66-1/2. He had been married to, Delia for 45 years. Delia carried on without her husband for another 20 years. She died Jan. 11, 1965. She had continued to live with her daughter Laura during this time on Bloomfield Road. She was buried beside her husband in the Calvary Catholic Cemetery in Mt. Pleasant. All of Edwin and Delia's children would join them in death by 1994. Anna Lucille, wife of Orlin M. Leonard, passed away on May 21, 1947; George Wayne was laid to rest beside his parents in the Catholic Cemetery on Dec. 26, 1973; Laura Mary (md. Thomas Leo Campbell) passed away Feb. 15, 1982 and lies in the family plot with her parents; Vergal Marie (md. Thomas James DuBois) passed away in Coleman, MI on Oct. 22, 1991; and Florence Vesta (md. Joseph Bernard Campbell) joined the rest of the family Sept. 18, 1994. She passed away in Menomonee Falls, WI.

WHITEHEAD FAMILY. George Washington Whitehead was the second son of William and Elizabeth (Bartee) Whitehead who immigrated to the United States from the Cambridge shire England area in 1851. George's parents were married in Spaulding, Lincolnshire County England in May 1841 and had two daughters, Mary (b. 1842) and Jane (b. 1849), and one son Charles R. (b. 1847) prior to coming to America. George was the first of William Whitehead's seven children to be born in the United States. He was born Sept. 18, 1852 in Union Township of Wayne County, NY. His parents had purchased a farm upon their arrival in the United States. George's mother died in 1861 in Wayne County, NY and his father married a widow, Ann Reed. She had a young daughter Susan (b. 1862). This marriage produced three more siblings for George: William (b. 1867), Joseph, and a sister Carrie (b. 1871).

The family moved to Isabella County in 1869 where George's father purchased a farm in the Union Township. George stayed on the family farm helping his father until he purchased his own 70-acre farm in 1876 in Sec. 29 of Union Township. A year later in September 1877 George married Sarah B. Lockwood (b. June 21, 1857) who was from Ontario County, NY. They had two sons, Edwin (Edward) Benjamin (b. Nov. 7, 1878) and Ernest (b. March 1883). She passed away Sept. 26, 1883, leaving him with two young boys to rear on his own.

George met a schoolteacher named Florence E. Wheeler and she became his second wife. They had four daughters: Florence B. (b. March 15, 1886), Rdella E. (b. Aug. 23, 1888), Vestah May (b. May 1892), and Gretchen (b. Jan. 20, 1897) and a son Alfred (b. August 1891). George passed away Jan. 11, 1921 of pneumonia at the age of 68. He is buried in the Mt. Pleasant Cemetery.

WHITEHEAD, George Wayne grew up in the farming country of Isabella County with his four sisters: Laura, Anna, Florence and Vergal. At the age of 24 he met his future wife, Tretha June Allen, from Shepherd. He had been introduced to her by his future brother-in-law, Walter Bun-

ker, who was married to her sister Donna. They were married on Sept. 25, 1939.

George worked on different farms in the Alma, Shepherd area for the next seven years until he found permanent work in 1946 on the Ken Myers farm located in Coe. He worked for Ken and Lois Myers for the next 25 years. Ken would cut back on his work force after the spring crops were in and he arranged for George to find work at a bee farm in Ann Arbor.

George and Tretha had six children during their 10-year-marriage: 1) Robert Wayne (b. Aug. 1, 1940 in Shepherd); 2) Shirley June (Oct. 6, 1941); 3) Jerry Wayne (b. Aug. 15, 1942, d. Aug. 18, 1942) is buried in the Shepherd Cemetery. His grave is marked with small simple cement cross-made by his father; 4) Duane George (b. Oct. 13, 1944) in Shepherd; 5) Judith Ann (b. July 15, 1946 in Alma); 6) Lois Jean (b. Nov. 4, 1947).

George and Tretha's marriage came to an end in 1949. She left with her five children and returned to Shepherd. She later moved to Alma where she met and married Harold C. Gallant. They moved back to the Shepherd/Mt. Pleasant area. George stayed at the Ken Myers farm for 20 more years. He met a woman named Edna whom he had a relationship with for several years. When George lost his farming job with Ken and Lois Myers, he moved to Onstead.

On Dec. 26, 1973 at St. Joseph Hospital, he succumbed to a brain concussion suffered from a job injury he received while working at Hubbard Apiaries. His sister Laura Campbell arranged for him to be interred in the family plot at the Calvary Catholic Cemetery in Mt. Pleasant. His two sons, Robert and Duane, along with his youngest daughter Lois attended the funeral services held at the Sacred Heart Catholic Church in Mt. Pleasant with Father John Thomas officiating. His other surviving daughter Judith Bendrat was unable to attend the service.

WHITEHEAD, Judy (b. July 15, 1946 in Alma, MI) md. Fred Bendrat Oct. 25, 1966 and divorced in 1980. Her mother was Tretha Allen (b. Feb. 18, 1923, Shepherd, MI) and father was George Whitehead (b. July 9, 1914 in Shepherd, MI). Tretha and George divorced in 1949 and Tretha married Harold Gallant in 1950.

Judy had five siblings; Robert, Shirley, Jerry, Duane and Lois. Judy left Michigan in 1955. On Nov. 25, 1966 Judy married Fred Bendrat and they resided in California then moved to Colorado in 1969. Judy and Fred have three children: Joanne (b. Oct. 23, 1967 in California); Fred (b. Aug. 25, 1970 in Colorado); and Heidi (b. Nov. 30, 1973 in Colorado). Judy and Fred divorced in 1980 and Judy moved to California.

Joanne married Doug Mailander on Feb. 17, 1991 and they have a son Andy (b. July 29, 1997 in California).

Heidi married Tom Barnes Feb. 16, 1991. They have two boys, Tom (b. Sept. 13, 1991 in California) and Tyler (b. Dec. 9, 1993 in California).

Fred married Cindy Ercanbrack Oct. 8, 1997. Cindy has two children, Noelle (b. Dec. 29, 1989 in California) and Robert (b. Jan. 17, 1993 in California).

Judy is now living in Las Vegas and spends a lot of time enjoying all her grandchildren.

WHITEHEAD, Lois Jean (b. Nov. 4, 1947 in Alma, MI) md. John Adams in October 1967 and they divorced in 1979. Her mother was Tretha Allen (b. Feb. 18, 1923, Shepherd, MI) and father was George Whitehead (b. July 9, 1914 in Shepherd, MI). Tretha and George divorced in 1949 and Tretha married Harold Gallant in 1950. Harold and Tretha will celebrate their 52nd anniversary this year.

Lois has five siblings: Robert, Shirley, Jerry, Duane and Judy Whitehead. Lois was reared in Shepherd, MI and worked in Mt. Pleasant, MI at the cleaners and the Coca Cola bottling factory through her teenage years. She attended Sexton High School in Lansing, MI. She moved to California in 1967 where she met and married John Adams in 1968. They have two daughters, Janet and Christina.

Janet Sher're Adams (b. July 26, 1969 in California) md. Gary Geier in 1991. They have four children: Brandyn Mark (b. July 28, 1991 in Nevada), Austin Lee (b. July 2, 1995 in Nevada), Trae Dalton (b. April 28, 2000 in Nevada), Kylie Jean (b. Sept. 13, 2001 in Nevada).

Christina Marie Adams (b. Oct. 27, 1978 in California) md. Ian Beatty in 1997. They have one son Christian Robert (b. Feb. 1, 1997 in Nevada).

In 1978 Lois and John relocated to Las Vegas, NV and divorced in 1979. Lois married Charles Schultz in 1984. Charles passed away in 1986. Lois was blessed with four handsome grandsons. She was then blessed with a beautiful granddaughter who is named after her. Lois is now living and working in Sandy Valley, NV. She spends her weekends and holidays with her five grandchildren.

WHITEHEAD, Robert Wayne was born Aug. 1, 1940 to George and Tretha Whitehead in the county hospital just north of Shepherd. He was the first of six children that the couple would have during their marriage. The first five years of his life the family moved several times to different farms in the Shepherd/Alma area. Then in 1946 the family of five settled on the Ken and Lois Myers farm just outside Coe. He started first grade at the one room school in Coe. His teacher was Lois Myers. She taught him for the next four years and became a life long family friend until her death in 2001.

At the age of 9 his parents divorced. He remained in the Alma, Mt. Pleasant, Shepherd area until the summer of 1951. His family moved to Orlando, FL where his aunt and uncle lived. Two months after their arrival they moved to Rock Island, IL. The next three years he attended school in the Rock Island-Moline-Davenport, IA area. In the spring of 1954 they moved to California and settled in the city of Anaheim.

He attended Anaheim Union High School and graduated in 1958, in a Class of 450 students. In July he enlisted in the U.S. Army and did six months of infantry training at Fort Ord outside of Monterey, CA and at Fort Bragg, NC in the famed 82nd Airborne Division. A leg injury ended his short parachuting career and he turned to his photography skills to work on the 18th Airborne Corps PIO staff during the last 18 months of his enlistment.

In July 1961 he returned to California with Nancy Burnett, his wife of five months. He began working as a commercial photographer for the next few months but grew tired of this profession. His next job was in aero space as an electronic inspector on the minuteman project. A daughter Terri Ann (b. May 25, 1964) was followed by Robert Wayne II (b. Dec. 14, 1963). This profession lasted two years when he turned to a childhood dream and joined the Anaheim Police Dept. on March 23, 1964. This was his profession for the next 30 years. He continued his education receiving an AA degree in police science in 1966 and BS in criminology, 1969.

Robert and Shirley Whitehead and granddaughter, Brandi.

On Jan. 8, 1968 another daughter June Ann was born. The following March 1969 he was transferred from the uniformed division to a detective position. At about the same time his marriage of nine years ended and he gained custody of his three children. He met his future wife, Shirley M. McCarrick, through his sister Lois. She had two children, Margaret (b. May 26, 1962) and John L. (b. Feb. 6, 1966) from a prior marriage. they combined the two families on Sept. 18, 1970. They raised their five children in the Catholic faith and sent them to parochial schools. They also became foster parents to newborns and before their service ended they had seen 125 babies pass through their home.

In September 1974 he was promoted to the rank of sergeant and returned to uniformed patrol. He served as field, desk and communication sergeant until August 1980. He was selected to supervise a team in the newly formed Crime Task Force. In 1983 he was asked to accept the burglary detail detective sergeant's position. In September 1984, 3-month-old granddaughter Brandi Nichelle McCarrick came to live with her grandparents. She attended Catholic school and was reared in that faith. A family death in 1987 saw the arrival of Shirley's teenage brother Paul Campbell into the family.

In 1991 he took over the Economic Crimes Detail (checks, credit cards and major fraud). His detail became involved in a three million dollar (twenty dollar bills) counterfeit seizure that year. He retired from the police department in this position on his wife's birthday Dec. 24, 1993.

In May 1994 he joined a high school friend Lt. Col. Robert Kreager, USAF, in London, England. For two weeks they toured the WWII D-day beachheads. His early retirement years have been spent rearing granddaughter Brandi, taking short vacations to visit family during school breaks. He kept in contact, through bi-weekly breakfast meetings, with the other retired police friends. He and his wife of 32 years are now looking forward to the high school graduation of granddaughter Brandi on June 1, 2002, then both of their retirements began.

WIEBER-REIHL. Henry and Helen (Naseman) Wieber, originally from Germany, were married around 1875 in the United States. They bought 318-1/2 acres on Weidman Road west of Winn Road from Alanzo Frisbee in 1898. They built a house and farmed the land. They had nine children: Mary, Margaret, Anna, Leo, August, Conrad, William, John and Joseph.

Wieber Family. Back Row, l-r: Leo, Henry, Conrad, Margaret, Walter, Regina. Front: Alexander, John, Rita, 1926.

John Reihl, originally from Germany, settled in Westphalia, MI. He bought 80 acres southeast of Beal City. John said one of the best times of his life was coming over from Germany on the boat. Before coming to Michigan he worked in tobacco fields in Kentucky and worked for a gardener in Ohio. He raised vegetables on his farm and hauled them to Weidman to be sold to the men working

Conrad and Margaret (Reihl) Wieber

in the lumber business and at the sawmills. Regina Miller came from Germany in the mid-1800s to live with an uncle and work for him. He built her a bureau that is still in use today. John Reihl and Regina Miller married around 1875. They built a log cabin and later added to the house. They had five children: Margaret, Anna, Mary, John and Leo.

Wieber Farm, 1960

Conrad Wieber married Margaret Reihl on Nov. 12, 1901. They bought 78 acres from his parents on Winn Road north of Weidman Road. They built a small house which was later enlarged. In 1915 relative and neighbors had a barn raising to house the livestock and feed. The crops were oats, wheat, corn, hay, beans, sugar beets, pickles and a vegetable garden. Pickles were picked by hand every other day for the three month season.

From 1903-22 they had seven children: Regina, Leo, Walter, Henry, Alexander, John and Rita. One of the children's jobs was to crawl along the rows of sugar beet, usually a five acre field, to weed and thin the beets.

Horses were used for farming until the late 1930s when a tractor was bought. A team of horses was kept until 1970 to haul firewood from the old-growth woods.

The older children went to a one-room school on the corner of Winn and Weidman Roads. John and Rita walked to St. Philomena school in Beal City a little more than a mile away. The teachers were nuns and there were two or three grades per room. The school burned Dec. 21, 1948 and was later rebuilt.

Regina, Walter, Alexander and John never married and stayed on the original farm, which had grown to 218 acres.

Leo and Henry, also bachelors, had their own farm in the area. John is the only survivor of these six.

Rita married Eldon Doerfer on Feb. 14, 1953. They moved to eastern Michigan and returned in 1998 on the property of the one-room school on Weidman Road west of Winn Road. They had three girls: Arleen, Susan and Brenda. Susan moved on the north end of the farm in 1997. In April of 2002 the farm was approved for a Michigan Centennial Landmark.

WILT-REED. Clara Belle Reed (b. March 2, 1886, d. April 16, 1971) was the daughter of Mary L. (Prentiss) and Charles Reed of Mulberry, near Blissfield, Lenawee County, MI. Her siblings were Harry Reed (b. Jan. 5, 1884, d. May 27, 1964 of Blissfield, MI); Edna (Reed) Brown (b. July 1, 1889, d. July 19, 1966 of Toledo, OH); Bessie Ann (Reed) Johnson (b. Feb. 18, 1891, d. Aug. 31, 1976, in Mt. Pleasant); Charley Reed (b. July 1, 1893. d. Aug. 24, 1893).

Clara spent her life on the farm. She was born in a log house with an addition built on it that had regular wood siding, her future home in Isabella County was of the same style. The family enjoyed the log house, it was warm, smelled of food cooking and just felt comfortable.

Clara married Page Wilt (b. April 30, 1881, d. Dec. 17, 1961) in May 1906. They lived with her parents a few months before coming to their farm home on N. Chippewa Rd. Her granddaughter Joyce (Wilt) Jenkins lives at that location today.

To my knowledge the only time Aunt Clara didn't live in a log home was between 1901 and 1907, when her parents built a large two story, four bedroom farm house. Then Clara and Page moved up north to N. Chippewa Rd., Wise Crossing, Isabella County.

Their children were Harry S. Wilt (b. June 7, 1910, d. Jan. 8, 1996); Marie (Wilt-Champion) Turkull (b. May 3, 1912, d. January 1990); and William Wilt (b. Oct. 14, 1917, d. Oct. 23, 1961).

WILTSE-ELKINS. Leon E. Wiltse was born July 18, 1939 in Vernon Twp. Isabella County to Wilbur Wiltse and Vilo (Ouderkirk) Wiltse. Shirley M. (Elkins) Wiltse was born Aug. 18, 1941 in Winfield Twp. Montcalm County, MI to Robert Elkins and J. Evelyn (Saunders) Elkins.

Leon and Shirley were married Nov. 10, 1960 in Big Rapids, MI. Leon has lived in Isabella County most of his life. He and Shirley have lived in the Mt. Pleasant area since their marriage. They have two children: Janet P. Wiltse (b. May 10, 1962 in Mt. Pleasant) and Everett G. Wiltse (b. Aug. 18, 1966 in Mt. Pleasant).

Leon worked in the grocery business until he went to work at Dow Chemical Co. in 1966 and retired from there in 1996. He is now working at Mountain Town Hobby's in Mt. Pleasant.

Shirley was a stay at home Mom and did the volunteer things such as Girl Scouts. Both Leon and Shirley have served as volunteer chaplains at Central Michigan Community Hospital. They are also very active in Community of Christ Church, Leon as a Deacon and Shirley as an Elder. Shirley was pastor for six years.

WILTSE-HOFFMAN. W. Garth Wiltse was born Sept. 20, 1937 at Vernon Twp. Isabella County to Wilbur F. Wiltse and Vilo P. (Ouderkirk) Wiltse. Teresa Marie (Hoffman) Wiltse was born July 18, 1941 at Coe Twp. Isabella County to Vincent H. and Mary C. (Siebeneck) Hoffman.

Garth graduated from Mt. Pleasant High School and went to the Army for two years. He served in the Honor Guard in Washington D.C.

Garth and Teresa were married July 22, 1961 in Shepherd, MI. Garth worked for Giant Super Market in Mt. Pleasant and Teresa worked at the Grant Store in Mt. Pleasant.

Garth died from cancer on Nov. 28, 1964 before their daughter Lori Lynn Wiltse was born March 17, 1965 in Mt. Pleasant.

WILTSE-OUDERKIRK. Wilbur F. Wiltse was born June 5, 1914 at Bethany Twp., Gratiot County, MI to Vern E. Wiltse and Mercy Viola (Armstrong) Wiltse. Vilo P. (Ouderkirk) Wiltse was born Oct. 26, 1918 at Vernon Twp. Isabella County to John H. and Della May (Tracy) Ouderkirk.

Wilbur's family moved to Colorado when he was six. He graduated there from Haxton High School and returned to Michigan in 1934 to work for his Aunt Pearl's husband who was Roy Ouderkirk. He went to work on the Ouderkirk farm and that's how he met and fell in love with Vilo Ouderkirk. They were married March 10, 1936 at Beaverton, MI. They had two sons, Wilbur Garth Wiltse (b. Sept. 20, 1937 at Vernon Twp. Isabella County, d. Nov. 28, 1964 in Mt. Pleasant) and Leon Everett Wiltse (b. July 18, 1939 at Vernon Twp. Isabella County).

Wilbur helped to build several barns in Isabella County. Wilbur went to work in a grocery store in Clare in 1939. He continued in the grocery business for many years. In 1959 he and Vilo opened Wiltse's Market on May St. in Mt. Pleasant. They operated it until 1967. Wilbur has worked at the Hardware Store on High St. in Mt. Pleasant now Gilroy's since 1972. He still works part time there. Vilo worked with him in many of the grocery stores besides their own. When they closed their store

she became a full time homemaker. She was a great cook and made the best apple pie. She sold lots of baked goods.

Wilbur and Vilo have both been very active in the Community of Christ Church (formerly Reorganized Church of Jesus Christ of Latter Day Saints). Vilo has been women's leader and church school director. Wilbur was treasurer for many years and served as pastor 1974-76. He holds the priesthood office of Elder.

WILTSE-PERHNE'. Everett G. was born Aug. 18, 1966 in Mt. Pleasant to Leon E. Wiltse and Shirley M. (Elkins) Wiltse. Robyn M. (Perhne') Wiltse was born April 25 in Lansing, MI to Cleona J. (Johnson) Cook and Gery L. Perhne'.

Everett and Robyn were married Aug. 3, 1996 at Sanford, MI. They have two daughters, Anastasya Nichole Wiltse (b. March 14, 2001 at Mt. Pleasant) and Natasha Marie Wiltse (b. June 19, 2002 at Mt. Pleasant).

Everett opened Mountain Town Hobby's in Mt. Pleasant in June 2002.

WOODIN-ROSE. Henry Woodin Jr. was a farmer also mill owner on Sec. 28 Sherman Twp. He was the son of Henry and Lydia (Earl) Woodin, natives of New York State. Henry (b. Nov. 6, 1827 in Monroe County, NY, d. June 26, 1899 at home on Drew Road) lived at home until the age of 19, receiving a good elementary education in the common schools. He was employed in various grist mills until 1853 when he and his family moved to Saginaw, MI.

Henry and Sarah Woodin

Henry met and married Sarah B. Rose in 1848 in Rochester, NY. Sarah was born Oct. 9, 1825 in Ontario County, NY to William and Anna (Barber) Rose and died at her home at Drew Road on March 13, 1897. Several of Sarah's family members also settled in this area .In 1869 Sarah and Henry moved to Isabella County where Henry selected a grist and saw mill site on the Chippewa River which he operated until his death at home on Drew Rd.

Henry and Sarah owned 1,050 acres of land with approximately 200 under cultivation. Three children were born to them: George (b. Aug. 11, 1848) was killed in a mill accident at the mill in 1878 at the age of 30; Anna A. (b. July 12, 1850, d. March 15, 1914); Louella E. (b. Aug. 10, 1860, d. June 9, 1937). Henry was selected supervisor on the Democratic ticket and held the office six consecutive years. Henry was also a member of the Masonic Order.

YARNELL-WHITE. Pearl "UV" (White) (b. Jan. 26, 1906 in Emerson Twp., Gratiot

County) was named after her Aunt UV (her mother's sister). She didn't find out until 1946 that her birth certificate had omitted the UV and listed her name as Pearl White. Her parents were Elmer and Lottie (Daub) White. Elmer was born on July 26, 1874 and Lottie was born on Aug. 7, 1876. They were married Dec. 3, 1893 and were farmers. Pearl's siblings include Daisy

Pearl White

(b. 1897, d. 1989), Clarence (b. 1900, d. 1983) and twin sisters, Emma and Amy (b. 1908).

Pearl has four children: Geraldine (now Dancer), Duane White, Maynard Danks, and Wesley Danks. In 1928, Pearl married Alton Danks. He passed away in 1932. Pearl now has 20 grandchildren, 25 great-grandchildren, and 21 great-great-grandchildren.

, In 1936, Pearl read in the newspaper that Otto Yarnell needed a housekeeper. She applied for the job, was hired, and moved to Coe Twp., Isabella County as Otto's housekeeper. Otto had two sons, George and Dean. In 1939, they moved from the Campbell farm on Wise Road to a 40-acre farm on Loomis Road where Pearl still lives. Pearl and Otto Yarnell were married in 1946. In addition to farming, Otto worked at Michigan Chemical in St. Louis, Central Michigan University, Coe Township Cemetery, and Wilcox Hospital in Alma. He died in 1976.

For a short time, 1946-47, Pearl worked at Ferro's Manufacturing in Mt. Pleasant.

Pearl has been active in a variety of organizations in Isabella County. In 1937, she joined the Meet-A-While group. Later she became a member of the Helping Hand. Pearl joined the Joe Ulsh VFW Post in 1961. She received the Medal of Recognition from Post 8215 for 21 years of dedicated service in the early 1980s.

ZUFELT. In March 1876, Henry (b. April 14, 1830, d. April 15, 1918) and Elizabeth (Giberson) (b. Dec. 16, 1832, d. Dec. 23, 1927) Zufelt came from Prince Edward County, Ontario, Canada and in the Spring of 1882 settled on a farm in Sec. 13 of Fremont Twp. in Isabella, County. Coming with them from Canada were their children: Grant (b. Sept. 23, 1870, d. Oct. 6, 1955); William (b. 1866, d. 1946); and Theresa. Emma and Alberta remained in Canada. Mrs. Zufelt lived in a log cabin on the farm of her son Grant after the death of her husband; then in Grant's home until her death at age 95. Henry and Elizabeth are buried in the Taylor Cemetery, Fremont Twp., Isabella County.

William married Anna Belle Noble April 3, 1890 at the Strickland Baptist Church parsonage. They celebrated their 50th wedding anniversary in 1940 at their farm in Fremont Twp. In later years they moved to Winn where they both died in 1946. Theresa married Mr. Hungerford, they had a son Floyd and moved from Isabella County.

Grant was a farmer and also broke horses. On May 8, 1898 in Dushville (Winn), MI, he married Cena Alice Richardson (b. Dec. 21, 1873, d. Dec. 5, 1957), daughter of Seth and Mary Richardson. Paul D. Huff was the officiating minister, and they were attended by Bert Adams and Clara A. Richardson. The family home of Grant and Cena is located on East Blanchard Road, 2-1/2 miles east of Winn, across from the present Morey Charter School.

Grant and Cena Zufelt, May 1953

Grant and Cena had three children: Howard (b. 1899, d. 1947), Atholl (b. 1902, d. 1963), and Retha Mae (b. 1906, d. 1991). Howard, Atholl and Retha attended the Davis Elementary School (Fremont Twp.), and two years of High School in Winn. Howard and Atholl graduated from Shepherd High School, riding their bicycles to Shepherd. Retha attended Mt. Pleasant High School for one year, attending Central Michigan Normal School for one year, earning her teaching certificate in 1925. She boarded in Mt. Pleasant with the George Bugbee family while attending school in Mt. Pleasant.

Grant, Howard, Athall, Cena and Retha Zufelt

Retha enjoyed horse-back riding, and rode her horse to school in Winn when attending there. She taught school for three years before her marriage to Milo Chapman.

Howard traveled West to seek his fortune, married Blanche L. Kenney, had one son, Raymond. Howard was found dead at age 47, and Raymond died the same year as a result of complications of rheumatic fever. Howard and Raymond are buried in Friends Cemetery, Newberg, OR.

Atholl married Gladys Bugbee, had one son, Robert, and retired from Dow Chemical Co. Atholl and Gladys are buried in the Green Cemetery, Lincoln Twp., Isabella County.

Retha married Milo Chapman, son of Burton and Lena (Densmore) Chapman (See Chapman biography)

Grant and Cena Zufelt are buried in the Green Cemetery, Lincoln Twp., Isabella County. *Submitted by Clara Chapman.*

INDEX

JOHN F MACDERMAID ©2003

Printed in the USA
CPSIA information can be obtained
at www.ICGtesting.com
JSHW060054150824
68134JS00032B/2728

9 781681 621906